THE HISTORY OF STANSTEAD COUNTY PROVINCE OF QUEBEC

With

Sketches of More than Five Hundred Families

Compiled by B.F. Hubbard

HERITAGE BOOKS
2009

HERITAGE BOOKS
AN IMPRINT OF HERITAGE BOOKS, INC.

Books, CDs, and more—Worldwide

For our listing of thousands of titles see our website at
www.HeritageBooks.com

Published 2009 by
HERITAGE BOOKS, INC.
Publishing Division
100 Railroad Ave. #104
Westminster, Maryland 21157

Copyright © 1874 1988 B.F. Hubbard

Pages 161-164 were missing from the original.

All rights reserved. No part of this book may be reproduced or transmitted in any form or by any means, electronic or mechanical, including photocopying, recording or by any information storage and retrieval system without written permission from the author, except for the inclusion of brief quotations in a review.

International Standard Book Numbers
Paperbound: 978-1-55613-123-3
Clothbound: 978-0-7884-7624-2

TO

COL. BENJAMIN POMROY,

ONE OF THE PIONEERS

OF THE

Settlements of Stanstead County,

WHOSE NAME IS CONNECTED

WITH THE

RAILWAY AND BANKING OPERATIONS

OF THE

EASTERN TOWNSHIPS OF CANADA,

AND

WHOSE PERSONAL EFFORTS HAVE CONTRIBUTED MATERIALLY

TO THE PROSPERITY OF THOSE TOWNSHIPS,

THE FOLLOWING PAGES

ARE RESPECTFULLY DEDICATED BY

THE COMPILER.

LIST OF ILLUSTRATIONS.

	Page
Wesleyan College	353
Outline Map	357

A pagination mistake occured in the original printing which resulted in the apparent loss of pages 161, 162, 163, and 164; actually, no text was lost. See the addenda on page 361.

TABLE OF CONTENTS.

Part First.

	Page
Early History and Settlement	1
County of Stanstead	6
Township of Stanstead	18
Sketches of Marlow Settlers	41
Hatley, by E. H. LeBaron, Esq	46
Magog and Barnston	50,51
Coaticook and Barford	56–58
Adventures and Experiences of Pioneers	62
Religious Denominations	81
Stanstead Seminary	104
Academies and High Schools	105,106
Stanstead Wesleyan College	106
Golden Rule Lodge	108

Part Second.

Sketches of Families of the early Settlers	114
The Family, its relations to society and genealogy	114
The Families of Stanstead	116
" " of Hatley and Magog	246
" " of Barnston, Coaticook and Barford	297
Additional Families	342
Mrs. Abigail Cass	345
Family Record	348
Notes in brief	351
General Index	362
Index of Families	363

Note. — Errors no doubt will be found in the compilation and printing of the History. The request is hereby made that they be promptly reported to the publisher.

INTRODUCTION.

THE original design of this enterprise was a Manual of the events connected with the settlement of the Township of Stanstead; but, with the advice of friends, it was thought best to attempt a History of the entire County.

At the first, one hundred pages would have been deemed sufficient to contain all that could be said or written in relation to the settlement of the County; but the materials have increased as the work has progressed, and it would have been easier to have written a larger volume than to have compressed the materials within their present limits.

The compiler is among the very few survivors of the pioneers of Stanstead County. His earliest recollections are associated with the beginnings of many of the early settlers, with whom he has sustained a part, though perhaps an humble one, in clearing away an almost entire forest, and in bringing this, our favored land, to its present state of prosperity. He would hope that other individuals may be induced, from convictions of duty to posterity, to gather up the fragments of the early history of the remaining localities of these Townships.

Having passed the time allotted to man in this world, and beginning to feel the infirmities of age, he has relinquished the labor of publication to the Rev. John Lawrence—with entire confidence that additions he may see fit to make to the book will be satisfactory to the public.

B. F. HUBBARD.

Stanstead Plain, P.Q.,
July 15, 1874.

In addition to what Mr. Hubbard has stated respecting the History of Stanstead County, now going to the press, it may be said that it gives me pleasure to contribute in any measure to the completion of a work which has taken much of his time and strength during the later years of his life, and which promises so much good fruit to those for whose gratification and profit he has labored.

He has written in a plain, clear style, well adapted to the subjects treated. Indeed there is little room for other than simple, truthful words, such as he has used. The arrangement is convenient, and quite satisfactory.

The portions giving incidents, adventures and experiences of individuals and families first on "the Frontier," and settling in the wilderness, have the freshness of close personal conversation, showing how facts, the realities of human life, often exceed the wonders of fiction and romance.

The number of families noticed is very large, and the sketches, it is hoped, will be found correctly drawn.

Anything added to the book (or in revision omitted) will, it is thought, be acceptable, as helping to secure a favorable recognition from the public, and render it of greater value to the present and coming generations.

JOHN LAWRENCE.

FORESTS AND CLEARINGS,

STANSTEAD COUNTY, P.Q.

PART FIRST.

EARLY HISTORY AND SETTLEMENT.

The Territory known as Lower Canada, Canada East, or the Province of Quebec, had been explored and partially occupied by the French before the close of the 16th century—some of the settlements having been antecedent to the New England colonies. The French settlements had, however, been confined mostly to that part of the valley of the St. Lawrence lying between Lake Champlain, Montreal and Quebec, and this territory had been divided into Seigniories for the purpose of representation in the government of the viceroyalty of France. This state of things continued until the close of the French war, in 1759, when the entire territory of Canada was ceded by the King of France to the British Government. In 1763, all the country lying north of the Western Lakes and the parallel of 45 degrees, north latitude, was set off by Royal Proclamation of George the Third, and distinguished among the British Colonies in America as THE PROVINCE OF QUEBEC. This Colony was placed under the administration of a Governor and a Council appointed by the Crown. In 1790, the Province of Quebec was, by Royal Enactment, divided into the Provinces of Upper and Lower Canada, known afterwards as Canada East and Canada West, but after the lapse of more than a century from the time of the conquest, or in 1867, a confederation of the British Provinces in America was formed, in which Lower Canada was denominated "THE PROVINCE OF QUEBEC."

In 1792, Lower Canada was subdivided into districts, counties, circles, or towns, and townships. Previous to that time, the territory of the Eastern Townships had been the hunting and fishing grounds of the St. Francis Indians, and no lines of demarcation had been drawn. The surveys were begun in 1792, and completed mostly before the close of that century.

The first Provincial Parliament of Lower Canada was organized in 1793, under the administration of Lord Dorchester, viceroy or Governor General. It was constructed on a basis similar to that of the Home Government—the Royal Prerogative being vested in the Governor and his Council, who were appointed by the Crown, and a House of Assembly of fifty representatives of the people—the districts and counties furnishing their appropriate numbers. In the division of the Province into counties, the seigniories of St. Ours and Rouville and all the territory lying east of the Richelieu River and north of the parallel of 45 degrees, north latitude, and extending south-easterly from the borough of William Henry to the eastern boundary of the Province were comprised in

THE COUNTY OF RICHELIEU.

The population of this newly formed county was, at the first, confined mostly to the old French settlements. A few enterprising families from New England had found their way into the Eastern Townships before the close of the past century, but isolated as they then were, they had little to do with Representation.—Indeed they were comparatively unknown to the administration, and, for a time, "every man did as seemed good in his own eyes."

From 1793 to the close of that century, beginnings had been made in the settlements on the eastern shore of Memphremagog Lake—at Judd's Point, Magog Outlet, Georgeville, and the Lake Shore, south from Georgeville—also at Stanstead Plain, Rock Island, East Hatley and Barnston. Beginnings were made in Bolton and Potton about the same time.

In the meantime there had been a liberal disposition manifested by the Crown and the provincial Governments in behalf of the settlers of the Townships, and large grants of land were made to companies and individuals with the view of encouraging settlement. About the beginning of the present century, associations were formed for obtaining grants of wild lands. Their petitions were favorably received. Two companies were started in Hatley—one by Capt. Ebenezer Hovey, and the other by Col. Henry Cull. These two companies received together a grant of 23,943 acres, March 25, 1803. Grants amounting to 7,197 acres were subsequently made to Moses Holt, Hon. W. B. Felton, and others.

The charter for Stanstead was obtained in 1800. The grant, amounting to about 20,000 acres, was made to Isaac Ogden, Charles Kilbon, Johnson Taplin, Israel Wood, Andrew Young, Abraham Friolt, and others.

In 1810, 107 lots, containing 21,406 acres of the wild lands of Stanstead, were granted to Sir Robert Shore Milnes. Lesser grants were subsequently made to other individuals.

Among the associates of Barnston were Robert Lester, Robert Morough, Joseph Bartlett and Clement Drew. Their grant, which comprised 20,000 acres, was made April 11, 1801. Grants were afterwards made to other individuals; among these were the Philips' Lands. These have been a source of litigation in our Courts of Justice for many years.

The Township of Barford, though settled at a comparatively recent date, was early parcelled out to individuals. A charter was issued April 15, 1802, granting 20,000 acres to Isaac Clarke, Abner Wooled, Thomas Ferguson, Hannah Vaucamp, James Green and their associates.

The parties comprising the different companies of associates were generally poor. Only one or two in each company were able to sustain the expense of obtaining their charters. These men did as many would do at the present time. They reserved "the lion's share" for themselves, surrendering but one lot of 200 acres to each of the others. The land thus secured by Isaac Ogden, in Stanstead, and by others in the other townships, were sources of wealth to their owners. Many of the original grantees sold their lots and left the country, but a great number are still occupied by the descendants of those grantees.

In some instances the grants that were made to Government officials and other individuals proved a curse rather than a blessing; for not being practically acquainted with "roughing it in the bush," they exhausted their capital, became poor, and were compelled to leave the country. Large amounts of money were expended in clearing land and in other improvements to very little purpose. Several families had come in from the States and had made beginnings upon what were then unclaimed lots, with the hope that they would be allowed to retain them as first settlers; but some years afterwards the authorities at Quebec, not having been apprised of the circumstances, had made appropriation of their farms to Sir Robert Shore Milnes and others. In after years, some of the original emigrants were able to buy back their farms at an upset price, but others were compelled to dispose of their "betterments" as they best could, and leave the country. In many cases vexatious and expensive lawsuits have been the result of the enforcement of the claims of the original grantees or their heirs.

In the early days of the settlements the inhabitants had access to each other and the surrounding country, only by paths through the woods. An Act had been previously passed by the Provincial parliament, for making and repairing roads and bridges under the supervision of a Grand Voyer, but it was not till their number and their means increased, that the early settlers could avail themselves of the privilege of establishing roads. The laying out of highways was attended with much expense. The Grand Voyer for the County of Richelieu then resided in Montreal. The following was the tariff allowed for his services in laying out the early roads in Stanstead County:—

For	Publishing Petition	$1.00
"	Travelling expenses	53.60
"	Attending Meeting of Petitioners	3.00
"	6 days time at $2.50 per day	15.00
"	Visit to the place and examination	6.00
"	Proces Verbal and description of Plan	8.00
"	Copy of Proces Verbal and Enregistration	3.00
"	Homologation of Proces Verbal	4.00
"	Order for Publication of Proces Verbal	1.00
		——94.60

Besides these charges there were usually contingencies which brought the amount up to $100. Bridges had previously been built across the Narrows, Barlow and Negro Rivers, and causeways of logs were laid in different marshy plains. Some of the roads which had been cut out and partly worked before the advent of the Grand Voyer were afterwards adopted by regular survey.

The first advent of the Grand Voyer was an affair of some note. Indeed, the Grand Voyer was a *great man*—weighing 300 lbs., avoirdupois. An ox team was sent to bring him and his attendant from Shefford. Prince Albert did not in more modern days, probably, produce a greater sensation.

Highways were laid out in Stanstead, Hatley and Barnston in

1808, and worked by assessment upon the inhabitants. Emigration from the New England States was steady, but the number of Europeans was comparatively small. For many years, however, there was but little consolidation or union of effort in the settlements; each neighborhood in the different townships managed its own local affairs, and formed a kind of community in itself, working its own roads and sustaining its own schools. Churches were organized in different localities, but the religious element was far from being a prominent one in society.

The want of Courts of Justice was a grievance which was long felt by the early settlers. A few magistrates were here and there appointed, and these were to a certain extent serviceable in preserving the peace of the community; but all matters of civil process had to be carried to the courts at Montreal or Three Rivers for adjustment. This state of things subjected the honest and industrious man to imposition and losses—inasmuch as he often chose to suffer wrong, rather than seek redress from a tribunal so far distant, and attended with very great expense. These inconveniences might, however, have been productive of some good ; for lawsuits were rare—men of litigious propensities could not upon the slightest provocation expose their neighbors to the rigors of the law with the same facilities as in more modern days. There are not unfrequently found in our communities individuals of this stamp, who by their frequent appearance as plaintiffs in our courts of justice prove conclusively that the law, like many other blessings, may be perverted to a prolific source of evil.

For many years, no alteration was made in the judiciary of the townships, but in process of time, Commissioners' Courts were established in all the towns and parishes that petitioned for them —thus affording an easy and expeditious way of collecting small debts. These Courts have been continued under various modifications to the present time.

As nothing had occurred to check the progress of the settlements up to 1812, they had attained to a good degree of strength and prosperity. The population had increased a hundred fold, and men of enterprise had laid the foundation for large fortunes by trade and otherwise. During the American War of 1812–1815, a check was given to emigration from the south, and some of the timid settlers sold out and left the country. The cold seasons of 1816 and 1817 rendered the prospects of the country discouraging, and things for a time seemed to be going backward, but changes for the better occurred, and accessions to the population have been gradually made.

In 1821, a sub-division of districts for judicial purposes was made, and a part of the county of Richelieu was included in "The Inferior District of St. Francis," in which Sherbrooke was selected as the place for building a Court House and Jail, and holding Courts of Justice. This was one step in the right direction. In 1828, an Act was passed by the Provincial Government, by which the previously existing counties were sub-divided and new ones constituted—Stanstead, Hatley, Barnston, Barford, Bolton, and Potton, were taken off from the County of Richelieu, and formed

THE COUNTY OF STANSTEAD.

The immediate result of the creation of new counties was an increase of the number of members in the Provincial Parliament—of these, Stanstead County furnished from one to two. Among its representatives, up to 1847, were Hon. Ebenezer Peck, Hon. James Baxter, Marcus Child, Esq., Col. Wright Chamberlain, and Col. John McConnel.

A new division of Counties was made in 1847, in which the Township of Magog was constituted from the north-western part of Hatley and the north-eastern part of Bolton, and this new township with the remainder of Hatley, and Barnston, Barford and Stanstead, form the present COUNTY OF STANSTEAD. Since that time, this County has been represented by Col. John McConnel, H. B. Terrill, Esq., Hon. T. L. Terrill, Albert Knight, Esq., and C. C. Colby, Esq.

From 1828 to 1841, little change was made in the management of the general affairs of the County, or in the local interests of the different towns. In 1841, an ordinance was passed, under which District Councils were established—the Wardens of these Councils being appointed by the Governor General, and the Councillors elected by the different townships and parishes in the district, the different townships or parishes electing one or two members, according to the amount of their population.

The first District Council of Sherbrooke was formed Sept. 7, 1841, Hon. Edward Hale, Warden. The townships in Stantead County were each represented in this Council. Among the advantages derived from this administration, were the surveying and establishing of roads; which prerogative had been confined to the Grand Voyer.

The Act constituting District Councils was repealed in 1845,

THE COUNTY OF STANSTEAD.

and Township Councils and Parish Councils were introduced—each township or parish to elect seven councillors. In 1847 this Act was repealed, and another was passed, which gave rise to the system of County Councils. In forming these councils each township furnished its appropriate numbers. The Act constituting the County Councils has been subject to various modifications, but it remains essentially unchanged to the present day. The same may be said of the township and parish councils—the county councils being a kind of tribunal for the arbitration of difficulties in the township councils.

TOPOGRAPHICAL VIEW.

BOUNDARIES.—The boundaries of the present County of Stanstead are Orford, Ascott, Compton and Clifton on the north; Compton and Hereford on the east, the parallel of 45 degrees which separates it from Norton, Holland and Derby, in Vermont, on the south; and Lake Memphremagog and Bolton on the west. The entire county comprises an area of about 410 square miles, or about 263,000 acres.

FACE OF THE COUNTRY.—There are few parts of our country, perhaps, that present a greater variety of surface than Stanstead County. The land on the eastern shore of Memphremagog Lake and extending through Hatley, on the west side of Lake Massawippi, is hilly and broken. The most prominent elevations are the hills west of the Narrows and Bunker Hill, near Fitch Bay.

The courses of Barlow, Negro and Coaticook Rivers are marked by uneven banks and hilly ground which generally extends about a mile on each side. The greatest elevation in the eastern part of the county is Barnston Mountain. In many places the surface is undulating, and resembles the rolling prairies of the west, with no prominent hills. On Barlow and Coaticook Rivers are small but valuable meadows, varying from a quarter of a mile to half a mile in width. The greater part of the hilly ground is adapted to cultivation or pasturage: and with the exception of a small tract of marshy land near the outlet of Lake Massawippi, and a section of some 800 acres west of the Lake, called "The Burnt District," there is but little waste land in the county.

SOIL AND PRODUCTIONS.—The soil in its native state was highly fertile and productive. The hills and higher grounds were covered with a heavy growth of maple, beech, birch, white ash and leverwood; and the lower lands produced elm, basswood, cherry, butternut, poplar, hemlock, spruce, pine, cedar, fir and tamarisk. The expense of clearing varied from $10 to $15 per acre. Crops of Indian corn, wheat, rye, oats, barley, buckwheat, potatoes, turnips, peas, beans and grass were sure and abundant. Potatoes were largely manufactured into whiskey. Many of the early settlers supposed that, like the Western prairies, the strength of the soil would always continue; and their principal object was to extend their clearings. The consequence was that most of the county was stripped of its most valuable timber, leaving only very limited reservation for sugaries, firewood, building materials, &c. Experience has shown that much of their best timber has been destroyed, and their farms impoverished to very little purpose. Many of these farms would now command a higher price in the market if no improvements had been made upon them.

The value of real estate has increased with the general prosperity of the country. At the beginning of the present century, the price of wild lands varied from one dollar to two dollars per acre. Very many of the farms of the early settlers would now command from $25 to $50 per acre.

MINERALS.—Until within the few past years, but little attention has been given to the geological and mineral resources of the county. Granite and limestone of a superior quality are abundant in Stanstead and Barnston. Soapstone has also been found. As our limits will not admit a particular description of the geological features of the several townships, the reader is referred to the Report of Sir William Logan, late Provincial Geologist.

STATE OF SOCIETY.—The state of society in the townships has been subject to changes similar to those experienced in new settlements generally. Let the reader imagine a colony of families or individuals from different countries and walks in life, thrown promiscuously together under circumstances of mutual interest and dependence, and he will form a pretty good estimate of things at the beginning. Every man was then "as good as his fellow," and distinction or caste was comparatively unknown.

For a long time, the early settlers formed a kind of brotherhood, and the friendships which began in the days of their hardships and privations were continued during the remainder of their lives. In their visits to each other, made with ox teams, often to the distance of six miles through the woods, they doubtless experienced a satisfaction much greater than is usually enjoyed in the more splendid visits of modern days.

As the forests began to disappear and the circumstances of the people improved, they naturally sought to avail themselves of the privileges enjoyed in other parts of the country. Their first step was in the right direction—the introduction of schools as good as could be sustained at the time. Social libraries were started in some of the towns, and were a great benefit. Some of the families of the early settlers had been favored with the advantages of a good English education, and these, in general, furnished teachers for the pioneer schools. Some of these families had brought in a few books, and these were read and re-read throughout the different neighborhoods. For many years, the Bible, Bunyan's Pilgrim, Dodridge's Rise and Progress, and Watt's or Wesley's Hymns, formed the entire library of many of the most wealthy families. The old-fashioned toy books, with coarse wood cuts, such as The New England Primer, Jack the Giant Killer, Valentine and Orson, Mother Bunch, Blue Beard, and Tom Thumb, were sought for and prized by the children and youth of that age, vastly higher than the neat periodicals that are now poured, like an avalanche, into the laps of the rising generation. Reading in those days was, like study, conducted under difficulties, but it was thorough. Books were read and re-read with attention and profit.

The organization of Christian Churches followed the introduction of schools. The people, coming as they did from different countries and localities, were different in their religious training and belief, but, for the most part, they united in sustaining the ordinances of the gospel in accordance with their own views.

The foundations of society having been laid, its progress has been commensurate with the growth and prosperity of the settlements. As the circumstances of the people improved and their means increased, their attention was turned to those moral improvements that are inseparable from the enjoyments of civilized life. The character of the schools improved, the influence of the gospel began to be felt, newspapers and periodicals were circulated, public spirit and enterprise increased, and during the past forty years, the state of society in Stanstead County has compared favorably with that of any part of Canada or the New England States.

EDUCATION.—The early settlers of the different townships had, as has been before remarked, taken their first steps in the right direction. Schools were started in all the neighborhoods where fifteen or twenty children could be gathered. As early as 1800, some three or four of these schools were in operation in Stanstead—as many in Hatley, and one or two in Barnston. The schools were kept in the most central log houses or barns in the different neighborhoods, and were generally taught by the best educated young men and women in the settlements—three months in the summer, and as many in the winter—the wages of the teachers varying from $4 to $7 per month, and this paid mostly in grain or in articles of clothing of domestic manufacture. Spelling, reading, writing, and arithmetic were the only branches taught. English Grammar and Geography were sciences of a later date. These, though small, were the nurseries in which very many who have been distinguished in public and professional life in our own country and elsewhere, first learned to lisp their A, B, C. As the settlements increased in numbers and strength, school-houses were built, competent teachers were employed at increased wages—the higher branches of a thorough English education were introduced, and as early as 1818, the schools in Stanstead County ranked among the best in any of the towns in Canada or in Northern Vermont. These schools were sustained by the people, and the teachers "boarded around." The compiler remembers his experience in this line, and the reminiscences of other early teachers would probably fill many pages.

In 1800, an Act was passed by the Provincial Parliament, authorizing the establishment of Schools under what was termed The Royal Institute. For many years, this Act was comparatively a dead letter in the townships—few of them having the ability to comply with its requirements. By the provisions of this Act, any township or parish could by petition receive from the Legislature the sum of $240 as an annual salary for the teacher of a grammar school, upon the condition that a house furnishing ample accommodations for the school and for the family of the teacher should be built by the people. One of these schools was started in Hatley in 1818, and another in Stanstead, about the same time; but they were comparatively short lived—continuing a few years—and no better than the best district schools of the time.

During the succeeding ten years little change occurred in the condition of the schools of the county. From the first there had been a liberal disposition manifested by the Government for the encouragement of education in the townships, and, in 1829, the Elementary School Act was passed. This Act, with some modifications, has continued in force to the present time. Commissioners were appointed, the different townships divided into districts, those districts multiplied, and grants made for building new school houses, and for the support of teachers—each school receiving $80 per annum. 'I his sum was generally sufficient to pay the wages of the teachers of the winter and summer schools —the inhabitants merely providing for the board of the teachers, firewood and the other contingent expenses.

The following statistics, as supplied by Henry Hubbard, Esq., Inspector of Schools for the District of St. Francis, will show the present number of schools in Stanstead County :

" For the Scholastic Year ending July 1, 1867, there have been in operation within the limits of Stanstead County, seven High Schools or Academies receiving Government aid—three in Stanstead, viz., Stanstead Seminary, at Stanstead Plain, and the High Schools at Cassville and Georgeville; one at Barnston, one at Coaticook, one at Hatley, and a Model School at Magog. These schools report an aggregate attendance for the year, of about four hundred and twenty pupils. There has been in addition to these an independent School in connexion with the Episcopal Church at Coaticook.

" Of English Elementary or district schools, there have been seventy-six in operation: twenty-nine in Stanstead, twenty in Barnston, one in Coaticook, five in Barford, thirteen in Hatley, and eight in Magog. The total attendance at the schools in Stanstead was 976, in Barnston, 555; in Coaticook 45 ; in Barford,139 ; in Hatley, 425, and in Magog, 2.3 ; total, 2,353; thus making the whole number of schools (of all kinds), 84; total attendance, 2,833. The number of schools in operation and the attendance vary a small per cent. from year to year."

MILITARY SERVICE.

In 1802, Sir John Johnson was appointed Lieut.-Colonel of the third battalion, Eastern Townships Militia. The able men were gathered. Companies were formed, and officers appointed. They met once or twice in a year. Their " trainings " were usually held in the largest openings in the settlements. The men appeared upon parade in their homespun, every-day clothing. Some with old army guns, some with old fowling pieces, and some with guns " without locks, stocks, or barrels ! " Some of the officers of these companies had had experience in military affairs; but most of the others, like the privates, might have presented the appearance of " the awkward squad," in a regular drill.

Three companies were organized in Stanstead in 1803. The Officers were Charles Kilborn, John Ruiter, and Thomas Friolt, captains; Andrew Young, and Thomas Fyler, lieutenants; Johnson Taplin, ensign,and Benjamin Kilborn and Richard Copp, sergeants. This company numbered about 50.

One company was formed in Hatley in 1807. Ebenezer Hovey captain; Simon Kezar, lieutenant; and Jesse Wadleigh, ensign. It numbered about 50.

A company was formed in Barnston, in 1805. Joseph Bartlett, captain; John Heath, lieutenant; Levi Locke, ensign; George Aldrich, sergeant. Had about 50 men.

In 1812, there were seven companies in Stanstead, four in Hatley and three in Barnston. In the American War of 1812-1815 each of those companies supplied some 5 men by draft for the British forces. A cavalry company had been formed, and these, with most of the militia were employed at different times in the frontier service.

Subsequent to the Peace of 1815, but little attention was given to military affairs. One training or muster each year having been deemed sufficient. This state of quietude was, however, broken by the Rebellion of 1837-1838.

Although the operations of the Insurgents had fairly begun in 1837, no positive outbreak occured upon the frontier until January, 1838. In the meantime, a volunteer company had been formed comprising recruits from Stanstead, Hatley, Potton and Bolton. The officers were Alex Kilborn, captain; J. Langworthy and H. Mears, lieutenants; J. S. Walton, ensign; and J. W. Martin, sergeant. This company did good service. Among their exploits was the following, as related by J. S. Walton, Esq., their ensign:

" A simultaneous attack had, as it appeared, been planned upon all the towns and villages along the line or frontier of Lower Canada and many parts of Upper Canada, on some night in January, 1837. About one hundred men, principally from Stanstead and Barnston, gathered on the night in question at Derby Line for the purpose, as some of them afterwards stated, of burning the village of Stanstead Plain, and disarming the Volunteers of Captain Kilborn's Company. They were mustered near the flag staff on the brow of the hill, overlooking Rock Island by one Blanchard, who had printed a paper at the line for circulation in Stanstead and

Compton counties, with the view of stirring up the people to revolt. This worthy man was chosen to lead this gallant band to charge upon the unsuspecting people on 'the Plain,'—for so little was danger apprehended at that time, that no guard was kept, either day or night. Before making an effectual demonstration, it was thought best by those brave men to send a reconnoitering party to the Plain, and Blanchard and some three or four others are reported to have visited most of the buildings in the village and to have recommended an immediate attack, as there were no "lions" in the way. A part of the company were opposed to burning the village, and some of them did not exactly like to risk the attempt of taking the muskets from the volunteers, lest they, themselves, might be taken. A good deal of time was spent in discussing preliminaries, until one after one, the company began to drop away; and before day light, all had disappeared, verifying the lines :

"Full one hundred gallant fighting men
Marched up a hill, and then marched down again!"

The invasion of Potton was not quite so barren of results.— A part of Capt. Kilborn's volunteers lived in Potton, and the writer, as color sergeant, was ordered to that place to drill them. He started about daylight of the morning succeeding the above-mentioned gathering at Derby Line, but quite ignorant of what had been passing there. While on his way, ofter crossing the Lake, he was asked by several persons if Stanstead Plain had not been burned the previous night. On receiving his reply in the negative, they expressed great surprise, as they had learned that morning from Troy, Vt., that not only Stanstead Plain, but all the principal villages on the frontier of Canada had been burned. It afterwards appeared that a party of about thirty-five, the most of them residents of Potton, had gathered at North Troy, and being there joined by a few reckless sympathizers, and led by a desperate character by the name of Hadlock, who had resided in Stanstead, all armed and provided with sleighs, drove into Potton, with the intention of robbing the volunteers of their muskets. They commenced their operations at the house of a very quiet man, Charles Hand, who lived near the line. He gave up his musket, seeing that resistance against 30 or 40 armed men would have been useless. Having accomplished this gallant exploit, they next called at the house of Mr. Ralph Elkins, who lived two or three miles from the line. Salmon Elkins and his wife, an aged couple, then lived with their son, Ralph Elkins, who had two sons who were volunteers. Like truly loyal British soldiers, they refused to surrender their arms to a set of lawless brigands, and with their father repaired to the upper loft of the house — The lads planted themselves at the head of the stairs, with their weapons loaded, and the father with a heavy bludgeon placed himself on the stairs, ready to strike down any one who should come up, if the boys missed fire. The Rebels were warned that the first man who attempted to go up would be shot down. For some time no one ventured to ascend. In the meantime, threats were made outside of firing the building. At length the foolhardy Hadlock said with an oath that he was not afraid, and should go up. He had no sooner stepped upon the broad stairs, at the bottom, than both of the lads fired, and the contents of one of the muskets were sent through his body. He fell, and expired in a few minutes.

This tragical event seemed to take the courage out of the whole party. They placed the dead body of their companion in a sleigh and drove back to North Troy, threatening, however, to return and hold the place. Couriers were despatched to the neighboring towns where volunteers were stationed, and to Headquarters in Montreal, and in a short time, 400 or 500 volunteers from Sutton, Brome, Stanstead and Sherbrooke, arrived at Potton to meet and repel the invaders, should they again dare to cross the border. But beyond threatening, no further hostile demonstrations were made upon the frontier of Stanstead county.

The company of volunteers mentioned in the preceding pages remained in service until late in the spring of 1838, when they were discharged.

Soon after the intended uprising in Montreal and the attack of insurgents upon the loyalists at Beauharnois in November, 1838, Col. Robert Nickle was sent by Sir John Colborne to superintend the operations of the frontier forces at Stanstead. A company of infantry was again formed : Alexander Kilborn, captain ; M. Dixon and C. A. Kilborn, lieutenants; James Sweeney and Coffin Quimby, sergeants.

A cavalry company was soon after formed which did good service : Israel Wood, captain ; J. W. Martin and H. B. Terrill, lieutenants. Another cavalry company was subsequently organized: John Gilman, captain ; Samuel Gilman and E. D. Whitcher, lieutenants ; and T. L. Terrill, orderly.

Soon after the arrival of Col. Nickle, it was ascertained that a

MILITARY SERVICE. 15

party of disaffected Canadians and their American sympathizers was organized in Barnston, and that they held nightly meeting for drill under the command of Lovell McKeech and Asa Hollister both living in Barnston. Col. Nickle accordingly issued a secret order for the arrest of these two men (the country then being under Martial Law,) and entrusted the enterprise of their arrest to Capt. Kilborn of the Infantry, and Lieut. Martin of the Cavalry. They selected ten men each from their respective companies, and after seeing them well mounted, divided into two companies or parties. Capt. Kilborn's party were to go in search of McKeech, and Lieut. Martin was to arrest Hollister. The two parties left Stanstead Plain quietly one at a time after dark, and met for rendezvous, some two miles north of the village. In accordance with this programme, the two parties took different routes, and were to meet at Negro River. McKeech was not to be found, but they succeeded in arresting Hollister, who took the matter very coolly, and requested the privilege of changing his clothes; but on reaching his bed-room, he dodged out at a back door and escaped. Capt. Kilborn being vexed at the loss of their prisoner dismissed all the men and ordered them to return home. In the meantime, he and Lieut. Martin remained a while near Hollister's house, but when from the report of a gun and other signals, they found that men were gathering at no great distance from them, they thought discretion to be the better part of valor, and about mid-night started for home. On reaching Mosher Corner, they were fired upon by some 20 men from behind the fences and from an old cellar. Capt. Kilborn, though severely wounded, started his horse upon the run, reached home, and gave the alarm. He had seen Lieut. Martin fall from his horse, and from the number of shots fired supposed he must have been killed, and that the party would not have made this demonstration unless they had been fully prepared to carry out their previous threat of burning Stanstead Plain. Such a panic as that caused by the arrival of Capt. Kilborn on that eventful night has never before or since been witnessed in Stanstead. An attack was hourly expected; messengers were despatched to Hatley, Compton, Lennoxville and Sherbrooke, and before ten o'clock the next morning a military force of 1000 men was on the ground. In the meantime, Lieut. Martin escaped unhurt. His horse had received a shot in his head and had fallen; but he extricated himself and run for his life. Ho succeeded in reaching a house where he passed the remainder of the night unmolested. His horse had been kindly cared for by a neighbor, and early the next morning he set out for home. He was met by his wife, accompanied by a cavalcade of the military and friends who had gone with the intention of finding him, whether dead or alive Capt. Kilborn recovered from his wound, and in a few weeks resumed the command of his company.

In the spring of 1866, the frontier towns were alarmed by threatened invasions from parties connected with an association in Ireland and America, known by the name of Fenians. As the operations of this organization are matters of general history, it may suffice to say that it presented for a time, a formidable appearance, comprising much of the Irish element in Britain and America. A part of their plan was to send detached parties mustered in the United States through different frontier towns into Canada, to overrun and to plunder the inhabitants and get possession of the country. The Provincial Government, having been apprised of their movements, despatched troops to the different frontier posts. In the meantime, parties of those desperadoes, numbering from 200 to 2,000, invaded our frontier in different places in Canada West, and at St. Armand, P. Q. In most of those places, they were promptly met and repulsed by the Canadians troops. Similar attempts were made some three years afterwards, which resulted in entire failure. The Stanstead frontier was at times threatened, but, beyond threats, nothing occurred to disturb the peace of the community.

MAILS AND ROUTES.

Many years elapsed before the pioneers of the Eastern Townships enjoyed the advantages of postal communication with other parts of Canada and the United States.

The first mail route opened in this part of the country was from Wells River to Derby Line, Vt., in 1812. Previous to that time, the towns upon that route had been supplied by a post-rider who came to Derby Line twice in each month, and, as his business increased, extended his trips through Stanstead, Barnston, Hatley, and Compton. He was employed in circulating the Green Mountain Patriot and the North Star, then published at Peacham and Danville, Vt. These were almost the only newspapers read in the settlements for many years, and the sight of a Quebec or Montreal paper was a very rare occurrence.

From 1800 to 1817 there were no regular mails through the Eastern Townships. Whenever despatches were sent from the Government, special couriers were employed, as also with returning documents. In 1817, a mail route was opened from Stanstead to Quebec, via Melbourne, with a weekly mail which was carried on horseback. Post-Offices were established at Stanstead, Hatley, the "Lower Forks," now Sherbrooke, and Melbourne. In 1824, a weekly mail was started between Stanstead and Montreal, via Copp's Ferry, now Georgeville, and Magog Outlet, where Post-Offices were opened. The expense of the conveyance of this mail was sustained in part by individuals living on the route. Another weekly mail was subsequently started between Stanstead and Montreal, via St. Johns, and these two mails supplied a regular communication with Montreal and Western Canada for many years. In 1833 semi-weekly mails were introduced, and since that time, the facilities for mail correspondence have steadily increased, and the greater part of Stanstead County is now in daily communication with the principal towns in Canada and the northern cities of the United States.

LOCAL NEWSPAPERS.

In 1823 Silas H. Dickerson started a weekly paper, "The British Colonist," at Stantead Plain. This paper was a very respectable sheet for the time, and, as it was the only one then printed in the Eastern Townships, it obtained a large circulation. Politics and party were then matters of mere name. Up to that time, the attention of the Provincial Government had not been fully directed to the requirements of the increasing Settlements of the Townships. The particulars of the organization of the new District of St. Francis furnished materials for the columns of Mr. Dickerson's paper; and it might have been well, perhaps, if he had been contented with printing those particulars. The Presiding Judge of the newly constituted Court, though a learned and worthy man, was peculiarly sensitive and tenacious of his own professional dignity Mr. Dickerson had been trained in the school of American Republicanism, and in some of his editorials had animadverted rather strongly upon the decisions of the Judge in particular cases. His comments, though just, perhaps, in the main, were ill-timed, and brought him into direct collision with the Judge. The Judge was arbitrary, and he was unyielding.

Suffice it to say that he was repeatedly fined and imprisoned for "Contempt of Court," and followed for some three years by the

FORESTS AND CLEARINGS.

Judge with unrelenting persecution and severity. His property became reduced, and he was compelled to relinquish the enterprise of his paper, and leave the country. He returned to Stanstead in after years, however, and for some time sustained the office of Collector of Customs for that Port.

THE STANSTEAD JOURNAL.

This newspaper, published at Rock Island, was commenced in 1845. The enterprise was started under circumstances of discouragement by LeRoy Robinson, who still remains its proprietor and editor.

Other undertakings of a similar kind had been tried and had failed for want of patronage, but Mr. Robinson had brought to the work a practical knowledge of the business, health, industry and perseverance. The result has been a success. The journal has acquired an extensive circulation, second, perhaps, to none in the Eastern Townships, and ranks among the best of our country papers.

THE COATICOOK OBSERVER.

This paper was started at Coaticook in 1870. It is a highly respectable journal and has a good circulation,—is now published by Hunter Bradford.

TOWNSHIP OF STANSTEAD.

The name *Stanstead* is of Anglo-Saxon origin. In almost every nation, and among all classes of people names of persons and places have been more or less descriptive of the character or qualities of the individuals or localities to which they are applied.

The noun or word which denotes a locality is often combined with an epithet, descriptive of some circumstance, quality, or natural production of the place. To show in what a variety of connections a simple word of this kind is found a few examples are subjoined in which STONE is a component syllabe—*Stone, Stondon, Stoneham, Stonehouse, Stonton.*—The Anglo saxon orthography is STAN--whence *Stonage, Stanwix, Stanford, Stanfold, Stanbridge, Stanstead,*

From the *Imperial Gazetteer* it appears that three places in England bear the name of Stanstead. It was from one of these places that the Township of Stanstead, and subsequently the county, derived its name.

TOWNSHIP OF STANSTEAD.

The survey of Stanstead was begun in 1792 and completed in 1793. There is a legend handed down from the early settlers to the effect that, while at this work, the surveyors were in the habit of mixing more whiskey with their water than was consistent with strict temperance, and finding it difficult sometimes to keep either themselves or their compass at equilibrium, were accustomed to talk to the instrument telling it to "*stand steady;*" but, owing to their too frequent potations, were only able to articulate " STAND-STEAD !" and that this circumstance gave rise to the name of the town. The question may, perhaps, furnish scope for the future researches of the antiquarian.

The Township of Stanstead, which includes the villages of Stanstead Plain, Beebe Plain, Rock Island, Georgeville, Fitch Bay, and the Lake Shore, Glines' Corner, Griffin's Corner, Marlow, Ruiter's Corner, Magoon Point, Brown's Hill, Cassville, Boynton, Amy 'orner, Newville, and Caswellboro' settlements, is situated on the eastern shore of Memphremagog Lake, in 4 degrees 55 minutes east longitude from Washington. Its other boundaries are Magog and Hatley on the north, Barnston on the east, and the parallel of 45 degrees north latitude, which separates it from Holland and Derby in Vermont, on the south. Its extreme lengh from east to west is about eleven miles, and its breadth from north to south is ten miles, comprising an area of about 110 square miles, or about 70,000 acres.

LAKES AND RIVERS.

Lake Memphremagog, about two-thirds of which lies in Canada, forms the western boundary of Stanstead, and extends northerly nearly through the entire county. It lies in a semicircular form, partly among the mountains and partly in the valley which runs obliquely across the northern portion. The waters are limpid and remarkably clear, except in the seasons of the spring freshets, when the streams are swollen with the mountain torrents from the high surrounding country. Its principal tributary streams are Barton, Black, Clyde, John's and Cherry Rivers, and Marlow, Lewis, Gale, Taylor, Lee, Rollins, Perkins, Ward, Tuck, and Thompson's Mill Brooks. Magog River is the only outlet. This river, with a north-easterly course of about 20 miles, forms a junction with the St. Francis River at Sherbrooke, and thus the surplus waters of the lake are conveyed into the St. Lawrence. The extreme length of the lake from north to south is about 33 miles, its breadth varying from one mile to three miles. The water is in many places shallow, but very deep in others, having been sounded in some instances to the depth of sixty fathoms. The deepest place yet ascertained is near the foot of Owl's Head, which measured one hundred fathoms. Steamers drawing five feet of water have for many years made daily trips from Newport, Vt., to Magog Outlet and back during the Summer and Fall. Captain George W. Fogg commanded the Mountain Maid, the only steamer used on the lake for many years, and was distinguished for his kindness and courtesy to his passengers. The stopping places on the route were Harvey's Landing, the Mountain House, Georgeville and Knowlton's Landing.

During the few past years, this lake has been a resort for tourists from the United States and from different parts of Canada. Travellers are generally pleased with the scenery of the lake and its surroundings. They seldom fail of climbing Owl's Head. This mountain is the highest, except one, in the Eastern Townships, and its summit affords a clear view of the country south of the St. Lawrence from Montreal Mountain to the St. Francis River.

In passing down the lake from Newport, Vt., a fine view is presented of Indian Point, a promontory in West Derby, so called from its having been for some time the residence of the family of an Indian known among the early settlers as *Captain Jo*. He had in former days sustained the position of Chief, in his tribe. Whipple's Point, on the opposite shore, affords an interesting view. Province Island, lying partly in Vermont and partly in Canada, containing about 100 acres mostly cleared and improved, was the property of the late Carlos Pierce, Esq. There are several small islands in its vicinity, among which is Tea Table Island.

After passing Province Island, the surrounding country presents the appearance of an extended amphitheatre with the lake for its centre. Prominent to view on the east are Blackadder Point, so called from a family who settled upon it; Bodwell Point, now known as Cedarville, and Magoon Point, formerly called Black Point, and on the west, Owl's Head, Sugar Loaf, Gibraltar Point, and in the distance, northerly, Bolton and Orford Mountains.

Whetstone Island, near Magoon Point, contains about forty acres —some twenty-five acres of which have been cleared and improved. It derived its name from a quarry which furnishes whetstones said to be equal in quality to any imported oil stones.

SKINNER'S ISLAND, opposite Magoon Point and near the eastern shore, has been distinguished in fiction as a refuge for smugglers in the American War of 1812-1815—inasmuch as it has been selected by several of our modern story-tellers as the place where various scenes of robbery, murder, and love have been enacted. This island contains about ten acres—rocky and barren—is principally a granite ridge—a reef of which extends to Minnie Island, a distance of about twenty rods. *Skinner's Cave*, said to have been the smugglers' retreat, is an opening in a granite ledge above high water mark, and extending some fifty or sixty feet into the ledge—about eight feet high and about eight feet wide.

MINNIE ISLAND, containing about half an acre, rocky and barren, was long the fishing ground of David Heath.

Long Island, near the eastern shore, and opposite the place of the Hon. C. D. Day, contains about forty acres. It consists of a long and broken ridge of rocks—the south part of which is granite. The surface is in some places thinly covered with dwarf pines and shrubs. It is a place of resort in the "blueberry" season. The only object worthy of particular note is the "Balance Rock," a granite boulder of some ten or fifteen tons, poised upon a high ledge of the same kind of stone.

ROUND ISLAND, in this vicinity, contains about ten acres—surface broken, and covered mostly with white birch and dwarf pine.

MOLSON'S ISLAND, containing about fifty acres, and near the eastern shore, opposite the farm of A. W. Boynton, is broken and uneven. A part has been cleared and improved. Mr. Molson has built a house and barn, and the premises furnish a good sugar orchard.

Lord's Island contains about twenty-five acres, mostly cleared and furnishing good pasturage. It lies midway from east to west in the lake and about two-and-a-half miles below Georgeville. Stephen Lord made the first clearing and improvements. There are, also, other large islands in the vicinity of Magog village and other parts of the lake—some of which are used as fishing grounds.

LONG BAY, a branch of Lake Memphremagog, extends northeasterly from Whetstone Island about two miles. Its average breadth is three-fourths of a mile. About the year 1848, a transient man by the name of Sprague came from Vermont, appeared to be partially deranged, but was known to possess some $3,000 in bank notes, which he carried about his person. He spent several weeks—alternately at Stanstead Plain and Georgeville. Some time, late in the summer, he left his boarding place at "The Plain," as was supposed, to go to Georgeville, but was never seen alive afterwards. In the following spring, his body was found floating on the deep water of Long Bay. He had doubtless been waylaid and murdered. There was a deep cut in the neck, and wounds in different parts of the body. Weights had been fastened to the body with silk handkerchiefs, but the stones had worn through their covering and dropped. Different parties were suspected, and legal proceedings instituted. Two or three men were arrested, and though the public mind was strongly impressed with the belief of their guilt, they were discharged—the chain of circumstantial evidence not being considered complete.

A strait of about half a mile in length called "The Narrows," connects Long Bay with FITCH BAY. Fitch Bay has an average breadth of three-fourths of a mile, and extends two miles north-easterly, or a little beyond the concession line between No. 21, 5th range and No. 4, 6th range. This bay derived its name from Colonel George Fitch, an Englishman of some note who was among the early explorers of the township. Though not immediately connected with the operations of the surveying party, he appears to have been identified with their movements. He explored Long Bay and Fitch Bay, and Bouchette's map of that part of the town was probably constructed from his plan.

Col. Fitch was a genial, pleasant companion, and a lover of fun and jokes. Among the anecdotes related of him is one in which he "met his match." At the time the surveyors were engaged in running the concession lines east of Long Bay, he proposed to Joseph Kilborn a trial of the extent of their eye-sight for a wager of some five gallons of rum for the party. The challenge was accepted and the compass set and sighted. Col. Fitch made the first trial and pointed out a large tree as being the farthest object he could discern. When Mr. Kilborn made his trial, he admitted that he could not see any further than to the tree in question; but he insisted that an accurate measurement of the length of their *noses* (his was a very long one,) and the distance of their eyes from the compass sight should be made, and the result was that

LAKES AND RIVERS.

Mr. Kilborn won the wager by the distance of more than *half an inch!* Col. Fitch died at Missisquoi Bay in 1799. The first male child born in Stanstead received his name—George Fitch Copp.

LOVERING POND, about seven miles in length, with an average breadth of three-fourths of a mile, lying partly in Stanstead and partly in Magog, is connected with Fitch Bay by Lee's Mill Brook.

HUBBARD POND OR CRYSTAL LAKE, in the vicinity of Stanstead Plain, is about three-fourths of a mile in length, with an average breadth of one-fourth of a mile. Some 20 acres of land on the eastern shore have been appropriated for a public cemetery. There are two or three other small ponds in the town.

RIVERS.—Barlow River has its rise from a pond in Holland, whence it runs through the south-west corner of Barnston, and entering Stanstead about one mile north of the Province Line, takes a south-westerly course for about a mile to the Caswellboro' Settlement. Here it receives a branch of some five miles in length rising from Barnston Pond, then takes a north-westerly direction about two miles to the Ox Bow, on the farm of J. M. Hubbard. It then takes a south-westerly course about two miles further to Rock Island, whence it continues about due west, along the Province Line, to Beebe Plain, whence making nearly a right angle, it runs about three miles almost due north to Mack's Mills, and then taking a north-easterly direction continues its course through the remaining part of the breadth of the town, and empties into Massawippi Lake in Hatley after a serpentine course of nearly twenty miles. Some valuable mill seats are still occupied at Rock Island, Mack's Mills, Smith's Mills and Woollen Factory, and Libbie's Mills. Before the forests had been cleared away, this river was much larger than it now is, and was well supplied with fish, which were often taken in large quantities. The Colby farm, containing about 1000 acres, is situated on this river. It has large and valuable meadows.

The survey of Derby, Vt., was made in 1780, or about twelve years before that of Stanstead. Mr. Whitelaw, who afterwards constructed a map of Vermont and New Hampshire, was at the head of the party, and a man by the name of *Barlow* was among the surveyors. While engaged in running the northern line, they found that their stock of provisions was exhausted, and Barlow was sent off through the woods to Wells River for a supply. On his return, he found his friends encamped on the hill south of that part of the river which runs in Derby, and opposite the present railway station at Rock Island. They were thirsty and hungry, and were so overjoyed with their supply of a bottle of rum and provisions that they unanimously declared that the name of Barlow should be given to the river.

NEGRO RIVER, which derived its name from a family of negroes known by the name of Tatton, who settled upon its banks in Barnston in 1804, takes its rise in Holland, runs through Barnston, and after a course of about two miles across the north east corner of Stanstead, empties into Barlow River in Hatley. It has several good mill seats in Barnston, and Colby's Mills in Stanstead. Boroughs' Falls on this river afford a picturesque and highly interesting view.

FACE OF THE COUNTRY.—The surface of Stanstead is diversified, but mostly lies in undulating or rolling swells, with no prominent hills. The top of Narrows Hill and some parts of the adjacent Lake Shore Settlement are the highest elevations, and Bunker Hill, near Fitch Bay, is next in height. The land near the Lake and between the Lake and Fitch Bay is in many instances broken and uneven, but is generally well adapted to cultivation and pasturage. Many of the farms have valuable sugaries. The surface on the banks of Barlow River is in some instances broken and irregular, but capable of cultivation. There is but little waste land in Stanstead, and it is not surpassed by any of the Eastern Townships in richness of soil and in agricultural resources.

The Lake Shore south of Georgeville, extending to Magoon Point, furnishes several large quarries of excellent limestone. Between Fitch Bay and the south-western boundary of the town, extending easterly to Beebe Plain, are extensive developments of granite of a superior quality. There are also other quarries of limestone and granite in different localities, which have been worked. No mineral deposits of sufficient importance to pay the expense of working have as yet been found. The Silurian rocks form the foundation strata of the western part of the town, and the Devonian, consisting of limestone and clay slates, with protrusions of granite, predominate through the eastern part; hence it will be seen that the surface of the different parts of the town must furnish soils corresponding with those of similar formations elsewhere—subject only to the result of drift or other accidental deposits.

LAKES AND RIVERS.

The forests, in their native state, presented a grand and luxuriant appearance—the high lands being covered mostly with maple, beech and birch, interspersed frequently with spruce ridges, hemlock and white ash. The lower lands produced cedar, hemlock, spruce, fir, tamarisk, brown ash, elm, leverwood or ironwood, basswood, butternut, and poplar; white pine was found in some instances, but it has long since disappeared. There is no place in the Eastern Townships that was richer in building materials and lumber of all kinds than Stanstead, and there is certainly none where more recklessness has been exhibited in their destruction. The result has been that the town is comparatively stripped of its most valuable timber, and the wood lands that remain are a very inadequate supply.

For many years potatoes were the principle crop, some farmers cultivating ten acres, others twenty, thirty, or forty acres, with an average yield of from 150 to 200 bushels per acre. The potatoes were manufactured into whiskey, which then brought from 40 to 50 cents per gallon in the markets; a bushel of potatoes generally yielded about a gallon. In some instances the whiskey trade was profitable; but its general tendency was to exhaust the farms and blight the prospects of the early settlers. * * * * Those days of darkness have, however, been followed by brighter ones, and for many years the town has been steadily increasing in wealth and prosperity. Stanstead now occupies a prominent position among the agricultural districts of our country. The township is well adapted to grazing, and affords extensive pasturage and hayfields; its wealth has been derived from its exports of beef, pork, butter and cheese, and cattle and horses.

The sugar maple, which predominates in the higher lands, furnishes a supply of sugar equal, in most cases, to the wants of the community. How great soever the desire of the early settlers might have been for enlarging their clearings, they mostly reserved sugar orchards. Some of the original orchards are still worked, but in most cases the trees have decayed and have been replaced by a second growth.

The process of sugar-making in early days was no sinecure. The sugar season usually began about the first of April, when, in most cases, the snow was from three to four feet in depth. The primitive sugar places were set with troughs, made usually from the fir, by cutting trees some fifteen inches in diameter into blocks of about two feet in length and splitting them through the centre.

These troughs held about a pailfull, and a good chopper would make fifty of them in a day. Large troughs made usually from hemlock, and holding from forty to fifty pailfulls, served for storage. These troughs seldom lasted longer than through two seasons. In the early part of the season the sap was carried in pails to the boiling place on snow shoes. This spot was generally near the centre of some 200 or 300 trees. The process of boiling was simple. The snow, sometimes four feet deep, was cleared away a sufficient space, posts or crotches were set and a pole laid across them; a large tree was then felled, which served as the foundation for a fire; as fast as it burned away, the fixings were removed; firewood was then no object; the sugar-makers being desirous of clearing their land and getting rid of the timber. Their principal difficulty was in obtaining kettles for boiling; but notwithstanding their imperfect arrangements, they often made from 400 to 500 lbs. of sugar in a single season.

Within the past half of a century, sugar-making has been much improved; the troughs, gathering pails, sap-yoke, snow shoes, and small kettles, have been superseded by substantial buckets, holders or large tubs and convenient modern boilers; and in almost every sugar lot may be seen a neat and appropriate building for securing the articles in use during the year, for storing a good supply of dry wood, and furnishing a comfortable shelter for the workmen. Much of the maple sugar now made is equal in quality to the best muscovada or crushed sugars in the markets.

STANSTEAD PLAIN.

This Settlement, comprising an area of about nine square miles, was begun by JOHNSON TAPLIN. Some two or three families had found their way through the upper part of Vermont, then a wilderness, and had located near the west-end of the pond at Derby Centre. Among these was the family of the Hon. Timothy Hinman, whose log cabin afterwards became a stopping place for the pioneers of the Eastern Townships. Mr. Taplin and his family were fifteen days in getting through the woods from Newbury, Vt., where they had previously resided, to Mr. Hinman's, where they arrived March 5, 1796. Mr. Taplin beat a snow-shoe path from Derby Centre to Stanstead Plain the next day, and on the following day, March 7, drew his children through on a hand-sled, crossing the river on the ice. His wife accompanied him and carried a large bundle of clothing. They went to work, and after clearing away the snow, which was four feet deep, put up a temporary shelter with poles and hemlock boughs, in which they passed the night, and though in the midst of a dense forest, and at least six miles from any settlement, they doubtless enjoyed a degree of comfort and independence which a monarch might have envied. During the two following days, they brought in the remainder of their effects on the hand-sled and made some improvements in their cabin. This cabin was located westerly from the present main street, on the bank of a ravine which passes through the centre of the village from east to west, where is still found a spring of excellent water. They remained in this shanty until Fall, when they built a log house on the south side of this ravine, and opposite the site of the present Catholic parsonage. Mr. Taplin began his clearing where the present Catholic church stands, and partially cleared some three acres in the spring and summer of 1796. This was then the only opening in the eastern part of the town. He afterwards built a small frame house, and his place soon became the resort of emigrants from the south. He gradually increased his business by bringing in different articles from the nearest markets and opening a limited business in English goods and New England rum, which he sold at almost fabulous prices. Stephen Boroughs lodged here the first night he came to Canada, and bought a lot of gilt buttons from Mr. Taplin which he afterwards returned, minus their tissue paper coverings. His first counterfeit bills were printed on this paper.—They were on the Haverhill, N. H., Bank—denomination $3. In 1800, Mr. Taplin received the grant of his farm, No. 3, 10th range, as an associate. A part of this lot was divided into building lots, and comprises the central part of the present village. Mr. Taplin afterwards sold out and settled at Fitch Bay.

In 1797, Capt. Israel Wood settled on No. 4, 10th range, adjoining Mr. Taplin. He afterwards received a grant of this lot as associate. The building lots comprising the north part of the village were taken from this farm. Jacob Goodwin made a beginning on No. 2, 10th range, in 1797, but soon after sold his "betterments," and left the country; some of his descendants settled in other parts of the town, but they are mostly dead or have left the country. Reuben Bangs made a beginning on No. 5, 11th range, in 1797; cleared some 25 acres, and sold to Phineas Hubbard in 1803. Selah Pomroy pitched lots No. 3 and 4, 11th range, in 1798, and settled adjoining his brother-in-law Reuben Bangs. About that time, James Bangs settled on No. 6, 11th range, and sold out to Hazen Pomroy in 1819, and removed to Ohio.

Andrew Young was one of the associates, he drew No. 4, 9th range, and afterwards purchased Nos. 5 and 6 same range. Samuel Pomroy settled at Derby Line in 1797, and started a clothier's shop, within the limits of the village of Rock Island. Jonathan Morrill began on No. 5, 10th range, in 1801, and sold to Augustine Hibbard in 1806. In 1804, Charles Kilborn settled at Rock Island. Phineas Hubbard settled on No. 5, 11th range, in 1804. Levi Bigelow began trade at Derby Line in 1805, and soon extended his operations through the present limits of Stanstead County. Heman Bangs and William Salisbury began to trade about the same time. Jonathan Gordon pitched No. 1, 12th range, in 1800, but sold out soon after; some of his descendants are now living in Hatley.

In the meantime, the settlement of the village progressed but slowly, for until 1807 there were but three houses within its present limits. In 1808, the road was cut through the forest where the main street now runs, the travel having previously been by a crooked path considerably to the west. Wright Chamberlain opened a store in 1809, and was soon followed by Zabdiel Thayer, and Henry and Elijah Curtis; these have all died or left the country.

Ichabod Smith and Wilder Pierce opened a store in 1813, and subsequently separated and built brick stores; that of Mr. Smith has since been taken down, but that of Mr. Pierce is now occupied with the Custom house and the Eastern Townships Bank. Other parties engaged in trade, about that time, but soon sold out and left the country. The settlements in the township and in Hatley and Barnston had in the meantime been rapidly increasing and "The Plain" had become rather a general market. Trade was then profitable; and among the different merchants who established themselves in the town, only two failures occurred during more than half a century. In many cases large fortunes were amassed, which were afterwards invested in western speculations, and the amount of money thus furnished by Stanstead capitalists would seem incredible, considering the circumstances under which it was acquired. In the early days of the settlement, the transportation of goods was attended with much inconvenience and expense, owing to the bad state of the roads and the distance from the markets. Many packages of English goods and heavier articles were brought from Montreal and from the South on horseback, and merchandise of all kinds commanded high prices.

STANSTEAD PLAIN.

Calico, which could not now be sold for more than 12 or 15 cents per yard, then brought from 84 cents to $1.00; and dresses made from this material, six yards of which was considered an ample pattern, were a luxury, coarse and homely as it was, which was prized by the young ladies of those days as highly as the finest and most costly fabrics are at the present time. Cotton goods, such as shirtings and sheetings, which are now sold at from 8 to 20 cents per yard, then brought from 50 to 75 cents per yard, cut nails were sold at 25 cents per pound, 9 by 7 window glass at 12½ cents per square, and other goods in proportion. In the case of a man who had opened a store in a neighbouring town, he was asked at what rate per cent. advance he sold his goods. His reply was "*four per cent.*" The enquirer thought this was hardly a paying business, and told him so. He said he did not know exactly what he meant by *per cent.*, but that he sold his goods at "*four times the price they cost him.*" This could not, perhaps, be taken as a fair estimate of *all* the trade of those days, but the leading merchants generally started manufactories of pot and pearl ashes which then commanded high prices in the English market, and took in salts of lye in payment for their goods, thus realizing a large profit both ways. The salts were made by boiling the lye of hard wood ashes to such a consistence that when cold it might be carried in a trough or basket. In this condition the salts were carried to the manufactories, sometimes on sleds; but as sleds were rare, a less expensive vehicle was usually adopted. The market price for salts was variable, ranging from $3 to $6 per cwt., but they could always be sold at a fair price, and for cash. The credit or barter system of those days increased the price of goods. The usual terms of trade were that payment should be made in grain or other kinds of produce in the month of January, following the purchases, which if the customer failed to do, he was required to pay cash and interest within the succeeding year. Not having the fear of the "Maine Law" before their eyes, the early traders were accustomed to do a wholesale and retail business in rum, brandy, gin, whiskey, and other distilled spirituous liquors; and in those days of "temperate drinking," almost every one, high or low, rich or poor, indulged in these beverages; and the account books of the merchants shewed frequent instances of long columns of charges of rum, brandy, gin, whiskey, and ditto, against individuals in good standing and of high respectability. In addition to the large quantities of foreign liquors that were sold, there were at one time not less than twenty-six distilleries for the manufacture of potato whiskey in the town, and these turned out at least 3000 gallons of whiskey, each, annually. A considerable part of the quantity thus made was disposed of at Montreal and other markets, but the amount consumed at home told fearfully upon the prosperity of the settlement. The Temperance Reformation of subsequent years changed the aspect of this traffic, but not before many of the early settlers had become habitually intemperate, some of whom found the drunkard's grave, and others were stripped of their property and compelled to leave the country. In looking back to those days of darkness and gloom, it is pleasant to realize that the fires of those distilleries have long since been quenched, and that the traffic in distilled spirits as a beverage is now regarded as a nuisance.

During the time of the American War of 1812-1815, the inhabitants of Stanstead and Derby maintained a strict neutrality and continued their previous friendly relation to each other. As they had together and alike shared the difficulties and privations incident to new settlements, and as nothing they could do could affect the general issue between the two Governments, they succeeded in maintaining an interchange of visits between families, and, to a very great extent, their previous business intercourse. Smuggling was, indeed, carried on by parties on both sides of the Line; but this did not disturb the quiet and harmony of the two towns.

In 1855, Stanstead Plain was set off by the Provincial Legislature as a separate corporation, comprising lots numbers 2, 3, 4 and 5 in the 9th Range, and lots numbers 2, 3, 4 and 5 of the 10th Range of lots in the Township of Stanstead—the whole being supposed to contain an area of about three square miles. The present public buildings are a Wesleyan church, of which mention is made elsewhere, a Roman Catholic church, an Episcopal church, a Congregational church, a town hall, an academy, a district school house, 2 hotels, 4 stores, 2 groceries, a druggist's shop, a silvermith's shop, a tailor's shop, 3 blacksmith's shops, a carriage shop, 2 harness shops, a shoemaker's shop, a bank agency, a registry office, a post office, a telegraph office, a custom house, a masonic hall and a tin shop. There are four practising physicians, six advocates and seven clergymen. The number of houses is about 100, with a population of about 800. Among the elegant residences may be mentioned those of A.

Knight, Esq., Hon. T. L. Terrill, Rev. W. L. Thompson, C. A. Richardson, Esq., W. H. Hunter, Esq., S. W. Snow, Esq., Mrs. H. A. Robertson, Mr. Isaac Butters and the late Carlos Pierce, Esq. The enterprise of the new Wesleyan church was begun in 1864. Mrs. Carlos Pierce performed the ceremony of laying the corner-stone in 1866. The building was completed in 1868, when it was in due form dedicated and ceded to the Canada Conference, under the auspices of the Rev. W. M. Punshon, L. L. D., the exercises of the meeting having been conducted by the then superintendent of the Circuit, the Rev. E. B. Ryckman.

In the cavity of the corner-stone were deposited a brief account of the early settlement of the township, and the origin of the church enterprise, a copy of the Deed of Conveyance to the Conference, samples of the different coins of money then in circulation, and copies of several periodicals and newspapers of the time. To the historian of after years, these statistics may, perhaps, serve as a starting point.

ROCK ISLAND.

The settlement of this village was coeval with that of Stanstead Plain—both having been begun about the same time. In 1798, Selah and Samuel Pomroy, brothers, came from Massachusetts. Selah settled on No. 4, 11th Range, in Stanstead, where some of his descendants still reside. Samuel made a beginning on the bank of the river in Derby, about ten rods south of the Canada line. The State of Vermont had been surveyed previous to that time, but the line of demarcation had been so imperfectly defined that the early settlers hardly knew at first, whether they were in Vermont or in Canada. In process of time, however, as the settlements on the frontier began to increase, the parallel of 45 degrees was supposed to have been ascertained, but it was not finally determined till many years afterwards.

Mr. Pomroy cleared at first about an acre in a dense forest of heavy, dark timber, and built a log house, which served as a stopping place for emigrants from the New England States to Canada. The first tree that was fallen on the Canada side of the river, was a large pine—the stump of which is still preserved as a relic. This tree stood upon the northern bank of the river, some twenty rods below the present main bridge, and furnished the shingles that covered the roof of Mr. Pomroy's house, and the house of Mr. Taplin, at Stanstead Plain.

For more than a year, Mr. Pomroy had no neighbors nearer than Mr. Taplin, at Stanstead Plain, and Mr. Hinman, at Derby Centre. In the meantime he gradually extended his clearing to some five acres, which took in the present business part of the village of Derby Line, and afterwards built a house directly on the line—one half in Vermont, and the other half in Canada. This house was a place of resort for the early settlers of Stanstead and Derby—between whom the most friendly relations were sustained. Some of the Canada settlers were in debt when they left the United States, and from prudential motives did not choose to cross the parallel of 45 degrees. To meet the requirements of this class, a line was painted across the floor, dividing the two countries. Debtors and creditors could enter at separate doors—meet, and exchange friendly greetings, but there was "a gulf between them."

In 1801, Mr. Pomroy started a clothier's shop, on a small scale, on the north side of the river, about fifteen rods above the present main bridge, and, in connection with his brother Selah, carried on the business for two or three years. Some years afterward he sold his property at Derby Line, and removed to Montreal.

In 1800, Daniel Lee pitched No. 1, 10th Range of Stanstead, made a small clearing on the east side of the river, and built a log house. He afterwards relinquished his "betterments" to James Paul, who sold out to Jedediah Lee in 1804. This property was afterwards owned by his son, Erastus Lee, and is now in the possession of A. P. Ball, Esq.

In 1802, a temporary bridge, leading from Stanstead to Derby, was built across the river. This bridge has since been frequently rebuilt, but the location has not been materially changed. Previous to that time, the only crossing place had been a ford, some forty or fifty rods above the Falls.

In 1803, Col. Charles Kilborn who had previously drawn lots numbers 1 and 2, 9th Range of Stanstead, came on and with his brother-in-law, Andrew Young, cleared two acres on the north side of the river, put up a grist mill and a saw mill, and, to secure a water power, built a dam across the main stream at the head of the Falls, and cut a canal across the curve of the river which took in an area of some 4 or 5 acres. This canal furnishes a most valuable water power,—it supplies several mills and foundries, and might be rendered available for many more. The territory cut off by the curves of the river received the name of ROCK ISLAND, and takes in the principal business part of that village.

These mills were the first started in the south-east quarter of Stanstead. Col. Kilborn moved his family in 1804, and for a few years they were the only occupants of " the Island." They had, in the meantime, extended *their clearing to some* 50 acres, and Jedediah Lee had cleared about the same amount on the east side of the river.—These clearings took in the south part of Stanstead Plain.

"The Old Yellow Store" was built in 1809, by Hon. Timothy Hinman. It was first occupied by Nehemiah Colby, of Derby. The property has passed through various hands and is now owned by the heirs of the Hon. P. Baxter. The store has been successively occupied by Baxter & Chamberlin, Baxter & Edmonds, Judd, Bates & Holmes, Judd, Bates & Wood, Baxter, French & Haskell, P. & J. W. Baxter, and Porter & Wiley.

In 1810, Jedediah Lee built a large house on the east side of the river. This house was then considered as rather in advance of the times.

In 1815, Otis Warren built a large shop, using the water power from the canal, and carried on for many years an extensive business in wool carding, and in the manufacture of the various kinds of machinery required in the settlements. Mr. Warren sold to Harris Way in 1837 and removed to Montreal. Levi Mattison started an iron foundry in 1815, but soon sold out and left the country.

In 1818, Alexander Kilborn built a house at the south end of Stanstead Plain, into which he removed with his parents, who remained until the time of their death. He afterwards built at an expense of more than $30,000, but sold out to Carlos Pierce.

In 1823, Freeman Haskell purchased from the Kilborns the entire water power of the canal, with the saw mill, grist mill and clothier's works, and built a linseed-oil mill. He began with good prospects, but was unfortunately killed by falling against the saw in his mill. His arm was cut entirely off, and he survived the accident but a few days. His brother, Sylvanus C. Haskell, succeeded him in the business, but soon after sold out and left the country. Carlos F. Haskell, the son of Freeman Haskell, was five years old at the time of the death of his father. His mother, a woman of energy, had trained him in business habits; and at an early age, we find him engaged in trade, first as clerk, and afterwards as principal. He was cut down in the midst of his years, but not before he had laid the foundation for a large fortune. He built "The Mammoth Store," was succeeded in the business by C. H. Kathan.

In 1827, Harris Way purchased from the heirs of Freeman Haskell the clothiers' shop and a greater part of the other property, and subsequently bought the shop and other real estate of Otis Warren. Mr. Way continued in business until 1855, and then sold out to Ozro Morrill.

In 1828, Stephen Foster, in company with Col. J. Langdon, of Montpelier, Vt., built a store upon the site of that now occupied by the Spalding Brothers. They continued the business until 1833, when Col. Langdon withdrew, and Levi Spalding came in. In 1844, Mr. Foster withdrew, and since that time the business has been in the hands of the Spalding family. It may by mentioned here that Mr. Foster was the first merchant in the Eastern Townships that abandoned the sale of distilled spirits.

Other stores have been built and occupied by different parties, prominent among whom have been Ozro Morrill, Austin T. Foster, W. H. Holmes, Holmes & Morrill, Cass & Jendro, and Charles Morrill.

Three brothers, John, Samuel and Stephen Reed started a paper mill about 1832, and for a few years sustained a large and profitable business in paper, books and general stationery; but the abundant supplies of those articles from the southern markets at very low prices, and the general depression of the times, compelled them to relinquish the enterprise. They had built at an expense of $5,000. The property has since passed into the hands of Ozro Morrill.

In 1834, Walton & Gaylord printed the various school books used in the townships. Webster's and Marshall's Spellers, Emerson's and Adams' Arithmetics, The Canadian Reader and a Geographical and Historical View of Canada. These books were used in our schools for several years. Mr. Gaylord afterwards started the making of paper hangings with good success. Mr. Walton removed to Sherbrooke, where he started "The Sherbrooke Gazette," one of the best local papers in the country. This paper is continued to the present time.

From 1834 to 1840, but little change occurred in the settlement. Willard Wood, Benjamin Wyman and others were actively engaged in business and acquired property. Charles Pierce, an enterprising mechanic, built extensively, and laid the foundation for a large business in the manufacture of boots and shoes. He died suddenly, and the business passed into the hands of Austin Foster. Hon. Portus Baxter built a store which has been successively occupied by Butler & Gilman, Gilman & Holmes, Gilman & Jones and George R. Holmes.

From 1840 to 1850, there were few changes. The limits of the village were gradually extended to the north, and across the river, taking in an area of nearly a square mile. A few enterprising traders and mechanics begun during this time—among whom were A. A. Barry, David White, Stilman Ray, E. Eastman, David Libbee, A. W. Morrill, and C. W. Drew. The Stanstead Journal, a weekly paper which was started by L. R. Robinson in 1845, has been continued to the present time. In later years George James bought the stand occupied by Benjamin Wyman, and carried on an extensive business in tanning and making boots and shoes. He afterwards sold out to Ozro Morrill, and the business has since been continued by Morrill & Judd. Among the latest business men have been A. W. Ovitt, T. & H. A. Pierce, L. C. Bates, J. H. Holton and Carpenter Brothers.

The present limits of the village contain 8 stores, 3 groceries, 3 boot and shoe factories, 2 cabinet shops, 2 planing mills, a door and sash factory, an iron foundry, a grist mill, a machine shop, a last and shoe peg factory, a blacksmith's shop, a tailor's shop, a harness shop, a hatter's shop, a drug store and jeweller's shop, a book store, post office, and hotel, a printing office, a school house and about 50 dwelling houses. Population about 450.

For more than a quarter of a century, the business of this village was tributary to Stanstead Plain, but during the past 25 years it has been in the ascendant. The facilities for water power will ever render it an eligible business place, and with the advantages of The Spur connecting with the Conn. & Pass. and V. M. Railway, it is probably destined to occupy a prominent position in the commercial operations of our country.

BEEBE PLAIN.

This settlement was begun by David and Calvin Beebe in 1798. The name of the village is commemorative of these men. The earliest settlements within the present limits of the village were mostly on lot 1 in the 7th Range of Stanstead. This lot was bought by Sampson Davis from David Beebe about 1802, and sold back to him some time afterwards. Subsequently, the two lots, numbers 1 and 2, 7th Range, passed into the hands of Zadok

Steele. No. 1 was afterwards purchased by Solomon Steele, and No. 2 by Sanford Steele, two of his sons. These farms have passed into other hands, and are now owned by Anson Beebe, John L. House, Horace Stewart, Samuel Bigelow, and one or two other parties. Jesse Willey purchased some 10 or 15 acres, built, and engaged for a time in mercantile business but sold out to John L. House and removed to Derby, Vt.

For many years, the settlement presented the appearance of an opening of some 100 acres in a dense forest, in which might have been seen one or two low frame houses, and some six or eight log cabins; but, like many of our modern towns, it has during the past quarter of a century grown to be a thriving and prosperous village, and is distinguished for the wealth and enterprise of its inhabitants. The completion of the M. V. Railroad forms a new era in the history of Beebe Plain. From its local advantages it bids fair to become a large and flourishing village, and second, perhaps, to none upon the frontier.

In 1872 Beebe Plain was set off from the south-west quarter of the township of Stanstead, by Act of the Provincial Parliament of Quebec, and constituted an independent Municipality.

LINEBORO'.

This settlement is but a part of Beebe Plain. It derived its name from the post office lately established upon the the Boundary line between Canada and Vermont. It is a railway station. Its interests will, probably, be hereafter identified with those of Beebe Plain.

BROWN'S HILL.

This settlement was begun in 1800, by two brothers, Theophilus and Sherborn Brown. The neighborhood was then a dense forest —no clearings nearer than Stanstead Plain and the Lake Shore and the beginning of the Nine Partners of Cassville. In 1799 Thomas Ayer had begun on No. 9, 1st Range of Hatley, at the place known as Ayer's Flat. In 1803 Amos Shurtliff and Willard Ayer moved their families in from New Hampshire. They were followed, in 1806, by Levi Brown and his family, and in 1807, by Jonathan Foss and Benjamin Bartlett. Eleazar Clark, Asa Cole and Thomas Cole came in with their families from Vermont in 1810, and John Brown and his family in 1818.

CASSEVILLE. 37

The early settlers of this neighborhood were generally active and enterprising men. Like the pioneers of Cassville, they had to carry their bags of grain on their shoulders to Fitch Bay and thence to West Derby by water to mill, or go some 15 miles through the woods. As they had made their beginnings without negotiating for titles, they were obliged many years afterwards to purchase their farms from the assignees of Sir Robert Shore Milnes, to whom the original grant had been made. Changes have occurred in this settlement during the past half century, but many of the farms are now occupied by the descendants of the first settlers, with many of whom the compiler was well acquainted. They were mostly self-made men, but for sterling worth and integrity they were surpassed by few in any country.

CASSVILLE.

This settlement comprises about six square miles, and was begun in 1799 by an association of emigrants from New Hampshire, who were known as THE NINE PARTNERS. Their names were Simon Cass, Theophilus Cass, Abraham Cass, Wm. Tripp, Wm. McCleary, John Langmaid, James Moses, James Locke, and Abraham Libbee. They began their clearings in 1799, and moved their families in 1800. On their return home in 1799, they carried with them a large number of sable skins they had taken during the summer. These were made into caps, muffs, tippets, &c., and were of substantial service to themselves and their wives in after years. When they came in with their families, the country was an unbroken wilderness. They had to cut their way for their teams, and were two days in getting from Stanstead Plain to the place where the Cassville Church now stands. They built a shanty in that vicinity, in which seven families lived together until they could build log houses for themselves. No blacksmith nearer than Brownington, Vt., and no mills nearer than West Derby, where a small clearing had been made and a grist mill and saw mill had been built. The only way they could get bread for their families was to take their bags of grain upon their shoulders and carry them through the woods to Fitch Bay, a distance of some six miles, and then take a canoe, and row up the Lake to Duncansboro', (now Newport, Vt.) the distance of about 20 miles, where they would again shoulder their bags and carry them to the mill about two miles further. The men usually took their turns in doing the milling of the neighborhood, each would carry his bag to Fitch Bay, and then one of their number would take a canoe and proceed down the Lake with his cargo, and when arriving at Derby Landing, opposite Newport, would carry the bags one at a time to the mill. By the time he arrived with his second bag, the first would be ground; and thus by carrying both ways, he generally succeeded in accomplishing his business and returning the same day. In building their first houses, they had to work at equal disadvantage, for having neither boards nor nails, they had to hew planks for floors and to cover their cabins with bark, or fasten shingles with wooden pins, as they best could. Glass windows were "few and far between." These inconveniences were only lessened as the settlement increased. The lands in the north part of the town were at that time unchartered, and the settlers went on and made improvements without negotiating for titles to their farms, supposing that they would be allowed to retain them on account of their early settlement. In the meantime, the authorities of Quebec, having little knowledge of the state of affairs, had made grants of those lands to Sir Robert Shore Milnes and others connected with the administration of the Government.

This was the case particularly with the settlements of Cassville and Brown's Hill. The grant to Sir Robert Shore Milnes was made in 1810, and the others about the same time; but it was not until some 15 or 20 years after, that the claims of the real owners were enforced. The owners or their assignees were generally fair with the occupants, setting their lands at their supposed value in their wild state, varying from $1 to $4, per acre. Most of the occupants were able to buy at the upset prices, but some were obliged to relinquish their betterments or dispose of them as they could. The early settlers of Cassville were generally upright and conscientious men, and, if honest and successful industry and unquestioned piety are virtues to be commended, to their posterity there is much cause for gratitude, if not for pride.

FITCH BAY.

Among the early settlers of this neighborhood were the Gustin, Davis, Taplin, Rickard, Doloff, Packard, Lee, Hoover, Clefford and Shurtliff families. The locality was then known as "the Head of the Bay," but was sometimes distinguished by the not very euphonious name of "Sucker City," from the abundance of that kind of fish taken from the Bay and its inlet brooks.

THE MARLOW SETTLEMENT.

A post-office was established here in 1855, which was named after the first explorer of the Bay, Col. George Fitch. The name of Fitch Bay was then adopted for the village. For many years, the settlement presented the appearance of an area of some four square miles of dense forest of heavy dark timber, dotted here and there with small openings. As several families had made beginnings within the limits of the present village, the ground was gradually cleared, and mills and manufactories were introduced, the water power from Lee's mill brook furnishing ample facilities. Within the few past years, a respectable village has arisen, in which are two churches, a school-house, two stores, a post-office, a gristmill with three runs, a saw mill with planing machines, a cabinet shop, a carriage and sleigh shop, two blacksmiths' shops, a harness shop, a boot and shoe shop, and an iron foundry. The number of dwelling houses is about forty-five.

RUITER'S CORNER.

This settlement comprises about four square miles, and consists of some 20 neat farm-houses. It derived its name from Capt. John Ruiter, of whom mention is made elsewhere. This settlement comprises a school district.

GRIFFIN'S CORNER

Derived its name from one of its early settlers. The settlement comprises an area of about four square miles—contains about 50 farm-houses. In the early days of its history it was a place of some little promise, but can hardly be called a village. The present public buildings are a church, a school-house, a blacksmith shop, and a tavern.

THE MARLOW SETTLEMENT.

In 1799, John Gustin, jun., Elisha Miller, Wm. Lanphier, John Gustin, sen., Josiah Gustin, and Abijah Mack, of Marlow, N. H., made a tour through the woods, a distance of 150 miles to Stanstead, and, after examination, decided upon locating near the Lake Shore. They had brought apple seeds, and planted three nurseries: one at Magog Point, one on No. 9, 4th Range, and the other on No. 6, 6th Range. Several fine orchards were afterwards produced from them.

In March, 1800, John Gustin, jun., Abijah Mack, and Elisha Miller, returned again to Stanstead with a two-horse team, loaded with farming implements and other necessaries. They were followed by Caleb White and Dexter White. These five put up a a shanty which they occupied together until Fall.

Having found that there were several unclaimed lots in the vicinity of their encampment, they agreed that, before exploring, the choice of the different parties should be determined by lot. The numbers were then put into a hat and drawn. It was somewhat remarkable that every one was pleased with the lot that had fallen to him.

In the meantime these pioneers had purchased a yoke of oxen, a cow and a grindstone in common, and in June began their operations—each beginning a clearing of his own.

They had previously sowed and planted a piece of ground which they had hired on shares, and their share of the crop furnished them with provisions for the ensuing year. In the Fall they secured their harvest, built a log house on the premises of Abijah Mack, and returned to their friends in New Hampshire. The next winter, 1801, Abijah Mack and Elijah Miller moved their families in, and in March following,, Caleb and Dexter White returned. They all resumed their labors upon their farms, and were made comfortable in Mr. Mack's cabin.

The Spring was unusually forward. ' Abijah Mack sowed two bushels of wheat in March. No crop has been sown so early in the Eastern Townships since that time. Their labors that year were rewarded by an abundant harvest. Gustin, Miller and Caleb White built log houses on their own premises. Comfort Carpenter and Simeon Glidden built a grist-mill and a saw mill near the present site of Smith's Factory on Barlow River. Constant White, a millwright from Charlestown, N. H., superintended the work. He settled in Stanstead.

In February, 1802, John Gustin and Caleb White moved their families in. The first part of the winter had been unusually open —no sleighing until the latter part of February. They improved the first fall of snow and started; but a thaw came on and left them on bare ground, almost at the beginning of their journey. The women and children had to walk over many of the rugged hills for which Vermont is distinguished. Mr. Gustin's ox team was thirteen days on the road, and the horse team was eleven days. This long journey served in some measure to render their log cabins acceptable homes. They were pleased with the attentions paid them by their new neighbors who came to welcome them—each seeming desirous of cheering and encouraging them by a particular relation of the difficulties through which they themselves had passed. They soon found that they were all engaged in the same enterprise—that they were placed upon a level and moved as equals, and that their interests were in a great measure identified. Consequently, the early settlers soon became strongly attached to each other, and the foundation of future society was thus gradually formed.

In the meantime, Hosea White had come in and made a beginning on the east half of No. 11, 5th Range. In April, 1802, Rufus Lanphier, Daniel Miller, and Benjamin Bingham, settled in the neighborhood. In 1804, Ira Miller settled on No. 7, 4th Range, with his brothers Elisha and Daniel. In 1806, Silas Mack purchased a part of No. 6, 4th Range, on which he located. In after years, his two brothers, Asa and Franklin Mack settled on No. 13, 4th Range. These were the last emigrations from Old Marlow to Stanstead. The name Marlow was given to the settlement as commemorative of the native town of its first settlers.

The beginning of the settlement was attended with much prosperity. A log school-house was built in 1805, and in 1817, a new house, much in advance of the times. This house has since been destroyed by fire. For many years the Marlow school ranked among the highest in the Eastern Townships. Many of the teachers of this school are still living, and some of them enjoy high positions in society.

The Marlow settlement comprises an area of about four square miles, extending easterly from the Lake Shore to the Griffin Corner settlement. It contains some thirty or forty neat farm houses, and a school house. The land ranks among the best in the Township.

SKETCHES IN BRIEF.

BY ELISHA GUSTIN, ESQ.

Our knowledge of the ancestry of "The Gustin Families" is very limited. Tradition says that two brothers of that name settled in America—one in Connecticut, the other in Maine. Samuel Gustin, a descendant in the third generation of the Connecticut branch, was a Baptist clergyman; married Mary Thomas; six sons and three daughters were the issue of this marriage; four of the sons were in the Army of the American Revolution; Samuel, the eldest, died of small pox; John, the second son, was among those who captured General Burgoyne; Josiah, the third son, was taken captive by the Indians at the battle of the Cedars—was taken to Montreal and afterwards exchanged. Elisha, the fourth son, was a "mighty hunter." In one of his excursions, hearing a cry from a favorite dog, he hastened to his relief, and found him under a large log which partially secured him from the jaws of a large panther that was standing over him, with his attention engrossed in cat-like play with his victim. "Uncle Lish," as he was called, sprung forward and grasped the panther by the tail, and by a violent jerk brought him to a "right about face." At this critical moment, his companion fired and killed the panther. John, the second son, followed the sea for several years, but afterwards settled upon a farm in Marlow, N. H., where he passed the remainder of his life. He married Lydia Mack. He lived to the age of 71 years. She died July 20, 1847, aged 101 years. Their children were Clarinda, John, Lurany, Sebre, and Abijah. These all married and had families—a part of those families settled in Canada.

John Gustin, jun., eldest son of John Gustin, as before mentioned, was born in Lyme, Conn., Sept. 27, 1768. He was a good English scholar, and excelled as a mathematician, and was for many years employed as a practical land surveyor. In early life he married Esther Way. In 1802 they settled in Stanstead—were useful and valuable members of the community.

WILLIAM MACK, ESQ.

All of the Mack families in America are supposed to be descendants of three brothers that came from Scotland early in the 17th century, having been compelled to leave that country on account of religious intolerance and persecution. As these men were proscribed, and a price set upon their heads, it has been difficult to trace the genealogies of their descendants. In 1755 Ebenezer Mack was ordained a Baptist preacher in Lyme, Conn. He married Abigail Davis. Their children were William, who married Ruth Gee, Abigail, m. Wm. Gee, Lydia, m. John Gustin, Zophar, m. Phebe Miller, Lurany, m. Zacchens Beebe, John, m. Grace Howard, Silas, m. Mary Brown, and Elizabeth, who married Ripley Bingham. Some of the descendants of these families settled in Stanstead. The Mack, Gustin, Miller, Beebe, Bingham and Ball families were directly related to each other by marriage.

WILLARD MACK, M. D.,

Was the eldest son of Abijah Mack, and came to Stanstead with his parents when about 7 years old. His early opportunities, like those of other young men of the settlement, were limited; but he had acquired a good English education, and taught in various district schools with acceptance and usefulness. He studied medicine under the direction of Drs. Whitcher and Colby, and graduated at the Medical Department of Yale College in 1819. He commenced practice in Stanstead, and was soon employed in the neighboring towns. Though young he had attained to a high stand in his profession, but he was cut down in the prime of life and usefulness. A severe cold, the result of exposure in his long winter rides, settled upon his lungs, and he died of pulmonary consumption, October 9, 1822, aged 28 years.

With many of the sciences and much of general literature he was familiar—was a proficient in the use of musical instruments—was well instructed in the principles of Masonry and rendered much valuable assistance to Golden Rule Lodge, of which he was a highly esteemed member. In his religious belief he was a Universalist.

ELISHA GUSTIN, ESQ.,

The eldest son of John Gustin, jun., came to Stanstead with his parents when a lad. He was from childhood an apt and promising scholar, but, with the exception of some assistance from his father and Mr. Harvey, one of their teachers, he may be said to have been self-taught. He had to labor constantly upon the farm, but, whether at home or in the field, a book was his companion. In this manner he succeeded in mastering the different branches of an English education, including the higher mathematics. He was early appointed to the office of magistrate, and sustained a prominent position in public affairs. He died March 28, 1868. In his religious belief he was a Universalist.

GLINES' CORNER.

This settlement derived its name from James Glines, one of the early settlers. It comprises an area of about one square mile, and contains about 20 farm-houses and a school-house.

THE LAKE SHORE SETTLEMENT.

(Communicated by Osmond Boynton.)

This settlement was begun in 1800, by the Merrill, Jewett Baird, Daily, Peaslee, Geer and Brown families.

No. 14, 1st Range, was occupied for some years by Samuel Brown, and, after passing through different hands, is now the property of Hon. C. D. Day. The place is distinguished for neatness and beauty of scenery, and bears the name of GLENBROOK.

No. 15, 1st Range, pitched by Isaac Brown, passed eventually into the hands of Hon. C. D. Day.

No. 16, 1st Range, was pitched by Elijah Baird—is now the property of Alexander Molson, Esq. Mr. Molson has built a splendid residence near the Lake Shore. His place is known by the name of FERN HILL.

No. 17, 1st Range, an associate lot drawn by Silas Peaslee in 1800. Upon his death and that of his wife, some 25 years afterwards, the property fell into the hands of their son-in-law, Luman Cheney. Mr. Cheney and his wife died in 1832, and the property was purchased by A. F. G. Channell, who sold to David Jewett, who sold to Abraham Boynton, who took possession in 1839. This farm is now the property of his eldest son, Adams W. Boynton.

No. 18, 1st Range, was pitched by a Mr. Norton, and, after passing through various hands, is now the property of William Davidson.

No. 19, 1st Range, was settled by Isaac Brown, and, after having changed owners some nine or ten times, is now the property of Henry Chapman, Esq., of Montreal. Mr. Chapman has built an elegant country residence. His place exhibits a degree of artistic taste and comfort which is seldom exceeded in our country. It is known by the name of BELLE MERE.

No. 20, 1st Range, being but a small part of a lot, was thrown in as a part of No 20, 2nd Range. This part was pitched by Elijah Geer, and after passing through several hands was bought by Alex. McEwen.

No. 21, 1st Range, was settled by William Winslow. He lived about two years with his family and then mysteriously disappeared from the settlement. No traces of him have ever been discovered. The farm is now the property of Alex. McPherson.

Nos. 22 and 23, 1st Range were settled by the Jewett family from Lisbon, N.H., and, after passing through various hands, became the property of W. N. Wood, who gave it the name of Woodland.

GEORGEVILLE.

The present name of this village was adopted in 1822—the settlement had been previously known as "*Copp's Ferry.*" The first settlement was made by Capt. Moses Copp in 1797. He had previously located in Bolton, but sold out and began upon a site near the centre of the present village. Elijah Baird had made a beginning about a mile to the south, and Jeremiah Lord, about a mile to the north. With these exceptions, the whole extent of the Lake Shore from Magoon Point to Magog Outlet was an unbroken forest. Mr. Copp long preserved the stump of the first tree he fell as a memento.

In the early stages of this settlement, its local situation rendered it a prominent place of business. It then commanded the trade of the western part of Stanstead, the western part of Hatley, and a large extent of territory on the western shore of the Lake. Several individuals engaged in trade and amassed large fortunes; among these were Joshua Copp, James C. Peaslee, and Chancey Bullock.

In process of time, however, as the country became gradually opened, much of the business of this village was diverted to other localities, and Georgeville has for several years remained stationary. The present village numbers about 40 dwelling-houses, 2 churches, 2 hotels, 2 stores, a post office, a stages, team-boat, and express office, a blacksmith's shop, a tanner and currier's shop, and a boot and shoe manufactory.

NEWVILLE.

This settlement comprises an area of about four square miles, consisting of lots numbers 17, 18, and 19 in the 13th and 14th Ranges of Stanstead.

It contains about 30 farm-houses and a school-house. Among the early settlers were the Fox, Ladd, Swain, Whitecomb, Sawyer, Jones, Norris, and Libbey families.

CASWELLBORO.

This settlement in the south-eastern corner of Stanstead contains about 10 dwelling-houses and a school-house. The Worth, Parsons, and Caswell families were among its early settlers.

FORESTS AND CLEARINGS.

HATLEY.

(Communicated by E. H. Le Baron, Esq.)

This township derived its name from a village of the same name in England. The survey determining its original boundaries was made in 1792. The subdivision into lots was made by James Rankin in 1795. The work was badly done. The division lines of the lots in the different concessions run in a zigzag direction, and some of the concessions are longer than others. In the eastern part of the town, there are twenty-eight lots in each concession, but in the western part the numbers diminish. The original limits of the town extended from Memphremagog Lake and Magog River on the west; but, in 1847, that part of Hatley lying west of the Tenth Concession Line was set off, and now forms a part of the Township of Magog. The present boundaries of Hatley are Magog and Ascot on the north, Compton on the east, Barnston and Stanstead on the south, and Magog on the west. Its length from north to south is ten miles, and its breadth from east to west is eight miles, giving an area of about eighty square miles, or about 51,000 acres.

LAKES AND RIVERS.—Massawippi or Tomifobi, lying near the centre of the town, is about nine miles in length, with an average breadth of about one mile. It has a crescent form, extending north-easterly and south-westerly from the west end of No. 4, 23rd Range to No. 8, 3rd Range. The water of Lake Massawippi is pure and transparent. The shores and bottom are generally sandy or covered with gravel, and free from marshes or bogs. In the early days of the settlement, fish of different kinds, such as shad, black salmon, maskilonge, pike, bass, mullet, and sturgeon, were abundant, and were often taken in large quantities. The fish thus taken formed no inconsiderable part of the sustenance of the families of the pioneers of Hatley. The building of mill-dams across the Massawippi and St. Francis rivers in later years, seems to have prevented the passage of sturgeon, salmon, and shad, up those rivers, and they are now seldom found in the Lake. Large quantities of pike, pickerel, and salmon-trout are, however, taken, especially in the spawning season, by torch-light and the spear; the best fishing-grounds being near the outlet and inlet of the lake. Two persons would often take three hundred pounds weight in a single night; but the result has been that the fish of different kinds have measurably disappeared from the

Lake. The late Protective Act of the Provincial Parliament has had the effect of preventing the taking of fish during the spawning season, and it is expected that there will soon be a plentiful supply.

The principal inlet to the Lake, is Bacon River, which is formed by the junction of Barlow and Negro Rivers, about two miles south of the Lake. The only outlet is Massawippi River, which runs through the north part of Hatley in a north-easterly direction and empties into the St. Francis, about one mile above the present village of Lennoxville, or about eight miles from its source.

These rivers and the country around the Lake had long been the hunting and fishing ground of the St. Francis tribe of Indians; and after the advent of the white settlers, companies of twenty-five or thirty Indians were often seen encamped in the vicinity of the Lake for the purpose of fishing, trapping sable, coon, mink, otter and beaver, and hunting moose and deer—all of which were then found in abundance. In later days, the forests have been cleared away, many interesting Indian relics have been found—such as stone arrow-heads and stone tomahawks with a groove for the handle. Nine of those tomahawks were ploughed up in the spring of 1861. They were found in a pile together. The origin of the race that first traversed this country must ever remain a mystery.

For many years after the settlement of the whites, the Indians continued their visits to the Lake and its surrounding country. They generally came early in the Fall and departed late in the spring. The writer remembers well their bark canoes and the many pleasant rides he had in them. The Indians were uniformly quiet and peaceable, unless irritated by injustice from the white men, or when heated by strong drink. As a general thing, the early settlers had far less trouble with the Indians than with many of their Yankee brethren.

LITTLE MAGOG LAKE, lying partly in Hatley, Magog, Oxford, and Ascot, is a beautiful sheet of water, about four miles in length, and varying from half a mile to three-fourths of a mile in breadth. The Magog River passes through it in its course to the north. It has two tributary streams—one from the north and the other from the south. There are several small streams that empty into the Massawippi Lake, but which are not worthy of particular notice.

FACE OF THE COUNTRY, SOIL AND PRODUCTIONS.

The surface of that part of the town east of the lake is generally undulating, with no prominent mountains or hills. With some few exceptions, the soil of the various farms will compare favorably with that of any part of the Eastern Townships. From the head of Massawippi Lake south-westerly to Fitch Bay, a distance of about four miles, is a ravine through which runs a small stream. A canal connecting Fitch Bay with Massawippi Lake might be constructed, and following the course of this brook, a passage for small steamers and other boats to the outlet of Massawippi Lake might be secured. This canal may perhaps be made at some future day. On the west side of this ravine is a ridge of land, known by the name of Bunker Hill, which, as it approaches the head of Massawippi Lake settles down into gentle slopes and declivities and then unites with the mountain on the west side of the Lake. This mountain is about four miles in length. Its eastern slope near the lake is steep, and in some places precipitous. In some few cases, the hills have been cleared and cultivated, but the remainder are covered with trees and furnish many excellent sugaries. The land west of the mountain is in some places undulating, but in others, nearly level. It is generally settled. The mountain is a place of general resort in the blackberry season.

Pic-nics are frequently got up here by the young men and maidens of Hatley and the adjoining towns for the double purpose of profit and pleasure. About two miles north-west of this mountain and east from Memphremagog Lake is a tract of some eight hundred acres of land that was covered with a heavy growth of spruce, pine, and tamarisk, but which was destroyed by a fire some 40 years ago—leaving only the blackened trunks of a few of the largest trees standing. The soil was in many places burnt almost entirely off. This almost barren waste is now covered with blueberry bushes, and is the yearly resort of many from almost every part of the country. Hundreds of bushels of these berries are annually gathered. Many French Canadian families devote their whole time to the business during the season, and camp in rude shanties on the ground. They find a ready sale for the berries in the neighboring towns.

MINERALS.—Deposits of iron, copper, and gold have been found, but not of sufficient value to defray the expense of working.

CHARLESTON, OR EAST HATLEY.

The Parish of Charleston, formerly known as East Hatley, was constituted and set off from the south-eastern part of Hatley and the northern part of Barnston by Act of the Provincial Legislature in 1818. The name, Charleston, was commemorative of Rev. Chs. Stewart, D.D., Bishop of Quebec.

The first settlement within the limits of this parish was made by Thomas McConnell, Jr., about 1800. Among the early settlers were Levi and Jabez Hall. For many years, the settlement presented the appearance of an opening in the forest of some 200 acres, with two small frame houses and three log cabins. In 1808 Robert Vincent built a small store, and began business in connection with Levi Bigelow, of Derby, Vt. Other families came in soon after—among whom were those of Ebenezer Bacon and Dr. John Weston.

In process of time, the settlement began to assume the appearance of a village, and during the American War of 1812–1815 was a place of business of some importance, particularly in the trade of salts of lye, pot, and pearl ashes. Mr. Vincent continued in trade more than twenty years.

He was a man of strict integrity, but not a successful merchant. Hollis Smith was associated with him in business some two or three years, but afterwards removed to Sherbrooke, P.Q. William G. Cook began in 1823, and continued in trade several years, and acquired a large property. Among the later inhabitants of the village were the families of Luther Hall, William Grannis, John Grannis, Major John Jones, Lovinus Kathan, Japheth Le Baron, J. L. Pool, John Woodward, G. W. Kennedy, Dr. F. D. Gilbert, Cyrus Whitcomb, and H. Haseltine.

This village now consists of an Episcopal church, a Methodist church, an Episcopal parsonage, a Wesleyan parsonage, an academy, one tavern, two stores, a post office, a blacksmith shop, a tin shop, and about 30 dwelling houses. Much of the business that was formerly done here has been transferred to Compton, Massawippi and North Hatley.

MASSAWIPPI, OR WEST HATLEY.

About 1800, Stephen Boroughs settled at the place now known as Borough's Falls in Stanstead, and a road was cut soon after from that place running through Hatley, east of Massawippi Lake, and the laying out of this road few years afterwards was the beginning of the present village of Massawippi. Simeon Cole had previously made a small clearing, and Appleton Plumley had built a saw mill. A grist mill was built soon after by Daniel Bacon. Stephen Burbank, one of the early settlers, bought the mills and built a distillery, and other distilleries were started in the neighborhood.

The evils entailed upon the community by these nuisances, were long severely felt. Through the confirmed influence of strong drink, many of the early settlers sunk to the most abject poverty, and were compelled to sell out and leave the country. The Mill Privilege below the present village was bought by Samuel P. Harvey, of Compton. He built mills, and in 1842, purchased the mills of the Burbank Estate, and built the mill now in operation in the village. Simon Kezar was then the only trader in the place. In this year, a clothier's shop, a blacksmith shop, and a shoemaker's shop were started, and a full store of goods was opened by Knight & Demick. In 1843, a tannery and three or four new dwelling houses were built. Since that time, the village has gradually increased in number of buildings and wealth. It now (1874) contains one church, one tavern, two stores, one tannery, a grist mill, a sawmill, a post office, two cabinet and wheelwright shops, two blacksmith shops, a tailor's shop and grocery, a harness shop, a boot and shoe shop, and about 40 dwelling houses, and numbers about 175 inhabitants.

NORTH HATLEY.

This settlement can hardly be called a village. There are a few neat farm-houses in the vicinity of Massawippi Outlet. A store has lately been built and a post-office established, and several new dwelling-houses are being erected. As a railway station it is probably destined to become a place of some importance. Branches of the Le Baron and Wadleigh families are now its principal inhabitants. Col. Henry Cull was among the earliest settlers of the neighborhood.

MAGOG.

The territory which now constitutes the Township of Magog was set off in 1847 by Act of the Provincial Parliament from the eastern part of Bolton and the western part of Hatley, and was organized into a municipality in 1855. More than half a century had passed since the time of the settlement of Ralph Merry at the Outlet. A more particular mention of Mr. Merry will be made hereafter.

Since that time a flourishing village has arisen. The present village of Magog, the northern part of which formerly belonged to the Township of Bolton, is built mostly on the street that crosses the river, and another that crosses this street and runs along the northern bank of the river. The river where it runs through the village is about 15 rods wide, and in the first half mile from the lake has a fall of about 25 feet, thus affording a water power amply sufficient for the operation of mills and factories upon a large scale. Mills and woollen factories had early been built, and in process of time, the Outlet had become a place of importance, particularly in the lumber trade, and in woollen, iron, and other manufactures. The village still continues to increase in prosperity, and numbers among its inhabitants several enterprising and wealthy men. The Mountain Maid, a small steamer, made daily trips from Magog Outlet to Newport, Vt., for many years. The Lady of the Lake, a splendid boat, built in 1867, and others now ply between those places.

The present village of Magog comprises about 100 buildings—including two churches, an academy, five stores, and two hotels. Besides these, there are two saw mills with circular saws, and planing machines, one grist-mill with three runs, a door, sash and window blind shop, a rake and snath factory, two cabinet shops, a carriage, sleigh, washing machine, and churn shop, two blacksmith shops, one wool carding and cloth dressing shop, three boot and shoe shops, and tailor's, jeweler's and milliner's shops.

During the past few years, the natural scenery around the village and along the eastern shore of the lake has been receiving artificial embellishment by families of wealth from the cities, who have made purchases of summer residences, and have done much in the erection of elegant buildings and in adorning their pleasure grounds.

BARNSTON.

The name of this town, like most of the other English settlements of Canada, was derived from a place of the same name in England. Its boundaries were determined by Royal Warrant in 1792, and are Compton and Hatley on the north, Barford on the east, the parallel of 45 degrees north latitude, which separates it from Holland and Norton, in Vermont, on the south, and Stanstead on the west. It is about ten miles in length and ten miles in breadth, and comprises an area of 100 square miles, or about 64,000 acres.

The survey dividing the town into lots was made in 1796, under the supervision of Jesse Pennoyer, Esq., of Compton, P.Q.,—the concession lines running north and south, and the range lines east and west. In the disposal of the lots, as of the other townships, one-seventh part was selected from different portions for the benefit of the Protestant Clergy, and another seventh part was reserved as the property of the Crown. These lots in both cases were designated in the surveyors' diagrams. They were not to be sold, but leased for terms of twenty-one years. In after years, many of these lots were pitched and improved, but before the expiration of the first twenty-one years, the Crown and Clergy Reserves were offered for sale and were mostly purchased by the original occupants.

FACE OF THE COUNTRY.—With the exception of Barnston and Pinnacle Mountains and the lands in their immediate vicinity and along the banks of the Coaticook and Negro rivers, the surface of the town presents an undulating appearance, with gentle swells and declivities, resembling in many places, the rolling lands west of the Mississippi—the higher lands and valleys running in a north-easterly and south-westerly direction. The highest of these elevations begins near the centre of the town, and extends about six miles north-easterly to Compton. The surplus waters even of the smaller springs are conveyed into the Coaticook River on the east, and into Negro River, on the west—to the distance in some instances of four miles. With the exception of Compton and Stanstead, this township is not equalled by any other in the country in richness of soil or the quantity of land adapted to cultivation. There is, indeed, little waste land in the town, as the most broken parts of its surface furnish good pasturage and sugaries. Granite is abundant in the vicinity of Barnston Mountain and in other parts of the town. Limestone is found in some places, but no minerals of importance have yet been discovered.

The first opening of the forest in Barnston was made by Capt. Joseph Bartlett, in 1796. Mr. Bartlett had previously resided in Danville, Vt. He started off on foot, late in the summer of 1796, and, after spending two or three days in the country around Stanstead Plain, pitched No. 12, 8th Range of Barnston—his nearest neighbors being the families of Mr. Taplin at Stanstead Plain, and of Capt. Ebenezer Hovey at West Hatley. After falling two or three acres of trees and putting up a log shanty, covered with bark, and without a floor, he returned to his family in Vermont. In the spring of 1797, he again set out for Barnston, accompanied by his second daughter and two elder sons. On their arrival at Stanstead, they sent back their hired team, loaded the hand-sleds they had fitted up with such articles of furniture and clothing as they could carry, and started off through the woods on snow-shoes. The snow was nearly four feet deep. Sally, the daughter, donned a pair of snow-shoes and fitted up a pack which in more modern days would have been ample load for the strongest young man, and in this manner they succeeded in reaching their future home. Mr. Bartlett and his sons began their operations by clearing off the timber he had previously fallen, and succeeded in getting in a small crop in the course of the spring. He was poor, and having no provisions in prospect until their crop could be harvested, was under the necessity of returning to Vermont and "hiring out" to get a present supply. In the meantime, he had arranged with a man in Derby for a temporary supply for the children, and had paid him for carrying the provisions through to Barnston; but, from dishonesty or carelessness, they were not forwarded. In the meantime, the children were reduced almost to starvation. For several weeks they had to subsist entirely upon leeks or wild onions, scraped birch bark, and such fish as they could take from the brook, and without salt. The return of Mr. Bartlett in August, with a plentiful supply of provisions, was hailed with joy by his famishing children. It is needless to say that the family were never again reduced to similar straits. Their little crops afforded an abundant harvest, and they were soon enabled by patient and persevering industry to have a comfortable home and a plentiful table in the wilderness. Previous to the return of Mr. Bartlett, the boys and their sister had succeeded in making some three or four hundred weight of salts of lye, which were afterwards exchanged for provisions. The father and the children remained together until the following winter—extending their clearing and improving their premises. In January, 1798, he again returned to Vermont, and moved in the remainder of his family. They stopped a short time at Stanstead—sent back their hired team, and again set out for their new home,—carrying their goods through on hand sleds. They were two or three days in effecting this last removal. Mrs. Bartlett was placed on a hand-sled with her babe of four months old, tucked up carefully with bed-clothes, and lashed or tied on the sled to prevent being shaken off in going over the rough road. Mr. Bartlett and a son returned the next day to take in the two young girls and some furniture. He put the two girls and a part of the goods on one sled, and the young man took the remainder. The weather was intensely cold, and before they had reached their home, the lad had become so chilled and tired that he entreated his father to let him lie down and rest a while in the snow. Knowing that to lie down and sleep under these circumstances was death, the father deposited a part of their loading in the woods—made the girls as comfortable as he could on his sled, and with a beech switch drove his son before him until they reached home. It was a fearful ordeal, but the life of the boy was saved. When they reached the house, he dropped down senseless. Several weeks elapsed before he recovered his usual strength and health.

Capt. Bartlett did not long remain " monarch of all he surveyed." He was soon followed by others from Vermont and New Hampshire.

Levi Baldwin, a native of Connecticut, was the second pioneer of the settlement of Barnston. He made a beginning in 1798 on No. 15, 16th Range, and moved his family in early in 1799. Their experience involved many hardships and privations; like their early neighbors, they were often reduced to very great straits for provisions while clearing their farm. Bread, the staff of life, must be had daily, at whatever price; and they were often obliged to go the distance of 10 and 20 miles and bring home bags of flour or meal upon their backs. During the first summer, while waiting for their crops to grow, they improved the time in making salts of lye for the purpose of buying bread. While engaged in that business, they had to subsist upon leeks, birch bark and fish. They succeeded in making about 16 cwt. of salts, which were worth at that time about 50 dollars. Having no team of their own, they entrusted the salts to a neighbor, who took them to market. On his return, he told them that the salts were worthless, and would not sell. Not satisfied with the statement of the man, Richard Baldwin, one of the sons, a lad of some 17 years, went to St. Johnsbury, where the salts had been taken, and found that they had been sold at $4 per cwt. In the meantime, the man had invested the money in Indian corn at one dollar a bushel, and brought the corn to Stanstead Plain and sold at the rate of four dollars per bushel. Without knowing the circumstances at the time, the Baldwins bought a bushel of this corn, for which they had to pay eight hard days work in falling trees.

BARNSTON CORNER.

The earliest settlers of this neighborhood were the Buckland, Parker, Converse, Cleaveland, Bartholomew, Davis, Norton, Cutting, White, and Bellows families. In the early days of the settlement, there were no regular roads through the towns. In 1804, a path had been cut through the woods from Stanstead Plain to the Aldrich, Clement, Mosher, Heath, and Locke settlement, now known as Mosher Corner, and soon after extended to the Bartlett, Baldwin, Hill, Child, and Bickford neighborhood. From this path, another was subsequently cut through, running north-easterly to the Bartholomew place, now known as the Davis Farm, and this was for several years the end of the road. These routes were with few alterations adopted and afterwards laid out by regular survey. Two roads running northerly and southerly across the town were laid out by the Grand Voyer in 1810, and two running easterly and westerly, soon after. The crossing of two of these roads forms the site of the present village of Barnston Corner. Previous to 1825, the settlement consisted of some 15 or 20 dwelling houses scattered over an area of about four square miles of forest with small openings. As the population of the different parts of the town increased, this locality became rather a central place of business, and for a time commanded the trade of the greater part of Barnston, the south part of Compton, and the new settlement of Barford. The Humphrey and Damon families and others of enterprise, came in about that time. The location of the Grand Trunk Railway in after years had the effect of diverting much of the business of this village to Coaticook, and but little progress has been made in the growth of the place during the past 15 or 20 years. John Mansur, the first postmaster, was appointed in 1832. Among the families of the later settlers were those of M. T. Cushing, Dr. N. Cleveland, Dr. N. Jenks, Eli S. White, and Page Remick. Among the successful merchants were Francis Judd, William G. Cook, A. A. Adams, John Thornton, S. B. Humphrey, and Hollis Shorey. The present village comprises about 50 dwelling houses within its limits. The public buildings are an academy, a Baptist church, a Wesleyan church, a tavern, two stores, a post-office, a telegraph office, a cabinet and wheelwright's shop, a blacksmith's shop, and a boot and shoe shop.

MOSHER CORNER, OR SOUTH BARNSTON.

This settlement, situated about 6 miles N.E. from Stanstead Plain, was begun about 1804, by the Aldrich, Bayley, Ball, Clement, Boroughs, Hanson, Heath, Locke, Mosher and Sprague families. The south-west quarter of the town, of which this locality forms a part, has progressed but little during the past half century. The greater part of the original settlers are dead or have left the country. There are, however, several thrifty farmers in the neighborhood, among whom are the Locke, Heath, Hanson, Clark, Boyle, Slater, McGookin, and Aldrich families. A post-office was established here in 1867, Francis Cooper, postmaster.

KING'S CORNER.

This is a settlement in the north-west part of Barnston, on the road between Stanstead Plain and East Hatley. Ira King, one of the early settlers, opened a tavern about 1810, and another hotel and store were afterwards built. For a time, Hiram Davis and branches of the King and Norton families were engaged in trade. The King family are mostly dead or have left the country. The neighborhood now contains the families of some 10 or 15 wealthy farmers.

WAYVILLE OR WAY'S MILLS.

This settlement, or small neighborhood of substantial farmers, derives its importance from its manufactories. The Way and Hollister families were among its early settlers. The buildings are a store, a grist mill, a saw mill, and a carding, spinning and weaving factory. From its local advantages, it is probably destined to become a business place of some importance. A post-office has lately been established, E. S. Southmayd, postmaster.

NEW BOSTON.

This settlement was begun about 1810, and was indebted to some Stanstead wag for its name. It comprises a few lots in the south west corner of Barnston. Samuel Burbank, William Blasdell, and some of the descendants of the Hartwell family were among the early settlers.

COATICOOK.

For many years, this settlement formed a part of the wild lands of Barnston. Richard Baldwin, jr., had made a small clearing in the forest, about 1840, and two small log-houses had been built. In 1842, Horace Cutting built a store and started business in connection with Marcus Child, Esq., who afterwards sold his property in Stanstead and removed to this place. A post-office was established in 1844, Mr. Cutting, postmaster. The name of the office suggested by Mr. Child was afterwards adopted as that of the village. For some years the settlement progressed but slowly; but the advantages derived from the location of the Grand Trunk Railway, the eastern portion of which had been completed, and which passed directly through the village, rendered it at once a place of importance, and its growth has been unprecedentedly rapid. Its local advantages and ample water privileges have been improved by active and energetic men who have contributed much to the growth and prosperity of the village. Among those may be mentioned Richard Baldwin, jr., Marcus Child, Horace Cutting, Lewis L. Sleeper, A. A. Adams, John Thornton, Dr. Benjamin Damon, and Amos K. Fox. The descendants of the Baldwin and Cleveland families of Barnston are among the business men of the place.

For many years after its settlement, the boundaries of the village had not been defined. In 1863, a plan of its present limits, made by Charles Merrill, was submitted to the Provincial Legislature, and Coaticook was constituted a municipality, separate from the township of Barnston. This new corporation comprises an area of about four square miles. The Coaticook river runs through it from north to south, and is so very tortuous, that a line following its course would measure nearly four miles before leaving the precincts of the village. The southern part of the village is now the centre of trade, but with its water-power and facilities for manufactories, the northern part must eventually be in the ascendant.

The present public buildings are an Episcopal Church, a Wesleyan Church, a Free Will Baptist Church, an academy building with a town hall, an Episcopal select school house, a district school house, seven stores, three hotels, one apothecary's shop, three blacksmiths' shops, a harness shop, a furniture shop, a machine shop, a saw mill, a grist mill, a tannery, a door and sash factory, a churn and washing machine factory, a hand loom factory, a mowing machine and rake factory, an iron foundry, a match factory, a post-office, and a telegraph office. The present number of dwelling houses is about one hundred and fifty; new streets are being opened, and settlement is rapidly increasing. To the historian of after years, the foregoing brief account may perhaps serve as a starting point.

BARFORD.

This township contains eleven concessions of seventeen lots each, is 10 miles in length from north to south, and about 6 miles in breadth, from east to west, and comprises an area of about sixty square miles, or about 38,400 acres. Its boundaries on the north are Compton and Clifton, Hereford on the east, the parallel of 45 degrees north latitude, which separates it from Norton, Vt., on the south, and Barnston on the west.

The survey determining the limits of the town was made in 1792, and the division into lots was made in 1801, the concession and range lines running in the same manner, and being a continuation of those of Barnston.

The surface of Barford is diversified. The Coaticook river runs through the town from north to south. The meadows along its banks are small but valuable. The remaining part of the town is hilly, and in some instances broken and uneven. The soil is rich and productive, with but little waste land. The farms in this town are not surpassed by any in the county in adaptations to cultivation and pasturage. To the traveller, the settlement presents the appearance of a number of neat farm-houses with comfortable surroundings along the course of the river and in other localities. Drew's mills, now Dixville, a small village on the Coaticook river, is the only place of business in the north part of the town. Here are a grist mill, a saw mill, a carding and clothier's shop, a post-office, and a store. A village has been started at the boundary line in the southern part of the town with favorable prospects. A small French settlement in the eastern part of the town is yet in its infancy.

A large share of the wild lands of this township was early parcelled out to Government officials and other individuals. About the year 1810, a grant of 2,500 acres was made by the Governor General to Mrs. Hannah Vaucamp, of whom mention has been previously made. With more energy than prudence, she commenced operations for settlement upon a large scale; suffice it to say that, after expending some $5,000 in clearing land and making roads to very little purpose, she relinquished the enterprise and returned to Quebec, where she died. This property was afterwards purchased by Dr. Ward, at a price much below its real value. Dr. Ward has since made valuable improvements on the premises.

Although this township was surveyed as early as the beginning of the present century, many years passed before any settlements worthy of note were made. Stanstead, Hatley and Barnston were the first points of attraction to emigrants; and it was not until the most eligible farms in these towns had been taken up, that attention was called to the forests of Barford. Indeed, many of the first settlements were made by the children of the pioneers of Barnston. Among these were the descendants of the Child, Baldwin, Cleaveland, Parker and Drew families. Leonard Martin and his family came in from Peacham, Vt., in 1823. Their children are settled mostly around them. Harba and Marcus Child, Esqs., grandsons of Harba Child, of Barnston, are among the most prominent public men of Barford. One of the descendants of the Drew family built the mills that still retain his name. This property has lately passed into the hands of Richard Baldwin, Esq., of Coaticook. Deposits of copper have been found in the eastern part of the town, but not of sufficient importance to justify the expense of working.

SQUIRE HOWE.

Was among the early settlers of Barnston. His father, Caleb Howe, had settled near Fort Dunmore, now Dummerston. That country was then new, and after the opening of the French War, the inhabitants were subject to frequent depredations from the Indians. Such was the insecurity of the place, that the women and children were kept in the Fort—the men cultivating the meadows in the daytime with their muskets by their side, and prepared to retreat into the Fort on the appearance of the Indians. Mr. Howe and two of his neighbors were surprised by an ambuscade of the Indians, while hoeing corn, and killed on the spot, and the Indians succeeded, by stratagem, in getting into the Fort, the women and children falling an easy prey. Among their captives were Mrs. Howe and her children. They were marched off through the wilderness to Lake Champlain, whence they were taken to Montreal, where after a delay of some months, they were ransomed and suffered to return home, after having passed through many hardships and sufferings. Squire Howe was four years old when the family were taken by the Indians. The Indian who claimed him as his property seemed to cherish a feeling of peculiar spite and malignity towards him during the whole of their journey. Often when the little fellow sunk down from fatigue or exhaustion he would rouse him by striking him on the head with the handle of his hatchet. The marks of this savage brutality were plainly to be seen during the remainder of his life. In his early youth the compiler examined the head of Mr. Howe, who was then an old man, and long and deeply indented scars were distinctly felt and seen. He settled in Barnston in 1804. Several of his descendants reside in that town.

ANTIQUITIES.

The relics of tribes of Indians, living anterior to any of whom we have knowledge, and who must have traversed our country at a very remote period, have already been noted in our account of Stanstead and Hatley. Relics of later years have, however, been found, which seem to have been connected with the exploration of the forests of our country by the English or French during the middle and the latter part of the past century. In 1800 Isaac Drew, one of the early settlers of Barnston, found, while hunting in the woods, a brass kettle embedded in the ground. He had stumbled over it by catching his foot in the bail. On raising it he found that the bottom was gone, but, being an ingenious mechanic, he made from it an excellent old-fashioned warming-pan, which has since remained as an heirloom in the family of one of his descendants.

In the township of Barnston unmistakeable traces have been found of the fate of a part of the company commanded by Major Rogers, sent from Londonderry, N. H., in 1758, by order of General Amherst, to destroy the Indian village of St. Francis. This company took their route by way of Lake Champlain and the rivers. They reached the settlement, and in the absence of the warriors, plundered and set fire to the village—the old men, women and children falling an easy prey. The act was retaliatory, on the part of the whites, for injuries done by that tribe to the inhabitants of New Hampshire: but in the sequel it proved to be dearly bought revenge; for the warriors, who had been out upon a hunting excursion, soon returned and were almost immediately upon their trail. Such was the haste with which they were pursued, that they were fain to drop their plunder and escape as they best could. They were overtaken on the north bank of Magog River, and a sanguinary battle was fought on the ground that now forms the north part of the village of Sherbrooke. The slaughter on both sides must have been fearful, judging from the relics discovered in after years. Major Rogers and a few of his men succeeded in making their escape, and taking the course through the wilderness west of Memphremagog Lake, they reached their homes, after passing through almost unparalleled hardships and sufferings. In their haste to escape, some plunged into the river and attempted to cross near the place where the G. T. Railway Bridge now stands. Not one of these men lived to tell the tale of his sufferings. A part were drowned, and the others escaped the tomahawk and scalping knife only to perish in the wilderness. Wounded, wet, and exposed to cold, hunger and fatigue, they followed the highlands through Ascot and Compton, until they reached the south-western part of Barnston, where, being exhausted by their accumulated sufferings, they laid down, as it appears, to die. * * * * * For more than a century, their fleshless skeletons were suffered to bleach in the forest, until they had been long covered by a soil made from the leaves falling from the trees. In clearing up that locality many years afterwards, relics were found, which, like "the testimony of the rocks" in modern geology, determine the fate of these unfortunate men. In one place human bones were ploughed up, and musket barrels with locks and brass trimmings—in one instance the lock showing that the gun had been discharged—the remains of powder-horns, clasp-knives, a razor, silver knee buckles and shoe buckles, remains of Indian mocassins, beads and other trinkets, camp kettles, musket balls and flints. In falling a large maple tree in Barford a gun barrel with the iron and brass work of a musket was found imbedded in the wood near the centre of the tree. The question may be asked, "How did it get there?" The probable solution is that the gun was left standing against a small tree, in which was a seam which secured it from falling, and in process of time grew around and covered it—the wood part decaying from exposure to the weather.

In collecting the substance of the following sketches, the compiler has enjoyed the pleasure of visiting most of the surviving pioneers of Stanstead County. Some had attained the age of more than 90 years—had served in the French War, and in the War of the Revolution; and in recounting experiences of by-gone days, their faces would light up with the ardor of youth, and, like Goldsmith's hero, they would "shoulder the crutch and show

how fields were won." These men form an important link between the past and the present, having lived during one of the most important epochs, perhaps, in the history of the world. With the events of the French War, the American Revolution, the French Revolution, War of 1812–1815, and the career of Nopoleon Bonaparte, they were familiar. They had seen the territory of the United States increased from a few British Colonies to a mighty nation—had been partakers of the hardships and privations attendant upon the work of opening out the forests of Canada, and had watched with wonder and admiration the numberless improvements of the age; and some of them almost expressed the wish that they could have a drink from "Rip Van Winkle's Flagon," and wake up a hundred years hence.

While much praise is due to the memories of our fathers, our mothers should have their appropriate share. They were a class of women that seldom find a parallel in modern days. Our fathers, indeed, toiled, but they were sustained and cheered by the patient, self-sacrificing and untiring industry of our mothers, who, by their intelligent, quiet influence, rendered their homes comfortable and happy, and who were instrumental, mainly, in moulding the characters that have distinguished many of their posterity. From several of these "mothers in Israel," the compiler has received valuable assistance in his work.

BY SAMUEL HOYT, ESQ.

My father, Samuel Hoyt, Sen., was a distinguished hunter, and used often to join the St. Francis Indians in their excursions around the Memphremagog Lake. He found them uniformly honest, upright and peaceable, except when under the influence of strong drink. In such cases, he was sometimes placed in rather equivocal circumstances, and was under the necessity of opposing force with force; but, in general, he had far less trouble with the Indians than with his white brethren. They sometimes hunted in company, and at other times agreed upon a division of the ground. Engagements of this kind were honestly kept by the Indians.

BY A. B. JOHNSON, ESQ.

Among the pioneers of the county of Richelieu, was Jonathan Johnson, Jr. He served in the American Army in the time of the

Revolution, was taken captive by the Indians, at the battle of Ticonderoga. A party of Indians had previously taken six or seven American prisoners, who had succeeded in killing their captors and making their escape. Mr. Johnson and six others were supposed by the Indians to be the party who had killed their companions, and their capture was in accordance with the customary system of revenge of the tribe. Mr. Johnson and his comrades were taken into the forest, and preparations were made for their death by burning by a slow fire, the captives themselves having been compelled to gather and prepare the wood for their own funeral pile. One of the number was a freemason, and in this extremity, he made the signal of distress. Providentially, the chief, or leader of the Indians was a mason, and this circumstance saved their lives. Through his influence, they were released from the stakes to which they had been bound, even after they had begun to feel the scorching effects of the fire. The authority of the chief did not extend any farther than the preservation of their lives; for during their subsequent course, they were treated with the utmost cruelty. Their route was down Lake Champlain and through the woods, to Montreal. At Montreal, they were subjected to the ordeal of "running the gauntlet." In this operation, the poor fellows had to make their way between two rows of Indians, squaws, and children —receiving their blows, or dodging them as they best could. This process was often repeated for the gratification of their tormentors, who seemed to take a fiendish delight in inventing new tortures, often compelling their victims to hold their fingers in red hot pipe bowls until the ends were in many cases literally burned off. Some of Mr. Johnson's fingers were so burned that the nails never again grew upon them. At one time during their pilgrimage, they travelled nearly forty days without any sustenance except the roots and berries which they gathered as they went along. As their route was through American Territory, the utmost quiet was observed by the Indians, and although they often encountered a plenty of wild game, they did not dare to hazard the firing of a gun.

From Montreal, Mr. Johnson and his comrades were taken to Quebec, where they were ransomed by the British Authorities, and held as prisoners of war. They were kept at Quebec three years, or until the general peace of 1783, when they were discharged and permitted to return to their homes in the United States. Mr. Johnson carried the scars and other marks of brutality he received from the savages to his grave. He settled in Hatley in 1802.

BY COL. JOHN MCCONNELL.

My father, Thomas McConnell, Jr., came to Hatley in 1796, and began on the shore of Memphremagog Lake, but subsequently removed to No. 6, 1st Range, and was one of the earliest settlers of the present village of Charleston. He was a man of energy, and, like Nimrod of yore, "a mighty hunter." Many of his exploits in that line would be worthy of note. In one of his solitary excursions in the almost boundless wilderness of the neighborhood, he had killed a large moose, but before he had finished the operation of skinning, night came on, and it was nearly dark. He was then at a great distance from any settlement, and had no resource but to camp out. The evening was mild, and wrapping himself snugly in the skin, with the hair inside, he laid down in the snow, and in the arms of the drowsy god, soon forgot his toils and his cares. During the night, the weather had changed, and the morning was intensely cold. When he awoke, he found that he was encased in a covering from which he could not extricate himself; and it was not until the perspiration and warmth of his body, caused by his desperate exertions, had measurably softened his covering, that he was able to cast it off. It was nearly night of the next day before he set out for home. Like the fox in the fable, he thenceforth adopted the maxim of never getting into a scrape without having well considered how to get out of it.

BY CAPT. SIMON BEAN.

My uncle, Capt. Simon Kezar, was very fond of hunting, often traversing the almost unbroken forests of Stanstead and Compton counties. Often in the days of my childhood and youth did I listen

> "Whene'er he spake of most disastrous chances
> Of hairbreadth 'scape and imminent deadly peril."

In one of his solitary excursions late in November, 1801, he took his gun, a supply of ammunition, an axe, a number of steel traps, a stock of provisions, and directed his course easterly to the Coaticook River; but not finding game to his satisfaction, continued his route up the river towards the pond at its source—in which region he had learned from the Indians that moose, deer, beaver, otter, and muskrat were plenty. As this tour was one of exploration, he left his traps and provisions in the woods in Compton, and taking his axe and gun and a supply of bread and meat sufficient for his dinner and supper, he started on up the river. In the afternoon, it began to snow, but he continued his course onward into Vermont several miles beyond the boundary line; the storm increasing and the night coming on, he thought it best to retrace his steps. The snow was falling fast, and this with the darkness of the night soon compelled him to stop. He had not time to make a camp, but set fire to a dry stub, and stood up all night under a leaning cedar near it, the snow continuing to fall fast all the time. In the morning, it had attained to the depth of two feet and a half, and continued to fall. He worked his way down the river, but his progress was very slow. The depth of the snow not being the only difficulty with which he had to contend—the trees and underbrush were loaded down with damp and heavy snow. He was then at the distance of at least thirty-five miles from his camp in Hatley, and became convinced that he should not be able to reach it, and must direct his course to one of the other settlements. The distance to the opening of Mr. Hinman in Derby he was certain was much less; and although he had no means of ascertaining the precise direction, he changed his course, and travelled all that day, and at night, drenched to the skin by the snow melting from the heat of his body, prepared to rest until morning. He trod down the snow, made a large fire from dry wood, and without having eaten anything during the day, laid down upon a bed of boughs with his back to the fire, and soon fell asleep. In the night he was awakened by the scorching effect of the fire—it having burnt the back part of his coat entirely out. During the night, the storm had abated, and as soon as it was light the next morning, he again set out. The snow was then three feet deep, and his progress slow and difficult. At about nine o'clock, the clouds broke away and the sun appeared. He then realized that it was indeed "a pleasant thing to see the sun"—inasmuch as he was assured that he was travelling in the right direction. Hope brightened, and he climbed a tree to take an observation, but no clearing or smoke from any point could be seen. Desponding and almost despairing, he continued his toilsome and painful journey until about eleven o'clock, when he came to a small opening. On brushing the snow from the stumps, he found that the trees had been recently cut, and that timber had been hewn on the spot. Cheered by this prospect, he proceeded with renewed energy, and soon after came to a hut where he found a woman with a family of small children. The husband had left home previous to the storm. By this time, he was nearly famished from hunger and fatigue; but after a slight repast, the best that the family could afford, he started for Mr. Hinman's place near Derby Centre. On the way, he met the man at whose house he had breakfasted, and another man with a team, breaking out the road. He staid at Mr. Hinman's that night, and the next day succeeded in reaching his camp in Hatley — much to the joy of his friends. His brother and some of his neighbors had started in search of him, but soon abandoned the attempt—believing that he had perished in the storm. His traps and provisions remained suspended from the limb of a tree in Compton until the following spring.

Among many reminiscences of my uncle, I might mention that in the month of December, soon after he settled in Hatley, he fell with his own hands, 30 acres of trees of heavy growth —a feat which few modern choppers can accomplish.

BY E. H. LE BARON, ESQ.

About the year 1802, a Mr. Bowen and his wife settled on the hill near the east end of No. 3, 6th Range of Hatley. After remaining four years at that place, they removed to No. 22, 3rd Range. In effecting their removal, Jonathan Cox took the family and their effects into a canoe, and rowed down the lake to the outlet, whence they went on foot to their new home. When on their way down the lake, they discovered upon the surface of the water an object which glistened and appeared to move. On approaching nearer, it was found to be a large black salmon basking in the rays of the sun. Mr. Cox allowed the canoe to drift quietly alongside without disturbing the repose of the "sleeping beauty," and succeeded in grasping her in his arms and depositing her safely in the canoe. In the meantime, the antics and demonstrations of his captive would have done honor to any modern circus-rider. The fish, when dressed, weighed about twelve pounds. Mr. Bowen left the country in 1815.

In the winter of 1798, Chester Hovey, then a young man, was sent by his father, Capt. Ebenezer Hovey, to Montreal with a span of horses and a sleigh for nails and other materials for building, and a supply of family groceries, including a barrel of rum. In crossing the lake on his return, his team broke through the ice near the foot of Owl's Head, where the water is nearly three hundred feet deep. He had barely time to cut the harnesses and clear the horses before the sleigh went down. He immediately slipped a halter around the neck of one horse and succeeded in drawing him out. He then attempted to get the other out, but was unable. Thinking further effort useless, he threw a blanket over the horse he had saved, and chilled and almost frozen, started for the eastern shore. After going a few rods, he heard the neighing of the horse left in the water, and resolved to make one effort more to save him. This time, he succeeded, and although drenched to the skin, and his clothes frozen stiff with ice, he reached home without further difficulty. The sleigh, with its load, remained at the bottom of the lake during the three following years, when it was fished up—all, except a few bags of salt. The barrel of rum was found entire, and was thought to pay amply the expense of the fishing.

BY MRS. ROXANA FLANDERS.

My father, Capt. Ebenezer Hovey, came to Canada in 1793, and pitched on the eastern shore of Memphremagog Lake at the place now known as Judd's Point, about three years before the survey of this locality was made. After making a small clearing and putting up a log shanty, he returned to Vermont, and in March, 1794, again set out for his new home with an ox team carrying his wife and eight children, with bedding, provisions, &c. They were accompanied by Joseph Ives, Joel Ives, Isaac Rexford, and David Chamberlin with their wives and children. They came by the way of Missisquoi Bay, and were seven days in getting through the woods from Frelighsburg to Memphremagog Lake. The snow was deep, and the women and children suffered much from cold and fatigue. When about half way through the woods, they found that they had eaten all their bread; but as necessity is the mother of invention, they succeeded in finding a ledge of rocks, where they made a temporary oven, in which they baked a supply of bread sufficient for the remainder of their journey. Beds were fitted up on their sleds for the women and children, but the men had to camp upon hemlock boughs in the open forest, sleeping as they best could—feeding their teams with browse and the small allowance of fodder they were able to bring with them. Their route for the greater part of the way was through a trackless wilderness. They had to cut and break their road. The larger streams were generally frozen, but the smaller ones and the marshy grounds were more open. Their teams often stuck fast in the mire, and they had frequently to help each other out. In many instances the women and children were compelled to unload and wade through the deep snow and water. In this manner, they progressed until they reached the end of their journey, Mr. Hovey's log cabin in Hatley. For a time, the different families managed to live together, but as soon as the snow went off, they set about making dwellings for themselves and began the work of clearing the forest. They were prospered, and as their circumstances improved and the settlement increased, the log cabins were superseded by neat and substantial frame houses and out-buildings. In 1804, my father removed to No. 11, 3rd Range of Hatley, and subsequently purchased several other lots. Three of the original farms remain in the possession of his descendants, but the remainder have passed into other hands. Among the inconveniences and privations of the early settlers was the want of comfortable clothing, especially for the winter season. Unlike the experience of the Israelites in their pilgrimage through the desert, their garments would wear out, and new ones had to be provided—the carding, spinning, weaving, and making up, all to be done within their own families. Coloring at the first was not regarded as a matter of much importance. Flax and tow formed the cloth for their summer clothing, but they often suffered for want of warm garments for the winter, as but few sheep could be kept on account of wolves and bears. These inconveniences were only lessened as their circumstances improved, and when from the increase of the settlements, carding and clothier's mills, and spinning and weaving factories were introduced into the country. My mother died in October, 1829. My father died, April 24, 1836.

BY MRS. LEMUEL FISH.

In the winter of 1795, my father-in-law, Joseph Fish, with his wife and their eldest son, Lemuel, then a babe of eight months, left their home in Reading, Vermont, and with an ox-team loaded with their household stuff and a limited supply of provisions, found their way through the woods to Durham, P. Q. After remaining a short time at that place, they sent back their team and set out on foot to seek a home on the eastern side of Memphremagog Lake—the mother carrying her babe all the way in her arms, and the father loaded with a pack of no small dimensions. After crossing the Lake and staying a day or two at the log cabin of Capt. Hovey, they directed their course to a place on Negro River, about a mile below Boroughs' Falls. Here they put up a temporary shanty on a rising ground near the river. The place is still known as "Shanty Hill." They were poor, and their hardships and privations were for many years very severe. Some time elapsed before they were able to clear land sufficient to raise their bread, and a still longer time before they could get their grain ground into meal. During the first seven years of their experience, there was not a grist mill within the distance of twenty miles from their dwelling. From 1795 to 1802, they pounded their grain in a large mortar made from a heavy block of maple. For variety, they sometimes boiled and ate their wheat and Indian corn whole. The supply of fish from the lake and river was abundant and contributed materially to their support. From 1802, their difficulties began to lessen. The wooden mortar was thrown aside, (although long preserved as a memento,) and they enjoyed the luxury of loaves baked from well-ground flour. The shanty had, meanwhile, been superseded by a substantial log house of limited dimensions, and which furnished them with a comfortable home. In 1795, Mrs. Fish was playfully called "the handsomest woman in the town," there being no other woman in the settlement. In the mean time, their family increased, and, by industry and economy, their means increased; and after residing some seven years in this locality, they removed to No. 9, 1st Range of Hatley, which lot Mr. Fish had drawn as an Associate. Here they passed their last days in comfort and prosperity, and lived to see their children and grandchildren well settled in life, and with hardly an exception sustaining respectable and useful positions in the community. All the families are exemplary members of the different Christian churches.

BY MRS. N. TAYLOR.

My father, Jeremiah Lovejoy, moved with his family from Danville, Vt., to Hatley, in March, 1797. There was then no opening at Derby Line, and but one house on Stanstead Plain. After leaving Stanstead Plain, we found an unbroken forest until we reached the opening of Joseph Fish, in Hatley. We remained with the family of Mr. Fish about a week, enjoying their hospitality and kindness, and then crossed the river on the ice, and moved into a log house, twenty by ten feet, with a stone and stick chimney in the centre and a fireplace on each side. In this cabin, two other families, viz., those of Samuel Fish and Ephraim Moore, found a home with us—making in all, six parents and fifteen children. Mr. Moore and his family remained a few weeks, but we did not leave until Fall. In the meantime, my father had made a small clearing, and sown and planted a crop, from which he raised a supply of provisions for the winter. He put up a log house during the season, covering it with long shingles. This was a splendid dwelling, compared with our previous one. We moved in as soon as the roof was covered and a sufficient part of the floor of hewn split logs was laid for one bed—no windows or chimney. It was about the middle of October. The day was stormy, with a heavy fall of snow. Mother made a fire against a temporary stone back in one corner of the cabin and cooked our supper, while father went back for the cow and the remainder of our furniture. By this time the children "were as hungry as bears." The kettle of hasty pudding was made, and rather than wait for the return of father with the cow, we chose to eat at once. We had each selected a clean spruce chip, on which mother gave us our supper of pudding and maple molasses. This was our first meal in our new home. Our beds were made of hemlock boughs spread over that part of our dwelling were the floor had not been laid. In this cabin, rude and homely as were its conveniences and surroundings, we enjoyed a happiness equal, if not superior, to that of the owners of any modern residences with the most costly furnishings. After laying the remainder of the floor and building a stone and stick chimney, father fitted up windows. This was done by cutting holes through the walls, in which he put square frames, covered at first with raw sheepskins strained on like a drumhead. Mother's outfit had been rather above those of her neighbors. After fitting up shelves on one side of the dwelling, she was able to display a set of twelve pewter plates, two large platters, and three basins of the same material. These were kept burnished after the old puritan style; next followed a number of wooden plates and bowls, which were for common use. For special occasions, she could furnish a table with six teacups and saucers, and as many white earthen plates, two pitchers, and a sufficient number of pewter teaspoons. Happy days of primeval simplicity! Well do I remember the old log house. Father had "caulked it with moss and plastered it with clay," and with ample fires built against the stone back, we could bid defiance to cold and care. Father improved the winter season in falling ten acres of trees, and after the usual process of "limbing and burning" in the Spring, planted among the logs Indian corn, beans, potatoes, squashes, pumpkins, cucumbers, and melons; and after our crop was harvested, we "fared sumptuously every day." We then considered ourselves rich. Our stock consisted of two cows, a pair of three year old steers and ten sheep. For these we had no pasturage but the wide forest around us, in which they often wandered far from home. Through the blessing of Divince Providence, we were not molested by wolves or bears. Led by the tinkling of the bell worn by one of the cows, father usually found them without difficulty; but in rainy or cloudy weather, he often came near losing himself in the woods. To avoid this dilemma he fitted up a large hollow log near the house, and one of the boys pounded upon it at intervals with a mallet. This was rather a novel mode of telegraphing, but answered the purpose. When winter came, our cattle were gathered home; and without any shelter except what nature gave them, were fed in a spruce grove near the house, and contented with their supply of corn-stalks, browse and other fodder, came out in good condition in the Spring. This arrangement continued until we were able to build a log barn and hovel, and enlarge our clearing so as to furnish hay and pasturage. By the time our stock had been wintered and father had sowed and planted his crop for the second Spring, our supply of provisions was exhausted, and he was under the necessity of going to Vermont and hiring out to get bread. During his absence we had to subsist upon very short allowance. The day before his return, mother had cooked the last morsel of food in the house. She made a small quantity of porridge from a handful of beans, and this served for our dinner and supper. The next day we had nothing to eat. In the evening, father returned, bringing a bag of cornmeal upon his back. A kettle of hasty pudding furnished us a good supper, and as we gathered around the family altar that night, thanksgiving to the beneficent Giver of our mercies might have been heard from the happy few in our humble dwelling. The meal which father had brought, with the milk from one of our cows, supplied us until the harvest season, and, from that time, we never again experienced the want of good and wholesome food. We raised a small crop of flax, which, with our wool, we worked into clothing—carding, spinning, weaving, coloring, and making up, all within our own family. Our summer clothes were made from flax and tow. The cloth, called tow and linen, was taken from the loom, and without bleaching, made up and worn, until, by washing, it had become white. We then colored our dresses with white maple bark and copperas. Mother was particular in having us neat and tidy on the Sabbath. She washed our clothes on Saturdays, and by pounding them on a flat stone or the surface of a smooth log with a mallet, they had a glossy appearance. No family in the settlement was better dressed than ours. Boys and girls, whether large or small, went to meeting barefooted. The young men and maidens generally carried their stockings and shoes in their hands, and would put them on before entering the place of worship, and take them off as soon as they came out. Our straw hats and bonnets, though coarse, were sufficiently fashionable. The winter clothing of father and the boys was made on this wise—the woollen cloth was taken from the loom and put into a barrel with soap and water, and fulled by pounding with a pestle. It was then colored with butternut bark, and made into trowsers, jackets, and spencers, as occasion might require. Our garments were homespun, but they were substantial and comfortable. Compared with the more ample dresses of modern date, they might have been considered behind the times; but it is much to be doubted whether the mothers of the present age would, if thrown upon their own resources and industry, be willing to make the efforts we did to sustain themselves and families respectably in honest poverty. Notwithstanding the disadvantages to which we were subjected, the table linen, pocket handkerchiefs, coverlets and other articles made by the mothers and maidens of those days would compare favorably with many of the best modern fabrics.

We had no schools nor ministers of the Gospel, but we had the *Sabbath*. Far away from the sound of "the Church-going bell," and the privileges of the sanctuary, we enjoyed the Divine presence and blessing in our day of rest. Several families had moved in about this time from the States, among which was that of Stephen Boroughs, of world-wide notoriety. He had previously been a Congregational preacher in Massachusetts, and he expressed a willingness to preach, if the settlers would meet. Their first meeting passed off favorably, but his second effort was not attended with so good results. His words were solemn and impressive; but no sooner had he closed the exercises of the meeting than he started off with a company of young men and boys, and spent the afternoon in a fishing excursion on the Lake. We did not ask him to preach again.

Among the early settlers of our neighborhood were the families of Samuel Fish, William Taylor, Jacob Taylor, Abraham Wells, Daniel Martin and Samuel Reed. These families continued to meet for divine worship in their different dwellings. Their meetings were usually conducted with reading, prayer and exhortations, by the professing christians who were present. Our singing, though not suited perhaps to the tastes of modern critics, was with the spirit and from the heart. Well do I remember the thrilling interest with which we used to join in singing Watts' and Wesley's hymns in the old tunes of Windham, Complaint, Sherburne, Northfield, Concord, Delight, &c.

The early settlers had generally enjoyed but limited opportunities of education, but they were desirous that their children might have those advantages that had been withheld from them. From the smallness of their number and their poverty, they were not able to sustain a teacher longer than two months in the summer, and two in the winter. The schools were generally taught by the best educated young men and women of the settlement—their wages varying from $3 to $7 per month, paid mostly in grain or in articles of clothing of domestic manufacture. These were primary schools in their fullest extent. Webster's Old Speller Webster's Third Part, and a few sheets of writing paper, comprising the outfit of the Scholar. Arithmetic, English Grammar and Geography were sciences of a later date. During the summer, the older boys and girls were kept out to assist in the work of the farm, or in the domestic arrangements of the family. In the winter, these might have been seen wending their way through the woods and the deep snow, with no other road but the path they themselves made, to the distance often of two miles, with such of the smaller children as could work their way through the snow drifts. On their arrival they might have been seen depositing their caps, hoods, mittens, dinner baskets, &c., in some corner of the room, and, after warming themselves well before a fire on which a quarter of a cord of wood had been piled taking their seats, upon rough boards or hewn split logs laid upon blocks of wood, and conning over the mysterious but valuable lore of spelling and reading. Writing was acquired under greater difficulties. There was usually but one window in the room, under which a temporary shelf or desk was made, and the larger boys and girls took turns in occupying it with paper not much better than our common wrapping, ink from the bark of the white maple, and the primitive goose quill. Many of the scholars thus educated have since been distinguished in public life in our own country and elsewhere.

In the fall of 1802 the small-pox broke out in the settlements, having been introduced, as was supposed, from the French settlements on the St. Lawrence. The disease spread through Hatley and the neighboring towns. Dr. Whitcher was fully employed in Stanstead, and we had no physician in Hatley. Stephen Boroughs had some knowledge of medicine, and he rendered himself more useful in this department than in that of theology. He set to work with untiring energy, and in almost every instance treated the disease successfully. Only three deaths occurred in Hatley.

From 1811 to 1814, the spotted fever prevailed throughout most of the settlements of the Townships, and swept off many promising young men and women and children in Hatley. In the Winter of 1843, several of our strongest men died of Erysipelas. With these exceptions, the neighborhood has been generally healthy, and subject to as few diseases as any part of our country.

In looking back upon the events of the past three fourths of a century, I seem to awake almost as from a dream. The transformation of the country can hardly be realized. Everything is changed. Instead of an almost boundless forest dotted here and there with small openings, large and well cultivated fields are presented, with a very limited reservation of woodland for sugaries and fuel; and on or near the sites of the primitive log cabins, elegant residences, with corresponding outbuildings, have arisen. The whistling of the railway locomotive and the clicking of the telegraph are heard. Truly this has been an age of progress! If the possibility of these improvements had been suggested in our younger days, we should probably have said with one of old: "Behold if the Lord would make windows in heaven, then might these things be!" I am now nearing the close of my earthly pilgrimage, and by the mercy of God, through the merits of my Redeemer, am looking forward to a glorious and happy immortality beyond the grave.

BY MRS. GRACE ABBOTT.

My two brothers, Ephraim and Paul Hitchcock settled in West Hatley in 1800. The next year, I followed them—being at that time about 20 years of age. I kept house for my brother Paul for some time, and afterwards married Abial Abbott, Jr., son of one of the first pioneers of Hatley.

In common with most of the other early settlers we had little to rely upon but strong hearts and willing hands, and the blessing Divine Providence. Our privations and hardships were severe, but we were sustained by the hope of better days to come, and in process of time we enjoyed a comfortable home in the wilderness, and had acquired a good property.

In 1814, my father's family sustained the loss of three of their number by the spotted fever. This disease, which assumed a most malignant type, and which seemed for a time to baffle the skill of the physicians of the country, prevailed to an alarming extent, and swept off many promising young people and children from the different settlements. Many of those who recovered were rendered partially, or entirely deaf. The disease usually commenced with chills and general prostration sudden and severe pain in the head and stomach, and vomiting. The brain soon became deranged, and generally continued in that state until death, purple spots or blotches appearing and covering the surface of the body.

EPHRAIM HITCHCOCK.

Ephraim Hitchcock and his wife settled on No. 6, 4th Range of Hatley, in 1796. During the first summer, he was obliged to bring all their grain and flour on his shoulders from Memphremagog Lake, and was suffering severely at the same time from ague and fever. Their food for the principal part of the first summer was fish and such vegetables as they could gather from the forest. With enfeebled health, coarse, and often scanty fare, in the midst of a dense forest, sixteen miles from any regular settlement, overtasked with clearing their land and in tending their small growing crops, nothing but the anticipation of brighter days in the future, could have sustained them. Joseph Fish and his wife had moved in some time previously, and Mrs. Fish improved the first opportunity that occurred to visit Mrs. Hitchcock. Their beginnings were about four miles distant from each other. They were then the only women in the southern part of Hatley. They were, of course, rejoiced to meet, and although strangers, a friendship began, which continued during the remainder of their lives. But where is the woman of sensibility who would not feel mortified to confess to an esteemed visitor who had come miles through the woods and swamps to see her, that she had not a morsel of food in her house? Necessity is, however, the mother of invention. Mrs. Hitchcock went out and gathered a few cowslips, which she boiled and salted. These, with a cup of tea, of which she found a small package, furnished their repast. This was the first female visit in Hatley—and although the circumstances might have been unfavorable, no one since that time has probably been made with more heartfelt joy to all parties.

SAMUEL REED.

Samuel Reed married Prussia Hitchcock—they were natives of Vermont. In the winter of 1798, they accompanied his brother-in-law, Paul Hitchcock, to Canada, with an ox team carrying a few articles of furniture and a small stock of provisions. After long and toilsome journey through the woods, they succeeded in reaching the opening of Mr. Hitchcock, in Hatley. In the meantime in prosecuting their journey through the rough woods of Northern Vermont, Mr. Hitchcock at one time lost his balance, and was run over by the oxen and sled. His leg was severely wounded, and he had to ride during the remainder of the journey. Many weeks passed before he recovered from the effects of the njury. Mr. Reed was a carpenter and house joiner, and hence, his family was of the migratory stamp. They remained in Hatley about one year, and afterwards, we find them making improvements successively in Compton and other neighboring towns. They were useful and valuable members of the community. He died in 1839, aged 68 years.

APPLETON PLUMLEY.

Appleton Plumley purchased the betterments of Simeon Cole. He built a saw-mill, but soon sold out to Daniel Bacon, who built a grist-mill adjoining the saw-mill. Another grist-mill was afterwards started at Massawippi, on which "hangs a tale." Jesse Wadleigh, a strong and athletic man, had brought his grist to the mill. The miller was all attention—put the grain into the hopper, and went below to hoist the gate, but the mill would not start. He examined the machinery, but it would not go. He then shut down the gate and went up stairs where uncle Jesse sat quietly smoking his pipe. Thinking that the joke had been carried sufficiently far, uncle Jesse explained the matter. He had grasped the upright shaft with all his strength, and was able to stop the entire machinery. The family of Mr. Plumley are mostly dead or have left the country.

EPHRAIM WADLEIGH.

Ephraim Wadleigh, with his wife and four children, settled on No. 10, 2nd Range of Hatley, in 1801. They were natives of New Hampshire. They came about 150 miles with an ox team, mostly through a new country, and were fifteen days upon the road. The land comprising the Old Episcopal Church, upon the hill, was a donation from Mr. Wadleigh in after years.

The Wadleigh families have been generally distinguished for energy and enterprise, and some of them have occupied prominent positions in the community.

COL. HENRY CULL,

Was born in Dorsetshire, England, in 1753. He was the youngest of a family of ten children. His brothers were most of them distinguished as officers in the British navy. Among the descendants of the families of his sisters was John Angell James, whose memory and praise are in all the churches. Mr. Cull pursued a course of mercantile studies at London, and engaged in business with a commercial firm of that city. After remaining some years in this business, he removed to Quebec, where he continued in trade until the close of the past century. About the beginning of the present century, he, in company with some twenty-five associates, obtained a grant of wild lands for settlement. The two charters, viz., those of Capt. Hovey and Col. Cull, comprised, together, 23,000 acres—an amicable division of the lots was made, and all parties were satisfied. Mr. Cull was, however, unfortunate in the selection of his own residence. He selected a large block of land at the outlet of Massawippi Lake in view of settling near his friend, Jesse Pennoyer, Esq., who had previously located in the western part of Compton. Like most European emigrants of his stamp, Mr. Cull was unacquainted with the practical manner of "roughing it in the bush." The greater part of his farm proved to be wet and cold, and was the poorest land in the township. With a capital far exceeding that of any of the other pioneers, he went on and made an extensive clearing and other improvements at great expense. The result, as might have been expected, was, that a large amount of money had been expended to very little purpose. Several of the early settlers of Hatley, Stanstead, and Barnston, who were then poor, but have since become wealthy, were glad to avail themselves of the opportunity of earning three shillings and four pence per day and their board, falling trees and clearing this farm. Owing to preliminary delays, Mr. Cull did not move his family in until 1806. He early received the appointment of magistrate, and that of Lieut.-Colonel of the third battalion of the Eastern Townships' Militia. His educational advantages had been much in advance of most of the other settlers. He was a correct scholar, and was familiar with the literature and most of the sciences of the age. He brought a well chosen library of some 500 volumes, comprising the best of the British classics, ancient and modern history and valuable miscellaneous works. There were then but few books in the settlement, and several of the most intelligent families in Hatley are the descendants of those whose tastes were formed from the use of this library. Mr. Cull was prepossessing in his address and manners, a genial companion, an efficient magistrate, and a popular military officer. He was in the Frontier service during the American War of 1812-1814, and by his prudent and judicious course, assisted by the influence and co-operation of others, quiet and harmony were in a good degree preserved on both sides of the Line. He had the confidence of the Government in a high degree, and had he been more selfish, could have secured for himself almost any personal advantages he might have asked. In his religious belief, he was an Episcopalian, but was not permitted to enjoy the ordinances of that church until near the close of his life. He was a kind husband and father, and was much respected in the community for his uprightness and hospitality. He died January 8, 1833.

MOSES BEAN.

Moses Bean pitched and began on No. 13, 2nd Range of Hatley, in 1798. He had brought a supply of provisions in his knapsack, and this, with his axe and a few dollars in change, formed the inventory of his property. He commenced operations by falling 4 or 5 acres of trees. Jesse Wadleigh and Taylor Little made beginnings in the immediate vicinity that year, and they together put up a shanty, in which they kept "bachelor's hall" for the two following years. In 1800 they each built log houses on their own premises. In 1802, Mr. Bean married Betsy Kezar, she had come to Hatley with her brother, Cap. Simon Kezar, jr., in 1800, and was the first school teacher employed in Hatley. They experienced the hardships and privations incident to new settlements, but, by persevering industry and economy, succeeded in acquiring a large property. Their family homestead is now owned by their eldest son, Simon Bean, Esq.

THE WOLF HUNT.

In the summer of 1840, the settlement of Stanstead was infested by wolves, particularly in the west part of the town. The wolves had been traced to a swamp south-east from Fitch Bay, and notice for a general hunt was given. On the morning of the appointed day, a party of more than 1000 men from different parts of the town assembled, and armed with guns, pitchforks, &c., surrounded the swamp, enclosing an area of about 12 square miles. The men were placed within hearing distance of each other, and were instructed to march straight forward towards the centre of the swamp, and to communicate with each other by concerted signals. As it was intended to surround the wolves near the east shore of the bay, the men upon that part of the circle remained nearly stationary, while the others advanced towards the centre of the circle. With these arrangements they began their march, and for a time pursued their course with regularity; some confusion afterwards arose, but they succeeded in coming to a close circle about half a mile east of the bay. The circle was about 20 rods in diameter, and strict orders had been given not to fire; no wolves were found, but seeing a deer, several of the most excitable ones shot at him without effect, and the result was that two promising young men, James F. Wood, and James Merrill were mortally wounded, Wood was killed almost instantaneously, and Merrill survived but a few hours, the deer escaped.

BY CAPT. RICHARD COPP.

My father, Capt. Moses Copp, was a native of Massachusetts, and was drafted into the service, in the American Revolution, when about 17 years old. He was with the American Forces at the time of the capture of Major Andre, and the discovery of the treason of Benedict Arnold. In 1785 he married Anna Mills. They resided in Warren, N. H., until 1796, when they came to Canada and pitched a lot in Bolton, which he afterwards drew as an Associate. Being a "stranger in a strange land," my father had some little difficulty in getting into the Association. He attended the meeting of the Commissioners, but not knowing the necessity of a proper certificate of character and qualifications, had not brought any. From this oversight he came very near losing his claim in the Company. At the place of meeting there was a good deal of rum, and noise, and fighting. In one instance two or three cowardly bullies were pitching into a poor sickly man. This was more than my father could bear, and, being a strong and muscular man, he at once laid the rowdies sprawling, and carried the sick man to a place of safety. After this demonstration the Commissioners decided that his credentials were amply sufficient. My father remained in Bolton until 1797, when he crossed the Lake and located on No. 26, 2nd Range of Stanstead, at the place which forms the centre of the present village of Georgeville. Not a tree had been fallen within the limits of that village and there were but two clearings upon that part of the Lake Shore—those of Elijah Baird and Jeremiah Lord. My father built the first boat that ran upon the Lake, and for many years our village was known by the name of "Copp's Ferry." He was early appointed captain of militia and was esteemed an upright and useful member of the community. He died in 1833. His wife died in 1845.

My brother, Joshua Copp, early displayed a genius for trade. When quite a boy he started on foot for Montreal and brought home a package of goods upon his back. He fitted up a shanty, sold his stock, and bought anew; and in this way he soon acquired a respectable capital. Suffice it to say, that he became a successful merchant, and realized a large fortune. He afterwards removed to Burlington, Iowa, where he died.

BY EDWARD WORTH.

I am a native of Cabot, Vt. Came to Stanstead with my brother, Joseph Worth, in 1798, at the age of 10 years. In 1817 I married, and settled on No. 3, 8th Range of Stanstead. Among my early recollections is the appearance of Stanstead Plain as covered with a growth of heavy timber, the central part being mostly maple, beech and birch; the outskirts hemlock, spruce and fir; and a dense cedar swamp on the west. My brother Joseph and Capt. Andrew Young were at one time neighbors. They each had a flock of sheep, and the two flocks were accustomed to run together in the woods. In the fall of 1802 the neighborhood was infested with bears that did much damage among the sheep. They made a raid upon our flocks at one time—killed some five or six, and drove the remainder through

RELIGIOUS DENOMINATIONS. 81

the woods to the south part of Derby, where they were found and driven home. My brother afterwards removed to the vicinity of Caswellboro, where some of his descendants still reside.

BY CAPT. ANDREW YOUNG.

I was born at Whitehall, N. Y., Nov. 5, 1771. Came to Stanstead in 1798, received the grant of No. 4, 9th Range, as an Associate, and afterwards purchased Nos. 5 and 6 of the same Range. Married and settled on No. 6 in 1803. Besides the work of clearing my farm I assisted my brother-in-law, Col. Charles Kilborn, in building his mill at Rock Island, in 1804. The first bridge connecting Rock Island with Derby Line Village was built in 1802. The Narrows bridge was built the same year. The settlement of Beebe Plain was begun in 1800 by the Beebe and House families. The first death that occurred in the town was that of a Mr. Beebe, who was killed by the fall of a tree. The first births were those of George Fitch Copp and Leonard Clarke. The first appointed magistrate was Gardner Green. As there were no resident Catholic or Episcopal clergyman during many of the first years of the settlements, the want of proper authority for the performance of the marriage ceremony was a grievance which was severely felt by the inhabitants. "As it was in the beginning," marriages and intermarriages would occur in the families of the early settlers; and the parties were under the necessity of either crossing the Line into the settlements of Northern Vermont, or to go through the woods, to the distance of 60 miles, to the older settlements of Canada, to meet the emergencies of their case. In this dilemma resort was had to the magistrates. They were not, of course, legally authorized, but under the circumstances, they assumed the prerogative, and some 200 couples were married in this manner in Stanstead. These marriages were afterwards legalized by a special Act of the Provincial Legislature. In later days this prerogative has been extended to all the ministers of the different Christian denominations.

RELIGIOUS DENOMINATIONS.

The following sketches obtained from Church Records, Clergymen and other individuals, will show the rise and progress of the different religious societies of Stanstead County.

EPISCOPALIANS.

The first missionary of the Church of England to the County of Stanstead was the Hon. and Rev. Charles Stewart, D.D. He came from England, and arrived at Quebec, Oct. 21, 1807. His first field of labor was at St. Armand, Missisquoi County, and in addition to the labors of that station, he established churches in Eaton, Sherbrooke, Lennoxville, Hatley, Stanstead and others of the Eastern Townships in the early days of their settlement.

STANSTEAD.

There were few of the early settlers of Stanstead who had been educated under the influences of the Episcopal Church, and it was not until their numbers increased by accessions from the States and England, that they were able to form themselves into a society. Through the influence of Rev. Dr. Stewart, the Rev. Richard Knagg was sent as a missionary to this station in 1819. The mission was an entire failure. Mr. Knagg retired in 1821, and no attempt was made to revive the interests of the church in Stanstead until about 1845, when the settlement of the Plain was occasionally visited by Rev. Mr. Doolittle, of Lennoxville, Rev. Mr. Reid, of Compton, and Rev. Mr. Jackson, of Hatley. In 1849, the attention of the Bishop of Quebec was directed to the station, and Rev. Henry G. Burrage, the successor of Mr. Jackson in Hatley, proposed to devote a part of his time to the society in Stanstead. This arrangement was adopted, and in February of that year, Mr. Burrage began to hold divine service in an upper room of the Brick Store formerly owned by Francis Judd, Esq. Mr. Burrage continued his labors with success until 1851, when a church was organized.

In his return made to the Bishop for 1852, Mr. Burrage gave as the average attendance at Public Worship on Sunday, from 50 to 60, and the number of communicants from 15 to 18.

M. Burrage was succeeded in 1857 by Rev. W.L. Thompson, who had been sent by the Colonial Church Society as a missionary to Stanstead Plain. It was during his incumbency that the present Episcopal Church edifice was erected, and much praise is due to him for his untiring labor and effort in the prosecution and completion of the enterprise. Mr. Thompson was followed by Rev. Henry F. Darnell, who after remaining about two years, removed to St. John, P. Q., and Mr. Thompson returned to Stanstead. He remained some two years longer in the ministry, and was succeeded by Rev. A. A. Allen, who was followed by Rev. J. Early. Mr. Early was succeeded in 1872 by Rev. A. J. Woolryche. The present incumbent 1874 is Rev. George Thorneloe.

HATLEY.

The origin of Episcopacy in Hatley was coeval with that of Stanstead—the Rev. Dr. Stewart, the pioneer clergyman and missionary of that denomination, having begun his labors in that place in 1817. As the early settlers of Hatley were mostly natives of Vermont and New Hampshire, and unacquainted with the doctrines and modes of worship of the Episcopal Church, Dr. Stewart soon set to work with untiring energy and perseverance in gathering a congregation and organizing a church. It is much to be regretted that the records of this organization have been lost. The first entry made by Dr. Stewart in the Parish Register was that of a baptism made on the 8th of February, 1818. The last entry was a marriage on the 16th of October, 1819. During the incumbency of Dr. Stewart a large and commodious church edifice was built upon the hill about a mile and a half north of the present village of Charleston—the expense of which was paid in part by the inhabitants, but mostly by himself. This building has since been remodeled, and is now occupied by the Adventists. In process of time, the people of the village finding this church an inconvenient place of worship, decided upon the erection of a new one, and a convenient church was subsequently built on a pleasant site in the village. Few men have perhaps performed more labor and under more self sacrificing circumstances than Dr. Stewart did in Hatley. His energies were directed not only to the moral, social and religious improvement of the people of his own immediate charge, but were extended throughout the entire circuit of the Eastern Townships. As he was unmarried, he made his home with the family of Ebenezer Bacon, Esq., during the time of his stay in Hatley. With this family, his name is a household word. They found him ever the kind and sympathising friend and judicious counsellor, and cherish his memory with reverence and affection.

In 1819, he was appointed visiting missionary in the diocese of Quebec, which then embraced the whole of the Province of Upper Canada.

Rev. Thomas Johnson became the successor of Dr. Stewart in 1819 and remained until 1830, and was followed by Rev Christopher Jackson, who continued in charge of the church until 1848, when from ill health, he was compelled to retire from the work of the ministry. He was succeeded by Rev. Henry G. Burrage, who remained in the ministry of the church until 1872, when he was followed by Rev. A. J. Balfour, who is the present incumbent.

From the absence of the church records, as before mentioned, we are not able to give particular statistics of the church in Hatley.

BARNSTON AND COATICOOK.

In 1862, Rev. John Foster was sent by the Bishop of Quebec as a permanent clergyman for Barnston and Coaticook. Up to that time, there had not been a single church edifice belonging to the Episcopal Church within the limits of his charge. In October of that year, a commodious church edifice was completed at Coaticook, and the Divine blessing seems to have attended the labors of Mr. Foster. The Episcopalians are increasing in numbers and respectability in and around Coaticook. A neat and substantial brick building designed for a school of a high grade, to be conducted under the auspices of the church, has been erected at Coaticook.

The Episcopal Church was organized at Coaticook in 1862. The number of communicants in 1867 was 56.

An Episcopal Church has been organized at Georgeville, Rev John Thornloe is the present incumbent.

METHODISTS.

Among the first Methodist preachers that came in from the United states, were Rev. J. R. Crawford, Rev. E. Sabin, Rev. T. Branch, and a Mr. Wells. The first appointment from the New England Conference on record, was that of Rev. Joseph Fairbanks, in 1804. About that time, a class was organized at Copp's Ferry, (now Georgeville,) Richard Packard, leader; T. A. Packard, Sally Packard, Artemisia Bullock, Miriam Bullock, Wm. Bullock, jun., Jeremiah Lord, Lois Lord, and Nancy Lord. Among the early preachers was an elderly man, known as "Father Carpenter." Mr. Fairbanks was succeeded in 1805 by Rev. S. Chamberlain, who was followed in 1806 by Rev. Philip Ayer. Rev. Levi Walker was sent to the Stanstead Circuit, then known as the St. Francis Circuit, in 1807: Rev. Charles Virgin in 1808, and Rev. Squire Streeter in 1809. From 1810 to 1812 the Circuit was supplied by Rev. R. Hayes and Rev. S. Briggs. Up to that time, Rev. Asher Smith, a local preacher, had labored with much usefulness in Stanstead and in other parts of the county. In 1812, Rev. Samuel Luckey and Rev. J. F. Chamberlain were sent from the New York Conference, but their appointments were withdrawn on acount of the war, and no other preachers were sent from the States until 1816, when Rev. B. Sabin was sent. The next appointment on record was that of Rev. S. B. Hascall and Rev. S. Norris, in 1819. They were succeeded in 1820 by Rev. Phineas Brandall. That year, the Stanstead Circuit was set off to the British Conference. Since that time, the records of the society can be distinctly traced. Many of the following particulars have been supplied by Rev. John Borland :—

In 1821, REV. JOHN HICK was sent by the Missionary Committee of the British Wesleyans to labor in Stanstead. Since that period, we are able to trace with accuracy and fulness the persons and labors of the Wesleyan missionaries who have been appointed to this Circuit or Mission. Mr. Hick, the first of this order, was an able and highly acceptable minister of the Gospel. He ministered not only to several congregations in Stanstead, but occasionally, also, to others in the towns adjoining. In accordance with the itinerant system prevailing in the Methodist Church, Mr. Hick was removed at the end of two years, and was appointed to Kingston, Ontario. The success of his labors and the strong hold he had gained on the affections of the community in general, led them to hail with pleasure his re-appointment to them in 1831. During his second term of residence he suffered the distressing bereavement by death of his wife who was buried according to her long cherished wish in the cemetery near Stanstead Plain.

In 1823, REV. RICHARD POPE became the Wesleyan minister of the Circuit as the successor of Mr. Hick. His period of service was extended over four years. A very extensive revival of religion which occurred under his ministry was, in all probability, the reason of this then extraordinarily long protracted stay. In 1827, Mr. Pope was removed to Quebec, where, his health having failed, he located. He resided in that city until 1832, when he became a victim of Asiatic cholera.

In 1827, REV. JAMES KNOWLAN became the successor of Mr. Pope. His time of ministerial service expired in 1829. He was a native of Ireland, and, having been destined for the Bar, was educated for that object. His talents as a preacher or a controversialist were of the highest order, and when circumstances conbined to arouse a naturally sluggish temperament, efforts of extraordinary power were sure to follow.

The REV. JAMES BOOTH followed Mr. Knowlan in 1829. It was during the incumbency of Mr. Booth that the Wesleyan Brick Church of Stanstead Plain was erected. To him belongs the praise of planning and superintending the work. At the time of building, this house was considered rather in advance of the times, at least for the country. Suffice it to say that it served as a commodious place of worship for more than thirtyfive years.

Mr. Hick's second appointment to Stanstead was in 1831, and terminated in 1833. Then commenced that of the REV. WILLIAM SQUIRE. Mr. Squire's period, like that of Mr. Pope, was one of four years. A similar reason led to this—a remarkable revival of religion, distinguished as " The forty days' meeting. " The extension of the work rendered it necessary that a colleague should be sent to assist Mr. Squire in his labors. Rev. John Raine and Rev. T. Campbell were sent. Mr. Raine's ministerial course was comparatively a short one. He labored with success until 1844, nearly completing his tenth year, when through death he entered the faithful minister's reward. Mr. Campbell - wards located at Hamilton, Ontario. Mr. Squire's ministry in Stanstead. as indeed it had been in every other place where he had labored, was that of an earnest, enlightened and eminently endowed servant of the Lord. In every case success, in a greater or a less degree, attended his efforts. It is a fact of rare occurrence that for many months, while in Stanstead, he preached four times each Sabbath day, besides several times on the week days, though far from possessing a strong and robust constitution.

In 1837, the REV. THOMAS TURNER received an appointment to Stanstead, and at the close of his term in 1840, was permitted by the Missionary Committee to return to England, the place of his nativity.

In 1840, REV. ROBERT COONEY, D.D., was appointed for Stanstead. His period extended to 1843. It was during this time that the doctrines of the sect called " Millerites " or " Adventists " were introduced into the neighborhood. Their prevailing belief was that the end of all things was then really at hand, and that the second coming of Christ would occur in 1843. Intense excitement and the most extravagant excesses were the consequence. As several of the members of the Methodist Church had fallen in with the views of " those who had turned the world upside down," the situation of Dr. Cooney was peculiarly trying. He sustained his position, however, with faithfulness, submitting his ways to God. His term of service expired in 1843.

The REV. HENRY LANTON was the colleague of Dr. Cooney from 1840 to 1841.

The REV. JAMES BROCK, the successor of Dr. Cooney, commenced his labors in Stanstead in 1843, and closed them in 1846.

The REV. EDMUND S. INGALLS succeeded Mr. Brock in 1846, and remained two years. Mr. Ingalls is a native of Dunham, P. Q., where, having been converted through the instrumentality of the Methodist Ministry, he united with that Church, and entered the Ministry in 1835.

The REV. JOHN BORLAND followed Mr. Ingalls in 1848, and remained until 1851. Mr. Borland is a native of Yorkshire, England.

His first advent to Stanstead was distinguished by a revival of religion, the fruits of which remain to this day.

In 1851, REV. JOHN TOMKINS was appointed to the Stanstead Circuit. His period of service extended to june, 1855. Mr. Tomkins is a native of Herefordshire, England. His early religious training was in connection with the Church of England, but at a mature age he was induced to attend the ministry of the Methodists, and having united with that Church, was soon employed as a local preacher.

His last conferential appointment was to the Hatley, P. Q., Station, in 1866. Having married in Stanstead, he decided to spend the evening of his life with the relations of his wife and his other friends in that place. Since the time of his retirement from active service, he has occasionally supplied different congregations in Stanstead, and has been instant in season and out of season in doing his Master's work; and is now, at an advanced age, awaiting the faithful minister's reward. As a preacher, he is plain, practical, and richly evangelical. The seed which he has sown has been watered by prayer, and will in due time doubtless, spring up and bear fruit to the honor and glory of God.

THE REV. MALCOLM MCDONALD followed Mr. Tomkins in 1855. He is a native of Scotland, but came to this country when quite young. His early religious training had been in connection with the Presbyterian Church; but, on becoming a subject of converting grace through the instrumentality of the Wesleyan Methodists, he was led to join their communion.

From an attack of hemorrhage of the lungs, he was compelled to withdraw from the ministry in 1857. He afterwards located at Stanstead Plain, and officiates occasionally as health may permit. During his active life, he had filled some of the most important offices in the Canada East District.

REV. W. H. BAKEWELL, succeeded Mr. McDonald in 1858. His term of service extended to 1860. His labours in Stanstead were attended with but little good. " Tekel " might have been written upon the borders of his garments.

The return of REV. JOHN BORLAND, in 1860, was a pleasant era for the church. He continued to labor with much acceptance and usefulness until 1863, when he was followed by the

REV. JOHN TOMKINS, who received a second appointment to the circuit. His term of service extended to 1866. It was during his second term of service that the project of the new Wesleyan Church was started. The old brick church had begun to decay, and it was thought desirable to build a new one. Subscriptions were obtained, and preparations for building upon a large scale were made. In 1866 Mr. Tomkins gave way to the appointment of

REV. W. R. PARKER.

It was during his incumbency that the new church was really begun and finished. Much praise is due to him for his untiring exertions in the progress and completion of the work. A revival of religion attended the first year of his ministry, and several were added to the church.

In 1867, a division of the circuit was made. The northern part was set off, and called the Cassville Mission; the southern part remaining, as heretofore, the Stanstead Circuit.

The REV. E. B. RYCKMAN succeeded Mr. Parker on the Stanstead Circuit, in June, 1869. In September, of that year, the new church was ceded to the Canada Conference with the customary forms, and dedicated to the worship of the Triune God.

THE REV. WILLIAM HANSFORD succeeded Mr. Ryckman in 1871. He was a native of Dorsetshire, England. Was employed by the Methodists as a local preacher in his own country at a very early age. At the age of 25 years he united with the

Canada Conference, and, after filling important stations in Canada West and Canada East, was sent to Stanstead. When at Perth, Ont., he experiened the distressing bereavement of the death of three of his children within the short space of four months. " They were lovely and pleasant in their lives, and in death they were not (long) divided. In 1874, he was returned for Stanstead as Governor of the new Wesleyan college and super intendent of the Circuit; the Rev. W. A. Allen having been sent as his colleague in 1873. The labors of Mr. Allen have resul ted in a very extensive revival of religion.

THE GEORGEVILLE CIRCUIT.

Georgeville in the early history of Methodism in this portion of the Eastern townships, formed a part of the Stanstead Circuit, and was supplied with religious ordinances by the ministers appointed from time to time to that station. For an interval of several years, the ministrations of the Wesleyan Church were withdrawn, and the people were dependant for spiritual improvement upon such means as circumstances afforded. In 1838, this lack of service was met by regular visits from Rev. S. G. Philips, of Bolton, and, at the close of that ecclesiastical year, a petition numerously signed by the inhabitants was sent to the Conference, requesting the appointment of a minister to that station. In answer to this call, the Rev. Edwin Peake was sent. During the incumbency of Mr. Peake, a neat and commodious church was begun and completed. Mr. Peake was succeeded in 1861 by Rev. John Davis, who was followed by Rev. John Thorneloe, who subsequently left the ministry for that of the Church of England. Mr. Thorneloe was succeeded by Rev. John Stewart, who was followed by Rev. Moses M. Johnson. Rev. Osborne M. Lambly is the present incumbent. Other preachers have occasionally supplied this station.

BARNSTON.

Among the early settlers of Barnston were the Baldwin, Cleaveland, Kilborn, Wheeler, and Boroughs families, who were Methodists. Their meetings, like those of the other primitive settlers, were held in the cabins and barns of the settlement. The first meeting of the Methodists was in the log cabin of Josiah Boroughs, in 1803, Rev. J. R. Crawford officiating. Subsequent to that time, the settlement was supplied by regular appointments from the ministers of the Methodist Episcopal Church, who were sent to the St. Francis Circuit by the New England Conference. In the meantime, Rev. David Kilborn, an itinerant preacher in New Hampshire and Vermont, had frequently visited his brother's family in this town, and had improved those visits in preaching in the different parts of the circuit. Although he was preceded by some one or two preachers, he may be justly termed the apostle of Methodism in Barnston. He was a native of New Hampshire, and was licensed to preach in 1805. Was made a presiding elder in 1815, and occupied high positions in the church during the remainder of his life. He died July 13, 1865.

A passing notice of SAMUEL DUNBAR may, perhaps, be due. He was a colored man; of his early history little is known. His family were among the early settlers of Barnston. He possessed good natural abilities, and had acquired the rudiments of a common English education. In common with many of his race, he early excelled in playing the violin, and had been extensively employed at the balls and merry-makings of the country; but having experienced religion under the preaching of the Methodists, he threw away his fiddle and devoted the remainder of his life to Christ. His after-life was distinguished by fervent and sincere piety, modesty and simplicity. He had been licensed by the M. E. Conference as a local preacher, and his labors in public, and in administering the consolations of religion to the sick and the dying, were abundant and were attended with much success. He was greatly respected and beloved.

After the transfer of the operations of the St. Francis Circuit to the British Conference in 1821, the church in Barnston was supplied occasionally by preachers from the neighboring towns and from the United States. The station was first taken up by the British Conference in 1827, when Rev. THOMAS TURNER was sent as a supply. He was followed by Rev. John P. Hetherington, who remained until 1829, and was followed by Rev. J. Graham, Rev. H. Lanton, Rev. John Raine, Rev. E. Botterel, Rev M. McDonald, Rev. J. B. Selley, Rev. Thomas Campbell, Rev. John Johnson, Rev. William Hume, Rev. Richard Garrett, and Rev. William Andrews, the most of whom had appointments in other stations. In 1856, Rev. John Davis, who had previously supplied the Georgeville Circuit, preached a part of the time in Barnston. He was followed by Rev. John Walton, who supplied

Barnston and Hatley, and remained until 1859. He was followed by Rev. J. B. Forsyth, Rev. S. G. Philips, Rev. Benjamin Cole, Rev. John Salmon, and Rev. John Evans. These all held appointments at Barnston, and some of them at Coaticook, which had been set off as a separate station, and where a neat and convenient church edifice had been erected. A new Wesleyan Church has lately been built at Barnston Corner.

HATLEY.

During the days of the early settlement of Hatley there were comparatively but few Methodist families in the town; these few were supplied occasionally with preaching by those ministers who were sent from the New England Conference. Many years elapsed before a Wesleyan Church was organized in this settlement.

After the transfer of the St. Francis Circuit to the British Conference by the New England Conference in 1821, Hatley was supplied by missionaries sent from England to the most prominent stations. These men extended their operations to different portions of the surrounding country, and in labors they were abundant. Mr. Hick, Mr. Pope, Mr. Squire, and their successors in Stanstead, had regular appointments in Hatley. In 1838, Hatley and Compton were set off as a separate circuit, and were supplied successively by Rev. E. Botterell, Rev. John Tomkins, Rev. E. S. Ingalls, Rev. B. Slight, Rev. Thomas Campbell, Rev. William Andrews, Rev. M. McDonald, and Rev. J. B. Selley. A change was afterwards made, and in connection with Barnston, the church in Hatley was supplied successively by Rev. John Davis, Rev. J. Walton, and Rev. J. B. Forsyth, until 1863, when Hatley became a separate circuit, and was supplied by Rev. Wm. Scales, who was followed successively by Rev. W. W. Ross, Rev. John Tomkins, Rev. Mr. Rowsom, and Rev. J. Clipsham.

CONGREGATIONALISTS.

Among the early settlers of Stanstead were a few families from Massachusetts and New Hampshire who had been trained under the influences of Congregationalism. These were followed by others of that denomination, but many years elapsed before their numbers and strength became sufficient for forming themselves into a society. Their first meeting for public worship was in 1796, in the log barn of Capt. Israel Wood, which stood near the site of the present Congregational Church on Stanstead Plain. Rev. John Taplin, brother of Johnson Taplin, officiating. The congregation numbered some ten adults and as many children. In 1804 the settlement was visited by Rev. James Hobart, of Berlin, Vt., who having a sister married and settled in the west part of the town, improved the times of visiting her by preaching in the different neighborhoods during the following twelve years.

From 1810 to 1816, Rev. Luther Leland, then settled in Derby, Vt., preached a part of the time in Stanstead. The meetings were usually held in the Old School House, which stood at the north end of the Plain, on the road leading easterly from the main street. When there was no other preaching in the neighborhood, the Congregationalists usually met here, and the meetings were conducted by the professing christians present. A Church was organized in 1816—the ministers assisting in the services were Rev. James Hobart, Rev. Chester Wright, Rev. David Sutherland, Rev. Luther Leland, and Rev. James Parker. The original church members were Levi Hooker, Mrs. Levi Hooker, Miss L. Hooker, Mrs. Amanda Smith, Miss Mary Ward, Dr. Israel Whitcher, Mrs. Dolly Whitcher, Mrs. Catherine Hubbard, Moses Montague, Mrs. Susan Montague, John Brown, Israel Brainard, William Arms, Pliny V. Hibbard, Reuben Bangs, Daniel Ludden, Mrs. Hannah Ludden, Mrs. Clarissa Nash, Adam Noyes, Richard Smith and Ephraim Clark. Many of these worthies were among the truly excellent of the earth, and their memories are hallowed by the most endearing associations.

The newly organized Church was supplied with preaching occasionally by Rev. Luther Leland and other ministers from the northern part of Vermont until the following year, 1817, when Rev. Thaddeus Osgood became their pastor. The Old Union Meeting House which stood at the junction of the road leading south from the Moulton neighborhood with that leading from the Plain through Cassville, had been completed the previous year, and by common consent of the proprietors, the Congregationalists were allowed to occupy it. The prospects under which Mr. Osgood began his labors were favorable. The appointments of the Wesleyan preachers from the South had been suspended, and the Methodists and Free Will Baptists united in sustaining the meetings. The congregations were large, and things went on prosperously for a time; but ere long, roots of bitterness sprang up and bore their appropriate fruit. Mr. Osgood was a moderate Calvinist; but as a part of the Church were ultra in their views, their differences were submitted to the arbitration of a council. The session continued two days. The Old Union Meeting House, which could furnish seats for 1500 persons, was filled to overflowing. The sympathy of the public and of the greater part of the Church and a majority of the council sustained Mr. Osgood—a small minority of the council voting for his dismissal. The disaffected members withdrew, however, from the meetings, and, for a time, attended the ministry of Mr. Leland, in Derby. Few men have been better known in the Eastern Townships than Mr. Osgood. His history is one of much interest, but our limits will permit only a very brief sketch.

At an early age, he began business in Massachusetts, and was on the eve of marriage with a lady of great personal attractions and merit. She was suddenly removed by death. For a time, he was but the wreck of himself. He afterwards recovered his health and reason, and having become a subject of Divine Grace, in a revival in his neighborhood, he determined to devote the remainder of his life to the service of his Redeemer. At the age of 28, he engaged in a course of preparatory study, and during his 30th year studied theology under the direction of Dr. Lathrop, of West Springfield, Mass. He was then ordained as an evangelist. His subsequent life was useful in an eminent degree, and he performed an amount of labor not surpassed by any individual since the days of Brainerd, Wesley, and Whitefield. He crossed the Atlantic many times and had travelled the entire circuit of the United States and the greater part of Canada and the Lower Provinces mostly on horseback. His efforts were directed especially to the improvement of the young, and to him belongs the praise of organizing the earliest Sabbath Schools in the eastern part of Canada. He was peculiarly happy in his efforts, and may justly be said to have been instrumental in moulding the character of many who have since been distinguished for usefulness. His motto, like that of Wesley, was, "The world is my parish;" and feeling himself circumscribed in Stanstead, he resigned his charge in 1818. He died at the advanced age of 84 years.

Soon after the resignation of Mr. Osgood, the Union Meeting House was occupied by an Episcopal Missionary, and during his stay of two years, the Congregationalists attended his meetings. In 1821, Rev. John Hick was sent by the British Wesleyan Conference to the Stanstead Circuit. The Congregationalists attended during the stay of Mr. Hick and his successor, Rev. Richard Pope, and then proposed a preacher of their own denomination for mutual support.

This proposal was not accepted, and they withdrew from the Methodists and again held their meetings at the old school house at Stanstead Plain. Deacon Reuben Bangs died in 1822, and Deacon Hooker having left the country, Selah Pomroy and William Arms became their successors. The meetings were regularly sustained, and when not supplied with preaching, were conducted by the deacons. In 1828, Rev. A. J. Parker, who had completed his theological studies and received his licensure, was invited to supply the church for a few months.

He afterwards settled in Danville, P.Q., where he was pastor of the church in that place, during nearly half a century. Mr. Parker was followed in 1829 by Rev. Andrew Rankin, also from New England. He was followed by Rev. Joseph Gibb, from Banff, in Scotland. The brick church at the north end of the Plain was completed in 1829. Mr. Gibb was installed pastor of the church early in 1830. Up to that time, the church had gradually increased in numbers and strength. They were united in their call to Mr. Gibb, and for a while, prosperity attended them. Mr. Gibb was an eminently endowed and useful minister of the gospel—as a theologian, he was excelled by few of the age. He had published several valuable treatises upon christian doctrine and practice, among which were a Dissertation on the New Covenant, Directions for Searching the Scriptures, and an Epitome of the First Principles of the Christian Religion. These books were well written, and were read with interest. By the majority of the church, and by the community in general, his worth and merits were measurably appreciated; but difficulties arising, partly from misapprehension, but mostly from the misguided policy of a faction, so wrought upon his sensitive mind that he sank under them, and died in June, 1833, in the prime of his strength and usefulness. His memory will be cherished by many with reverence and affection. After the death of Mr. Gibb, a part of the church members withdrew, and the remainder found themselves unable to sustain a minister. They were supplied successively until the fall of 1834, by different clergymen of the Hampshire County, Mass., Association. Among them were Rev. Mr. Clapp, of East Hampton, Rev. Mr. White, of South Hampton, and Rev. Mr. Beaman, of North Hadley. In the fall of 1834, Rev. A. O. Hubbard was sent by the A. H. Missionnary Society. He remained until the fall of 1835. The church at that time was small and much divided, but the labors of Rev. Mr. Curry from Montreal, resulted in measurably adjusting these differences, and in June, 1836, Rev. L. Sabin was sent by the A. H. M. Society. Mr. Sabin remained until June, 1837. During this year, the church enjoyed a season of comparative prosperity. The meetings were well attended, and some additions made to the church. There were at that time a good number of intelligent laymen, and the Prayer Meetings and Conferences were peculiarly interesting and profitable. Among these were the deacons, Selah Pomroy and Phineas Hubbard, Joseph and David Gibb, both of whom afterwards became distinguished ministers of the gospel, and who were early removed to a higher and holier sphere of usefulness, Dr. Henry Hayes, who died in the service of his country in the war of the late American Rebellion, and Phineas Hubbard, jr. Mr. Sabin was succeeded by Rev. R. V. Hall, who remained in the pastorate until 1854, or more than 16 years. In 1854, a small church was organized in the neighborhood of Brown's Hill, called the North Congregational Church, of which Mr. Hall became the pastor. Mr. Hall afterwards settled in NewPort, Vt. The North Congregational Church has since been remodeled, and is now in charge of Rev. L. P. Adams. In the meantime, the old church at "the Plain" had broken up, and the Meeting House remained closed until 1856, when the church was re-organized, and supplied by Rev. James Hay, who had been sent by the Canadian Cong. Missionary Society. The number of church members comprising the new organization was 25. Deacon Phineas Hubbard had died in 1842, and Deacon Selah Pomroy in 1856. Sanford Steele, John Christie, Stephen Allen, Quartus Pomroy, and John Moir, were the appointed deacons of the new church. Mr. Hay remained until 1858, when, from severe labor and feeble health, he was obliged to resign his charge and remove to a milder climate. He afterwards labored successfully as a missionary in Australia.

About this time, the new church sustained an almost irreparable loss by the death of Deacon Steele, a man of highly cultivated intellect, sound judgement, and sincere piety.

"But ere his sun had reached its noonday height,
Its glories sank in everlasting night."

In the fall of 1858, Rev. Alexander Macdonald was installed

pastor of the church. After that time, C. W. Cowles and Joseph Cheney were appointed deacons. Deacon Allen died soon afterwards, and Deacon Christie in 1864. He was a native of Banffshire, Scotland,—had been an active and useful member of a church in his native country, of which Mr. Gibb had been the pastor. From the strong desire of enjoying the privileges of his ministry during the remainder of his life, he had followed Mr. Gibb to Stanstead. He was a man of exemplary piety, and by his consistent life exerted an influence which was felt and will be long remembered in the neighborhood where he lived. He possessed a clear and sound judgment was familiar with the literature and many of the sciences of the age, and as a critical biblical scholar was excelled by few—whether laymen or clergymen.

Mr. Macdonald was succeeded by Rev. John Rogers, who was installed in 1865, and closed his ministerial labors in the spring of 1873. The church is now without a pastor. Rev. L. P. Adams still continues in the pastorate of the North Cong. Church, is settled at Fitch Bay, where a neat and commodious church edifice has lately been erected.

BAPTISTS.

Barnston.

Among the early settlers of this town were the Bartlett, Griswold, Bellows, Sutton, Jewett, Parker, Smith, White, and Hibbard families. These were Baptists. They were occasionally supplied with preaching by ministers from the New England States, but their meetings were generally conducted by their deacons—among whom were J. Griswold, P. J. Sutton, and J. Bellows.

About the year 1812, Elder Roswell Smith settled in the north part of the town, but after preaching four or five years, left the country. A church had been organized about that time, but after the lapse of a few years, it disbanded. In 1833, a new church was formed, consisting of some twenty members. In the meantime, preaching had been occasionally supplied by Elders John Ide, Harvey Clark, Marvin Grove, and others.

Several other members were soon after added, and the church was supplied for one year by four preachers alternately—Bros. Downs, Powell, Mitchell, and Baldwin. At the close of that year Bro. Baldwin removed his family to Barnston—was ordained pastor and remained in charge of the church about four years. He was followed by Elder A. H. House, who was succeeded some two years afterwards by Elder James Green, who continued in the pastorate until 1853, when he was followed by Elder H. T. Campbell, who was succeeded in 1856, by Elder James F. Ferguson, who remained until 1864.

For many years, the meetings of the church were held in the dwelling-houses and school-houses of the settlement, and it was not until a recent date that a meeting-house was built. Elder Israel Ide, like St. Paul, was by occupation "a tent maker," or in modern parlance, a carpenter and joiner. During the time of his stay in Barnston and Barford, he contracted with the society and built a neat and commodious edifice at Barnston Corner.

Barford.

The origin of the Baptist Church in this town is of recent date—the Church having been organized in 1837.

Elder Israel Ide was ordained as pastor in 1838. He was succeeded in 1847 by Elder Joseph Chandler. Mr. Chandler is the present incumbent. The Church is in a prosperous state.

The second Baptist Church of Barford was organized May 20, 1863. The assisting ministers were Elders J. Chandler, A. Gillies, J. F. Ferguson, and J. Lorimer.

Elder Alvin Parker was ordained pastor of the Church at the time of its organization.

Stanstead and Hatley.

The first Church organization within the present limits of Stanstead County was that of the Baptists, October 28, 1799. Abial Abbott, David Jewett, Moses Wells, Richards Packard, Ephraim Claflin, Francis Brown, Amasa Merriman, Martin Adams, Japheth Le Baron, Betsey Le Baron, Ruth Abbott, Mary Adams and Polly Chamberlin, united in forming a church. In after years, some of these individuals, with their families, went over to the Free-will Baptists and the Methodists. The Society held their meetings alternately in the dwelling houses of the early settlers along the Lake Shore from the present village of Georgeville to Magog Outlet, and were occasionally supplied with preaching by Elders Hibbard, Rogers, Butler and Marsh. Elder Marsh afterwards moved into the settlement, and supplied the Church three or four years. The increase of members was gradual. In 1817, they numbered about seventy-five. They were supplied principally by

Elder Harvey Clark for nearly twenty years. He left about 1830, but occasionally visited and supplied the Church a few years longer. From 1833 to 1837, Elders E. Mitchell and J. Baldwin supplied. In 1837, Elder Mitchell located near Georgeville, and since that time has sustained the pastorate of the Church, which has passed through the changes experienced by other Christian denominations in the country.

FREE-WILL BAPTISTS.

Stanstead.

In 1802, the settlement of Stanstead was visited by Free-will Baptist preachers from New Hampshire and Vermont. In 1803, Elders Robinson Smith and Joseph Boody gathered a Church of about twenty members.

From 1803 to 1806, the newly-formed Church enjoyed the occasional preaching of the Gospel, and additions were made to their number. In 1804, Elder Avery Moulton received license, and was ordained in 1806. This year, the old log meeting-house was built. William Moulton, Avery Moulton, Daniel Heath, William Rogers, and others, sustaining the expense. William Moulton was licensed to preach about that time. The compiler remembers the old log meeting-house. It was about 30 by 25 feet, built of unhewn logs, with one window on each of three sides, a stone back and stick chimney, and the door on the other side. Total expense probably about $75.

In 1811–12, the Church enjoyed a revival under the labors of Elders Avery Moulton and Robinson Smith. Among the accessions from this revival were the Cass, Locke, Wallingford, and Wallace families. The revivals extended to the Church in Hatley.

In 1823, the Wheelock, Vt., quarterly meeting held a session in Barnston, the result of which was a revival which extended to Stanstead. Among its fruits were Abial, Thomas P. and Albanus K., sons of Elder Avery Moulton, and several of his daughters. Up to this time, the Church had not enjoyed the privilege of a regular ecclesiastical order, and they connected with the Wheelock quarterly meeting.

Elder Abial Moulton was installed pastor of the 1st F. W. Baptist Church of Stanstead, July 22, 1834. It was during his incumbency that the Act authorizing the ministers of the F. W. Baptist churches to officiate at marriages and funerals, and to keep registers, was passed.

In 1835, the first Stanstead F. W. Baptist Church enjoyed a revival, and 36 were added to its number. This revival was followed in 1840-41, by another which bore good fruit. Up to this time, the Church had steadily increased until the seed of the doctrine of the Second Advent, as promulgated by William Miller, had been scattered broadcast, and had taken deep root in many of the F. W. Baptist churches—some of those churches, however, remained steadfast—among the faithful, was the church of which Elder Abial Moulton was pastor.

The summer of 1848 was a season of revival in the Cassville neighborhood, and several were added to the Church. The Freewill Baptists and the Wesleyan Methodists then united in building a Union meeting-house—each party to occupy it their due portion of time. This house was built principally from the materials of the old Union House erected in 1816. Elder Abial Moulton contributed liberally to the enterprise, and to him belongs the praise of superintending and completing the work. This Church has lately been ceded to the Canada Wesleyan Conference.

Hatley.

Christopher Flanders may be justly termed the apostle of the F. W. Baptist Church in Hatley. Though a layman, he possessed gifts of a remarkable order—was frequently called upon to officiate at funerals, and to administer the consolations of religion to the sick and the dying. His labors in connection with those of Rev. J. B. Crawford, a methodist misionary from New Hampshire, Rev. Avery Moulton and others, from Stanstead, resulted in 1802 in forming the nucleus of the Free Will Baptist church of after years. Deacon Taylor Little and Ephraim Wadleigh were among the first converts. The settlement was visited occasionally by Elder Joseph Boody, Robinson Smith and others, until 1809, when Elder R. Smith moved in with his family. Prosperity seemed to attend the Church, and revivals were frequent. In the meantime, Elder Avery Moulton had removed from Stanstead to Hatley, and his labors were greatly blessed for the good of the Church. In 1811, a general revival commenced, and extended to a good degree through the community. In 1823, the connection between the church and the Wheelock, Vt., quarterly meeting was dissolved, nd an organization with the Stanstead quarterly meeting was formed. The Church at that time numbered about 25 members. No particular changes occurred for many years. In 1836, Amos Tyler, a methodist preacher, settled in Hatley, and united with the F. W. Baptists. He preached some 4 years, and was followed by Elders Richard Parks and K. R. Davis, under whose ministry several were added to the Church. Rev. Abial Moulton preached often in Hatley. In 1840, Rev. Richard Parks was installed to the pastorate. He was followed in 1842 by Rev. Chester Heard, a licentiate from Eaton, P. Q., who by request had moved into the town;—soon after his arrival, several were added to the Church, but a dark day came, Millerism shook the Free-will Baptist Church to its foundation. Though young in the ministry, Mr. Heard sustained his position with a discrimination above his years, and has lived to realize the fruit of his labors in the comparative restoration of the Church in Hatley to its primitive state. About 1847, Elder Zebina Young settled in Hatley, and since that time he has been a co-worker with Mr. Heard, the utmost harmony of feeling and effort subsisting between them. The present number of members is about 75.

Barnston.

A Church had been early formed, which at a later date was supplied by Elder Abial Moulton and others, who labored with a good degree of success. In 1832, Elder Erastus Harvey, from Vermont, commenced preaching,—a revival soon followed and resulted in reconciling past difficulties and restoring order in the church. In 1835 a revival began and extended through the different parts of the town. In this revival Elders Harvey, Christopher Page, Abial Moulton, and T. P. Moulton were prominent and useful laborers. The number of Church members at that time was 120, and prosperity seemed to attend them. Elder Harvey had located in the town and for a number of years he labored with usefulness.

In 1842, a small Church of 11 members was formed by Rev: Abial Moulton, a part of the members residing in Barnston and the others in Barford. In 1854 they took the name of the Coaticook Church, and were supplied by Rev. A. Moulton, Rev. G. Sawyer, and others; enjoying a good degree of prosperity. June 27, 1855, Rev. Thomas P. Moulton was installed pastor. The following year, a neat church edifice was built at the expense of $2,300, including bell and other fixtures. This church occupies a pleasant site in the village of Coaticook.

UNIVERSALISTS.

Many of the families of the early settlers of the south-west quarter of Stanstead were Universalists. These were followed by others who located in different parts of the town. Their first meeting was held in the old Marlow school-house, the Rev. William Farewell, of Barre, Vt., officiating. For several years meetings were occasionally held in the different neighborhoods with preaching from Rev. J. Huntingdon, Rev. Joab Young, Rev. James Babbitt and Mr. John Gustin. In 1830, Rev. Joseph Ward settled at Griffin's Corner, and soon after a society of Universalists was formed which included the greater part of the advocates of that belief in the town.

This society held meetings, mostly, at Griffin's Corner, and were supplied with preaching for a few years, but afterwards disbanded. There are several influential men in the different townships of this belief. Many of their preachers have been distinguished for talent.

The number of Universalists in Barnston, Hatley and Magog is large; but no regular associations have as yet been formed in those places.

ADVENTISTS.

The views that distinguish this denomination were introduced into Stanstead County by the Rev. William Miller, of Low Hampton, N. Y., in 1835. In 1842 Rev. Josiah Litch and Rev. Columbus Green held a series of meetings in Stanstead and at Derby Line, and camp meetings in Hatley.

The belief of their proselytes was that the final consummation of all things would take place in April, 1843. Intense excitement and fanaticism were the result. In the fall of 1842, a number of families banded together, and took their bedding, provisions, &c., to the old Union meeting-house in Stanstead, where they intended to remain until the spring of 1843, when they believed the last trumpet would sound. A few even went so far as to prepare their ascension robes.

From the failure in the calculations of Mr. Miller as to "the time of the end," many of his followers apostatised, but a large number continued steadfast. From "the signs of the times," they viewed the event of the Second Advent of Christ as very near. In 1845 meetings were held at Derby Line and at different places in Stanstead County. In 1857, a church of 40 members was organised at Derby Line, of which the Rev. John M. Orrock became the pastor. A Church was formed at Fitch Bay in 1862, Rev. D. W. Sornberger, pastor. Churches have been formed in other places.

ROMAN CATHOLICS.

Stanstead.

The origin of this denomination in the County of Stanstead is of recent date. Many years had elapsed before their numbers became sufficient for the organization of churches. Their early meetings were held in the dwelling-houses of the different Catholic families, until 1859, when a purchase of two acres of land from No. 7, 11th Range of Stanstead, was made by the Bishop, on which a church was subsequently built. In 1842, the Bishop accompanied by the Rev. Messrs. P. Lafrance, C. H. Morrison. and J. Barret consecrated the church and burial-ground, and the name or title given to the mission was " The Sacred Heart of Jesus of Stanstead." In 1848, the Rev. J. B. Champeaux was sent as a resident missionary. He labored with acceptance and usefulness, and succeeded in gathering a large Church. In the meantime, as their numbers increased, and the interests of the Church required a more central place of worship, it was thought expedient to relinquish the church they had thus far occupied and to build another at Stanstead Plain. A purchase of eight acres of land from No. 3, 10th Range, was made in 1850, and a church edifice was soon after erected. This church stands upon the site of the first framehouse built in Stanstead, and contains some of the original timbers of that building.

The time of the incumbency of Mr. Champeaux extended to 1851. He was assisted during the last year by the Rev. M. Picte. Rev. T. Thibodier was sent in 1851, and was followed in 1852 by Rev. H. Bienvenue, who was assisted by Rev. J. A. Singer. Rev. O. Peltier was sent in 1853, and was followed in 1855 by Rev. H Millier who had Rev, J. J. J. O'Donnell for a colleague. Mr. Millier left in 1856, and Mr. O'Donnell occupied the station until 1859, when he made way for the appointment of Rev. M. Pigeon. Mr. Pigeon was followed in 1861 by Rev. L. N. O'Dominique, who retired in 1862, when Rev A. D. Limoges received the appointment which he filled with success and usefulness. Rev. L. Z. Mondor was for some time colleague to Mr. Limoges. Rev. M. McAuley is the present incumbent.

The increase of the Roman Catholic population and churches has been very great during the past quarter of a century. In 1839 the Church numbered but 75; in 1871 there are upwards of 1000 communicants.

Coaticook.

Previous to 1863 the labors of this mission were sustained by the Rev. Messrs. Daly, Germaine, and Browne. During that year, an eligible tract of six acres of land on the eastern bank of Coaticook river was purchased, and a neat and commodious church edifice erected. The number of communicants in 1863 was 120; in 1871, probably 500.

Barford.

The first missionary to this station was the Rev. James Daly. His term of service extended from 1856 to 1858, when he was succeeded by Rev. E. Germaine, who was followed by Rev. J. Browne. Rev. E. P. Gendreau was sent in 1862. In 1863, the charge of this mission was assigned to Rev. J. B. Chartier, who was assisted that year by Mr. Gendreau and subsequently by the Rev. Messrs. A. Desnoyer and J. Gravel. The mission has since that time been under the supervision of Mr. Chartier.

The number of communicants in 1862 was about 50, in 1871, probably 300.

Boundary Line.

A church edifice was built at this station in 1866 through the efforts of Mr. Chartier. The mission was begun in 1861, by Mr. Brown. Number of communicants in 1871, 500.

Magog.

In 1860, the Catholics at Magog purchased about three-fourths of an acre of land in the north-western part of the village, upon which they built a neat and convenient chapel, 50 by 36 feet. The expense, amounting to about $1,000, was raised partly by subscription, and partly through the exertions of an excellent lady residing at Magog. This chapel was dedicated in 1861 by His Lordship Bishop Jas. Laroque. The number of members confirmed at that time was 26. The first missionary was the Rev. A. E. Dufresne, who was followed successively by Rev. A. D. Limoges and Rev. Z. Mondor. Rev. F. X. Poulin is the present incumbent. This church is in a prosperous state.

STANSTEAD SEMINARY.

The lot comprising the site of this institution was given by J. Langdon, Esq., of Montpelier, Vt., and Wm. Grannis, Esq., of Stanstead. The building was begun and completed in 1829. The estimated cost, $2,500, was divided into shares of $25 each. The shares were all sold, but the estimate was not sufficient to finish the building, and the deficiency, amounting to $700, was made up by equal donations from Ichabod Smith, Wilder Pierce, and James Baxter.

In 1830, a grant of $800, was made by the Provincial Legislature to this institution. This allowance was afterwards reduced to $400 per annum. In 1855, an additional grant of $300 was made. The amount, $700, was received one or two years, but it gradually diminished. The allowance of 1872 was about $300.

For many years, this and the Academy at East Hatley, were the only classical schools in the Eastern Townships. Stanstead Seminary has always sustained a high literary character, and has furnished instruction to a very large number of students, many of whom have been successfully employed as teachers. Many, also, have been distinguished in public and professional life.

The directors for 1865 were: I. Smith, Wilder Pierce, Carlos Pierce, C. C. Colby, B. F. Hubbard, George Pomroy, and J. P. Lee.

The following persons have successively been employed as teachers:—

GENTLEMEN.

Thomas Brown,	John P. Connor,	Isaac Parker,
Lyman Stevens,	T. P. Redfield,	George G. Ide,
Rev. Jason Lee,	John A. Jamison,	Hugh Elder,
Daniel P. Jacobs,	Reuben Spalding,	Henry Hubbard,
Rev. Joseph Gibb, Jr.,	Rev. C. W. Bennett,	B. F. Hubbard,
Andrew Robertson,	George Robertson,	Denison Gage, Jr,
Rev. David Gibb,	Rev. N. P. Gilbert,	Charles Prentiss,
Rev. R. H. Howard,	Charles Merriman,	Rev. David Allison,
T. A. Garfield,	William H. Lee,	Rev. John P. Lee.
Rev. Edward Johnson,	Rev. A. L. Holmes,	

LADIES.

Miss Laura Webb,	Miss Harriet Ives,	Miss Sarah Giles,
" Frances M. Ives,	" Julia A. Mather,	" Laura A. Chase,
" Sarah M. Leverett,	" Lucretia Gilbert,	" Maria Whitcher,
Mrs. Anna B. Gage,	" Frances A. Bellows,	" Ruby Warfield,
Miss Phœbe Oakes,	" Hattie H. Child,	" A. M. Weare,
" Mary T. Bates,	" Laura M. Aubrey,	" Juliette A. Loomis,
" Elmira S. Bruce,	" Almira Hubbard,	" Amelia Hills,
" Emma L. Taylor,	" Elizabeth Dickerson,	" Mary Jane Parsons,
" Josephine H. Stevens,	Mrs. A. C. Johnson,	" Sarah Benham.
" Gertrude J. Holmes,		

CHARLESTON ACADEMY.

This Institution is co-eval with Stanstead Seminary—both having been founded the same year and under similar circumstances. In the commencement of their operations, the two institutions seemed to fraternise, and as evidence of their good feeling, the Stanstead people proposed to their Hatley brethren to make the academy at Charleston a school for young men, and that at Stanstead a seminary for young ladies during the five following years. This proposal, which offered Hatley a material advantage, was not accepted.

The academy is a neat, substantial two-story building, with a cupola, and bell—stands upon a rising ground, commanding an extensive prospect, and has a lawn, which, beautified with shade trees, affords a pleasant and valuable ornament to the village. The expenses of the building, amounting to about $3,000, were paid by subscriptions from individuals and donations from the Rev. Dr. Stewart and others.

The Academy at Charleston, like that at Stanstead, was endowed by grants from the Provincial Government. For some time this school received $800 per annum. This sum was afterwards reduced to $400, which is now reduced to about $200.

MAGOG ACADEMY.

This Institution was founded in 1856, by Ralph Merry, Samuel Hoyt, Calvin Abbott, M. W. Copp, E. D. Newton, A. B. Johnson, Charles Turner, George O. Somers and others.

The building is pleasantly situated in Magog village, on the northern side of the outlet—built of wood, two stories high. The property and interests of the Institution are vested in a board of five trustees, who are chosen annually. In 1857 a Model or Normal school was organised with a yearly grant of $80 from the Provincial Government. This grant has been continued to the present time.

BARNSTON ACADEMY.

The plan of this Institution was originally that of a Model or Normal school. The building was begun and completed in 1851, under the supervision of the Rev. James Green and N. Jenks, M.D. The expense of the enterprise amounted to $1200, of which $600 was paid by a grant from the Provincial Legislature; the remainder was made up by an assessment upon the municipality. The building, a neat and commodious one, is of wood—two stories with a cupola and bell. The school has been well sustained, and its literary standing has been highly respectable.

COATICOOK ACADEMY.

This Institution was begun in 1852. A grant of $150 per annum was then made, but for a time the Academy was identified with the District School. A large building was erected in 1864, with ample accommodations for a Town Hall and for both departments of the school, on a pleasant eminence in the village. The cost of the building, $2500, was paid by assessment upon the Corporation. T. T. Shurtliff, contractor.

A neat and substantial brick school house was built in 1866. This Institution is the property of the Episcopal church, but is open to other denominations.

GEORGEVILLE HIGH SCHOOL,

Was established December 27, 1854. The original legislative grant was $200 per annum, but has been subject to discount—will probably soon be discontinued. Among the trustees have been Increase Bullock, Esq., Levi Bigelow, Esq., Dr. S. S. Kendall and L. P. Merriman. Among the teachers have been John Monro, William Ives, Henry Hubbard, J. L. Terrill, Hazen I. Bullock, A. H. Moore, Malcolm Tuck, Adelia Arms, Naomi C. Hubbard, Marcella O'Connor and Lucy M. Gillies.

STANSTEAD WESLEYAN COLLEGE.

At a meeting of the Directors of Stanstead Seminary in 1865, a plan was proposed to raise by subscription and otherwise, the sum of twenty thousand dollars, and erect buildings suitable for an institution to supply the place of Stanstead Seminary, and furnish the facilities for a thorough collegiate education. A committee was appointed to raise the funds, and Carlos Pierce, with his accustomed liberality, proposed to donate ground for the site of the buildings. The enterprise of the new Wesleyan Church had, in the meantime, involved an expense much greater than was at first anticipated, and the Directors were compelled to abandon the project.

STANSTEAD WESLEYAN COLLEGE.

In the winter of 1870-1871, a few Wesleyan ministers met at Sherbrooke, P. Q., and discussing topics relating to the moral progress of the country, it was proposed to start a plan for securing a college for the Eastern Townships. The suggestion was at once adopted, and a meeting of friends called, the result of which was the issue of a Prospectus setting forth the necessity and design of a collegiate institution suitable to the wants of the present day for youths of both sexes—the minimum amount to be raised for the enterprise $20,000. A Joint Stock Limited Company, with shares of $25 each, to be formed, and managed by a Board of twenty-one Directors.

At this meeting, Rev. J. Wakefield, Rev. E. B. Ryckman, Rev. G. Washington, Wesleyan ministers, with Col. B. Pomroy, G. Williams, Esq., W. R. Doak, Esq., and E. Lawrence, Esq., were constituted a Provisional Committee, with power to determine the location of the College—subject, however, to the approval of the Canada Wesleyan Conference. Compton intimated its readiness to subscribe $10,000, but Stanstead, notwithstanding its pecuniary embarrassments, offered $15,000. The project was brought before the Conference in June, 1871, and met their entire approval. The location of the College at Stanstead was confirmed and the Rev. William Hansford was assigned to that Station with the view of promoting the interests of the enterprise. Among the stipulations were —that the institution could not go into operation before the minimum sum of $25,000 should be raised—that it should be proprietary—that the affairs of the Joint Stock Company should be managed by a Board of twenty-one Directors, seven of whom to be Wesleyan clergymen, and appointed yearly by the Conference; the remaining fourteen to be chosen yearly by the shareholders, seven of whom to be lay members of the Wesleyan Church, and the Chief Officer or Governor of the College to be appointed yearly by the Conference.

The canvass for raising the $15,000 that had been pledged for Stanstead and its vicinity involved much effort and perseverance on the part of Mr. Hansford and other individuals, but it was successfully completed in the month of August, 1871. The canvass was then extended by Mr. Hansford and his clerical assistants through the Eastern Townships and also through the cities of Montreal and Quebec and the frontier towns of Ontario. The first Stockholders' meeting was held in Stanstead, December 19, 1871, when the " Stanstead Wesleyan College Association was organized,

—Rev. Wm. Hansford, President. In October, 1872, it was found that subscriptions to the amount of $25,000 had been secured, and a meeting of the Shareholders was convened. The contract for the building was awarded to G. W. Bryant, Esq., of Sherbrooke, P. Q. He at once commenced operations, and the corner stone was laid with appropriate ceremonies by the Rev. William Morley Punshon, LL.D., then President of the Canada Wesleyan Conference, on the second day of December following. December 24, 1872, the College was incorporated by Act of the Provincial Parliament at Quebec.

The first Board of Directors were Rev. S. D. Rice, D.D., Col. B. Pomroy, Charles W. Pierce, Esq., Rev. G. Washington, A.M., Stephen Foster,Esq.,C. C. Colby,M.P.P., Rev. Geo. Douglass,LL D., W. L. Thompson, Esq., Wm. Sawyer, M.P.P., Rev. Wm. Hansford, Hon. T. L. Terrill, A. A. Adams, Esq., John McLaren, LL.B., John Meigs, M.D., Rev. J. M. Hagar, M.A., Rev. Leroy Hooker, W. H. Lee, M.A., C. W. Cowles, M.D., A. P. Ball, Esq., James Macpherson, Esq., and Rev. J. Wakefield.

The Officers of this Board were Rev. Wm. Hansford, President; Col. B. Pomroy, Vice-President; A. P. Ball, Esq., Treasurer; W. H. Lee, M.A., Secretary.

Rev. W. Hansford was appointed Governor of the College in 1873 and re-appointed in 1874.

MASONIC.

Golden Rule Lodge.

About the beginning of the present century Freemasonry became general through the United States; and Lodges were opened in most of the towns and country villages.

In 1803, Lively Stone Lodge, No 22, was organized and opened at Derby Line, where many of the leading men of Derby and Stanstead met and held fraternal intercourse. The Charter members were Hon. Timothy Hinman, W.M.; Luther Newcomb, S.W.; Rufus Stewart, J.W.; Ebenezer Gould, Eliphalet Bangs, Elijah Strong, Nehemiah Wright, Timothy Rose, Levi Aldrich, Leobens Chase and Charles Kilborn.

The most friendly relation was sustained between the brethren on both sides of the line until the time of the American War of 1812-1815. At that time politics were predominant on both sides of the line, and the Canada brethren deemed it expedient to withdraw and to have a lodge of their own. A Charter was obtained from the Grand Lodge of Freemasons of England, and GOLDEN RULE LODGE, No. 19, was installed at Stanstead Plain, February 23, 1814. Phineas Hubbard, Esq., W.M.; Ezra Ball, Esq., S.W.; Timothy Rose, Esq., J.W.; Oliver Nash, Secretary; James Weston,Treasurer.

As the most amicabie intercourse had all along subsisted between the two Lodges, they were able conjointly to interfere and to prevent much of depredation and plunder upon the frontier that might otherwise have occurred, so that a good degree of order and harmony was maintained between the inhabitants on both sides of the line.

From the high estimation in which Masonry was then held, applications for admission were numerous. Although character was always carefully scrutinized, many were admitted who brought discredit upon the brotherhood. This yielding or compromise was the *first* error in the management of the Lodge, and was afterwards a prolific source of evil.****

In accordance with general custom, spirituous liquors were introduced into the Lodge as "refreshments." This was their *second* error. Many of the brethren, however, were opposed to the measure and were among the first to join the Temperance Movements of after years ; but others continued their homage to " the enchanted cup," and were expelled from the Lodge.

The termination of the war in 1815 produced depressing changes in the business of the country. The circulation of money, which had been abudant, was suddenly checked,and a very great scarcity followed; applications for membership in the Lodge became less frequent, and its finances were seriously affected by the scarcity.

From 1815 to 1818, the affairs of the Lodge continued prevail ingly in a prosperous state. Amongst its presiding officers were Selah Pomroy, Esq , W.M. ; Elias Lee, W.M ; Isaac Whitcher, M.D., S.W., and Elisha Gustin, J.W. In 1818, a Mark Lodge with an unlimited charter was organized in connection with Golden Rule Lodge. The Mark Lodge soon became a flourishing institution, comprising most of the influential members of Golden Rule, Lively Stone, and Rural Mark Lodges—the last of which had been established in Hatley. The funds arising from the Mark Degree were for a time kept separate from those of the Blue Lodge, but annual reports and regular settlements were neglected, and the result was—their affairs became involved, and a large deficiency was found in the treasury. This was the *third* important error in the institution.

In 1821, a Royal Arch Chapter was opened at Stanstead Plain. The officers were Hon. Wm. Howe, H.P.; Ichabod Smith, K.; Wilder Pierce, S.; Wm. Verback, C.H.; F. W. Adams, P.S.; M. F. Colby, R A.; C. S. Haseltine, G.M., 1st V.; Marcus Chi'd, G.M., 2nd V.; Wm. Arms, 3d V.* * *

But little change occurred in the administration of affairs until 1823, when the meetings of the lodge were removed to Georgeville. During this year, a rivalry which had for some time subsisted between the cities of Montreal and Quebec resulted in severing the masonic relation heretofore existing between them, and in the organization of a new Provincial Grand Lodge for the District of Montreal, by which Golden Rule was required to be represented in that body, and to return their warrant and jewels, James Peaslee was appointed to transact the business, which he performed successfully; the result was that the jewels were returned to Golden Rule, and a new charter issued where it was designated No. 6 Provincial Registry and 785 English Registry. The lodge began to work under this dispensation in 1824, and during the following three years nothing of particular importance transpired, Among the presiding officers were James C. Peaslee, Chancey Bullock, Joel H. Ives, Joshua Copp, Sebre Mack, Franklin Mack and Ephraim Wood.

The history of James C. Peaslee is an instance where moral power obtained distinction under the strongest physical embarrassments and difficulties. Having lost his right arm when a boy, the pain of amputation brought on "lock jaw," and he was never able afterwards to move his lower jaw. The only way in which food could be introduced was by breaking out his front teeth. He remained in this state during the remainder of his life. He was the son of a poor widow, and feeble and helpless as he was was literally driven from his maternal home by a brutal stepfather. By the sympathy and assistance of a few friends, he was placed at school where he succeeded in acquiring a respectable English education. He afterwards taught in various district schools. Metallic pens were then unknown, and he had to hold his quills between his knees and shape their points with his left hand. With his scanty wages, he began to buy and to sell, and by saving all, succeeded in process of time in building up a business equal to any in the county, and amassed a large property. He died a few years ago in Illinois.

In tracing the history of Golden Rule Lodge, we find that it experienced, in common with other institutions of the kind, the disastrous effects of the Anti-Masonic excitement of the time. This excitement, under the form of a political engine, was instrumental in closing nearly all the lodges in North America—hurling from office every mason who would not renounce the order—silencing ministers of the gospel, and pursuing the brethren even into their domestic circles with unrelenting persecution and severity. Under these circumstances, the brethren of Golden Rule surrendered their charter, pronounced their valedictory, and disbanded. Little did they imagine, at the time, that twenty long years would intervene before the institutions would be revived.

* * * * *

In 1846, a number of superannuated masons met accidentally at Derby Line, and were deploring the extinction of Golden Rule Lodge and the consequent dispersion of the craft. Many of the members had withdrawn during the time of the Anti-Masonic troubles—some had left the country, and others had "passed that bourne from which no traveller returns." The result of their deliberations was the calling of a meeting to reorganize the Lodge.

Such was the influence of the Anti-Masons, even at this late date, however, that they had to maintain the utmost secrecy in their movements; and, indeed, female curiosity had, in two or three instances, nearly developed their mystery; but they succeeded in effecting their meeting, which consisted of thirteen superannuated masons—formerly members of Golden Rule and Lively Stone Lodges. The decision of the meeting was the reorganization of Golden Rule, and a petition signed by twenty-two of the brethren was sent to the Grand Lodge at Montreal for a new dispensation.

In the meantime, the jewels, books, furniture, &c., &c., of the old lodge, which had remained at Georgeville since 1829, had been brought to Stanstead Plain. Their petition for a dispensation was granted, and Joseph Breadon, M.D., was instructed from the Grand Lodge at Montreal to invest the officers and install the Lodge. Their charter proved to be the same document as that granted by the Duke of Sussex to Elisha Gustin and others in 1824.

Golden Rule Lodge, No. 517 E. R., and No. 8 P. R., was installed in due and ancient form by Dr. Breadon, in 1849. The officers were Elisha Gustin, W.M.; Samuel Reed, S.W.; Stephen Haseltine, J.W.; Franklin Mack, Secretary; M. Bachelder, Treasurer;

William Verback, S.D.; Asa Gaylord, J.D.; W. R. Andros and Joseph Brown, Stewards; and Stephen Reed, Tyler.

The emotions of the brethren at their first meeting may, perhaps, be better felt than described. In looking back through the twenty long years and contemplating the changes time had effected, not only among the fraternity, but in the affairs of the entire country, they found themselves much in the predicament of poor Rip Van Winkle when awaking from his long sleep. Politics and the general state of society had changed, and they themselves had changed. From young men in the prime and strength of life, they found that age, old age was fast creeping upon them. With subdued feelings, "mournful, yet pleasing to the soul," they separated—realizing the full enjoyment of re-union and the truth of "Behold how good and pleasant it is for brethren to dwell together in unity!"

From this date, the interests of the Lodges steadily progressed, and soon attained a prominence never before occupied in the Eastern Townships.

In 1848, an attempt was made to recover the records of the old lodge, which had been mislaid or lost, but without success.

Nothing worthy of particular note occurred during the following seven years. In 1855, a general movement was made by the principal Lodges in Canada for the establishment of a Grand Lodge in their own country. This movement was regarded as the harbinger of better days to come; for the exaction of dues and fees by the Grand Lodge of England had long been considered a grievous burden. In the meantime the movement of the Canada brethren for a Grand Lodge of their own was regarded as schismatic by the Grand Lodge of England. The question involved a meeting of delegates from the various Lodges in Canada, in which it was urged that the Canada brethren had the legitimate right of secession, and that the Grand Lodge of England had no right to follow them with claims of authority or jurisdiction. The result of this meeting was a compromise, by which the different lodges retained their charters and were dismissed from the Grand Lodge of England. Golden Rule was represented at this meeting by H. J. Martin and E. B. Gustin, in a manner highly creditable to the Lodge and themselves.

In 1856, the junior members succeeded in carrying a vote for the purchase of Robert Morris' Universal Library. The seniors were at first opposed to the measure. They thought the young men of the present age would do well if they equalled the founders of the Lodge in masonic skill and knowledge. The counsels of the young men, however, prevailed—the library was bought, and has been of great value to the institution. In this year, Past Master Gustin represented the Lodge in Grand Lodge at Hamilton, Ont., and Golden Rule was visited by the Grand Master, the Deputy Grand Master, and several brethren from Montreal. The work of the Lodge, which is the Ancient York Ritual, met their entire approval, and the brethren went to work with the cheering hope that brighter days were in store for Masonry in Canada.

In 1857, a Dispensation was obtained by which the brethren were allowed to hold a regular communication on the top of Owl's Head Mountain once in each year. A meeting was held at that place in September, and an inscription commemorative of the event was cut in a rock upon the top of the mountain. The same year, the Corner Stone of the Episcopal Church of Stanstead Plain was laid with masonic ceremonies. The Royal Arch Masons obtained a Dispensation for a Chapter, and received this Charter that year. The officers for the Chapter were: Elisha Gustin, H.P.; E. B, Rider, K.; Jos. Woolley, J.; H. J. Martin, Scribe E.; William Verback, C.H.; A. Bodwell, R.M.; F. Mack, P.S., and E. Bodwell, Janitor.

A Masonic Hall was built at Stanstead Plain in 1860. In 1864, the Lodge celebrated its semi-centenary anniversary. Father Gustin was elected W.M. The meeting was largely attended—was one of much interest, as Mr. Gustin was one of the original founders of the Lodge. In 1870, Golden Rule dissolved its connection with the Grand Lodge of Canada, and united with the Grand Lodge of Quebec, and was classified as Number Four.

The affairs of the Lodge are now (1874) in a prosperous state —number of members more than one hundred and fifty. The Masters who have presided over the Lodge since 1846, have been: Elisha Gustin, Stephen Haseltine, E. B. Gustin, H. J. Martin, Andrew Bodwell, E. B. Rider, W. B. Colby, C. S. Channell, R. P. Stewart, Thomas Stevenson, Robert C. Parsons, and Horace M. Hovey.

PART SECOND.

GENEALOGICAL SKETCHES OF THE FAMLIIES OF THE EARLY SETTLERS OF STANSTEAD COUNTY.

THE FAMILY, ITS RELATIONS TO SOCIETY, AND GENEALOGY.

In date and form it is *primeval*, as divinely ordained in Eden by God, in the creation of man, male and female; and their union in marriage, whereby they became one flesh, was the first manifestation of the human race in social relations and duties.

The family is *dual* as to parentage, or persons joined in marriage, while primeval and a unit in form. Adam and Eve, the first, were also the *only*, persons created as progenitors of mankind. One man and one woman were thus divinely constituted the parents of the race.

Moreover, it is *normal*, as being the only established and lawful state of social union and life for mankind.

This union of man and woman, and state of those one in heart, obligations, and duties, is alone normal and adapted to the wants and welfare of the race.

The family is *germinal*, — the seed-bud or appointed means for the propagation of the human race. God blessed the man and woman created and joined in marriage by him, and said "Be fruitful and multiply, and replenish the earth." Hence, "marriage is" not only "honorable in all," but the family state is the only one approved of God, and lawful to man, for the propagation of his species. While, therefore, the race germinates in the family, and is propagated from generation to generation, a thousand social relations, duties, comforts, and delights spring up therein to bless mankind.

The family is *essential*, as without it the world would be a mere chaos of human beings. The domestic state is indispensable to the health and comfort of mankind.

It is essentially necessary to that moral purity in the sexes required by God, and alone respectable among men. It is the substratum or ground-work of all social relations, domestic comforts, and good manners in society.

THE FAMILY A TYPE.

It is specialy *typical,* as it foreshadows, — first: the *School,* in the nurture and education of children. Home education is all some children ever have. Second the *State.* Family government was the first known.

The father was a prince or ruler in his house, as Abraham and the patriarchs. Children were subjects of government, first in the family. Obedience to parental authority insures obedience in the State. Equity and law in the family are such in the State.

Third, the *Church.* Indeed, in the first ages of the race, piety, fear and worship of God, were confined to the family. Naturally enough has the father been regarded both a prince and a priest in his own house; and as far as children are trained in the love and service of God, so far is there hope for the Church of Christ.

The conclusion of the subject is, that the family, as constituted in man's creation and condition in Eden, is *universal.* Not for Adam and Eve only, and their posterity to the deluge; not for Noah and his sons only, in their generations,— but for the human race in all time, was the family state ordained, that every man and woman might share and enjoy its blessings. How else shall the people of our land and the world have homes? How else shall the tender and endearing relations of kindred be perpetuated? How, without the family, can domestic happiness be preserved in the earth?

GENEALOGY.

Marriage and parentage thus unite, in the providence of God, to form and maintain the family, which furnishes both the occasion and material for Genealogy, this being simply "an enumeration of ancestors and their children in the natural order of succession."

The most ancient and important record of the kind, unparalleled indeed in its nature, is the genealogical table given in the New

Testament; extending, as recorded in one case, from Abraham, and in the other from Adam, to Christ, a period of four thousand years.

"Mary, the noble virgin of David's royal race," of whom the Saviour was born, terminates the long series of generations, which sustained by life-giving power, like a golden chain extends onward through the whole course of development preceding the advent of Christ. No other nation but hers could furnish such a genealogy; no other Book than the Bible publish it to the world.

J. L.

STANSTEAD.

The Wood Family.

The ancestors of this family came from England in 1744, and settled in Massachusetts. CAPT. ISRAEL WOOD, b. in Dracut, Mass., in 1761, m. *Abigail Curtis*, a native of Methuen, Mass. They settled on No. 4, 10th Range, now forming a part of the village of Stanstead Plain. He afterwards received a grant of this lot as an Associate. He was the third pioneer in this settlement, having begun in 1797. He received the appointment of Captain of Cavalry in 1811, and was engaged in the Frontier Service in the American War of 1812. He d. in 1815. His wife d. in 1814. Their children were Israel 3d, Ephraim, Abigail, m. *Schuyler Johnson*; Sarah, m. *Dolphin Mitchell;* David, m. *Charlotte Snow;* Mary, m. *Rev. William Squire;* Alonzo, m. *Charlotte Weston;* Hiram and Persis, who died young.

Capt. Israel Wood, 3d.

ISRAEL WOOD, 3D, b. April 19, 1787. Came to Stanstead with his father's family in 1797. In 1809 m. *Lucy Bangs*, b. December 29, 1789. They settled on No. 18, 14th Range of Stanstead. He sustained the office of Captain of Cavalry, and was engaged in the Frontier Service during the time of the Rebellion of 1837-38. He d. Feb. 2, 1843. His wife d. June 20, 1862.

CHILDREN.

CLARISSA W., b. April 7, 1814—m. *Lovinus Kathan*.
HIRAM O., b. Oct. 2, 1816—m. *Lucy A. Wheeler*.

FAMILY OF DEA. REUBEN BANGS.

LAURA A., b. Oct. 7, 1818.
LUCINA, b. Aug: 5, 1820—m. *Seth H. Flanders.*
ISRAEL 4th, b. June 24, 1822—m. *Lydia M. Moulton.*
REUBEN B., b. April 21, 1824—m. *Rhoda M. Lee.*
ISAAC W., b. July 13, 1826—m. *Mary A. Phelps.*
LUCY B., b. Oct. 31, 1828—d. October 17, 1850.
CHARLES, b. Jan. 27, 1831—d. January 23, 1858.
ABIGAIL C., b. April 21, 1833—m. *Hiram Woodward.*
Two children died young.

Ephraim Wood.

EPHRAIM WOOD, b. September 10, 1789. January 17, 1816, m. *Agnes Moore*, b. Nov. 30, 1795. They settled in the vicinity of Georgeville—were consistent and exemplary members of the Congregational Church. He d. June 19, 1844. She afterwards m. her 2nd husband, *Capt. Richard Copp*, of Georgeville.

CHILDREN.

ABIGAIL, b. Nov 17, 1816.
MARY, b. April 18, 1819.
JAMES F., b. May 27, 1821—was killed at a wolf hunt in 1840.
HIRAM A., b. April 26, 1823.
MARK W., b. Jan. 25, 1826—d. April 12, 1833.
GEORGE W., b. July 18, 1828—d. October 22, 1856.
ELIZABETH, b. Feb. 27, 1831.
MARK W. F., b. Feb. 4, 1834.

Family of Dea. Reuben Bangs.

REUBEN BANGS, b. in Barnstable, Mass., December 9, 1760. Served in the American army two years previous to the close of the Revolution. In 1780 m. *Lucy Thayer*, b. in Williamsburgh, Mass., March 30, 1762. They settled on No. 5, 11th Range of Stanstead in 1798; sold to Phineas Hubbard in 1804; removed to Hawkesbury, Ont., and returned to Stanstead in 1813, and was appointed deacon of the Congregational church organised in 1816. He was an exemplary Christian, and was prominent in sustaining religious meetings when the regular ministry of the gospel was not enjoyed. In the families of his descendants and with others who knew him, his memory will be cherished with reverence and affection. He d. July 11, 1822. His wife d. December 13, 1848.

CHILDREN.

DOLLY, b. Aug: 6, 1782—m. *Dr. Isaac Whitcher.*
SUSANNA, b. March 4, 1784—m. *Capt. Enoch Bayley.*
REUBEN H., b. July 4, 1787—m. *Clarissa Teal.*
LUCY, b. Dec. 29, 1789—m, *Capt. Israel Wood*, 3rd.
CLARK T., b. Feb. 17, 1792—d. September 3, 1822.
JASON, b. April 24, 1794—m. *Eunice Brown.*
ELI, b. Sept 17, 1796—m. 1st, *Achsah Lee* 2nd, *Asenath Tilton.*
SUBMIT, Dec. 29, 1798—d. in March, 1835.
ABIGAIL, b. Oct. 21, 1802—m. *Luther Lowell.*
ABEL T., b. Sept. 14, 1806—m. 1st, *Olive Bartlett*; 2nd, *Judith Abbott.*

Capt. James Bangs.

JAMES BANGS, b. in Williamsburgh, Mass;, April 2, 1769. In 1790 m. *Martha Nash*, b. April 9, 1774. They settled on No. 6, 11th Range of Stanstead in 1800. He received the appointment of Captain of Militia in 1806; sold to Hazen Pomroy in 1819, and removed with his family to Sandusky, Ohio. He d. February 11, 1853. His wife d. January 1, 1850.

CHILDREN.

THEODORE S., b. June 18, 1791—m. 1st, *Mary Glines;* 2nd, *Narcissa Sawyer.*
HENRY L., b. in 1793—m. *Almira Carter.*
SAMUEL C., b. in 1797—m. *Electa Adams.*
ELISHA N., b. April 10, 1800—m. *Abigail Wallace.*
MARTHA, b. in 1802—m. *Elisha Sevrance*
HORTENSIA, b. in 1804—m. *Isaac Herrick.*
HORATIO N., b. in 1806—m. *Lydia Parks.*
HARRIET, b. in 1808—m *Hiram Parks.*
CLARISSA, b. in 1810—d. in 1827.
JAMES S., b. in 1812—m. *Louisa Gilbert.*
MARY, b. in 1814—m. *Webster B. Stone.*

Col. Heman Bangs.

HEMAN BANGS, b. in Barnstable, Mass., m. *Susan Hallett*, a native of Williamsburgh, Mass. This family resided many years at Stan-

FAMILY OF DR. ISAAC WHITCHER.

stead Plain, but they are mostly dead, or have left the country. Their children were Thankful H., m. *Col. Alexander Kilborn*, Lavinia, Heman, Edward, Charles, Nancy, Amanda, Susan, Eliza and George.

Oliver Bangs.

OLIVER BANGS married *Betsey Weare*. She died soon after their marriage. He left the country in 1812. One child, Dr. John E. Bangs, settled in Stanbridge, P.Q.

Family of Dr. Isaac Whitcher.

ISAAC WHITCHER, b. in Methuen, Mass., October 7, 1770, commenced practice in Danville, Vt., in 1791. Came to Stanstead in 1799, and in 1801 married *Dolly Bangs*, b. August 6, 1782. For many years he was the only practising physician within the limits of Stanstead County, and he was often called to the settlements in Barnston, Hatley and Compton, as well as to those on the east and west shores of Magog Lake. As the country was then an almost unbroken wilderness, the labor and fatigue he had to endure were such as would have broken down many men of the present generation. In several instances he was called to go in the night, to the distance of 12 or 14 miles, and had to follow a guide through the woods on foot, by the light of a torch or lantern. He was distinguished for his kindness to the poor, often making long journies and furnishing medicines for the sick without any prospect of compensation. He died in 1832, after a successful practice of more than 39 years. His wife d. in 1866. They were members of the Wesleyan Church.

CHILDREN.

MARIETTA. b. May 7, 1802—m. *Ballard Clark*.
CLARISSA, b. June 9, 1804—d. March 31, 1811.
MARIA, b. March 29, 1806—m. *Rev, John Tomkins*.
LORENZO, b. April 7, 1808—m. *Abiah Sargent*.
ERASMUS D., b. April 11, 1810—m. 1st, *Lavinia Davis;* 2nd, *Rachel Chamberlin*.
MARY JANE, b. April 13, 1813—m. *David Wallingford*.
CYNTHIA T., b. April 28, 1815—m. *Arba Fitts*.
LAURA, b. Jan. 20, 1817—m. *J. E. Pell*.
ISAAC N., b. June 23, 1819—m. *Almira Fox*.
CLARK T., b. Sept. 4, 1821—m. *Nancy Peaslee*.

Family of Andrew Patton.

ANDREW PATTON was born in Paisley, Scotland, Feb. 15, 1780 He m. *Lydia Weston*, and settled in Stanstead in 1804. She d. June 12, 1814. In 1820 he m. his 2nd wife, *Susan Dustan*. Was employed in public affairs for many years, having filled several places in the Customs Department, was Surveyor of Customs for the Port of Stanstead. He and his wife died in 1870. The family are Episcopalians.

CHILDREN.

LYDIA W., b. May 12, 1821—m. *Robert Gillespie*.
SUSAN A., b. July 5, 1823—m. *John Wyman*.
ANDREW F. B., b. Nov. 16, 1825—m. *Jane Chamberlin*.
WILLIAM M., b. Jan. 26, 1828—m. *Mary E. Dibble*.
EDWIN D., b. Nov. 28, 1832.

Family of Augustine Hibbard.

AUGUSTINE HIBBARD, b. in Windham County, Conn., April 7, 1748, graduated at Dartmouth in 1774. Studied theology. Served as chaplain in a regiment stationed near Boston for some two or three years, and afterwards settled as minister of the Episcopal Church in Claremont, N.H. Jan. 7, 1777, he m. *Eunice Ashley*, b. in Claremont, Dec. 28, 1751. She d. Aug. 1, 1800. He afterwards m. *Sophia Stone*. They settled on No. 5, 10th Range of Stanstead, in 1807. He had previously retired from the ministry, and during the latter part of his life was mostly employed in public affairs. He d. Dec. 4, 1831. His wife d. May 4, 1842.

CHILDREN.

HORATIO G., b. Oct. 14, 1777.
AMELIA B., b. Nov. 28, 1778—m. *A. Kimball, Esq*.
HORACE, b. Sept. 10, 1780.
ASHLEY A., b. Jan. 12, 1782.
BENJAMIN D., b. June 23, 1784.
VALERIAN O., b. Nov. 21, 1785.
PLINY V., b. Jan. 16, 1790.
THERESA P., b. Sept. 21, 1791—m. *Stephen Haseltine*.
EUNICE A., b. Jan. 5, 1795, d. in May, 1831.

FAMILY OF AUGUSTINE HIBBARD. 121

Pliny V. Hibbard.

PLINY V. HIBBARD m. *Sibyl Nelson*. She d. Feb. 9, 1823. Aug. 12, 1823, he m. *Hannah Labaree*, b. in Charlestown, N.H., July 21, 1788. Mr. H. was for many years employed as an evangelist by the Canadian Board of Protestant Missions. Was an active and useful laborer in his Master's vineyard. He d. in 1859. His wife d. March, 1874.

CHILDREN BY FIRST MARRIAGE.

ORPHEUS, b. in 1808, d. in 1813.
OSMOND, b. March 18, 1811—drowned June 8, 1825, in Browning, Vt.
SOPHIA A., b. June 3, 1815—m. *William Benton*.
FRANCES W., b. May 8, 1819—m. *Isaac Atwater*.
HARRIET, b. July 19, 1817—m. *John Truesdale*, of Manchester, N.H.
EUNICE A., b. Jan. 19, 1821—m. *Peter Middlemas*—not living.
AUGUSTINE, b. Feb. 9, 1823. Went west—not living.

CHILDREN BY SECOND MARRIAGE.

SIBYL, b. June 16, 1824, d. in New Orleans in 1857.
BENJAMIN, b. Aug. 20, 1825—m. *Susan Fisher*, lives in Stoneham, Mass.
ASHLEY, b. March 27, 1827—m. *Sarah Perry*. Mr. Hibbard has been a successful merchant, and has been variously employed in public affairs in Montreal.
WILLIAM R., b. Nov. 25, 1828; engaged in mercantile business in Montreal. He m. *Sarah Cameron*.
MARY, b. April 30, 1832—m. *Peter Middlemas*. She is his second wife.
ELIZABETH, b. Oct. 12, 1834.
One child by first marriage died young.

Oliver Nash.

Was born in Williamsburgh, Mass., Oct. 10, 1780—m. *Clarissa May*, and settled on No. 7, 10th Range of Stanstead, in 1805. They were members of the Congregational Church. He d. in 1849, she d. in 1859—no children.

Moses Montague.

Was born in Sunderland, Mass., June 9, 1782. Settled on the east half of No. 7, 11th Range of Stanstead in 1805. In 1808 m. *Susan Lee*, b. Jan 29, 1787. The were members of the Congregational Church. She d. Aug. 19, 1819. One child died young. He returned to Sunderland, and m. *Mary Pomroy*, of Williamsburgh, Mass. They had five children.

The Pomroy Families.

These families are of Norman French extraction. One of the barons, who came over to England in the days of William the Conqueror, had for his coat of arms, the inscription " POMME ROI," or *Royal Apple*," which was afterwards adopted by his descendants as a surname. The orthography has in some instances been changed, but all those families in America who spell their name "*Pomroy*," are supposed to be the descendants of three brothers, viz., Eldad, Medard, and Ammi Pomroy, who came from England in the 17th century, and formed part of the old Plymouth colony of Puritan memory. Eldad subsequently removed to Connecticut. The brothers married and had families, and their descendants are scattered widely over the United States and Canada. Some have attained to high positions in the army; and others in commerce and in the various departments of public and professional life.

Selah Pomroy, Esq.

SELAH, a great grandson of Eldad Pomroy, was born in Northampton, Mass., Oct. 7, 1775. In 1795, he married *Hannah*, daughter of *Capt. Abel Thayer*, of Williamsburgh, Mass. The ancestors of Mr. Thayer belonged to the old Plymouth colony. Mr. Pomroy and his wife settled originally in Brookfield, Vermont; removed to Stanstead in 1798, and located on numbers 3 and 4, 11th Range —then a dense forest—no clearings nearer than those of Johnson Taplin, and Israel Wood, at the Plain.

For many years Mr. Pomroy sustained the office of magistrate. He was variously employed in public affairs, and was distinguished for his regard for law and order and for his efforts for the suppression of intemperance. In 1843, his house, barn, and other outbuildings were set on fire and destroyed by an incendiary whom he had convicted and fined for selling spirituous liquors without license. In 1817, he united with the Congregational

THE POMROY FAMILIES. 123

Church, in which, for more thân twenty-five years, he sustained the office of deacon. Like "Barnabas," he was a good man, and his Christian example and counsels will be long remembered by those who knew him. His wife died in 1821. In 1823, he married the widow *Mary Lawrence*, of St. Johnsbury, Vt. She died in 1837. In 1839, he married the widow *Harriet H. Buck*, of Montreal. She survives him. He died Dec. 23, 1856.

CHILDREN BY FIRST MARRIAGE.

HAZEN, b. April 20, 1796.
QUARTUS, b. Feb. 20, 1798.
BENJAMIN, b. Dec. 28, 1800.
CORDELIA, b. Jan. 27, 1804.

Hazen Pomroy.

HAZEN, the eldest son of Selah Pomroy, Esq., was b. April 20, 1796 and m. Oct. 26, 1819, *Lois* dau. of Capt. Daniel Mansur. They settled on No 6, 11th Range. They have celebrated their golden wedding and are now enjoying comfortable circumstances and health.

CHILDREN.

Their childen, NANCY M.,—b. July 31. 1820, m. 1847, Horace Wells, Esq., in Syracuse, N. Y., now living in Hoyleton Illinois; GEORGE b. June 25, 1822, m. May, 1845, Azubah Lee. Children,—*Ernest A.*, b. Feb. 4, 1846, deceased;—*Adel F.*, b. May 20, 1848; *William H.*, b. Aug. 1853. Mr. Pomroy settled on No 13, 12th Range, sustains the office of Capt. of Militia and holds various places of trust in the community.

CHARLES, b. May, 22, 1824—m. Mary Calkins in Lowell, Mass. d. at Watertown Mich., 1849. Children,—*Mary C.*, b. Mar. 1855, *Charles*, b. 1858, lives in Michigan.

ADELIA, b. May 9, 1826—m. Feb. 1st, 1853 in Utah, Alabama, Lewis Harper, M.D., and has *William L*, born Mar. 4, 1854 ; *Annie*, b. June 20, 1857, d. Aug. 1858; *Ernestine A.*, b. Feb. 1859 ; *Louisa A.*, b. 1860 ; *Arthur P.*, b. 1868. Dr. Harper died in Brunswick, Germany, Mar., 1874. His family still resides there.

LOUISA, b. June 2, 1828—m. Sept.,1855 in Chicago, Oliver B. Green, of Worcester, Mass. Children, *Mary P.*, b. April 26, 1857 ; *Olivia P. and Louisa P.*, twins, b. Feb. 1860 ; Louisa P. d. an infant, and Andrew H., b. Nov. 1870, in Chicago, residence of family.

ESTHER, b. July 30, 1830.—d. Oct. same year.
ELLEN, b. Sept. 16, 1832.—m. July, 1858, Quartus Bliss, Esq., Compton, and has *Olive Louisa*, b. Sept. 8, 1859; *Lyman Quartus*, b. Sep. 3, 1861; *Sarah A.*, b. Nov. 19. 1862, and *Ellen P.*, b. Aug. 14, 1866.
HAZEN, b. April 26, 1834—m. 1870 Nellie Clark, lives in Peru, Indiana.
BENJAMIN, b. Sep. 4, 1836, lives at Home.
SELAH W., b. April 4, 1839, has lived in Boston, now in New Jersey.
COURTLAND, b. May 28, 1844, m. Charlotte Smith, lives near the old homstead, has a son *Courtland*, b. 1862.

QUARTUS, 2d son of Selah Pomroy, was born Feb. 20, 1798. In 1822, he married *Aliva*, daughter of *Nathan Stearns*. They settled on No. 4, 12th Range, but afterwards sold out. He has for many years sustained the office of deacon in the Congregational Church. He lives in the house occupied by his father during the later years of his life.

CHILDREN.

HANNAH, b June 1, 1823,—d. July 22, 1845.
WILLIAM H. b. July 29, 1828—d. Sep 17, 1830.
LUCY L., b. Nov. 13, 1829—d. Sep. 21, 1842.
WRIGHT, b. July 27, 1833—m. *Adeline*, daughter of *Capt. James Young*, lives in Caswellboro, a daughter *Lucy*, b. 1863. One child died in infancy.

Benjamin Pomroy.

BENJAMIN, 3d son of Selah Pomroy, was born Dec. 28, 1800. Received his preparatory training as clerk, with Ichabod Smith, Esq., at Stanstead, began mercantile business at Sherbrooke, P. Q., in 1823, returned to Stanstead in 1824, and married *Lucy*, daughter of *Jedediah Lee*. In 1830, they removed to Compton, where he soon after gave up trade and commenced farming. He served during the Rebellion of 1837, 1838, as Captain of the Queens Mountain Rangers, and subsequently received the appointments of Major of Militia and Colonel of the 2d Battalion of the County of Compton. He was one of the pioneers in the construction of the Grand Trunk Railway, and his name is identified with the rise and progress of many of the other railroads of our country. He was a prominent mover in the establishment of the Eastern Townships Bank; of which he was elected President in 1859.

FAMILY OF LEONARD K. BENTON.

This was the first chartered bank put into operation in the Townships. It is located at Sherbrooke; has an agency at Stanstead Plain; A. P. Ball, Esq., son-in-law of Col. Pomroy, is the manager of this agency. In 1854 he experienced a distressing bereavement by the death of his wife, under most afflictive circumstances. She was killed by being thrown from a carriage; the horse having been frightened by a train of cars passing near the highway. In his public and private life Col. Pomroy has been distinguished for his liberal donations to benevolent institutions and objects.

CHILDREN.

SELAH J., b. Jan. 1, 1825—m. *Victor*, daughter of *A. A. Adams, Esq.*, of Coaticook.

MARY LEE, b. Aug. 16, 1827—m. *A. P. Ball, Esq.*

Mr. Ball was for many years engaged in mercantile business at Sherbrooke; but subsequently removed to Stanstead Plain, where, in addition to the business of the bank agency, he sustains the office of magistrate, and is otherwise employed in public affairs.

ERASTUS LEE, b. June 3, 1837, d. May 6, 1841.

Family of Leonard K. Benton.

LEONARD K. BENTON was b. in Langdon, N. H., Feb. 1803. He m. Feb. 22, 1830, *Cordelia*, dau. of Selah Pomroy, Esq., and was engaged in mercantile business until 1836, when he sold out and removed to the Pomroy homestead, where he has been engaged in farming. In 1850 he received the appointment of magistrate, and for many years has been actively engaged in the municipal and educational affairs of the County. His wife d. Jan. 2, 1874, leaving a tender and faithful husband in deep sorrow and loneliness, and affectionate children to mourn over a loss which no human sympathy could repair. Her life was devoted to her family and the good of others, and in death she had hope and peace in Christ, her Redeemer, whose presence and glory in heaven she will forever enjoy.

CHILDREN.

SARAH A., b. April 15, 1831, m. 1851 *T. H. Dozier* and has *Martha P. D.*, b. 1852, m. 1871, had 2 children d. March, 1873, and a son *William B.*, b. Oct. 1861. at Union Springs, Ala.

LEONARD K., b. Nov. 1832, d. in infancy.

CYNTHIA H., b. March 27, 1834, m. June, 1857, *Capt. James K. Gilman*, has *Cordelia B.*, b. Aug. 3 1859.

MARY C., b. Jan. 27, 1836, m. June, 1857. *Henry G. Pierce, Esq.* He died in 1870. Children, *Nancy A.*, b. April, 1858 *Henry F.*, b. Jan. 21, 1862, and *Rose Mary*, b. April 23, 1865, in Stanstead.
WILLIAM L., b. Aug. 8, 1839, d. March, 1864.
HARRIET P., b. Jan. 5, 1841, m. Dec., 1866, *Eugene Morrill*, and has *Jennie E.*, b. Aug., 1867, d. Jan., 1874; *Benjamin B*, b. Nov. 1868. GILBERT E., b. Jan., 1873, d. Aug. same year. *William*, b. May, 1874.
EMILY WILLISTON, b. Aug. 15-1843, m. Nov. 1866, *Charles E. Channell*, and has *Leonard S.*, b. April 8, 1868, *William E.*, b. March 31, 1871; a dau. b. Jan. 3, 1873, d. Feb. 14 same year; *Mary A.*, b. March 26, 1874, in Montreal.

The Hubbard Family.

GEORGE HUBBARD emigrated from Southampton, England, in the early part of the 17th century, and settled in Massachusetts. His descendants are numerous, and scattered widely over the Northern States and Canada.

PHINEAS HUBBARD, in the 7th generation, in a direct line from George Hubbard, was b. in Sunderland, Mass., March 22, 1775, m. June 22, 1797, *Catherine Nash*, b. in Williamsburgh, Mass., May 17, 1779. They settled in Sunderland, where their three eldest children were born, removed to Stanstead in 1805, and located on No. 5, 11th Range. He was soon after appointed magistrate, and as there were no regular clergymen in the settlement, had to officiate in most of the marriages that occurred during the first ten years of his residence. He was employed in public affairs, several years, was deacon in the Congregational Church. He d. Feb. 2, 1842; his wife d. July 13, 1858.

CHILDREN.

BENJAMIN F., b. June 9, 1798. Studied at Peacham Academy, Vt., spent several years in teaching in Maryland and Pennsylvania, returned to Stanstead in 1830, and settled on the east part of No. 7, 10th Range. Oct. 19, 1831, m. *Harriet Nash*, of Williamsburgh, Mass. In 1847, sold his farm and commenced the business of Drugs and Medicines at Stanstead Plain. He was appointed postmaster in 1847, and has sustained other places of trust and responsibility. Harriet, his wife, d. Jan. 29, 1862. Dec. 25, 1862, he m. his 2nd wife, *Annette D. Cummings*. She was b. April 17, 1813.

REV. AUSTIN O., b. Aug. 9, 1800. Graduated at Yale in 1824. Studied theology under the direction of the Baltimore Presbytery, spent some time as a student, and afterwards instructed in biblical literature in Princeton Seminary—preached three years in the vicinity of Taney Town, Md. In 1832, m. *Mary Graydon*, of Harrisburgh, Penn. She d. in 1833. He labored three years as a missionary in Melbourne, P.Q. In 1839, m. *Julia A. Hayes*, of South Hadley, Mass. In 1841, he was installed pastor of the Cong. Church in Hardwick, Vt., took the charge of the church in Barnet, Vt., in 1845, and in 1855 settled in Craftsbury, Vt. He published a small English Grammar and five discourses on the Sabbath. He d. Aug. 8, 1858. His wife d. Aug 7, 1857.

SOPHRONIA, b. Sept. 6, 1802, m. *William P. Spencer.* He d. in 1854. She d. in 1865.

PERSIS S. b. Jan. 22, 1805, m. *Luke Hurd.* They settled in Newport, P.Q. He was a farmer. D. 1873.

PHINEAS, JR., b. July 10, 1808. Began his mercantile career as clerk, at an early age. In 1832, engaged in trade in company with J. Foss, of Eaton, P.Q. In 1836, m. *Zilphia White* of Williamsburgh, Mass., and began business in his own name at Stanstead Plain. He received the appointment of postmaster and that of magistrate— was actively employed in public affairs, was a liberal contributor to benevolent objects, and was distinguished for his unflinching adherence to his convictions of justice and right. He d. Dec, 27, 1846. His wife d. May 12, 1864.

JOHN M., b. June 9, 1810, m. *Lucy M. Field.* She d. in 1839. In 1841, he m. *Lucy D. Wood.* They settled on the family homestead. He is a farmer.

ACHSAH H., b. Oct. 15, 1812, d. Sept. 3, 1833.

CATHERINE, b. May 28, 1816, m. *Samuel A. Hurd, Esq.* They resided in Eaton, P.Q., where he was engaged in mercantile business, and occupied a prominent position in the management of public affairs, and was a deacon in the Cong. Church of that place. Deacon Hurd now lives in Sherbrooke in feeble health.

SAMUEL N., b. April 24, 1820, d. April 3, 1831.

HENRY, b. July 1, 1825. Studied mostly at Stanstead Seminary and St. Johnsbury Academy, Vt. Received the honorary degree of A.M. from the University of Vermont, was employed several years as principal of the Academy in Craftsbury, Vt. In 1854, m. *Lois F.*, dau. of *Rev. David Carr*, of Waterford, Vt. In 1856, removed to Barnston, P.Q., where he remained principal of the Academy two years, when he removed to Danville, P.Q., where he continued in charge of the Academy until 1859, when he received the appointment of inspector of schools for the District of St. Francis, in the place of M. Child, Esq., deceased. He resides in Sherbrooke, P.Q., where he has been honored with other offices of trust and responsibility.

Shipley W. Snow, Esq.

Was b. in St. Johnsbury, Vt. April 7, 1816. Settled in Stanstead in 1836, m. *Jane*, dau. of *Capt. W. S. Hunter*. He was engaged for several years in the saddle and harness making business, and was connected with mining operations. He was elected Mayor of the Corporation of Stanstead Plain in 1859, and has been otherwise employed in public affairs.

Family of Wilder Pierce, Esq.

This family is of English extraction. The orthography has in some instances varied, but all those families in America who spell their names Pierce, or Pearce, can trace their ancestry back to the earliest colonists of New England.

WILDER PIERCE, b. in Westmorland, N.H., Jan. 3, 1788, commenced mercantile business at Stanstead Plain in 1816. In 1817 m. *Nancy*, dau. of *Israel Parsons*, of Hatfield, Mass. He retired from trade in 1837, and employed the declining years of his life in the cultivation of his farm. He was early appointed magistrate, and was for many years actively employed in public affairs. He and his wife were consistent and exemplary members of the Wesleyan Church. He was among the largest contributors in building the two Wesleyan churches and Stanstead seminary. He d. Sept. 29, 1866. His wife d. Jan. 10, 1853.

CHILDREN.

CHARLES W., b. April 23, 1818. A successful merchant. Settled in Boston, Mass. M. *Mary*, dau. of *Rev. J. Horton*. They are members of the Wesleyan Church. He was among the largest contributors to the erection of the new Wesleyan Church and the Wesleyan College of Stanstead, and has been liberal in sustaining benevolent institutions and objects.

SARAH P., b. March 14, 1820—m. *Hon. Henry Keyes*. She d. Dec. 8, 1853.

EMILY, b. Oct. 29, 1821—d. Feb. 26, 1832.

JOHN A., b. Sept. 12, 1823—d. July 20, 1861.

GEORGE, b. Aug. 31, 1825. A successful merchant. Was connected in trade with his brothers Charles W. and Carlos, in Boston, for some time. He m. *Mary M.*, dau. of *G. P. Clapp, Esq.* They were members of the Wesleyan Church. He d. Dec. 12, 1864. The organ in the new Wesleyan church of Stanstead was given as a tribute to his memory, by his brother Carlos Pierce.

HENRY G., b. June 9, 1827—m. *Mary C.*, dau. of *L. K. Benton, Esq.* They settled on the family homestead. His farm ranked among the model farms of the county. He was active in promoting the agricultural interests of the Townships, was a liberal contributor to benevolent institutions. He and his wife were members of the Wesleyan Church. He d. Oct. 9, 1870.

JULIA ANN, b. April 5, 1829—m. *George L. Goodwin*, a merchant of Boston. They are members of the Wesleyan Church.

CARLOS, b. May 20, 1831. Began his career in business at a very early age. When very young, he was the subject of a very remarkable Providence. In 1848 a large granite store in Federal street, Boston, fell down with a crash, burying everything in its ruins. He had been employed in the store, and after the confusion was not to be found. A large gang of men went to work to remove the broken timbers and merchandise, but with little hope of finding him alive. After a while, faint groans were heard, and guided by the sound of his voice, they finally succeeded in rescuing him, more dead than alive; having been imprisoned for nearly five hours. When found, he was lying with a large bale of flannel resting on his legs, and protected from death by two beams which formed a sort of arch over his body. In his fall from the upper loft, his frock had been turned up over his head, and when he had reached the place where he was found, he was in danger of perishing for want of air. Happening to have a pair of scissors in his pocket, he managed to cut holes through the frock, sufficient to let in air to sustain life. When found, he was very much exhausted, though but little hurt. Several weeks elapsed, however, before he was able to engage again in business. Soon after this occurrence, he engaged in business with his brothers Charles W. and George, in Boston. June 24, 1858, he m. *Mary Ann*, dau. of *Col. W. Mills*, of Bangor, Maine.

Previous to the time of the late American war, he had steadily increased his substance, and from several investments and contracts which he made at that particular time, realized a large property. He returned to Stanstead in 1863, and bought the Kilborn farm and other pieces of land, amounting in all to 600 acres, which, with the buildings and improvements he made, involved an expense of $150,000. He was an amateur farmer, and his farm ranked among the very first in the county in cultivation and crops. He was a liberal contributor to the agricultural interests of the county; having bought and fitted the former Race Course of the village at the expense of about $5,000, which he gave to the County Agricultural Society as a place for their annual fairs, subject to the condition that in the event of the removal of the annual meetings to another locality, this ground was to become the property of the Corporation of Stanstead Plain, to be fitted up and improved as a public park. His donations to Crystal Lake Cemetery and other public improvements were liberal, and in his contributions to benevolent objects, he was ever among the foremost. In the erection of the new Wesleyan Church, which involved an expense of more than $60,000, he paid at least $50,000. He had, with several others, engaged in a large purchase of wild lands in Kansas. The business of obtaining a charter for a railroad to pass through these lands was entrusted mainly to Mr Pierce; and such was the labor attending his efforts that his overtasked system gave way, and he died of brain fever, Aug 20, 1870.

In the Wesleyan church, of which he was a consistent member, he was distinguished for his efforts in sustaining the ordinances of the gospel, and for his interest in the improvement of the rising generation. He was, during the last years of his life, superintendent of the Sabbath School, in which his wife was a faithful teacher. Their memory will be long cherished in Stanstead.

EMMA FRANCES, b. September 17, 1832.—m *Hon. Henry Keyes.* She was his second wife. The name of Mr. Keyes is identified with the history of most of the railroad operations in Vermont during the past quarter of a century. He was a proprietor and Director in several: and for a long time President of the Conn. & Pass. Road, to the stock of which he was a heavy contributor. He invested largely in other roads, the supervision of which was, entrusted to him. He filled successively the place of Representative from Newbury in the Vermont Legislature, and that of State Senator at Washington, and was the Democratic candidate for Governor in 1857. Had he seen fit, he could have occupied any of the prominent offices in the country. In his domestic life he was an affectionate and tender husband, and a kind and indulgent father. He was a member of the Congregational Church at Newbury; a liberal contributor for the support of the ordinances of the gospel, and among the very first in sustaining the benevolent institutions of the age. He d. September 24, 1870.

MARTHA, b. March 1, 1836—m. *Isaac Butters*, his third wife. He was for many years engaged in mercantile business in Montreal, from which he retired, and was a liberal contributor to the erection of the Wesleyan church.

MARY, b. April 2, 1838—m. *Walter C. Cobb, Esq.* Mr. Cobb was a successful merchant. He d. in 1871. A son, *Walter A.*, b. Sept. 29, 1867, d. Sept. 4, 1868.

Family of Wright Chamberlin, Esq.

COL. WRIGHT CHAMBERLIN was born in Thetford, Vt., 1779. He commenced mercantile business as agent for Levi Bigelow, at Derby Line, in 1805; began in his own name at Stanstead Plain in 1809; continued in trade several years and afterwards retired and engaged in farming, having acquired a large property. He received his first military appointment in 1809 and was promoted successively to the rank of Lieut.-Colonel. In his business transactions he was distinguished for his uprightness and integrity. His word was as good as his bond. In the abodes of sickness and suffering he was ever ready to sympathize and succor. In 1814 he m. *Rachel*, dau. of *Mr. M. Camp*. She d. April 25, 1852. He d. March 13, 1860. They belonged to the Wesleyan Church.

CHILDREN.

SUSAN, b. June 20, 1815—m. *R. V. Burt*, has children, lives in Hyde Park, Mass.

MARY A., b. April 8, 1817—m. *S. M. Herbert, Esq.*

WRIGHT, b. March 24, 1819—m. *Mary Bangs*, d. November 20, 1872. A daughter, music teacher in Granby, P. Q.

RACHEL, b. April 6, 1821.

ASHER, b. February 5, 1823.

HANNAH, b. May 25, 1826.

LAURA, b. October 13, 1827, m. *Royal Chamberlin, Esq.*, of Lockport, N. Y.; has two children.

JANE, b. February 5, 1829—m. *A. F. B. Patton, Esq.*

HARRIET, b. February 25, 1830, m. *Hon. T. L. Terrill*, and has children:—William Lee, b. May 14, 1852, lives at home; George Frederick, b. July 3, 1868.

WILLIAM, b. in August, 1833—d. May 22, 1838.

Family of Ichabod Smith.

ICHABOD SMITH, ESQ., was born in Surry, N. H., April 24, 1788, removed with his father's family to Brownington, Vt., in 1798; came to Stanstead in 1810, and opened stores at Georgeville, Barnston and Eaton: began business at Stanstead Plain in 1813 in company with William Baxter and Wilder Pierce. In 1814 m Amanda, dau. of *Nathan Ward, Esq.* She was born in Springfield Vt., May 2, 1789. Mr. Smith re-commenced business in 1816 In 1824 built a large brick store at the north end of the village and in 1836 sold that property, retired from business and removed to the south end of the street. He early received the appointment of magistrate, and was for many years actively employed in public affairs, was long a prominent and influential member of the Wesleyan Church, and a liberal contributor to benevolent institutions. He was one of the founders of the Stanstead Seminary, and for many years president of the Stanstead County Bible Society. He d. in January, 1867. She d. in March, 1871.

CHILDREN.

GEORGE, b. July 28, 1815—d. at Hamilton, C. W., October 4, 1834.

MARY W., b. February 20, 1817—m. *Hon. 1. F. Redfield.* She d. July 24, 1839, in Cavendish, Vt.

LUCY B., b. June 15, 1820—d. June 16, 1836.

HARRIET A., b. February 25, 1823—in 1843 m. *George R. Robertson, Esq.* Mr. Robertson was an advocate, resided in Sherbrooke, P. Q. He d. in 1871. Children, James S., b. April 23, 1845, d. 1865; Mary Amanda, b. September 11, 1846; George S., b. April 1, 1849; Josephine, b. December 25, 1850; William Duncan, b. July 4, 1853; Gordon F., b. February 9, 1855; Isabella F., b. February 16, 1857; Katherine E., b. February 6, 1859 and Margaret Selina, b. March 28, 1863. The residence of the family is at Stanstead Plain.

CHAUNCY W., b. May 27, 1825—d. in infancy.

Family of Albert Knight, Esq.

ALBERT KNIGHT, son of Capt. Samuel Knight, was born in Waterford, Vt., February 12, 1817. He began his career as clerk

FAMILY OF CAPT. SAMUEL KNIGHT.

in mercantile business, at an early age; commenced business for himself at Stanstead Plain in 1837, and after continuing in trade for several years, sold out and retired. He then built a very commodious family residence which is justly admired for its elegance and utility. He has successively sustained the offices of Director of the Conn. & Pass. Railroad and President of the Stanstead Branch of the Eastern Townships' Bank. In 1861 he was elected to represent Stanstead county in the Provincial Parliament. In 1839 he m. *Julia Ann*, dau. of *Timothy Rose, Esq.* They belong to the Society of Universalists.

CHILDREN.

ALBERT TIMOTHY, b. February 22, 1840, d. January 7, 1852.
JULIA M., b. April 21, 1844—m. *Henry Marshall*, and has Julia Rose, b. January 12, 1871.
LELIA O., b. May, 26, 1848, m. September 14, 1869, *Samuel O. Shorey*. A son, Albert K., b. August 22, 1870; and a dau., Laura P., b. April 28, 1872.
LEWIS R., b. June 12, 1852—d. July 27, 1853.
CLARENCE A., b. October 3, 1855.
WINFIELD S., b. April 30, 1851—d. January 30, 1874.
FLORENCE, b. August 20, 1859.

Family of Capt. Samuel Knight.

CAPT. SAMUEL KNIGHT, b. in Athol, Mass., December 9, 1783. In 1808 m. *Mehitable Goss*, who was born in Hartland, Vt. February 2, 1787. They settled on No. 9, 13th Range of Stanstead in 1823; and afterwards removed to No. 6 in the same Range. Mrs. Knight d. September 16, 1863. He d. December 5, of same year.

CHILDREN.

LOVISA, b. May 29, 1811—m. *Dr. John E. Bangs.*
CHARLES S., b. Sept. 23, 1813—m. *Sally Bachelder.*
ALBERT, b. Feb. 13, 1817—m. *Julia Ann Rose.*
EMILY, b. May 8, 1819—m. *James McCaw.*
SAMUEL, b. May 8, 1825—m. *Julia A McDuffee.*
JOSEPH, b. May 24, 1821—m. *Emeline Morse.*
IRENE, b. March 27, 1827—m. a *Mr. Colby.*

134   FORESTS AND CLEARINGS.

BENJAMIN F., b. Sept 22, 1833—m. *Charlotte R. Gilman.*

Family of Capt. Andrew Young.

ANDREW YOUNG, b. in Whitehall, N. Y., Nov. 5, 1771, was one of the 25 Associates, and drew one lot of 200 acres, and subsequently purchased two more, making Nos. 4, 5 and 6 in the 9th Range of Stanstead. In 1801, he married *Polly Currier*, b. in Unity, N. H., Aug. 24, 1779. He was appointed Captain of Militia. He was an industrious and successful farmer, honest and upright in his dealings, and hospitable and kind to the poor. He d. Dec. 8, 1860. His wife d. Nov. 27, 1851.

CHILDREN.

ALEXANDER, b. June 29, 1802—m. *Mary Drew.*
JAMES, b. Oct. 6, 1803—m. *Mary B. Mears.*
ALBERT, b. Feb. 10, 1807—d. Feb. 14, 1811.
HANNAH, b. March 6, 1808—d. Feb. 17, 1811.
ANDREW, b. Feb. 11, 1810—m. *Abbie S. Smith.*
HANNAH, 2d, b. Feb. 14, 1812—m. *James Lovelace.*
JARED, b. April 2, 1814—m. *Lucinda Bartlett.*
ALBERT, 2d, b. May 26, 1816—m. *Martha Lewis.*
LUCINA, b. April 17, 1818—d. March 27, 1821.
BETSEY, b. June 24, 1821—m. *Hugh H. McCaw.*
MARY, b. April 11, 1823—m. *Michael Mc Adam.*
HORACE, b. July 4, 1825—m. *Maria Jenkerson.*

Alexander Young.

ALEXANDER YOUNG, b. in Stanstead, Jan. 29, 1802.—m. *Mary Drew.* She was b. April 1, 1801. He d. Aug. 8, 1851.

CHILDREN.

ALEXANDER ALONZO, b Sept. 26, 1826.—m. *Elsie McDuffee.*
MARY JANE, b. July 5, 1833.
GEORGE, b. July 4, 1835.
JOHN, b. March 29, 1838, engaged in the practice of law.
JULIA A., b. Oct. 25, 1840—m. *R. Tomlinson, Esq.*

Major James Young.

JAMES YOUNG, b. in Stanstead, Oct. 6, 1803—m. *Mary B. Mears* She was b. April 9, 1810. Mr. Young has successively held the offices of Captain and Major of Militia.

CHILDREN.

LUCINA, b. July 7, 1831—d. June 28, 1858.
ADELINE, b. March 6, 1834—m. *Wright Pomroy.*

FAMILY OF TIMOTHY ROSE.

JAMES, b. May 1, 1836.
ANDREW, b. March 4, 1838.
MARY, b. June 24, 1840—m. *Hiram W. Emerson*, of St. Johnsbury, Vt., who d. 1863; a dau. *Arabell, M.*, b. Jan 28, 1864. Mrs. Emerson m. Milo W. Hale, of Waterford, Vt.
WARREN M., b. July 10, 1842—d. May 1, 1843.
WARREN M., 2d., b. June 18, 1844.

Andrew Young, jr.,

Was born in Stanstead, Feb. 11, 1810—in 1849, m. *Abbie S. Smith*—b. April 13, 1821. Hé was actively employed in public affairs for many years. In their domestic circle, they experienced the affliction of being le childless, three promising children having been taken away by death at an early age. Mr. Young died in 1869.

The Rose Families.

These families are the descendants of *John Rose*, whe came from England and settled in Massachusetts in the latter part of the 17th century.

EDWARD ROSE, in the 5th generation from John Rose, b. in 1746.—m. *Sibyl Walker*, b. in 1745. They came to Stanstead in 1800, and resided with their son, Timothy Rose. He was a member of the Methodist Church, and was distinguished for his uniform and consistent piety. He d. in 1835. She d. in 1827. Their children were *Timothy, Edward,* and *Sybil*. Edward was killed by a fall from a horse.

Family of Timothy Rose.

TIMOTHY ROSE, b. in Deerfield, Mass., May 15, 1775.—m. *Sally Albee*, b. in Rockingham, Vt., Feb. 16, 1781. They settled on No. 7, 13th Range of Stanstead, in 1800, and afterwards removed to No 6, 12th Range. In 1805, he built a tannery, the first started in the Eastern Townships, and succeeded in acquiring a large property. He received the successive appointments of Lieutenant, Captain of Cavalry, and afterwards that of Magistrate. He d. Aug. 15, 1840. His wife d. July 20, 1855.

CHILDREN.

LEWIS E., b. Nov. 16, 1799—one of the wealthiest men of Stanstead County, d. in 1870.
HIRAM, b. Oct 31, 1801—d. Dec 25, 1814.
ESSEBA, b. June 18, 1804—m. *Hiram Bishop.*

HARRY, b. in July 1806—d. Dec. 26, 1815.
SARAH, b. in 1809—d. Dec. 22, 1814.
JULIA ANN, b. Nov. 15, 1817—m. *Albert Knight, Esq.*
LUCRETIA, b. May 4, 1821, m. *Freedom Whittaker.*
GEORGE H., b. June 14, 1824, m. *Nancy Fox.*
Five children died in infancy.

Family of James Saunders.

JAMES SAUNDERS, b. in Salem, Mass., July 12, 1757, m. *Elizabeth Little*, a native of Newbury, Mass. They settled on No. 2, 12th Range of Stanstead in 1804, sold out, some years afterwards, and left the country. He d. Dec. 14, 1830. She d. April 18, 1838.

CHILDREN.

WILLIAM, b. Oct. 17, 1775, m. *Lois Rowell.*
NATHANIEL, b. Aug. 7, 1777, m. *Mary Woodbury.*
BENJAMIN, b. Sept. 4, 1779, d. Jan. 10, 1802.
HENRY, b. Aug. 1, 1802, m. *Sarah Edwards.*
THOMAS, b. Sept. 8, 1784, m. *Sarah Woodbury.* They settled in Stanstead in 1806, afterwards left the country.
SAMUEL, b. Aug. 18, 1791, m. *Mehitable Hopkins.*
ELIZABETH, b. Oct. 22, 1786, m. *Luke Woodbury.*
JAMES, b. Nov. 20, 1789, d. in June, 1806.
DAVID, b. Nov. 17, 1793, d. July 28, 1839.
DANIEL, b. June 20, 1796, m *Phebe F. Abbott.* He came to Stanstead with his parents in 1804—served an apprenticeship in the cloth dressing business, and at the age of 21, settled at Andover, Mass. From a careful examination of the Fall in the Merrimac River, he conceived the plan of securing a water power in his own immediate vicinity, and keeping his project to himself, made purchases of all the lands he could secure near the proposed location. He then laid his scheme before several capitalists in Lowell. They at once joined in the undertaking, and a company was formed, called "The Merrimac Water Power Association," of which, he was the principal manager and agent. In 1845, an act of incorporation was granted by the Legislature of Mass. to him and his associates. From this beginning, the present city of Lawrence has arisen. He deservedly became the possessor of an immense fortune. Daniel Saunders, Jr., his son, was associated with him in the enterprise. He was educated for the profession of law, has been several times elected to the Legislature of Mass., serving in the House and Senate. He was Mayor of Lawrence at the time of the falling of the Pemberton Mills.
CALEB, b. Nov. 10, 1798, m. and settled in Illinois.

Family of Adam Noyes.

ADAM NOYES, b. in Acton, Mass., Jan. 22, 1774, m. *Mehitable Tuttle*, b. Nov. 29, 1780. She d. Sept. 29, 1815. In 1816, he m. *Lucy Tuttle*, b. Aug. 3, 1778. They settled at Stanstead Plain in 1812, afterwards removed to Georgeville. They were members of the Congregational Church. He d. Nov. 25, 1843. She d. Oct. 14, 1829.

CHILDREN BY 1st MARRIAGE.

HENRY W., b. Dec. 28, 1799, m. *Frances Williams*.
THOMAS R., b. Aug. 21, 1801, d. April 4, 1814.
ADAM S., b. Dec. 18, 1802, m. *Sarah Martin*
MARIA M., b. Feb. 17, 1807, d. March 27, 1814.
CHARLES A., b. March 31, 1809 d. July 18, 1833.
JARVIS W., b. Dec. 7, 1811, m. *Laura Reed.*
THOMAS R. P., b. March 28, 1815, d. March 24, 1856. One child d. in infancy.

2nd MARRIAGE.

JOSEPH, b. July 27, 1823, d. Aug. 2, 1854.

Family of Stephen Foster, Esq.

The ancestors of this family came from England in the 17th century, and settled in Massachusetts.

STEPHEN FOSTER was b. in Montpelier, Vt., July 12, 1806. He commenced mercantile business in company with Col. J.Langdon, at Derby Line, in 1828, and they opened a store at Rock Island in 1830. In 1831, he m. *Maria*, dau. of *Asa Kimball, Esq.*, of Barton, Vt. Col. Langdon withdrew in 1833, and the busisess at Rock Island was continued under the firm of Spalding & Foster until 1844, when Mr. Foster withdrew, and was afterwards appointed cashier of the People's Bank, at Derby Line. His wife, d. in 1854. In 1855, he m. *Carrie B.*, dau. of *D. Evans, Esq.*, of Providence, R. I. He was that year elected Mayor of the Municipality of Stanstead, and has sustained other offices of reponsibility and trust. He has been among the foremost in the support of the ordinances of the gospel and in his contributions to benevolent objects, and it is perhaps worthy of note that he was the first dealer in the township that banished the sale of ardent spirits from his business.

CHILDREN.

ORREN, b. June 3, 1835, d. Feb. 6, 1836.
WILLIAM S., b. June 4, 1837, m. *Maria,* dau. of *Elias Cheney,* of Sherbrooke, P.Q.
CHARLES H., b. Sept. 4, 1839, d. Sept. 10, 1840.
OSCAR A. G., b. Sept. 26, 1841, d. Aug. 29, 1842.

Family of Freeman Haskell.

FREEMAN HASKELL m. *Fanny Kathan.* Their children were CARLOS F., who m. *Martha Stewart,* and LOUISA.

Family of Francis Judd, Esq

FRANCIS JUDD was b. in Reading, Vt., Aug. 12, 1792, m. *Rosanna Marsh.* Mr. Judd was for several years engaged in successful trade in Barnston, Hatley and Stanstead, sustained the office of magistrate, and was otherwise employed in public affairs. His wife d. Aug. 6, 1863. The family are Episcopalians.

CHILDREN.

FRANCIS, b. April 19, 1827. An Episcopal clergyman, laboring with much acceptance and usefulness in Iowa City, Iowa.
JAMES H., b. March 13, 1831, m. *Jenett Winn.* He is engaged in mercantile business at Rock Island, P.Q.
WILLIAM B., b. Dec. 8, 1832, d. in Feb. 1833.
WILLIAM B., 2nd, b. 1834.
ELLEN R., b. July 8, 1836, d. in Dec. 1840.
CHARLES E., b. April 21, 1838.
THOMAS A., b. July 2, 1847.

Family of Chester Cowles, M.D.

This family are the descendants, in a direct line, from the Puritans that landed on Plymouth Rock in 1620.

CHESTER W. COWLES was born at Peacham, Vt., May 26, 1822; studied medicine with Drs. Josiah Shedd and Justus Cobb, at Peacham, and graduated at the University of New York; commenced practice at Stanstead Plain with M. F. Colby, M.D., in 1846. September 24, 1850, m. *Hortense,* dau. of *Gardner Chase, Esq.* He has an extensive and lucrative practice, and stands high in his profession. His family belong to the Congregational Church, in which he sustains the office of deacon. He lately received the appointment of magistrate.

FAMILY OF H. BAILEY TERRILL.

CHILDREN.

GENEVIEVE H., b. January 20, 1853.
JULIA E., b. December 4, 1854.
EUGENE C., b. January 17, 1860.

Charles A Richardson, Esq.

Was born in Quebec, October 16, 1804, where he acquired the profession of notary. In 1827 he married *Jane T. McKay*, of Quebec. She died in 1831. He came to Stanstead in 1829, and about 4 years afterwards removed to Lennoxville, where he m. *Louisa B.*, widow of *J. C. Butterfield*, of Walpole, N. H. He was appointed Postmaster at Lennoxville in 1836, but resigned the office and returned to Stanstead in 1844. He holds the office of Registrar for Stanstead county. Was for some time Mayor of the village corporation. Three promising children were removed by death, and they are left childless. His family are Episcopalians.

The Terrill Family.

This family are the descendants, in the 7th generation, from Roger Terrill, of Puritan memory. He was among the pioneers of the settlement of Woodbury, Conn. in 1672. We find no record of this family, but he "begat sons and daughters," and his posterity are scattered widely over the New England States and Canada.

Joseph H. Terrill, of the 6th generation from Roger Terrill, was among the earliest settlers of the Eastern Townships. He came to Canada with his father in 1800, subsequently married *Betsey*, dau. of *Capt Orsamus Bailey*, of Eaton, P. Q. They settled in Sherbrooke, P. Q., where he died in 1859. Their children were H. Bailey, Timothy Lee, Frederick, Preston, William, Amelia, Eliza and Jerusha. Of these only two settled in Stanstead.

Family of H. Bailey Terrill.

H. BAILEY TERRILL, oldest son of J. H. Terrill, was born in Sherbrooke, P. Q., December 2, 1811. He pursued the regular course of English, Classical and French studies at Quebec; studied law under the charge of Messrs. Peck & Short, Esqs., at Sherbrooke; was admitted to the bar in 1835, and in 1836 commenced practice at Stanstead Plain. In 1851 he was elected to represent Stanstead county in the Provincial Parliament and began his political career with the most brilliant prospects of success and usefulness, but was cut down and died of Asiatic Cholera at Quebec, October 29, 1852, in the 40th year of his age.

Mr. Terrill became early distinguished for his legal attainments and abilities, and at the time of his death was among the very first of the profession in Canada. His active and comprehensive mind seemed at once to grasp any legal point before him. With jurisprudence and with the politics of our country he was equally familiar; and, as an advocate, was a most formidable opponent. In person he was tall and elegant, rather inclined to corpulency; voice clear and pleasant; articulation distinct, and his address prepossessing and commanding. If he had lived to the usual age of man he must have become eminently distinguished in the highest departments of public life. In his private life he was tender and affectionate, kind and indulgent, and a valuable citizen. In early life he married *Laura*, dau. of *A. Farnham*, of Hardwick, Vt.

CHILDREN.

FREDERICK W., b. December 2, 1836—m. *Ellen*, dau. of *A. W. Kendrick, Esq.*, of Compton, P.Q.; is an advocate, has a good practice in Montreal.

EDWARD C., b. November 16, 1838—m. *Rachel A. Norton*; commenced the practice of law under bright prospects but was cut down in early life.

JOSEPH L., b. June 12, 1841; pursued the usual course of study of law; was admitted to the bar in 1865. He m. *Josephine*, dau. of *G. R. Robertson Esq.*; has a good practice at Stanstead Plain.

THOMAS B., b. December 16, 1842, engaged in mercantile business at Cookshire, Eaton, P. Q.

HAZZARD BAILEY, b. October 1, 1852.

Timothy Lee Terrill.

TIMOTHY LEE TERRILL, 2nd son of J. H. Terrill, was born in Sherbrooke, P. Q., in March, 1815. He pursued the study of law under the charge of his brother, H. Bailey Terrill, and was admitted to the bar in 1840. He joined the volunteer Forces in 1838, and remained in the service during the time of the Rebelion: settled at Stanstead Plain in 1844, and in 1850 m. *Harriet*, dau. of *Col. W. Chamberlin.* In 1852 he was elected without opposition to serve in the Provincial Parliament for Stanstead county and re-elected in 1854, 1856 and 1858. In 1854 was appointed Queen's Counsel, and in May, 1856, received from the Governor General the appointments of Registrar of the Province. Provincial Secretary and member of the Executive Council of the Province of Canada, which offices he resigned in 1857. From the failure of his health, he was induced in 1861, to retire from political life, after a successful career of more than eight years. He has for some time devoted his attention to farming, and is connected with the agricultural interests of the county.

Family of William Arms, Esq.

WILLIAM ARMS, b. in Deerfield, Mass., May 28, 1794; in 1818 m. *Miranda,* dau. of *Rev. J. Haven,* of Croydon, N. H. He was engaged for many years in the manufacture of axes and ploughs at Stanstead Plain; was appointed deacon of the Congregational church in 1821. In 1836 he removed to Sherbrooke, where he built an extensive iron foundry, and carried on a successful business for several years; received the appointment of magistrate in 1841; took an active part in public affairs, and was a liberal contributor to benevolent objects. He d. February 4, 1853. His wife d. in 1870.

CHILDREN.

ADELINE, b. July 27, 1821—m. *Samuel Tuck,* of Sherbrooke. A son d. in the late war; another m. a dau. of Judge Sanborn, and is in business.

MIRANDA, b. April 16, 1827—m. *Thomas Goldsmith,* lives in Troy, N. Y.

ADELIA, b. July 20, 1829—m. *J. McNicol,* of Sherbrooke.

CALISTA, b. September 19, 1831—m. *Lemuel Farwell,* of Sherbrooke.

Two children died young.

Family of Joseph Worth.

JOSEPH WORTH, b. at Hampton Falls, N.H., Nov. 9, 1768—m. *Susan Taplin.* They settled in Caswellboro'. She d. April 1, 1801. Jan. 2, 1803, m. *Polly Sawyer.* He d. May 20, 1823. Their children were Jacob, Susan, Lydia, Columbus, Miriam, Betsy, Roxana, Lucy and Shubel.

Family of Hugh McCaw.

HUGH McCAW married *Agnes McElroy*. They were natives of Ireland. Settled in Stanstead in 1828; removed to Reach, Ont., in 1855. They were worthy and useful members of the community. He d. Feb. 19, 1865, aged 91 years.

CHILDREN.

MARY, m. 1st, *Mr. Steele;* 2nd, *Joseph Walker.*
JAMES, m. 1st, *Sarah Taylor;* 2nd, *Emily Knight.*
JANE, m. 1st, *Reuben Taylor;* 2nd, *John Bailey.*
HUGH H., m. *Betsey Youug.*

Matthew Dixon, Esq.,

Was b. in Northumberland County, Eng., Jan. 27, 1810. He came to Canada in 1832, and after remaining four years at Quebec and Montreal, came to Stanstead in 1836. In 1837, he m. *Elmira*, dau. of *Henry Lee*. He joined the volunteer forces in 1837—was engaged for the service during the time of the Rebellion, and for some time held a lieutenant's commission. In 1846, he received the appointment of Preventive Officer in the Customs department, and was stationed successively at Stanstead Plain, St. Regis, Georgeville, and Lineboro', or the Boundary Line, north of Derby, Vt. Mr. Dixon is an efficient and faithful officer. In 1858, he was elected Mayor of the Corporation of Stanstead Plain. His wife d. in 1873. In 1874, he m. *Amelia House.*

Family of Harris Way.

HARRIS WAY, m. *Abigail Evans*. Their children were CHARLOTTE, m. *Ozro Morrill*. AURELIA, m. *Austin T. Foster*. ALANSON, m. a *Miss Bemis*. ELLEN, d. young.

Silas C. McClary, M.D.,

Was born in Hillsborough, N.H., July 29, 1792. Feb. 8, 1818, m. *Pluma Hammond*. She was b. in Thetford, Vt., May 23, 1792, and d. Feb. 15, 1841. Aug. 11, 1850, m. *Sarah Doolittle*, b. June 4, 1801, d. Sept. 22, 1863. April 24, 1864, m. *Cynthia Baldwin*. She was born March 31, 1798.

Dr. McClary commenced practice at Stanstead Plain, in 1817. He was a popular physician, and generally successful in practice; was a correct scholar, and well informed in most of the departments of literature and science; was a member of the Congregational Church. He d. October 11, 1864. Three children by first marriage.

Family of Amos Amsden.

AMOS AMSDEN, b. in Henniker ,N.H., Sept. 10, 1792—m. *Abigail Dustan*, b. in Dorchester, N.H., Aug. 19, 1793. They settled at Stanstead Plain in 1819. She d. June 18, 1852. They were members of the Wesleyan Church.

CHILDREN:

HIRAM A., b. March 26, 1818—m. *Sarah Hill.*
FREDERICK A., b. Sept. 23, 1822—m. *Adelaide Thomas.*
ABBIE A., b. Nov. 29, 1828—m. *William Sharp.*
CAROLINE A., b. April 25, 1835—m. *Edward Sharp.*
Two children died young.

Family of J. W. Martin.

JOSEPH WINTHROP MARTIN, of the sixth generation of the American branch of the family, is the descendant of an old family in Somersetshire, England. Members of the family came to New England as early as 1635, and located at Weymouth and Hingham. They united with the colony that settled Rehoboth in 1644, and Swansey in 1667, in the latter towns their descendants are still to be found, occupying the same farms possessed by their ancestors for over two hundred years.

In 1796, Mr. Martin's family removed from Rehoboth, Mass., into the then unsettled portion of northern Vermont, and finally located in Caledonia County. The subject of this sketch was born at St. Johnsbury, 12th January, 1801.

An elder brother having settled at East Stanbridge, L.C., where he still resides, Mr. M. concluded to follow him, and on the 1st May, 1822, he reached Stanstead, where he finally settled. For some time he carried on the saddle and harness business, but for many years he has devoted himself to farming.

On the 26th January, 1839, he was commissioned by the Governor General, Sir John Colborne, Lieutenant of Cavalry, which office he retained until the close of the Rebellion. While on an expedition, in command of Col. Alexander Kilborn, to secure some prisoners, they were fired upon by a company of men in ambush. Col. K. was dangerously wounded, and Lieut. M. escaped almost by a miracle; several balls grazed his head and body, and his horse shot under him, but owing to the darkness o the night, he succeeded in effecting his escape unhurt.

On the 28th February, 1845, he was appointed one of the Commissioners of Small Causes for the Township of Stanstead, and on 21st October of the same year he was appointed a Justice of the Peace, but declined serving. He was again appointed on the 11th May, 1860.

Mr. M. has at various times been a member of the County and Village Councils.

On the 3rd March, 1828, he m. *Almira Deborah*, youngest child of *William* and *Deborah* (*Buell*) *Baxter*, of Rutland, Vt., and has had

CHILDREN.

HENRY JOSEPH, b. 13th Nov., 1828.
CAROLINE AGNES, b. 24th Jan., 1832—d. 8th June, 1832.
EDGAR, b. 10th April, 1834—d. 3rd Jan., 1836.
CAROLINE LOUISA, b. 16th June, 1837.

His son, Henry J., is a resident of Washington, D.C., and his daughter Caroline Louisa, resides at home with her parents.

The Child Family.

Families of this name are found in Great Britain and are scattered widely over the United States and Canada. The orthography has in some instances been changed, but all those who spell their name *Child* or *Childe* probably sprang from the same source. We find the name *Childe* in England nearly as far back as to the time of the adoption of surnames in that country. The letter *e* has in most instances been dropped. The immediate progenitors of the subject of the following notice settled in Worcester, Mass.

Marcus Child, Esq.,

Came to Stanstead in the early days of the settlement, and was employed for a few years as clerk in the business of Levi Bigelow, at Derby Line. At a later date, he engaged in partnership with Dea. Levi Hooker in the business of drugs and medicines on Stanstead Plain. Mr. Child bought out the concern, and continued the business for several years. Was early appointed postmaster and magistrate. He succeeded in acquiring a large property, was one of the founders of Stanstead Seminary, and a liberal contributor to the interests of the Wesleyan Church. Was among the early members who represented Stanstead County in the Provincial Parliament.

In the Revolution of 1837-1839, he was identified with the Radical or Reform Party. For a time, he was among the proscribed, and was compelled to leave the country; but this party soon came again into power. Mr. Child returned, and was again elected to the Provincial Parliament for Stanstead County.

His interests had for several years been connected with the then new settlement of Coaticook. The name of its Post Office was given at his suggestion, and it was afterwards adopted as that of the Municipality. He removed to that place, a few years before the close of his life, and held the office of School Inspector for the District of St. Francis. He was "a ready scribe," and while at Stanstead, was Secretary or Corresponding Secretary for the Stanstead Bible Society, Stanstead Seminary, and other institutions of the kind.

In early life, he married *Lydia Chadwick*, a native of Massachusetts. Of their children, two only, survived to maturity: *George M.*, who settled near Coaticook, and *Elizabeth*, who married Lewis L. Sleeper, Esq. She died in the prime of life and usefulness, much beloved and deeply lamented. During the last years of his life, Mr. Child and his family were connected with the Episcopal Church.

Family of Stephen Allen.

STEPHEN ALLEN, b. in Wendell, Mass., Jan. 30, 1800—m. *Melissa Arms*, who was b. May 24, 1807. They settled at Stanstead Plain in 1828, and subsequently removed to Cassville. He was a deacon in the Congregational Church. He d. Jan. 3, 1861.

CHILDREN.

JOSEPH S., b. May 1, 1830.
GEORGE A., b. July 2, 1834.
SARAH B., b. March 20, 1837.
JAMES F., b. Dec. 30, 1841.
CHARLES H., b. Oct. 28, 1845.
CLARA A., b. Aug. 31, 1848.

L

Dolphin Mitchell.

DOLPHIN MITCHELL married *Sarah Wood*. They were among the early settlers of Stanstead Plain. She d. in 1824. He afterwards m. *Almira Cook*. He d. in 1835.

Family of Frederick Holmes.

FREDERICK HOLMES, b. in Stonington, Conn., Feb. 19, 1790—m. Nov. 24, 1814, *Abigail Pettes*. He settled originally in Stanstead.

CHILDREN.

GEORGE R., b. Aug. 18, 1815. Engaged in mercantile business.
DENISON F., b. April 10, 1817—m. 1st, *Sarah Lee*; 2d, *Olive Cummings*.
MARY ANN, b. Jan. 15, 1820—d. May 24, 1834.
WILLIAM F., b. Sept. 14, 1821.
SIMON O., b. Dec. 12, 1825.
ANNA M., b. March 24, 1829—m. *Horatio C. Blake*. One child died young.

The Meigs Family.

(Communicated by John Meigs, M.D.)

The first authentic account we have of the name of Meigs is that Peveril Meigs married into the male line of the Churchill family about 50 years before the birth of John Churchill, Duke of Marlborough.

The American account of the family is that Vincent Meigs and his son, John, came from Dorsetshire, England, with the first settlers of Connecticut in 1638. Vincent settled at Hamanosset Neck, East Guilford, Conn., where he d. in 1658–John, son of Vincent Meigs, died in 1713, leaving 5 children—*John*, b. in 1670, d. in 1718; *Joanna*, b. in 1672, d. in 1739. *Ebenezer*, b. in 1678; *Hannah*, b. in 1677, and *Hesper*, b. in 1680 John Meigs, the grandson of Vincent Meigs, had 7 children : *John*, a physician, b. June 10, 1697, who d. in 1770; *Stephen*, b. Oct. 10, 1699 ; *Recompense*, b. Dec. 11, 1701; *Irene*, b. March 10, 1704; *Samuel*, b. Aug. 22, 1705; *Phineas*, b. Sept. 21, 1708, and *Sarah*, b. Dec. 10, 1713. The children of Dr. John Meigs, great grandson of Vincent Meigs, were *Dr. Abner Meigs*, b. in Woodbury, Conn., in 1750, d. in 1835 ; *Dr. Phineas Meigs*, b. July 11, 1760 ; and *Rebecca, Jesse* and *Irene*. The children of Dr. Abner Meigs, great great grandson of Vincent Meigs, were, *Heman*, b. June 14,

1780, who d. in 1855, *Sarah, John*, a physician, *Lorenzo, Anson* and *Church*. The children of Heman Meigs, the 5th generation from Vincent Meigs, were *Church Meigs*, who was b. in 1804, d. in 1866, and *John Meigs*, b. Feb. 16, 1810, *Chastina, Selonia* and *Josephine*.

John Meigs, M.D.

In the 6th generation from Vincent Meigs, was b. in Wheelock, Vt., Feb. 16, 1810, studied medicine under the direction of Dr. Phineas Spalding, of Lyndon, Vt, graduated at the Institute in Woodstock, then in connection with the College in Middlebury, Vt. Commenced the practice of medicine in Stanstead. 1836, and was subsequently admitted a member of the College of Physicians and Surgeons of the Province of Quebec. In Jan., 1843, he m. *Elizabeth*, dau. of *Wm. Grannis, Esq.* She was b. in Hatley, P.Q., April 19, 1822. Dr. Meigs sustains a high standing in his profession. The family are Episcopalians.

CHILDREN.

ALICE L., b. April 26, 1847.
ELIZABETH S., b. May 20, 1854.

Family of William Grannis, Esq.

WILLIAM GRANNIS, ESQ., b. in Claremont, N. H., in 1781, m *Nancy M. Dustan*, a native of Claremont, N. H., and b. in 1791. They settled in Hatley, 1816, removed to Stanstead in 1829. He was one of the founders of Stanstead Seminary. He d. in 1833. The family are Episcopalians.

CHILDREN.

SARAH, b. March 2, 1809—m. *Dr. R. Parmelee*.
JANE, b. Jan. 21, 1812—d. in 1830.
HARRIET, b. Dec. 28, 1814—m. *Sidney P. Redfield, Esq.*
ELIZABETH C. T., b. Sept. 19, 1822—m. *Dr. John Meigs*,
HELEN W., b. Feb. 16, 1818—m. *Timothy P. Redfield, Esq.*
WILLIAM C., b. March 30, 1826—m. *Lucia Baldwin*.

Family of Abraham F. J. Channell.

ABRAHAM F. J. CHANNELL was b. in London, Eng., Nov. 24, 1748. At an early age he was apprenticed to a tailor in that city, but before the expiration of his indentures was impressed on board a British man-of-war, and was afterwards transferred to a frigate laden with stores for the supply of their forces in America. This vessel was captured by an American Privateer, and taken into

Boston Harbor. Mr. Channell subsequently enlisted on board the privateer and remained in the Continental service during the time of the Revolution; was engaged in several battles, particularly in that of Sullivan Island. At the close of the War, he began business in Boston as a tailor. In 1780, he m. *Abigail Burnham.* She d. June 21, 1794. He came to Canada in 1810, and commenced business at Georgeville. In 1815, he m. *Wealthy Cox.* He d. Jan. 9, 1858, having attained to the age of 110 years. The children by his 1st marriage were *Fanny C., Abraham, Sally, Betsey, Abigail* and *Robert.*

CHILDREN BY 2nd MARRIAGE.

SUSAN, b. June 3, 1816, m. *John C. Tuck, Esq.* He is a Preventive officer in the Customs department at Georgeville.

LEON L., b. May 25, 1818, m. 1st *Harriet Goodrich*, 2nd *Harriet Gibb*, is engaged in mercantile business in Clinton Co., N. Y.

CHARLES S., b. March 26, 1820, m. *Mary A.*, dau. of *David Webster, Esq.* She was connected with the family of the Hon. Daniel Webster. Mr. Channell was engaged in mercantile business for many years at Georgeville, sustained the office of postmaster, and was otherwise employed in public affairs, received the appointment of magistrate, removed to Stanstead Plain in 1861, and was appointed collector of Customs for that Port, in 1870.

Family of Hon. James Baxter.

HON. JAMES BAXTER was descended in a direct line from Rev. Richard Baxter of Nonconformist memory, and was b. in Norwich, Vt., Dec. 21, 1788. He commenced mercantile business at Stanstead Plain in 1817 and Sept. 14, 1819, m. *Caroline*, dau. of *William Baxter, Esq.* of Rutland, Vt. She was b. Feb. 10, 1795. In 1829 he was elected to the Provincial Parliament, and was the first member sent from Stanstead County. In 1832 he was appointed by the Governor General a member of the Legislative Council, which office he held until the time of his death, Nov. 13, 1837. *Caroline*, his wife, d. April 18, 1865.

CHILDREN.

HARRIET, b. Oct. 4, 1821, m. *William B. Palmer, Esq.* She d. April 18, 1845.

GEORGE W., b. July 1, 1824.

CHARLES B., b. Jan. 5, 1826.

JAMES, b. July 28, 1831.

Family of George T. Gates.

GEORGE T. GATES, b. in Hanover, N. H., Jan. 9, 1795, m Elizabeth Cook. She d. May 17, 1818. May 21, 1821, m. Fanny Wright, b. in Hanover, N. H., Jan. 27, 1797. They settled at Stanstead Plain in 1823. One child by 1st marriage, Elizabeth, m. Silas Shaw.

CHILREN BY 2nd MARRIAGE.

LEONORA, b. Nov. 4, 1822—d. Sept. 4, 1823.
FANNY, b. April 2, 1824—m. Albert M. Dow.
GEORGE W., b. Dec. 16, 1825—m. M. F. Currier. Mr. G. was for several years connected with the management of the Conn. & Pass. railroad, is now superintendant of the Eastern Division of the Western Union Telegraph Company at White River Junction, Vt.
HENRY E., b., June 21, 1827—m. A. E. Phelps, lives in Chicago.
HARTLEY, b. Dec. 29, 1828.
CHARLES W., b. May 8, 1830—d. Sept. 21, 1854.
ANN E., b. March 24, 1832—m. Lockhart K. Hall.
AMANDA, b. May 13, 1836—d. April 28, 1854.

Family of Rev. Joseph Gibb.

REV. JOSEPH GIBB, b. in Aberdeenshire, Scotland, in 1776—m. Elizabeth Strachan. She was a woman of much mental and moral worth and of consistent and devoted piety. They settled at Stanstead Plain in 1829. He d. June 14, 1833, she d. Jan. 28, 1860.

CHILDREN.

JOSEPH, JR., b. Feb. 19, 1810; graduated at Mareschal College, Aberdeen, Scotland, was engaged in teaching for some time in England. Studied and completed his theological course at Highbury College, London. He followed his father's family to Canada in 1831. In 1834 he received a unanimous call from the Cong. Church in Haverhill, N. H., was ordained, and entered upon his duties under the most favourable auspices. He was almost idolized by his church and people, and they cherish his memory with the strongest affection. His talents were of the very first order, and in pulpit eloquence and in plain and practical illustration of the truths of the Gospel, he was surpassed by few of the age. He died of consumption, April 11, 1837.

ANNA, b. April 12, 1812—m. Henry Hayes, M.D. Dr. H. emigrated from Scotland in 1831.

DAVID, b. June 25, 1814. Graduated at Dartmouth, N. H. Studied theolgy at Andover, Mass. Was afterwards ordained pastor of the Cong. Church in Russelltown, P.Q. He subsequently became pastor of the Cong. Church in Granby, P.Q., where he died, March 16, 1848. Like his brother Joseph, he was much beloved by his people, and, like him, was compelled to lay down his armor in the midst of success and usefulness. He m. *Catherine*, dau. of *Rev James Robertson*, of Sherbrooke, P.Q.

MARGARET INNES, b. April 25, 1817—m. *M. S. Field.*

ELIZABETH, b. Dec. 2, 1819—d. April 11, 1854.

JAMES, b. Sept. 18, 1825—m. *Mary Wells.*

Family of Rev. Robert V. Hall.

REV. ROBERT V. HALL, b. in Stanstead, Jan. 10, 1810. Aug. 12, 1835, m. *Laura*, dau. of *C. Newton, Esq.*, Shoreham, Vt. She was born April 29, 1808. She d. Dec. 4, 1858. Jan. 10, 1861, he m. *Adelia L. Ellis*, of Bedford, P.Q.

CHILDREN BY FIRST MARRIAGE.

ROBERT N., b. July 26, 1836, graduated at the University of Vermont; studied law; was admitted to the bar in 1861. He m. *Laura*, dau. of *A. W. Kendrick, Esq.*, of Compton, P.Q. He settled at Sherbrooke, P.Q.; has a good practice, and stands high in his profession.

WILLIAM S., b. April 1, 1839; graduated at the University of Vermont; studied law. M. *Sarah*, dau. of *Levi Spalding, Esq.*, of Derby, Vermont.

MARY K., b. Sept. 14, 1842, d. Oct. 8, 1856.

JAMES R., b. March 12, 1845; is engaged in the business of drugs and medicines, in Newport, Vt.

Family of Silas H. Dickerson, Esq.

SILAS H. DICKERSON was a native of New Jersey, and b. May 12, 1799. At the age of fourteen was apprenticed to a printer in Kingston, Ont., and afterwards was a journeyman printer with Nahum Mower, in Montreal, where he m. *Mary Price*, b. at Elizabethtown, N.J., Sept. 25, 1797. In 1823 they removed to Stanstead, where Mr. Dickerson started the *British Colonist*, a weekly newspaper. This paper was the only one published in the Eastern Townships for many years, and had an extensive circulation. He was appointed Collector of Customs in 1853, and in 1857, was elected Mayor of the Corporation of Stanstead Plain. He d. Oct. 23, 1857.

THE COLBY FAMILY.

CHILDREN.

MARY, b. March 20, 1824—m. *Jacob Winn.*
CHARLOTTE, b. July 31, 1826—m. *John R. Wells.*
WILMOT H., b. Sept. 19, 1828—m. *Sarah Butin.*
ELIZABETH, b. Dec. 12, 1831; was for some time preceptress in Stanstead Seminary.
CAROLINE, b. Feb. 22, 1830.
JULIA, b. July 30, 1837—d. July 23, 1858.
HELEN R., b. Sept. 24, 1838.

The Colby Family.

We have no authentic account of the ancestry of this family Tradition says that two families of this name came from England in 1632, and settled in Old Salisbury, Mass. One of these families afterwards removed to Chester, N.H. SAMUEL COLBY, a descendant in the sixth generation from this family, m. *Ruth French.* They were natives of Candia, N.H. Settled originally in Thornton, N.H.; removed to Derby, Vt., in 1798, and were among the pioneers in the settlement of that town. They were intelligent and useful members of the community. Their children were NEHEMIAH, who m. *Melinda Larabee;* SARAH, m. *Dea. Wm. Verback;* MOSES F., m. *Lemira Strong;* RUTH F., m. *Dr. David French;* and EMILY, who m. *Dr. S. S. Kendall.* Of these Moses F., only, settled in Canada.

Moses French Colby, M.D.,

Was born in Thornton, N.H., July 2, 1795. His early opportunities for education, like those of other pioneers, were limited to the common schools of the time; but he succeeded in laying the foundation of that knowledge for which in after life he was so eminently distinguished.

In 1814, he commenced the study of medicine under the charge of Dr. Newcomb, of Derby, Vt., attended the lectures of the Medical Department of Yale College in 1817, entered the Medical Department of Dartmouth in 1820, and graduated in 1821. Commenced practice in Derby, that year; was uniformly successful, but not being satisfied with present attainments, he relinquished his practice for a time, and, in 1828, entered the School of Practical Anatomy at Harvard College, where he pursued the regular course with attendance at the hospitals. During that time, he formed the acquaintance of Dr. Gould, the late President of the Massachusetts Medical Society, and one of the most eminent *savans* of the age, with whom he sustained an interesting correspondence for many years, some parts of which have been published. In this connection, it may perhaps be worthy of note that while a few months are now deemed by many as amply sufficient time to complete the education of medical men, Dr. Colby was willing to devote fourteen years of the best part of his life to this science. Indeed he was a *student* during the whole of his life. On his return from Cambridge, Mass., he again commenced practice in Derby; and such was his success, that his circuit soon extended over Orleans and Stanstead Counties. In 1832, he removed to Stanstead, and after having passed a rigid examination before the Medical Faculty at Quebec, and obtaining licensure, commenced practice. In 1837, he received the honorary degree of A.M. from Dartmouth College, and about the same time was elected a member of the Provincial Parliament for Stanstead County. He served during the time of the Rebellion as surgeon for the Militia and Volunteers of the County. At the close of the Rebellion, a union of the two Canadas was effected, and the election of the member for Stanstead County for the New Parliament was one of the most exciting events in its political history. The election was contested by Dr. Colby, the candidate of the Conservative party and Marcus Child, Esq., of the Liberals. The poll was kept open at Hatley twelve days; and during that time both parties worked with a desperation not exceeded in any election. The result was that Mr. Child had a small *nominal* majority, but the friends of Dr. Colby claimed a majority of legal votes.

The character of Dr. Colby was one of peculiar interest. While the science of medicine was his *forte*, he was familiar with the various branches of a liberal education. His contributions to the Boston Medical and Surgical Journal and other distinguished periodicals exhibit an acquaintance with the theory and practice of medicine much in advance of the age in which they were written.

In Northern New England and the Eastern Townships of Canada, he stood decidedly at the head of his profession, and his memory is cherished with respect and esteem. In his religious views, he embraced the doctrines of the Reformation, and exhibited the spirit of the Gospel in his daily walk and conversation, and was ever a liberal contributor to benevolent enterprises. July 10

1826, he married *Lemira Strong*, of Pawlet, Vt., b. May 9, 1806. Dr. Colby died May 4, 1863, aged 67 years. Mrs. Colby lives with her son C. C. Colby on the Plain.

CHILDREN.

CHARLES C., b. Dec. 10, 1827,—m. *Harriet H. Child.*
EMILY, b. April 23, 1830,—d. March 9, 1832.
WILLIAM B., b. Jan. 23, 1833,—m. *Malivna A. Wallingford.*
EMILY, 2d, b. April 10, 1836,—m. *Wm. T. White, Esq.* She d. July 12, 1866.

CHARLES C. COLBY, b. in Derby, Vt., Dec. 10, 1827, graduated at Darmouth in 1847; studied law. Commenced practice at Stanstead in 1855. In 1867, he was elected to represent Stanstead county in the House of Commons of the Legislature of the New Dominion of Canada, as convened at Ottawa, Ontario—was re-elected in 1871. Dec. 21, 1858, he m. *Harriet H.*, dau. of *J. Child, Esq.*, of Weybridge, Vt. She was for some time preceptress of Stanstead Seminary. The political career of Mr. Colby has been a prosperous one.

CHILDREN.

ABBY J., b. Sept. 27, 1859.
JESSIE M., b. Nov. 11, 1861.
EMILY S., b. Feb. 1, 1864,—d. Sept. 17, 1865.
CHARLES W., b. March 25, 1867.

WILLIAM B. COLBY, b. in Stanstead, Jan. 23, 1833, m. *Malvina Wallingford*, b. in Stanstead, Nov. 13, 1832. Mr. Colby has been variously employed in public affairs.

CHILDREN.

MARY, b. Oct. 23, 1862.
MARTHA S., b. Aug. 21, 1865.

The Kilborn Family.

COL. CHARLES KILBORN was born in Litchfield, Conn., March 3, 1758. He was a descendant of Thomas Kilborn, who emigrated from England with his family in 1635, and settled in Weathersfield, Conn.

In the beginning of the American Revolution, the subject of this notice was drafted into the Continental service, though much against his own will. He served, however, through one campaign, and was engaged in several skirmishes with the British. He subsequently enlisted in the British army, and was taken prisoner in an engagement with a detachment of the American forces. He succeeded in making his escape, and, after a series of vicissitudes and adventures, found his way to Canada, on foot, by a long route through an uninhabited country. Before peace was concluded he had become a captain in the British service. In February, 1784, he married *Margaret Young*. They afterwards resided 17 years at Caldwell's Manor, and two years at Alburgh; removed to Stanstead, in 1804 and settled on Rock Island, where he built a grist mill, a saw mill, a carding and clothiers, factory, and a linseed-oil mill.

He drew lots Nos. 1 and 2, 9th Range as an Associate, and purchased others, but lots and mills have passed out of the hands of the family.

At the commencement of the American war of 1812 Mr. Kilborn held the office of Major in the British service, and at the close of the war, retired with the rank of Lieut.-Colonel. He sustained the office of magistrate many years, and was a prompt administrator of justice, without fear or favor of party. The following incident is illustrative of his promptitude and energy. Some time in the early days of the settlement, the noted counterfeiter, Stephen Boroughs had begun his operations at the place now known as Borough's Falls, and had fitted up a shop in his barn in such a way that there was no entrance into it except by a hole through the hay mow. His retreat having been discovered, Mr. Kilborn went with two others, to arrest him. As only one could go in at a time, he said to the others," if he kills me, don't let him come out alive." At his entrance into the room, Boroughs presented and snapped his pistol, which fortunately missed fire Boroughs said it was the first time he had ever known the pistol to miss fire. By this time, Mr. Kilborn had things pretty much in his own way, and succeeded in bringing Boroughs and his deeds of darkness fully to light. A large number of spurious bank notes, and the implements for counterfeiting upon a large scale were found, and the nest was thoroughly broken up. Col. Kilborn died, June 19, 1834. *Margaret*, his wife, died Aug. 21, 1841. Their children were *Lucy*, m. *John Savage*; *Betsey*, m. *Henry Curtis*, *Benjamin*, m. *Sophia Cooley*; *Alexander*, m. *Thankful Bangs*; *Sally*, d. at the age of 17 years; *Joseph*, d. young, *Mary*, m. *Daniel Remick*;

THE LEE FAMILY.

Nancy, m. *Stephen Cobb*; *Matilda*, m. *Eliphalet Bodwell*, jr.; and *Lydia*, who m. *E. F. G. Studdert*.

COL. ALEXANDER KILBORN, b. April 5, 1791, m. *Thankful H. Bangs*. He early had a predilection for the military service, arose from the place of Sergeant to that of Lieut.-Colonel of militia. At the breaking out of the Rebellion in 1837 he had the command of a company of volunteers. In the winter of 1837-1838, while on his way to secure some prisoners, he received a severe wound in the abdomen, which very nearly proved fatal. He was one of the founders of Stanstead Seminary; 2 children, Susan L. and Charles A. Susan died Nov. 21, 1868, aged 53 years. Colonel Kilborn, d. April 20, 1872.

CAPT. JOSEPH KILBORN was b. in Litchfield, Conn., Feb. 15, 1771. Studied the art of surveying, and was appointed Deputy Surveyor of the Province of Quebec in 1792, and, as such, assisted in surveying nearly all the Eastern Townships. He was afterwards appointed Military Surveyor and Draftsman, with the rank and pay of Captain in the regular army. He died Nov. 15, 1814, aged 43 years.

Family of Daniel Holmes.

DANIEL HOLMES, b. in Stonington, Conn., September 17, 1787— m. *Malinda Lee*. They settled in Stanstead. Both deceased.

CHILDREN.

HORACE, b. in 1811—d. in 1820.
LEWIS F., b. in 1815—d. in 1820.
WILLIAM H., b. April 25, 1814—m. *Julia G. Small*.
ALONZO H., b. in 1817.
HORACE D., b. February 8, 1821—m. *Mary Ann Bailey*.

The Lee Family.

These families are of English extraction, and, like the *Browns* and *Smiths*, are ubiquitous, being found in almost every part of Britain and America. The earliest record of the Stanstead branch is that Jedediah Lee deeded to his son, Elias Lee, in 1744, fifty acres of land in the town of Ellington, Conn., and that in 1745 Elias Lee married Sarah Royce, and settled on that farm. Their children were Sarah, Lucy, Mary, Elias, Daniel, Lucy 2nd, Jerusha, Ruth and Jedediah. Of these Jedediah and Daniel settled in Stanstead.

JEDEDIAH LEE b. in Ellington, Conn., April 7, 1755—m. *Elizabeth Wood* in 1776. Two children were the issue of this marriage, one of whom died young. Mary married James Paul, and was the mother of 12 children. Mr. Lee subsequently m. *Mary Perry*, She d. in 1793, leaving one child, Malinda, who m. Daniel Holmes, March 1, 1797, m. *Mary Denison*, widow of Jeremiah Holmes. He d. October 24, 1824; she d. April 29, 1828. The children by the third marriage were Erastus, b. 1797—d. unmarried, March 21, 1866. He was a consistent and exemplary member of the Wesleyan Church, and a liberal contributor to benevolent objects. Lucy, b. January 1, 1801—m. Col. B. Pomroy. She was killed by being thrown from a carriage in 1854.

DANIEL LEE, b. in Ellington, Conn., January 20, 1753—m. *Sarah Whittaker*. They settled on No. 10, 10th Range of Stanstead in 1797, where they lived to a good old age, and were much respected for their uprightness and exemplary piety.

CHILDREN.

ELIAS, b. April 18, 1777—m. *Rhoda Morrill.*
HENRY, b. in 1780—m. *Sarah Davis.*
JOSIAH, b. June, 24, 1782.
SARAH, b. March 1, 1783—m. *Theodore C. Pool.*
JONATHAN, b. April, 12, 1785—m. *Mary Moulton*, 2nd, *Mrs. D. Morrill.*
SUSAN, b. January 31, 1787—m. *Moses Montague.*
BETSEY, b. October 5, 1788—m. *Theodore C. Pool;* she was his second wife.
DANIEL, b. June 1, 1790—m. *Judith Morrill.*
EDE, b. October 1, 1791—m. *Mary Pinkham.*
MARY. b. June 1, 1794—m. *Archibald Morrill, Esq.*
WHITTAKER, b. in 1795.
IRA, b. in 1796.
AZUBAH, b. in 1798—m. *Jeremiah Morrill.*
ACHSAH, b. in 1800—m. *Eli Bangs.*
JASON, b. June 27, 1803—m. *Ann M. Pitman*, 2nd, *Lucy Thompson.*

ELIAS LEE, eldest son of Daniel Lee, was born April 18, 1777 —m. *Rhoda Morrill*, b. September 14, 1780. They settled on the family homestead. Mr. Lee was for many years actively employed in public affairs. The family were consistent and exemplary members of the Wesleyan Church. He d. April 16, 1855; she d. September 18, 1856.

CHILDREN.

DANIEL LEE, b. in 1806—m. *Maria Weare*, is an acceptable and useful minister in the Wesleyan Church.

ELIAS, b. in 1810—m. *Asenath Davis*, was for some time publisher of the *Frontier Sentinel*, at Stanstead.

SUSAN M., b. May 5, 1814—m. *Benjamin Atkinson.*

SARAH W., b. September 7, 1816—m. *Denison Holmes.*

LAURA ANN, b. June 19, 1819—m. *J. F. Harvey.*

JOHN PARKER and AMANDA, twins, b. January 15, 1821. John P.—m. *Loella Pinkham;* Amanda,—m. *E. Hodgden, Esq.* They both held prominent positions as teachers in Georgia. He was for some time principal of Stanstead Seminary; is a licensed Wesleyan preacher.

RHODA M., b. December 25, 1823—m. *Reuben B. Wood.*

CLARA G., b. December 14, 1826—d. July 24, 1854.

JONATHAN LEE, b. April 12, 1785—m. *Mary Moulton.* She was b. in Loudon, N. H., June 6, 1792. They settled on No. 11, 11th Range of Stanstead. She died September 8, 1822. Their children were Alonzo, Elvira, Addi, Rosina and Mary. Alonzo and Mary married and had families, but they died before they had reached the meridian of life. June 5, 1823, Mr. Lee m. *Deborah Thrasher*, widow of David Morrill. Four children were the issue of this marriage: Julia A., Jonathan, David M., and Joseph Y., all deceased. Mr. Lee d. October 31, 1829.

HENRY LEE, the second son of Daniel Lee, was born in Strafford, Conn., in 1780—m. *Sarah Davis*, a native of Barrington, N. H.; located on the western half of No. 10, 10th Range of Stanstead in 1804. The family are mostly members of the Wesleyan Church. He d. in 1848; she d. in 1846.

CHILDREN.

LEONARD, b. in 1806—d. in 1822.

MOSES M., b. in 1808—m. *Elmina Symonds.*

LUCY, b. in 1809—m. *George House.* She d. November 5, 1844.

EDE, 2nd, in 1811—m. *Orpha Quimby.* He d. March 13, 1858.

ELMINA, b. in 1812—m. *Matthew Dixon, Esq.*

WILLIAM L., b. in 1814—m. *Deborah Sears*, a successful merchant.

ORENDA, b. in 1816—m. *Rev David Worthington.*

AZUBAH, b. in 1818—m. *Capt. George Comroy.*

JOSIAH, b. in 1820—m. *Roxelana Davis.*

ARVILLA, b. in 1822—m. *Henry Pond.*

EDE LEE, 1st, was born in Strafford, Conn., October 7, 1791. In 1816 m. *Mary Pinkham*, and settled near Fitch Bay. She d. April 18, 1843. He d. in 1872.

CHILDREN.

ELECTA A., b. November 5, 1818—m, *Hiram Peaslee.*
EDE W., b. March 21, 1820—m. *Dalinda M. Wilson.*
MARY P., b. April 4, 1822—m. *Albert Clefford.*
DOROTHY O., b. June 4, 1824—m. *Ezra B. Rider.*
SOPHRONIA, b. June 20, 1826—d. August 5, 1832.
ALLADIN, b. March 20, 1828—m. in Iowa.
TIMOTHY W., b. February 10, 1830—m. *Elmira N. Hubbard.*
ERASTUS, b. February 15, 1833—m. *Mary M. Clefford.*
BETSEY A., b. Sept. 10, 1834—m. *G. A. Rider.*
CLARINDA, b. June 4, 1838—m. *Emery O. Clefford.*

Moses M. Lee.

Son of Henry Lee, was b. June 23, 1808—m. *Elmina Symonds*, b. Aug. 13, 1810. They settled on the family homestead; are consistent and exemplary members of the Wesleyan Church.

CHILDREN.

WILLIAM HENRY, b. March 5, 1836—m. *Josephine H. Stevens.* They were for some time, Principal and Preceptress of Stanstead Seminary.

LUVIA, b. Dec. 31, 1834—m. *Thaddeus O. Davis.*
GEORGIA, b. Oct. 7, 1845—m. *Rev. John D. Stuart.*

Rev. Jason Lee,

The youngest son of Daniel Lee, was b. June 27, 1803. He united with the Wesleyan Church of Stanstead in 1826. His early opportunities of education had been confined to the common schools of the settlement, but, in 1830, we find him among the scholars in the higher English and classical studies. He subsequently attended the Methodist Institute at Wilbraham, Mass— was licensed by the New England Conference, and, in 1833, engaged in the mission among the Indians west of the Rocky Mountains. His labors as a missionary have been noted in the Book entitled "*Ten Years in Oregon*," to which the reader is referred. He crossed and re-crossed the Rocky Mountains many times—" enduring hardness as a good soldier of Christ."—July 16, 1837, he m. *Anna M.*

Pitman. She accompanied him to Oregon, where she d., June 26, 1838. He afterwards m. *Lucy Thompson.* She d. in 1842. In 1844 he returned to Stanstead, with his constitution broken and his health impaired by physical hardships, and found an asylum among his relatives and friends. He d. March 12, 1845, "rejoicing in hope of the glory of God and a blessed immortality beyond the grave."

The Lee Families of Stanstead have generally been a prolific race, and their connexions by intermarriages are numerous and scattered over the county. Many individuals of these families have been distinguished for talents and enterprise; and, with few exceptions, they have all been active and useful members of the community.

The Morrill Families.

The ancestors of these families were of English descent, and were among the early colonists of Newhampshire and Massachusetts.

PAUL MORRILL, b. in Amesbury, Mass., m. *Dorothy Blount*, b. in Pembroke, N.H. They settled originally in Chichester, N.H.,— removed to Stanstead in 1803—and were much esteemed for their integrity and uprightness. Their children were *William, Jonathan, Nathan, Isaac, Paul, David, Sarah, Abigail, and Joseph.*

WILLIAM, eldest son of Paul Morrill, was b. in Pembrooke, N. H., Sept. 22, 1768—m. *Hannah Rogers*, b. in Chichester, N.H., Nov. 9, 1773. They came to Stanstead in 1800, and settled on No. 15, 11th Range. Mr. Morrill soon succeeded in making a comfortable home for his family in the wilderness. He acquired a good property and lived to more than 96, at the time of his death, and his wife to be over 90. Their last days were spent with their son, *Archibald Morrill, Esq.*, on the farm upon which they began in 1800. They retained their mental faculties to the last, and the compiler received valuable assistance from them in gathering up incidents connected with the experience of the early settlers.

Their children were *Fanny*, m. *Moses Heath ; Archibald*, m. *Mary Lee; Esenath*, m. 1st, *Nathaniel Tilton*, 2nd *Eli Bangs ; Abigail*, m. *Eliphalet Cass ; Dorothy*, m. *James Corrill* and *Jeremiah*, who m. *Azubah Lee.*

ISAAC MORRILL, b. in Loudon, N.H., Nov. 2, 1778.—Dec. 12, 1805—m. *Mary Thrasher*, b. in Falmouth, Maine, Dec. 20, 1786. They settled on No. 12, 12th Range of Stanstead in 1806. He d. Aug. 4, 1845.

CHILDREN.

ELI, b. Oct. 20, 1806—m. 1st *Sally Davis*, 2nd *Lydia Moulton*.
DAVID R., b. July 9, 1815—m. 1st *Clarissa Cass*, 2nd *Sarah Roberts*.
MARY JANE, b. Nov. 20, 1808—m. *Adoniram Dutton*.
HARRIET, b. Nov. 20, 1817.
CHARLOTTE, b. July 24, 1822—m. *Gabriel Standish*.
ALPHEUS, b. April 27, 1825—m. *Mary E. Glidden*.
MARIA, b. June 28, 1828—m. *Nelson Bartlett*.
JERUSHA, b. Sept. 20, 1820—m. *Canborn J Bartlett*.
DAVID MORRILL, b. in Loudon, N.H., Feb, 19, 1781—in 1807— m. *Deborah Thrasher*, b. in Falmouth, Maine. Aug. 14, 1788. They settled in Stanstead in 1809. He was killed in the American War in 1814—She afterwards married Jonathan Lee. Mr. Morrill had 4 children.
BENJAMIN I. b. in 1808—m. 1st. *Mary Lee*; 2nd, *Malvina Farley*.
LOUISA D., b. April 4, 1810.
MALONA, b. March 10, 1812—m. *Coffin M. Quimby*.
ORRIN, b. Oct. 8, 1813,—d. in March, 1815.

Archibald Morrill,

Eldest son of William Morrill, was b. in Loudon, N. H., Feb. 29, 1794, and was about 4 years old when his father settled in Stanstead. He m. *Mary*, dau. of *Daniel Lee*, b. in Strafford, Conn., June 1, 1794. He remained with his father until he became of age, and then assumed the charge of the family homestead. He has sustained the office of magistrate for many years, and has been variously employed in public affairs.

CHILDREN.

OZRO, b. Dec. 21, 1819, m. *Charlotte*, dau. of *Harris Way*; has for many years been extensively engaged in mercantile business, and taken an active part in the management of public affairs.
LAURA ANN, b. Feb. 21, 1821,—m. *John McGaffee*.
LUCINA L., b. Nov. 9, 1823—d. Aug. 23, 1858.
ABIGAIL C., b. May 14, 1825—m. *Osborne Clark*.
SUSAN R., b. April 23, 1829.
JENETT V., b. Sept. 2, 1833.
JULIA S., b. Nov. 15, 1837.
Five children died in infancy.

THE MOULTON FAMILY.

Family of Abner Morrill.

ABNER MORRILL married Sarah Hoyt. They were natives of Chelsea, Mass. They resided for some time in Methuen, Mass. and Danville, Vt. Came to Stanstead in 1800, and located on No. 5, 10th Range. Mr. Morrill removed to the Newville settlement in 1808. His wife died about that time, and after her death he spent the remainder of his life with his daughter, the mother of the Hon. Thaddeus Stevens, in Peacham, Vt. The children of Abner Morrill were Hannah, m. a *Mr. Clements*; Sarah, m. *Joshua Stevens*; Jonathan, m. *Deborah Hoskins*; and Rhoda, who m. *Elias Lee*. The children of Jonathan Morrill were *Eveline*; m. *Hale Rix*; Deborah, m. *James Corey*; Nancy, m. *Hills Welch*; and Lewis, who m. *Lucy Flint*. Lewis Morrill studied medicine.

Family of Nathaniel Tilton.

NATHANIEL TILTON married Sarah Sanborn. They were natives of Gilmanton, N. H.; were among the early settlers of Stanstead. Their children were Sarah, m. John Boynton; Joseph, m. Charlotte Barnard, and Nathaniel.

Nathaniel Tilton, jun, married Asenath Morrill. She survived, him, and m. her 2nd husband, Eli Bangs, both deceased. The children of Nathaniel Tilton, jun., were George, who m. Sophronia Hungerford. Washington, who m. a Miss Snow; Eleeta, m. Joel Carr, Orpha, Sarah, and Ozro.

The Moulton Family.

These families are of English origin. Their ancestors were among the early New England colonists and settled in New Hampshire.

WILLIAM MOULTON b. in Amesbury, Mass., March 6, 1768, 1791 m. *Judith Ladd*, b. in Loudon, N.H., Nov. 5, 1771. They settled on No. 12, 10th Range of Stanstead in 1798. In early life, he united with the Free Will Baptist Church, and was ever distinguished for his active and exemplary christian life, and for his efforts for the improvement of the rising generation. His wife Judith d. April 25, 1822. In 1824, he m. *Grace House*. He d. in August, 1843.

CHILDREN BY 1ST MARRIAGE.

MARY, b. June 6, 1792—m. *Jonathan Lee*.
HARRIS, b. Oct. 2, 1793—m. *Sarah Davis*.
SARAH, b. July 15, 1796—m. *Joseph Pinkham*.

M

JUDITH, b. June 28, 1798—m. *Rev. W. B. Mack.*
JOHN L., b. July 9, 1800—m. *Lydia Bachelder.*
LOUISA, b. Dec. 15, 1801—m. *Philip Rogers, Esq.*
ALICE, b. Oct. 26, 1804—d. Sept. 6, 1806.
ELSIE L., b. Sept. 12, 1806—m. *Rev Hiram Kinsley.*
NAOMI, b. July 14, 1808—m. *John M. Quimby.*
RUTH, b. April 25, 1810—m. *Samuel Wallahan.*
SUSANNA, b. April 16, 1813—d. Aug. 26, 1828.
JULIA G., b. Aug. 30, 1814—m. 1st, *David Small, Esq.*; 2d, *Wm: H. Holmes.*

CHILDREN BY 2ND MARRIAGE.

JOSEPH, b. in August, 1825—d. Feb. 1, 1858.
MARY, b. in November, 1829.

AVERY MOULTON, b. in Amesbury, Mass., March 8, 1770. In 1793—m. *Lydia Proctor*, b. in Kingston, N.H., Oct. 24, 1776. They settled in Stanstead in 1800. In 1805, he was ordained a minister in the Free-Will Baptist Church, and labored in this connection many years with acceptance and usefulness—not only supplying the church of which he was the pastor, but preaching in various settlements in the neighboring towns, and travelling extensively in Vermont and New Hampshire. His efforts were continued with faithfulness unto the end, for after having been broken down by paralysis, he was taken to the place of meeting, and during the last years of his life, he was accustomed to preach sitting in his chair. He d. in 1828.

CHILDREN.

LYDIA, b. May 27, 1794—m. *Howard King.*
FANNY, b. April 17, 1796—m. *Rev. J. J. Bliss.*
ABIAL, b. May 31, 1798—m. *Fanny Wallingford.*
ALONZO, b. Aug. 3, 1800—m. *Priscilla Prescott.*
SALOME, b. Nov. 23, 1803—m. *Silas A. Davis*
SOPHRONIA, b. May 6, 1806—m. *Thomas Wells.*
THOMAS P., b. April 19, 1808—m. *Louisa Moore.*
ALBANUS K., b. Sept. 27, 1810.
LUCINDA, b. March 8, 1813—m *Joel Adams.*
WILLIAM A., b. Oct. 8, 1816.
PANTHA L., b. June 8, 1819—m. *Albert Hilbard.*

ABIAL MOULTON, b. in Gilmanton, N.H., May 31, 1798. March 14, 1820—m. *Fanny Wallingford*, b. in Hopkinton, N.H., Oct. 4,

1798. They settled in Stanstead. Mr. Moulton engaged early in the work of the Free-Will Baptist Church ministry, and during the past 30 years has labored in Stanstead and the neighboring towns.

CHILDREN.

DAVID W., b. Jan. 6, 1821—m. *Betsey Bachelder.*
LYDIA M., b. Nov. 27, 1822—m. *Israel Wood.*
ABIGAIL W., b. Feb. 23, 1825—m. *Wilder P. Boynton.*
HIRAM, b. April 6, 1827—d. June 6, 1832.
ORRIN N., b, Feb. 27, 1829—m. *Asenath Lyford.*
FANNY, b. Feb. 9, 1831.
MORRILLA, b, Aug. 1, 1833—m. *Leonard L. Bangs.*
EMMA E., b., Nov. 5, 1835—m. *Lucius J. Bangs.*
GILBERT M., b. April 20, 1838—m *Martha W. Hall.*
MARY E., b. Feb. 2, 1841.

Family of Joshua Libbee.

JOSHUA LIBBEE, b. in Portsmouth, N,H., Aug. 7, 1777—m. *Sally Grant,* b. March 5, 1779. They came to Stanstead in 1804, and settled eventually at the place called by their name—Libbee Town. He d. June 26, 1858. She d. the same year.

CHILDREN.

ISAAC, b. June 5, 1802—m. 1st *Lucy Sherburn,* 2nd *Mrs. C. S. Knight.*
HANNAH, b. April 7, 1806—m. *Nicholas Carpenter.*
DAVID C., b. May 17, 1809—m. *Lucinda Hyatt.*
SARAH, b. in 1811—m. *Benjamin Currier.*
CHARLes, b. Jan. 27, 1813—m. 1st *Relief Dresser,* 2nd *Martha Miner.*
GILMAN, b. Dec. 25, 1816—m. *Zelia Blodget.*
OLIVE, b. in 1818—m. *Sylvanus Griffin.*
WILLIAM, b. Dec 15, 1820—m. *Jane Harvey.*
JAMES, b. March 11, 1822—m. 1st *Harriet Spencer,* 2nd *Sarah Miner.*

Family of James Paul.

JAMES PAUL m. *Mary,* dau. of *Jedediah Lee.* They settled on No. 1, 11th Range of Stanstead in 1800. Afterwards removed to No. 13, 14th Range. These farms subsequently passed into the hands of Jedediah Lee. Mr. Paul d. in April, 1842. Mary his wife in June, 1860. Their children were *John*, m. *Mehitable Massey ; Daniel*, m. *Sarah Clark ; Philura*, m. *Marshall Pope; Esther*, m. *Solomon Smith ; Warram*, m. *Sarah Crown ; Elias L.*, m, *Susan Flanders: Jeremiah H.*, m. *Martha Rix; Cordelia*, m. *Zenas Carrington; Mary*, m. *John Rix ; James*, m. *Lucy C. Bangs ; Jerusha*, m, *Porter Norton ; Elisa*, and *Marshall*. These were mostly parents of large families.

Family of John Quimby.

JOHN QUIMBY, b. in Chester, N.H., in 1769—m. Mary Moore, b. in Georgetown, Mass., in 1774. They settled on No. 27, 10th Range of Stanstead in 1808. She d. in 1838. He d. in 1860 (having had 12 children, 62 grand children, 77 great grand children, and two great great grand children) aged 91 years.

CHILDREN.

COMFORT, b. in 1792—m. *William Boynton.*
NANCY, b. in 1795—m. *Gardner Boynton.*
JACOB, b. in 1797—m. *Nancy Carr.*
MARY, b. in 1799—m. *William McCaffee.*
MARTHA, b. in 1801—m. *David Hildreth.*
JOHN M., b. in 1803—m. *Naomi Moulton.*
SALLY, b. in 1805—m. *William Brown.*
COFFIN M., b. in 1807—m. *Malona Morrill.*
BENJAMIN, b., in 1809—d. in 1833.
AMOS, b. in 1811—m. *Louisa Sargent.*
ORPHA, b. in 1813—m. *Ede Lee*, 2nd.
CLARISSA, b. in 1816—d. in 1856.

Family of Daniel Curtis.

DANIEL CURTIS was born in Stoughton, Mass. March 20, 1770. He married *Mary Aikin*. They came to Stanstead in 1800, [and settled on No. 8, 10th Range. He d. Oct. 17, 1833. She d. July 28, 1836. The family are mostly members of the Wesleyan Church.

CHILDREN.

HIEL, b. July 20, 1801—m. *Harriet Knowlton.*
MOODY, b. Nov. 14, 1802—drowned July 9, 1826.
JULIA, b. May 1, 1805—d. Sept. 21, 1829.

SMITH, b. June 16, 1807—m. *Clarissa Pond.*
LUCIA, b. Feb. 28, 1810—m. *Archelaus Hill.*
DEBORAH, b. March 16, 1813.
MARY ANN, b. July 7, 1815—m. *Amos Bigelow.*
JOHN C. b. June 9, 1818—m. *Almira Morrill.*

Family of Jonathan Field.

JONATHAN FIELD, b. in Leverett, Mass., Jan. 25, 1786. He came to Stanstead in 1808, and began on the east part of No. 3, 11th Range, which he had purchased from Selah Pomroy. In 1810, he married *Elizabeth Lothridge*, who was b. in Leverett, Mass., in 1783. She d. in 1849. In 1851, m. his 2nd wife, *Ruth Dustan*, widow of *Israel Parsons*. She d. in 1869. The family belong mostly to the Wesleyan Church.

CHILDREN.

MOSES, S., b. June 9, 1811—m. *Margaret I. Gibb.*
LAVINIA, b. Sept. 14, 1812—living at home.
LUCY MARIA, b. Feb. 26, 1815—m. *J. M. Hubbard*, d. in 1839.
ALONZO, b. Feb. 27, 1817—lives on the homestead.
SUSAN M., b. Oct 7, 1818—m. *Henry McGaffey*, b. in Lyndon, Vt.
ARVILLA, b. Dec. 1, 1820—m. *Seth F. Ball* of Leverett, Mass. a dau. b. and d. June, 1851, and Charles D., b. Oct. 5, 1859.
POLLY, b. Oct. 6, 1823—d. Nov. 9, 1830.
CLARISSA, b. Nov. 10, 1825—d. Feb. 6, 1827.

Family of Major Camp.

MAJOR CAMP, b. in Sharon, Conn., Jan. 26, 1771—m. *Phebe Curtis*, b. in Dracut, Mass., Feb. 13, 1771. They settled originally in Tunbridge, Vt. Came to Stanstead in 1800; some 20 years afterwards, they removed to Berlin, Vt. She d. May 22, 1838. He d. June 2, 1855.

CHILDREN.

ALMIRA, b. March 4, 1792—m. *Solomon Nye.*
RACHEL, b. Aug. 9, 1793—m. *Col. W. Chamberlin.*
LYMAN, b. Feb. 15, 1795—m. *Prudence Clark.*
IRA, b. Dec. 24, 1796—m. *Harris Davis*; 2nd, *Mary A. Adams.*
CHARLES D., b. Dec. 18, 1798—m. *Larona Cotton.*
MARILLA, b. Dec. 18, 1800—m. *William Clark.*
SAREPTA, b. Nov. 18, 1802—m. *Horace Wilson.*

170 FORESTS AND CLEARINGS.

ZEBINA, b. Feb. 6, 1805—m. *Hannah Thompson.*
ALONZO, b. Nov. 23, 1806—m. *Mary Hubbell.*
DIANA, b. Sept. 4, 1808—m. *Jesse Scott.*
ERASTUS, b. April 30, 1812—m. *Eliza Hubbell.*
ARABELLA, b. Oct. 24, 1814—m. *Samuel E. Emerson.*

Family of Nathaniel Rix.

NATHANIEL RIX, born in Landaff, N.H., in 1753. In 1775, m. *Esther Clark*, b. in Hopkinton, N.H., in 1758. They settled in Landaff, N.H., where their children were born—removed to Stanstead in 1799, and located on No. 6, 12th Range. They afterwards sold out and left the country. He d. Oct. 12, 1828. She d. July 18, 1834.

CHILDREN.

NATHANIEL, b. Nov. 26, 1777—m. *Rebecca Eastman.*
ESTHER, b. Sept. 27, 1779—d. Jan. 11, 1843.
JOHN, b. Dec. 25, 1781—m. *Martha Boroughs.*
EBENEZER, b. Feb. 1, 1784—m. *Mary Clark.*
POLLY, b. May 15, 1787—m. *George Rose.*
GEORGE W., b. May 14, 1789—m. *Lydia Kelly.*
RUTH, b. Aug. 8, 1791—m. *Seaborn Eastman.*
CLARK, b. Aug. 2, 1795—m. *Laura Savage.*
HALE, b. Jan. 25, 1798—m. *Evelina Morrill.*
MARGARET, b. Nov. 16, 1799—m. *Nahum Crane.*

NATHANIEL RIX jun. b. in Landaff, N.H., Nov. 27, 1777. m March. 3, 1802, *Rebecca Eastman*, born in Bath. N.H., Sept. 23, 1780. They settled upon the same farm with his father in Stanstead, but afterwards removed to Littleton, N.H., where he was for many years employed in public affairs. He d. Oct. 21, 1857.

CHILDREN.

GUY O., b. Dec. 14, 1802—m. *Martha Gates.*
LUCRETIA, b. Oct. 16, 1804—m. *Joel Eastman.*
NARCISSA, b. Jan. 3, 1807—m. *Nathan Underwood.*
PERSIS, b. Aug. 19, 1809—m. *Aaron Gill.*
WILDER P., b. Jan. 13, 1812—m. *Mary Rose.*
BENJAMIN H., b. July 28, 1815—m. *Mary E. Bryant.*
CHARLES, b. June 6, 1818—m. *Susan Eastman,*
REBECCA JANE, b. March 25, 1821—m. *Clark Rix*, 2nd.

Family of Daniel Mansur.

DANIEL MANSUR, born in Methuen, Mass., Dec. 5, 1769. m. March 6, 1798, *Nancy Davis*, b. in Barrington, N.H., Jan. 18, 1776. They came to Stanstead in 1801, and settled on No. 2, 11th Range. Mr. Mansur built a blacksmith shop—the first started in the east part of the town, and carried on the business in a limited way, while attending to his farm. He afterwards purchased No. 7, in the same Range, to which he removed. This farm is now owned and occupied by his grandson, *David A. Mansur, Esq.* Mr. Mansur d. June 12, 1832. Nancy, his wife, d. May 22, 1863.

CHILDREN.

LOIS, b. Sept. 7, 1799—m. *Hazen Pomroy.*
JOHN, b. July 2, 1802—m. *Huldah Peaslee.*
DANIEL, b. Aug. 7, 1804—m. *Hannah Clark.*
RUTH, b. March 14, 1806—m. *Charles Sargent* d. 1864 in Seward, Ill.
HORACE, b. March 20, 1808—m. *Susan Sargent.*
NANCY, b. Aug. 8, 1811—d. in 1814.
VALERIA, b. May 27, 1814—m. *Rev. Richard Hutchinson.*

DANIEL MANSUR, JUN, b. Aug. 7, 1804—m. *Hannah Clark*, b. Sept. 24, 1803. They settled on the family homestead. She d. Sept., 1870. He d. Sept., 1873.

CHILDREN.

BETSEY, b. Feb. 4, 1826—m. *Hiram Davis.*
DAVID A., b. Feb. 5, 1827—m. *Maria C. Clark*, children *Mary W.*, b. July 4, 1870 and *Charles*, b. Oct., 1871.
HENRY, b. Aug. 12, 1829—d. Aug. 11, 1835.
DANIEL, b. Jan. 10, 1832—d. Oct. 22, 1865.
MARY, b. Nov. 28, 1834—m. *David Wilkie.*
NANCY, b. May 10, 1838—m. *Charles Fogg.*
JULIA, b. Nov. 27, 1840—d. March 18, 1857.
LUCIUS, b. Nov. 26, 1846.

Family of Peter Weare

PETER WEARE, b. in 1760—m. *Hannah Nason*, b. in 1763. They were natives of Andover, Mass., and settled in Bolton near the Lake Shore in 1793, removed to Stanstead in 1803, and settled on No. 7, 11th Range. He d. in January, 1828. She d. in Dec., of the same year. Their children were *Jonathan,* m. *Nancy Austin* ; *John,* m. *Cynthia Ashley* ; and *Betsey,* who m. *Oliver Bangs.*

JOHN WEARE, 2nd son of Peter Weare, b. in Andover, Mass., March 28, 1791, was about three years old when his father settled in Bolton. He m. *Cynthia Ashley,* b. in Claremont, N.H., Aug. 8, 1791. They settled eventually at Cedar Rapids, Iowa, where he d. April 6, 1856. She d. June 16, 1842.

CHILDREN.

BETSEY A., b. April 11, 1812—m. *John S. Sherman.*
SAMUEL A., b. Sept. 16, 1813—d. March 9, 1816.
JOHN, b. Oct. 5, 1818—m. 1st, *Martha Parkhurst* ; 2nd, *Martha Rogers.*
HENRY, b. April 22, 1817—d. June 2, 1846.
MARY, b. July 25, 1819—m. 1st, *Alex. L. Ela,* 2nd, *John F. Ely.*
LYDIA, b. Jan. 22, 1822—m. *Elisha C. Ely.*
SARAH, b. Jan. 11, 1825—m. *S. C. Carpenter.*
CHARLES, b. Jan. 29, 1828—m. *Catherine Cornell.*
HARRIET S., b. Aug. 1, 1829—m. *Lowell Daniels.*
GEORGE, b. Dec. 3, 1834—m. *Mary Carpenter.*

Family of Seth Caswell.

SETH CASWELL, b. in Littleton, N.H., March 15, 1792— m. *Mary Venan,* b. in Wheelock, Vt., Oct. 7, 1800. They settled on No. 9, 13th Range of Stanstead in 1820. He d. in 1871.

CHILDREN.

HARVEY L., b. March 28, 1820.
WILDER P., b. Jan. 9, 1822.
ALONZO F., b. March 7, 1824—m. *Martha Ladd.*
ALMA L., b. Feb. 9, 1826—m. *Joel Bishop.*
LYDIA L., b. Feb. 8, 1828—m. *Lucius Paul.*
HORATIO G., b. Dec. 17, 1829—m. *Eda T. Shattuck.*
FRANCKLIN, b. Oct. 17, 1831.
GEORGE R., b. May 26, 1833—m. *Mary Hackett.*
LODEMA, b. April 26, 1835—m. *Joel Nutter.*
HENRY H., b. Oct. 17, 1838.
ELLEN A., b. June 21, 1843.—d. March 22, 1846.

Family of Jessee Farley.

JESSE FARLEY, b. in Hollis, N.H., in 1767—m. *Mehitable Hall,*

FAMILY OF REUBEN TAYLOR. 173

who was b. May 28, 1776. They settled on the north half of No. 6, 13th Range of Stanstead in 1803. He d. in June, 1836. She d. Feb. 19, 1843.

CHILDREN.

LUCY, b. in 1798—d. Jan. 7, 1850.
MEHITABLE, b. Nov. 6, 1800—d. Feb. 6, 1827.
LOUISA, b. April 18, 1803—d. June 7, 1859.
ORIN C., b. May 1, 1805—d. Sept. 21, 1814.
HORACE H., b. June 15, 1807—d. Aug. 8, 1815.
FRANKLIN, b. May 7, 1810—d. May 19, 1812.
SUSAN A., b. Feb. 11, 1815—d. Dec. 23, 1838.
MALVINA P., b. Sept. 23, 1818—m. *B. T. Morrill.*

Family of Amos Farley.

AMOS FARLEY, brother of Jesse Farley, m. *Lucy Hall.* They settled on the south half of No. 6, 13th Range of Stanstead, in 1803, but sold out in 1820, and left the country.

Family of Silas Taylor.

SILAS TAYLOR, b. in Reading, Vt., June 6, 1758—m. *Sarah Farley,* b. in Hollis, N.H., June 15, 1760. They settled on No. 5, 13th Range of Stanstead in 1805. He d. Nov. 12, 1825. She d. June 8, 1840.

CHILDREN.

SETH, b. Dec. 6, 1793—d. June 30, 1868.
REUBEN, b. Feb. 28, 1801—m. *Jane McCaw.* He d. Aug. 20, 1840 In 1844, she m. her 2nd husband *John Bailey.*
SARAH, b. June 10, 1804—m. *James McCaw.* She d. in 1842.

Family of Reuben Taylor.

SARAH, b. March 29, 1832—m. *Francis Baldwin.*
HENRY S., b. April 9, 1833—m. 1st, *Susanna Rogers;* 2nd, *Jenett Clark.*
MARY, b. June 9, 1836—m. *William Barron.*
NANCY, b. June 18, 1838—m. *James Taylor.*
ELLEN, b. May 5, 1839—d. in 1850.
SUSAN, b. Dec. 17, 1841.

Family of John Roberts.

JOHN ROBERTS, b. in Meredith, N.H., in 1768—m. *Hannah Clark*, b. Nov. 22, 1788. They settled in Stanstead. He d. Feb. 3, 1830. She d. Nov. 10, 1864.

CHILDREN.

LOUISA, b. Nov. 4, 1819.
LUCETTA, b. March 16, 1827—m. *William Onthank.*
SARAH J., b. Aug. 5, 1824—m *David R. Morrill.*
JOSEPH, b. May 5, 1829—m. *Nancy Ball.*

Family of Dr. Samuel Clark.

SAMUEL CLARK, b. in Billerica, Mass. Studied medicine in his native town, served in the American Army during the Revolution, afterwards received a pension from the American Government. He m. *Betsey Burt*, and settled in Stanstead in 1797. The family subsequently removed to the west. He d. in 1845, aged 80. She d. in 1829. Their children were Hannah, m. *John Roberts* : Susan, m. *Joseph Smith ;* Betsey, m. a *Mr. Marston ;* Lucy, m. *Daniel Roberts,* Joel, Samuel, John, and Ira.

Family of Oliver Hartwell.

OLIVER HARTWELL m. *Hannah Kelly.* They were natives of Dummerston, Vt., were among the early settlers of Stanstead. Their children were *Mary, Amos, Lewis, Ira, Malinda, Miranda, Warren, Sally, Hannah, Sophronia, Tyler, Oliver* and *Flora.*

Family of Elliott Sawyer.

ELLIOTT SAWYER, b. in Rowley, Mass. m. *Lucy Young*, b. in Lisbon, N.H. They settled in the neighborhood of Newville in Stanstead in 1804. Their children were Narcissa, m. *T. S. Bangs ;* Elliott, m. *Lydia Abbott ;* Maria; m. *Ogden Fox ;* Ruth, m. *Samuel Webster,* Mary, m. *James McDuff* ; Betsey, m. *Albert Woodward ;* Lucia, Joseph, Jerusha, and John.

Family of John Webb.

JOHN WEBB, a Chelsea pensioner from England, settled in Newville, Stanstead, in 1827. Children—*John, Henry, George H., Thomas, William, Robert* and *Emily.*

Family of Uriah Fox.

URIAH FOX, b. in Campton, N.H., Sept. 15, 1760. Served in the American Army during the time of the Revolution. In 1784, he m. *Mary Smart.* Came to Stanstead in 1803, and settled on No. 14, 13th Range. She d. June 26, 1839. He afterwards m. *Elizabeth B. Prouty*, who d. June 19, 1844. He d. June 6, 1849.

CHILDREN.

POLLY, b. Nov. 11, 1785—m. 1st, *Raphael Cook*; 2nd, *Eli. Howe.*
URIAH, b. Oct. 23, 1787.
AUGUSTINE W., b. Oct 29, 1789—m. *Pamela Nash.*
AMOS, b. May 15, 1792—m. *Eunice Kilborn.*
BETSEY, b. Oct. 31, 1796—m. *Lovell McKeech, M.D.*
MATILDA, b. May 13, 1788—m. *Ira Jones.*
MARTHA, b. Aug. 3, 1800—m. *Samuel G. Ladd.*
SAMUEL S., b. July 2, 1803—d. Dec. 10, 1814.
OGDEN, b, Sept 3, 1805—m. *Maria Sawyer.*
SALLY, b. Sept. 16, 1808.

AMOS FOX, son of Uriah Fox, was b. in Campton, N.H., May 15, 1792. Came to Stanstead with his father's family in 1803. In 1819— m. *Eunice Kilborn*,b. Aug. 11,1801. They settled at Stanstead Plain. Mr. Fox received his first military appointment in 1812, was appointed Major in 1847, and subsequently Lieut. Colonel of Militia He was otherwise employed in public affairs. He d. in 1867.

CHILDREN.

HONESTUS, b. March 18, 1821—d. Aug. 20, 1838.
AMOS K., b. Aug. 13, 1824—m. *Huldah Baldwin.*
MARIA E., b. Dec. 7, 1817—m. *George Rogers.*

Family of Silas Fox.

SILAS FOX, b. in Campton, N.H., m. *Mary Cheney*, a native of Newburyport, Mass. They came to Stanstead in 1800, and settled on No. 16, 15th Range. He d. April 8, 1832. She d. Aug. 30, 1832 Their children were Winthrop, m. *Betsey Cook*; Sally, Moody, m. *Nancy Clark*; and Jane who m. *Daniel Patterson.*

MOODY FOX, b. May 4, 1793—m. *Nancy Clark.* She was a native of Bethlehem, N.H. He d. in 1870.

CHILDREN.

ALMIRA, b. Nov. 8, 1816—m. *Isaac N. Whitcher.*
MINERVA, b. March 29, 1818—m. *Gilbert Wallingford.*
NANCY, b. June 19, 1827—m. *George H. Rose.*
MARY, b. Feb. 1, 1830—m. *William Thomas.*
JANE, b. June 14, 1840—deceased.

Family of Ebenezer Lincoln.

EBENEZER LINCOLN, b. in Taunton, Mass., July 9, 1775. June 9, 1802, m. *Sarah Willis*, b. in Norton, Mass., April 10, 1777. They came to Stanstead in 1807, and settled on No. 17, 12th Range. He d. May 17, 1844.

CHILDREN.

SARAH, b. July 11, 1803—d. Aug. 2, 1854.
SUSAN, b. Feb. 15 1806—m. *Simeon Brown.*
EBENEZER, b. April 27, 1808—m. *Mary Jane Hawkins.*
WILLIAM G., b. March 26, 1810—m. *Sylvia Webster.*
BETSEY, twin sister of William G., resides in Michigan.
NANCY, b. March 7, 1812—d. April 18, 1829.

Family of Nathaniel Ladd.

NATHANIEL LADD married *Polly Smith.* They were natives o Epping, N.H., settled on No. 15, 11th Range of Stanstead in 1800. He d. in 1827. She d. in 1844. Their children were Polly m. *Robert Rowe*; Louisa, and Samuel G., who m. *Martha Fox.*
SAMUEL G. LADD b. in Sanbornton, N.H. in 1790—m. *Martha Fox*, b. in Stanstead, Aug. 3, 1800. She d. in 1852.

CHILDREN.

OZRO, A., b. Aug. 9, 1818—m. *Lasura Fox.*
AMANTHA, b. July 12, 1821—m. *Stephen A. White.*
AMANDA, b. July 5, 1823—d. in July, 1827.
MARTHA, b. Aug. 17, 1826—m. *Alonzo Caswell.*
URIAH G., b. Feb. 28, 1829—m. *Eleanor Mason.*
SAMUEL G., b. March, 27, 1831—m. *Eliza Bigelow.*
MARY S., b. April 27, 1833—m. *Roswell Blanchard.*
CARLTON C., b. Aug. 22, 1835.
PAMELIA, b. May 4, 1839—m. *Ozro Bartlett.*

Family of Thomas Swain.

THOMAS SWAIN, b. in Saco, Maine, March 19, 1785. M. Oct. 28, 1806, *Lois Moulton*, b. in Loudon, N.H., June 16, 1785. They

FAMILY OF ABRAHAM LIBBEE. 177

settled in Stanstead in 1807, but subsequently removed to Illinois. He d. Aug. 9, 1850. She d. May 19, 1860. Their children were James, Alvina, Nancy, Sylvia, Amanda, Lois, Sarah, Thomas, and Elizabeth.

Family of Richard C. Hoitt.

RICHARD C. HOITT, b. in Northwood, N.H., Aug. 22, 1779. Settled in Barnston. M. *Abigail Drew* in 1806. She was b. April 9, 1789. They subsequently settled on No. 15, 11th Range of Stanstead. He was employed in teaching during the winter seasons, for nearly 30 years; was a practical and surveyor. They removed to Whitby, Ont.

CHILDREN.

EZRA, b. July 3, 1807—m. *Electa Bachelder.*
RICHARD, b. Feb. 28, 1809—m. *Ruth Glidden.*
JAMES D., b. Jan. 27, 1811—m. *Elizabeth Dickey.*
STEPHEN, b. Sept. 24, 1812—m. *Helen Dickey.*
John L., b. Oct. 11, 1814—d. Aug. 22, 1840.
ALONZO, b. Jan. 15, 1817—d. Oct. 30, 1838.

Family of Abraham Libbee.

ABRAHAM LIBBEE, one of the Nine Partners in the Cassville settlement, was born in Epsom, N.H., June 10, 1776, M. *Abigail Pearson,* who was b. in Baffield, N.H., July 27, 1772. He d. Jan. 10, 1839. She d. April 5, 1858.

CHILDREN.

NATHAN—b. June 1, 1801.
WILLIAM, b. Feb. 26, 1803.
PEARSON, b. Jan. 24, 1806.

NATHAN LIBBEE, b. June 1, 1801—m. *Mehitable Massey.* He d. June 9, 1839.

CHILDREN.

RUHANNAH, b. Jan. 14, 1823.
BARTON b. Feb. 12, 1825—m. *Eliza Wells.*
CHARLES, b. Sept. 10, 1827—d. in 1859.
MARY, b. Feb. 28, 1831.
ABRAHAM, b. Oct. 19, 1833.

178 FORESTS AND CLEARINGS.

Alva, b. Aug. 19, 1835.
John, b. Aug. 4, 1837.
John, b. Jan. 9, 1839.

William Libbee, was born, Feb. 26, 1803. March 3, 1831, m. *Dianthe Jane Sinclair.*

CHILDREN.

Alfred W., b. Oct. 3, 1832—m. *Mary E. Lockwood.*
Louisa, b. April 30, 1834—m. *Alfonso Stoddard.*
Royal, b. May 17, 1836.
Elsimena, b. May 29, 1839.
Lizzie P., b. May 20, 1855.

Pearson Libbee b. Jan. 24, 1806. Dec. 14, 1832, m. *Sophia,* dau. of *Theophilus Cass.*

CHILDREN.

Olive, b. April 7, 1845.
William P., b. Aug. 26, 1849.

Family of John Langmade.

John Langmade one of the Nine Partners in the Cassville settlement, was born in Chichester, N.H., March 4, 1776. He came to Stanstead in 1798, and began a clearing on No. 19, 11th Range, returned to New Hampshire in 1799, and married *Hannah Seva,* who was b. in Rye, N.H., Jan. 9, 1774. In 1815, they removed to Hatley. He d. in 1837. She d. July 9, 1848.

CHILDREN.

Bela, b. July 9, 1801—m. *Betsey Ayer.*
Leon and Lemira, twins, b. in Feb. 1804, Leon m. *Eliza Haines.* Lemira d. May 2, 1830.
Lucinda, b. in June, 1806—m. *Nathan Morrill.*
Hannah, b. in Sept., 1808—d. in Sept., 1817.
Sarah, b. in Feb., 1812— m. *Roslin A. Henry.*
Edward S., b. April 27, 1814. In 1840, m. *Anne Kendrick.* They reside in Georgia, where he is employed in the profession of law, and in public affairs.
John S., b. in Sept., 1818—m. *Eliza Kendrick.* They reside in Georgia.

Family of James Locke.

JAMES LOCKE, one of the Nine Partners in the Cassville settlement, was born in Epsom, N.H., March 4, 1775. The early part of his life was spent in teaching in Virginia. He returned to his native town in 1799, and married *Abigail Sherman*, b. June 17, 1775. They came to Stanstead in 1800, and settled on No. 19, 12th Range. They were consistent and exemplary members of the Wesleyan Church, and were much respected in the community. His death, which was caused by the kick of a horse, occurred March 29, 1855. His wife d. Sept. 29, 1859.

CHILDREN.

LOUISA, b. May 15, 1801—d. Oct. 12, 1818.

JAMES M., b. Oct 15, 1804—m. *Sarah*, dau. of *Theophilus Cass*. He received the appointment of magistrate in 1855, and for many years occupied a prominent position in the management of public affairs—was an exemplary and influential member of the Wesleyan church. He d. in 1869.

MARIN, b. Aug. 4, 1806—m. *Ives Wallingford*.

WILLIAM S., b. April 28, 1808—entered the Wesleyan Ministry when about 21 years old, was an itinerant for many years supplying different circuits under the directions of the New England Conference. Aug. 27, 1833, m. *Caroline Tibbets*, and afterwards located in Manchester, N.H.

EDWARD J., b. March 30, 1810—d. Jan. 30, 1814.

FLORINDA, b. March 6, 1812—m. *Oscar Wyman*.

EMELINE, b. April 27, 1813—m. *C. W. Copp, Esq.* This his 2nd wife.

EDWARD J., 2d, b. May 2, 1820.

Family of William McClary.

WILLIAM McCLARY, one of the Nine Partners in the Cassville settlement, was born in Epsom, N.H., July 8, 1769. Aug. 16, 1795, m. *Isabella Dickey*, b. April 28, 1771. They came to Stanstead in Feb., 1798, with one child, about two years old. They at first settled on No. 14, 12th Range, about half a mile north of the old Elm Tree on the Morrill Hill. This lot had been previously pitched by another party, but afterwards abandoned, leaving the walls of a cabin without a roof or a floor. Mr. McClary shoveled away the snow, built a fire against the stone back which had been built at one side, and they remained in this condition until he could make a temporary covering of poles and hemlock boughs, many months passed before boards and shingles could be obtained. The shingles used in making the roofs of the earliest cabins were fastened on with wooden pins, there being no nails in the settlement. Mr. McClary resided upon this farm for several years, but afterwards sold out, and removed to Barnston. He d. Oct. 31, 1846. His wife d. March 25, 1835.

CHILDREN.

ANDREW, b. July 8, 1796—m. *Hannah Folsom*, b. May 3, 1799 ; d. June 1, 1821. He afterwards m. *Caroline Wallis*, b. Jan. 11, 1806. The issue of this marriage was 3 sons and 6 daughters.

DAVID, 2d son of William McClary, married *Abigail Caton* of Coaticook, P.Q.

Family of Charles McClary.

CHARLES MCCLARY, b. in Epsom, N.H., in 1791—m. *Betsey Cass*. They settled on No. 13, 12th Range of Stanstead, afterwards removed to Libbee Town, in Barnston. Their children were John, m. *Marcella Bangs* ; Harly, m. *Cynthia Taylor*; Chester, m. *Malvina Cass*; Charles, m. *Jane McClary*; Eliphalet, m. *Miss Shaw*; and Nancy A., who m. *Erastus Paul*.

Family of Jacob Taylor.

JACOB TAYLOR married *Sophia Beach*. They were natives of Vermont, settled on the north-east corner lot of Stanstead, in 1801, removed to Cassville in 1816, and subsequently, to Derby, Vt. He had served in the War of the American Revolution, and during the last years of his life received a pension from the United States Government. He d. in 1848. She d. in 1835.

CHILDREN.

ALICE, b. in 1790—m. *Ira Cole*.

JACOB, b. Jan. 15, 1792—came to Stanstead with his father, in 1801. June 1, 1814 m. *Sarah Haines*. They settled on No. 17, 12th Range. She d. May 17, 1857. He d. Jan. 23, 1872.

JAMES, b. in 1794—m. *Abigail Heath*.

REUBEN, b. in 1797—m. *Judith Currier*.

DAVID, b. in 1800—m. *Nancy Sias.*
TIMOTHY, b. in 1804—m. *Dorcas Harvey.*
CHANCEY, b. in 1807—d. in 1828.

Family of Jacob Goodwin.

JACOB GOODWIN, a native of Boscawen, N.H., came to Stanstead with his family in 1798. They were the 2nd family of pioneers in the settlement of Stanstead Plain. Located on No. 2, 10th Range, but, after a few years, sold out and left the country. The children were *Philip, Ebenezer, David, Sarah, Jacob, John,* and *Roswell.* Jacob was a physician. These all married and had families. Only a few of the third generation remain in Stanstead County.

Family of Moses Wells.

MOSES WELLS, b. in Chester, N.H., Feb. 10, 1768. June, 1790, m. *Mary Moore,* b. in Goffstown, N.H., May 15, 1773. In the spring of 1798, Mr. Wells came to Stanstead on foot, and in the following summer returned and took his family with as many of their effects as they could carry on horseback through the woods to Duncansboro, now Newport, Vt., from whence they proceeded down the lake in a canoe to the place that forms the present village of Georgeville, then an opening of two acres in a dense forest. At that time there were but two other families in the settlement—those of Capt. Moses Copp and Richard Packard. The three families dipped their water from the same spring, and baked their bread in the same oven. The oven was built of stone, and stood "out of doors." Mr. Wells was the first blacksmith that began business in the township. He made all the iron work of Borough's Mill at Borough's Falls from heavy bar iron with his own hands, a work which few of our modern mechanics could accomplish under similar circumstances. He afterwards removed to Hatley, where his wife d. in 1833. He d. Feb. 10, 1855, aged 86 years. They were worthy members of the Free-Will Baptist Church.

CHILDREN.

THOMAS, b. March 5, 1792—m. *Sophronia Moulton.*
MARGARET, b. June 12, 1793—d. in 1827.
WILLIAM, b. Dec. 24, 1794—m. *Martha Mirick.*
ELIZABETH, b. in May, 1797—m. *Thomas Osgood.*
MARY, b. in 1801—m. *Capt Willard Ayer.*

IRENE, b. in June 1803—d. in June, 1816.
ROBERT M., b. in May, 1805—m. *Olive Chamberlin.*
CATISTA, b. in Sept., 1807—m. *G. French.*
JAMES, b. in April, 1809—m. *Caroline Herriman.*
CYRUS, b. in Aug., 1812—d. in Sept., 1814.
MISSOURI, b. in Feb., 1817—m. *Calvin Hall.*

Family of David Wallingford, 2nd.

DAVID WALLINGFORD, 2nd, b. in Hollis, N.H., Oct. 22, 1778. In 1798, m. *Abigail Stoker*, a native of Hopkinton, N.H. Began business at that place as a clothier, but just as he was beginning to realize the avails of his labors his entire property was swept away by fire. After struggling in vain for many years to retrieve their losses, they removed to Stanstead in 1806, and located on No. 20, 13th Range. Misfortune seemed to have followed them; for the great hail storm of 1807 destroyed the greater part of their first crop. They succeeded, however, by industry and perseverance in placing themselves in comfortable circumstances. He was a good English scholar, and usually spent the winter seasons in teaching. He and his wife were members of the Free-Will Baptist Church, in which he sustained the office of deacon. He was actively engaged in the temperance movements of his time, and a warm supporter of Sabbath Schools and the cause of missions. He d. in 1836; she d. Feb. 13, 1859.

CHILDREN.

FANNY, b. Oct. 4, 1798—m. *Rev. Abial Moulton.*
ESTIS, b. Aug. 24, 1800—d. Aug. 3, 1813.
ROXANA, b. June 19, 1802—d. Oct. 12, 1804.
IVES, b. April 9, 1805—m. *Maria Locke.*
DAVID, 3rd, b. Nov. 29, 1807—m. *Mary Jane Whitcher.*
SAMUEL S., b. May 28, 1810—m. *Louisa Rogers.*
CALVIN, b. Aug. 8, 1812—m. *Elvira Lee.*
GILBERT, b. Feb. 17, 1815—m., 1st, *Emeline LeBaron*; 2nd, *M. Fox.*
ESTIS, 2nd, b. Dec. 27, 1819—m. *Catherine McCurdy.*
LYMAN J., b. April 3, 1825—m. *Lucy Ann Sheppard.*

The Lyford Families.

JAMES G. LYFORD, m. *Molly Hardy.* They were natives of Exeter,

N.H., settled in Canterbury, N.H., whence they removed to Stanstead in 1802, and located on No. 13, 10th Range. Mr. Lyford afterwards purchased No. 7, 10th Range, which he sold to Oliver Nash in 1804. Their children were James, Dudley, Riley, Zebulon, Jonathan, Polly, Jeremiah and Nancy. Polly, m. *Abraham Cass;* Nancy, m. *John Cass;* Zebulon, m. *Sarah Buswell;* these last three settled in Stanstead, the others left the country.

Zebulon Lyford,

b. in Canterbury, N.H., m. *Sarah Buswell*, a native of Gilmanton, N.H. They settled in Stanstead in 1802. He d. March 16, 1816; she d. March 8, 1857. Their children were John, Nathaniel and Susan.

John Lyford,

Eldest son of Zebulon Lyford, was b. July 23, 1797—m. *Asenath Glidden*, b. Jan. 20, 1800. They settled near Cassville—were members of the Wesleyan Church. He has for many years sustained the office of magistrate, and has been variously employed in public affairs. Asenath, his wife, d. Aug. 2, 1871.

CHILDREN.

WILLARD J., b. Dec. 22, 1819—m. *Harriet Erskine.*
JOHN, b. Sept. 25, 1821—m. *Nancy Ames.*
SIMEON G., b. April 22, 1823—m. *Sarah Pressey.*
JANE, b. April 19, 1825—m. *Willard Cole.*
EDWIN, b. May 12, 1827—d. July 14, 1827.
EDWIN, 2nd, b. Jan. 1, 1830—m. *Ellen Libbee.*
ASENATH, b. Oct. 26, 1832—d. Aug. 17, 1838.
WRIGHT C., b. Aug. 22, 1834—m. *Sarah C. Mitchell.*
RUTH, b. Feb. 25, 1836—m. *L. A. Stearns.* She d. in 1861.
ASENATH, 2nd, b. Aug. 21, 1838—m. *Orrin N. Moulton.*
SARAH, b. Dec. 25, 1840—m. *L. A. Stearns.*
CHARLES, b. March 13, 1842.
HARLEY, b. Dec. 3, 1844—m. *Ellen Ladd.*

NATHANIEL LYFORD, 2nd, son of Zebulon Lyford, was born in March, 1799. In 1819, married *Mary Glidden.* She d. in 1827, leaving 4 children, Mary, Zebulon, Noah, and Betsey, m *Susan Rogers,* in 1831, d. in March, 1851. He was a member of the Congregational Church. The children by the 2nd marriage were *Benjamin F., Alonzo G.,* and *William F.*

Family of Peter Heath.

PETER HEATH, a native of England, came to America near the close of the past century, settled in Bridgewater, Mass., where he married *Abigail Crawford*. They removed to Stanstead in 1804, and located on No. 10, 11th Range. He d. in 1817; she d. in 1830. Their children were *Daniel, John, Nathaniel, Abigail, Isaac, Peter,* and *Moses*.

Daniel Heath,

Son of Peter Heath, b. in Bridgewater Mass., in 1772, m. *Judith George*, b. in 1772. They settled in Stanstead in 1804. He d. Nov. 1847; she d. in 1846.

CHILDREN.

ABIGAIL, b. June 17, 1798—m. *James Taylor*.
POLLY, b. March 23, 1800—m. *Paul Morrill*.
JUDITH, b. May 20, 1804—m. *Richard Walker*.
ELIZA, b. Oct. 27, 1808—m. *Jonathan Dustan*.
DANIEL G., b. Feb. 24, 1810—m. *Zeruiah Rogers*.
ELISHA, b. March 20, 1812—m. *Sally Brown*.
JOHN S., b. Aug. 14, 1814—m. *Sylvia Hall*.
REUBEN, b. June 11, 1816—m. *Mary Jones*.
GEORGE, b. Dec. 3, 1818—m. *Ellen Cleaveland*, 2nd *C. Richardson*.

Moses Heath,

Son of Peter Heath, b. in Bridgewater, Mass., m. *Fanny Morrill*, b. in Danville, Vt. They settled on No. 14, 11th Range of Stanstead, in 1804.

CHILDREN.

ELECTA, b. in 1812—m. *Carlton Cass*.
WILLIAM, b. in 1815—m. *Sally Simpson*.
ASENATH, b. in 1818.
MARIA, b. in 1821—m. *William Aldrich*.
ARCHIBALD, b. in 1825—m. *Zelinda Morrill*.
ERASTUS, b. in 1828—d. in 1832.

Family of Theophilus Cass.

THEOPHILUS CASS, one of the Nine Partners in the Cassville settlement, was b. in Epsom, N.H., Dec. 26, 1777. Dec. 18, 1799,

m. *Jane M. Sanborn*, b. Feb. 24, 1778. They were consistent and exemplary members of the Free-Will Baptist Church, and much respected in the community. He d. Dec. 27, 1861, aged 84; she d. in 1872.

CHILDREN.

ELIPHALET, b. May 12, 1803—m. *Abigail Morrill*, 2nd *M. W. Johnson*.
SARAH S., b. Jan. 28, 1805—m. *James M. Looke, Esq.*
HORACE, b. July 4, 1809—m. *Mary Willey*.
SOPHIA, b. Dec. 12, 1806—m. *Pearson Libbee*.
CARLTON, b. May 15, 1812—m. *Electa Heath*.
STEPHEN S., b. Nov. 14, 1816—m. *Lestina Brown*.
RACHEL, b. Feb. 10, 1820—m. *Elisha Swett*.
ELIPHALET CASS, b. May 12, 1803. Oct. 23, 1828, m. *Abigail Morrill*, b. June 22, 1805. She d. March 25, 1855. He m. *Mary W. Johnson*. They are worthy members of the Free-Will Baptist church.

CHILDREN BY 2ND MARRIAGE.

MARY A., b. Nov. 27, 1837—m. *Alvin McGaffee*.
MARTHA J., b. March 17, 1839 m. *Thomas Langmade*.

Family of Francis Cass.

FRANCIS CASS, son of Simon Cass, b. April 11, 1777—m. *Mehitable Wallace*, b. September 22, 1775. They were natives of Epsom, N. H. Settled in Stanstead in 1800. He d. January 14, 1856; she d. January 19, 1835.

CHILDREN.

NANCY, b. June 24, 1797.
JOHN, b. November 9, 1799.
SOPHRONIA, b. August 27, 1805—d. in 1835.
HEPZIBAH, b. in 1809—d. in 1814
EMILY, b. in 1811—m. *William Perry*.

JOHN CASS, son of Simon Cass, was born in Epsom, N. H., October 29, 1791—m. *Nancy Lyford*, b. in Exeter, N. H., January 25, 1795. They settled near Cassville. He d. November 28, 1846; she d. July 4, 1838.

CHILDREN.

MARY, b. July 6, 1813—m. *Collins Bartlett.*
BETSEY, b. June 9, 1815—m. *Alonzo Brown.*
GILBERT, b. August 5, 1817—m. *Semantha Bartlett.*
JOHN, b. June 28, 1819—m. *Sabrina C. Perkins.*
THOMAS, b. September 16, 1823.
HIRAM, b. July 25, 1833.

LEVI CASS, son of Simon Cass, b. in Epsom, N. H., in 1785—m. Betsey Mosher, b. in Grafton, N. H., July 4, 1785. They settled in the vicinity of Brown's Hill. He d. November 20, 1829.

CHILDREN.

HARRIET, b. May 25, 1808—m. *Hiram Bean.*
LORENZO D.; b. June 16, 1810.—m. *Abigail Butterfield.*
ERASTUS, b. January 29, 1812—m. *Almina Fisk.*
LEVI, b. March 8, 1814—m. *Sarah Weare.*
LOUISA, b. January 12, 1816—m. *John M. Mosher.*
JUDITH, b. April 11, 1818—m. *Lewis Aldrich.*
SIMON, b. May 24, 1821—m. *Elsie C. Belknap.*
FRANCIS, b. October 16, 1823.

Family of Joseph Aldrich.

JOSEPH ALDRICH m. *Lavinia Hatch.* They settled in Stanstead in 1806. He d. in 1813; she d. in 1829. Their children were Mandana, Caroline, Lavinia, Harriet, Lewis, who m. *Judith Cass,* and Emily.

The Rogers Families.

These families are the descendants of *Daniel Rogers,* who emigrated from England in the days of the Puritans and settled in Massachusetts. He was a grandson of John Rogers, the martyr.

Family of Joseph Rogers.

JOSEPH ROGERS, b. in Chichester, N. H., April 12, 1777. In 1800 m. *Judith Bachelder,* b. in Loudon, N. H., February 4, 1782. They settled on No. 13, 10th Range of Stanstead in 1802. He d. in May, 1846; she d. in February, 1833. They were members of the Methodist Church.

CHILDREN.

PHILIP, b. November 10, 1801—m. *Louisa Moulton.*
HANNAH, b. in 1803—m. *Ballard Clark.*
JUDITH, b. in 1808—m. *Joseph Davis.*
BETSEY, b. in 1814—m. *Cushman Clark.*
ZERUIAH, b. in 1816—m. *Daniel G. Heath.*
GEORGE, b. in 1817—m., 1st, *Maria Fox;* 2nd, *Eliza Haney.*
DEAN, b. in 1819—m. *Hannah Coburn.*
JOSEPH, b. in 1821—d. in 1853.

The Boynton Families.

These families are of English extraction, and are scattered widely over Britain and America. The orthography of the name has sometimes been changed, being found Boynton, Boyington and Byington; but these different families have doubtless sprung from the same source.

MAJOR WILLIAM BOYNTON m. *Mary Gibson.* They were natives of Canterbury, N.H. Settled in London, N.H.; removed to Bolton, P.Q., in 1795. In 1797 crossed the lake and located in Stanstead, near the place now called Libbee's Mills. This was about two years previous to the beginnings at Brown's Hill and Cassville, and the whole neighborhood was then a dense forest. They made a shanty on the bank of the river, covering it with hemlock boughs. While living in this shanty, their youngest son, Jesse P. Boynton, was born. When he was about a week old, there came a heavy shower of rain, which raised the water in the river so that it overflowed its banks, and reaching the shanty, floated the bed, Mrs. Boynton, " baby and all," into four feet of water. This happened in the night, and it was with some difficulty that Mr. Boynton succeeded in rescuing them in a canoe.

For some two or three years, they had to subsist mostly by hunting and fishing. Moose and deer were plenty in the forests and fish were abundant in the lakes and rivers. In the meantime, they gradually extended their clearing, and the family began to assume the appearance of a thriving colony. As early as 1805, they built a grist mill and a saw mill. These mills have since been rebuilt, and have passed into other hands. Major Boynton and his wife were respected and useful members of the community. He d. September 8, 1830; she d. December 5, 1831. Their children were Deborah, Edmund, James, William, John, Gardner and Jesse P.

Family of Gardner Green.

GARDNER GREEN, b. in Concord, N.H., February 23, 1767. May 20, 1790, m. *Deborah Boynton*, b. in Loudon, N.H., February 22, 1777. In 1795 they settled in Bolton, P. Q., where he was appointed magistrate. They removed to Stanstead in 1799. He was drowned in 1808 in attempting to cross Lake Champlain in a storm. Deborah, his wife, afterwards m. *Ezra Ball, Esq.* She d. December 18, 1858. Her children by her first marriage were Sarah, m. *Sylvester Ball;* Catherine, m. *Samuel Folsom;* Nathaniel, m. *Hannah Varnum;* William, m. *Filey Hanson;* and Mary, who m. *Charles Rogers.* Her children by her second marriage were Ezra Ball, jun., m. *Lucy Rexford*, and Deborah Ball, who m. *Edmund Boynton, Jun.*

EDMUND BOYNTON, b. in Loudon, N.H., May 19, 1779, was 18 years old when his father settled in Stanstead. He m. *Betsey Weston*, b. in Peacham, Vt., October 3, 1787. He sustained the office of captain of militia for many years. He d. May 30, 1847.

CHILDREN.

EPHRAIM, b. February 24, 1809—m. *Harriet Morrill.*
JERUSHA, b. October 3, 1811—m. a *Mr. Hollister.*
LYDIA, b. May 9, 1814—m. *William Davis.*
NATHAN, b. March 4, 1816—m. *Margaret McClure.*
EDMUND, b. March 24, 1818—m. *Deborah Ball.*
LEWIS, b. August 28, 1822—m. *Catherine Folsom.*
GARDNER BOYNTON, b. in Loudon, N.H., June 4, 1792. May 26, 1814, m. *Nancy Quimby*, b. February 10, 1795. They settled on the family homestead—were worthy and exemplary members of the Wesleyan Church. He d. January 5, 1873.

CHILDREN.

CAROLINE, b. March 30, 1817—m. *Benjamin Atwood.*
MARY ANN, b. June 4, 1819—m. *Samuel C. Burns.*
JULIA M., b. June 6, 1821—m. *Truman A. Quimby, Esq.*

FAMILY OF CAPT. JOHN BOYNTON.

JESSE, b. in August, 1823—m. *Olive A. Curtis.*
WILDER P., b. February 13, 1826—m. *Abigail Moulton.*
LYMAN R., b. February 5, 1829—m. *Hortense Cook.*
JESSE P. BOYNTON, the youngest son of Major William Boynton, was b. in Stanstead, July 27, 1799. February 7, 1830, m. *Susan Davis*, b. June 25, 1806. They belong to the Wesleyan Church.

CHILDREN.

THOMAS, b. March 25, 1831—d. July 13, 1852.
CORDELIA, b. September 8, 1832—d. November 23, 1848.
STEPHEN D., b. December 25, 1836.

Family of Capt. John Boynton.

CAPT. JOHN BOYNTON, b. in Newhampton, N.H., May 4, 1756—m. *Lydia Dow*, b. in Gilmanton, N.H., in 1762. They settled on No. 3, 12th Range in 1805 and afterwards sold out, and removed to Windsor, P.Q., where he d. in 1841. She d. Dec. 10, 1840.

CHILDREN.

BENJAMIN, b. April 2, 1790—m. *Mary Burt.*
LYDIA, b. Aug. 15, 1791—m. *Moses Blount.*
JOHN, b. April 1, 1793—m. *Isabel Nelson.*
NANCY, b. Oct. 11, 1794—m. *Asa Blount.*
ABRAHAM, b. March 17, 1796—m. *Amanda Pope.*
DAVID, b. Oct. 6, 1799—m. *Betsey Vinton.*
WILLIAM, b. in Feb., 1800—m. *Harriet Curtis.*
MARY, twin sister of William—m. *Joseph Thomas.*
NOAH, b. in 1801—m. *Lucinda Vinton.*
HANNAH, b. Oct. 7, 1803—m. *Hiram Moor.*
RICHARD, b. Oct. 18, 1805—m. *Mary Davis.*
SARAH, b. July 10, 1806—m. *Johnson Lunt.*

ABRAHAM BOYNTON, son of Capt. John Boynton, was b. March 17, 1796—m. *Amanda Pope.* They settled on the Lake Shore, near Georgeville. He d. Sept. 12, 1855. She d. Jan. 14, 1861. They were members of the Methodist Church.

CHILDREN.

RUTH, b. Sept. 22, 1825.
JAMES, b. Oct. 14, 1827—d. March 15, 1845.
ADAMS W., b. July 4, 1830—m. *Anna G. Christie.* They reside on the family homestead, No. 17, 1st Range of Stanstead.

190 FORESTS AND CLEARINGS.

OSMOND, b. June 15, 1833—m. *Mary G. Hubbard*. He was engaged in mercantile business with his father-in-law, B. F. Hubbard. He d. Jan. 20, 1867; she d. Nov. 30, 1870.
LUTHER W., b. Sept 24, 1836—d. Nov. 14, 1864.
AMANDA, b. April 15, 1839.

The Taplin Families.

The ancestors of these families emigrated from England in the 17th century and settled in Vermont.

Family of Johnson Taplin.

JOHNSON TAPLIN, b. July 1, 1766—m. *Miriam Haseltine*, b. in Newbury, Vt., Feb., 9, 1771. They were the pioneers of the settlement of Stanstead. He was one of the first militia officers appointed in the township, and served as captain for many years. After residing at the Plain 15 years, he removed with his family to the vicinity of Fitch Bay.

CHILDREN.

SALLY, b. Oct. 17, 1789—d. March 10, 1792.
JOHN H., b. March 20, 1791—m. *Susan Davis*.
BETSEY, b. June 23, 1794—d. June 23, 1813.
ALBERT and ALVIN, twins, b. Sept. 20, 1800. Albert d. Feb. 22, 1811. Alvin d. Dec. 28, 1814.

John H. Taplin

Was b. in Corinth, Vt., March 20, 1791. He was three or four years old when his father came to Stanstead Plain, and for two or three years, was the only child in the settlement east of the Lake. He remained with his father until he became of age, and afterwards m. *Susan Davis*. They settled near Fitch Bay. He d. Sept. 25, 1859; she d. in 1861.

CHILDREN.

HORACE, b. May 17, 1813—d. in infancy.
JOANNA, b. May 2, 1814—m. *Samuel Rexford*.
BETSEY, b. April 10, 1816—m. *William Suttle*.
WILLIAM, b. March 21, 1818.
LAVINIA, b. Jan. 10, 1820—d. in infancy.

FAMILY OF ABNER RICKARD. 191

JOHNSON, b. March 6, 1822—m. *Lavinia Ayer.*
HORACE, 2nd, b. April 21, 1825—m. *Comfort Tilton.*
SUSAN, b. Aug. 29, 1827—m. *Emmons Hemminway.*
SARAH, b. May 1, 1829—m. *Wellington Rawson.*
ALVIN, b. Nov. 5, 1833—m. *Lizzie Peeble.*
ALBERT, b. July 6, 1835—m. *Rebecca Green.*

Family of Samuel Doloff.

SAMUEL DOLOFF, b. in Conway, N.H., June 3. 1792. June 1, 1819, m. *Laura W. Packard,* b. in Newport, Vt., July 13, 1797. They settled near Georgeville, but subsequently removed to the vicinity of Fitch Bay. He d. March 20, 1862. She d. July 22, 1857.

CHILDREN.

HAMDEN, b. June 9, 1820—m. *Luthera Gage.*
BETSEY, b. Jan. 28, 1822—m. *William C. Ladd.*
ARTEMISIA P., b. Feb. 25, 1824.
FERDINAND S., b. April 24, 1826—m. *Sarah J. Israel.*
FLORILLA, b. Jan. 3, 1831.
ERASTUS P., b. April 9, 1838—d. April 12, 1842.

Family of Josiah Doloff.

JOSIAH DOLOFF, b. in Conway, N.H., May 20, 1789. He m. *Abigail Sherwin,* b. Sept. 29, 1786. They settled near Fitch Bay. He d. Nov. 19, 1852.

CHILDREN.

WILLIAM, b. Sept. 13, 1819—m. *Betsey Lorimer.*
EMILY, b. Jan. 1, 1822—m. *Jeremiah Harris.*
DENNIS B., b. Aug. 4, 1823—m. *Lucy Ann Oliver.*
ADELINE, b. Feb. 19, 1825.
ANGELINA. b. Feb. 15, 1827.
HANNAH, b. Sept. 12, 1829—d. in 1854.

Family of Abner Rickard.

ABNER RICKARD, b. in Plymouth, Mass., in 1771. M. *Lydia King,* a native of the same town. They settled in the vicinity of Fitch Bay. He d. Dec. 12, 1856; she d. in 1855.

CHILDREN.

LUCINDA, b. 1791—m. *Lebbeus Smith.*

THOMAS, b. in 1793—m. *Clarissa Ainsworth.*
HARVEY, b. in 1795—m. *Patience Blake.*
JESSE, b. in 1799—m. *Betsey Chase.*
LYMAN, b. in 1801—m. *Polly Niles.*
SOPHIA, b. in 1805—m. *Alva Blodgett.*
ALVA, b. in 1808—m. *Betsey Richardson.*
LYDIA, b. in 1810—d. young.
ABNER, b. Oct. 16, 1814—m. *Sarah Pool.*
SIMEON b. Oct. 6, 1816—m. *Almira Hunt.*
ABNER RICKARD, JUN., b. Feb. 16, 1814—m. *Sarah Pool.* She was b. Feb. 23, 1817. They settled near Fitch Bay.

CHILDREN.

THEODORE, b. Dec. 14, 1839.
BETSEY, b. Nov. 5, 1842.
CATHERINE, b. Sept. 28, 1844.
ESTHER, b. Dec. 18, 1847.

Family of Richard Clefford.

The ancestors of this family were among the earliest of the English colonists in America. The orthography is sometimes changed, but all the families that write their name either *Clefford*, or *Clifford* have undoubtedly sprung from the same origin, and can trace their ancestry as far back as to the fair but ill-fated *Rosamond Clifford* of England. Richard Clefford, the subject of this notice, was born in Strafford, Conn., May 19, 1793. April 4, 1820, m. *Eleanor Shields*, b. in Newbury, Vt., June 19, 1794. They were among the earliest settlers of Stanstead, located near Fitch Bay.

CHILDREN.

MATILDA, b. Dec. 26, 1821—m. *Obadiah Wilson.*
ALBERT, b. May 1, 1823—m. *Mary Lee.*
JONAS, b. April 11, 1824—d. April 13, 1843.
SAMUS S., b. May 25, 1825—m. *Sarah Davis.*
RUBY, b. Feb. 14, 1827—m. *Chester Wilson.*
SURECTY, b. June 19, 1828.

The Amy Families.

WILLIAM AMY and his wife were natives of Connecticut. They settled in Stanstead in 1800, at the place called by their name, *Amy Corner.* He early received the appointment of magistrate, was a prominent freemason. He d. in 1847. Their children were William, Gratus, John, Anderson who m. Olive Clefford, Sarah, Betsey and Vena. The children of Anderson were Sarah, who m. Joseph Abbott; Jacob, who m. Sarah Wade; and Joseph, who m Ann Dewey.

Family of Elijah Geer.

ELIJAH GEER, b. in Norwich, Vt., Feb. 23, 1786, m. Cynthia Jewett. They settled in Stanstead near the Lake Shore. She d. in 1831. He subsequently m. a 2nd wife. The children by the first marriage were Sarepta, b. July 14, 1810, m. C. Bryant; Abel C., b. Feb. 9, 1812, m. Elsie B. Remick; Sarah b. in 1816, m. a Mr. Baldwin; Ann J., b. in 1818, m. John Whidden; Hannah, b. 1820, m. A. S. Dwetty; Cynthia, b. in 1822, m. a Mr. Porter; Caroline, b. in 1828, m. a Mr. Chaddock; Luman, Lucinda, and Laura. 11 children by 2nd marriage.

Family of Luke Perry.

LUKE PERRY married Irene Patrick. They settled in Stanstead in 1804. He d. Oct. 26, 1824. She d. in 1856. Their children were William, m. Emily Cass; Emily, m. Charles Haines; Irene, Patrick, Maria, Mathews, Edwin, Hannah, Pluma, and Calvin.

WILLIAM PERRY married Emily Cass. They settled near Brown's Hill in Stanstead. Perry Corner is called after their name.

CHILDREN.

FRANCIS, b. Sept. 9, 1833.
CALVIN, b. March 19, 1838.
ADELINE, b. Nov. 19, 1839.
ELLEN, b. Aug. 23, 1841.
EMELINE, b. Jan. 5, 1846.

The Merrill Family.

In March, 1800, David Merrill with his wife and twelve children left Fishersfield, now Newbury, in New Hampshire, to find a home in Canada—his wife on horseback, and he and the children with an ox team. They were 25 or 30 days in getting through the woods to Duncansboro, now Newport, Vt. At Newport, they put themselves and their team on board a scow, and proceeded down the lake to the place where the Mountain House now stands, where they encamped for the night. They continued their course down the lake, the next day, and disembarked on the eastern shore, some three miles below Georgeville. Here they pitched their tent, made a small clearing, and built a log house. They afterwards sold out and in 1803, located on No. 21, 3rd Range in Stanstead. This was the first settlement made between Georgeville and Fitch Bay. David Merrill d. in Dec., 1831. The advent of his family was rather a case of wholesale emigration, as all the children settled in Stanstead. They all married and had large families. Israel Merrill, the 2nd son, had 12 children. Mary G., who m. Isaac Winn; Rev. David H., who lives on the family homestead, and his four children; Esther B., who m. Heman Phelps; Jacob G., Israel B., Collins J., Sarah P. W., Jeremiah H., Clifton G., and Victoria A. Israel Merrill, sen., d. in Jan., 1853.

Family of Theophilus Brown.

THEOPHILUS BROWN, b. in Candia, N.H., Sept. 14, 1775. Settled on No. 26, 9th Range of Stanstead, in 1800. In Feb., 1807, m. *Mary Varnum,* b. Jan. 22, 1784. They were worthy and useful members of the community. He d. in 1867.

CHILDREN.

JAMES, b. May 12, 1808—d. in infancy.
ROSAMOND, b. June 17, 1809—m. *Israel Brainerd, jun.*
ANN, b. Aug. 5, 1811—d. Sept. 30, 1833.
JOHN Q., b. June 18, 1813—m. *Abigail K. Gustin.*
THEOPHILUS, b. Feb. 25, 1816.
MARY, b. March 14, 1817—m. *Lyman Gustin.*
SOPHRONIA J., b. in Feb., 1821—m. *Timothy D. Brainerd.*
JONATHAN D., b. Sept. 25, 1825—m. *Jane Lewis.*

Family of Sherburn Brown.

SHERBURN BROWN, b. in Candia, N.H., April 7, 1778. Settled on No. 27, 9th Range of Stanstead, adjoining his brother Theophilus Brown, in 1800. March 2, 1807, he m. *Catherine Dodge,* b. May 3, 1783. She d. July 17, 1823. In 1824, he m. his second wife.

CHILDREN BY 1st MARRIAGE.

SANBORN, b. April 6, 1808.
ORRIN, b. Nov. 2, 1809.

CATHERINE, b. Dec. 26, 1810—m. *Carlton Ayer.*
LOUISA, b. Nov. 14, 1813—d. Jan. 12, 1817.
SHERBURN, b. April 12, 1816.
MARIA, b. Aug. 2, 1818—m. *E. H. LeBaron, Esq.*
ELVINA, b. July 20, 1820—d. in infancy
NELSON, b. Nov. 3, 1821—d. young.
PAMELIA, b. July 17, 1823.

CHILDREN BY 2nd MARRIAGE.

SEWELL, b. Dec. 4, 1824—d. Aug. 1, 1838.
ALBERT, b. April 22, 1826.
SUSAN, b. July 12, 1827.
ALMIRA, b. Dec. 13, 1828.
SARAH A., b. Aug. 12, 1830.
WILDER, b. April 2, 1832.
NEHEMIAH, b. July 9, 1835.
OZRO, b. March 7, 1838.
ADELINE, b. Jan. 14, 1840.

Family of Levi Brown.

LEVI BROWN, b. in Candia, N.H., Sept. 9, 1782—m. *Jemima Osgood.* They settled on No. 26, 10th Range, in 1806. He d. in 1843. She d. in 1860. Their children were Amelia, m. *Mark Farley;* Levi, m. *Sarah Sheppard;* Aaron, Evelina, who m. *John S. Cole;* and Betsey A., who m. *Joseph Johnson.*

Family of Amos Shurtliff.

AMOS SHURTLIFF, b. in Tolland, Conn., June 22, 1775, m. *Nancy Brown,* who was b. in Candia, N.H., Nov. 25, 1770. They settled on No. 28, 10th Range of Stanstead, in 1803. He d. March 3, 1837; she d. March 9, 1837.

CHILDREN.

LATHROP, b. Sept. 19, 1804—m. *Harriet Hopkins.*
JONATHAN B., b. Aug. 6, 1807, sustained the office of magistrate for many years, and was actively employed in public affairs.
NANCY, b. Sept. 20, 1818—m. *Chester W. Brown.*
3 children died young.

Family of Thomas Ayer.

THOMAS AYER, the pioneer of the Ayer's Flat Settlement, was a native of Weare, N.H. He m. *Sylvia Wright*, a native of the same state. They located on No. 1, 9th Range of Hatley, in 1799. This lot is the site of the present village of Ayer's Flat. For many years their trials and privations were severe, but they succeeded eventually in acquiring a large property. He d. in 1842; She d. in 1860. Their children were Roxana, m. A. Rexford; Willard, m. Mary Wells; Osgood, Betsey, m. Bela Langmade; Gardner, m. Matilda Lanphire; Carlton, m. Catherine Brown; Louisa, m. Ira Wright, and Wilder, who m. Mary Hovey.

Willard Ayer.

WILLARD AYER, b. in Weare, N.H., Dec. 9, 1776. M. *Betsey Coburn*, b. March 11, 1774. They settled on No. 28, 11th Range Stanstead in 1803. He d. Aug. 10, 1858; she d. Feb. 15, 1853.

CHILDREN.

WARREN, b. Jan. 30, 1801—m. *Lucinda Boynton*.
MIRANDA, b. May 28, 1802—m. *Noah Glidden*.
FREDERICK, b. Nov. 7, 1803—m. *Mary Eaton*.

Carlton Ayer.

CARLTON AYER, b. July 17, 1811—m. *Catherine Brown*, b. Dec. 29, 1811. They settled at Ayer's Flat, where Mr. Ayer has been variously employed in public affairs.

CHILDREN.

HELEN M., b. Nov. 28, 1839—m. *Stephen Davis*.
EDGAR C., b. Sept. 26, 1842.
CORDELIA L., b. Jan. 1, 1845—m. *Charles G. Beckett*.
HOMER, b. April 20, 1847.

Family of Jonathan Foss.

JONATHAN FOSS b. in Chester, N.H., December 20, 1780, m. *Margaret Skinner*, who was b. in Wolton, Conn., in 1787. They settled on No. 23, 9th Range of Stanstead, in 1807. He d. in 1854.

CHILDREN.

JOSEPH, b. March 1, 1805—m. *Sarah A. Moore;* 2nd, *Almira Rogers*.
JONATHAN, b. May 21, 1807—m. *Anna Clark*.

MARGARET, b. January 22, 1809—m. *Ozias G. Brown.*
LAURA, b. in June, 1811.
AUSTIN, b. January 9, 1813—m. *Phebe Hibbard.*
LYDIA, b. May 7, 1815—m. *Reuben Emerson.*
MARY, b. January 22, 1818—m. *Edward Oliver.*
CLARISSA, b. January 4, 1820—d. April 9, 1825.
EMILY, b. March 8, 1822—m. *Carlos Rider.*
HIRAM, b. May 2, 1824—m. *Martha Davis.*
SMITH, b. May 28, 1829—m. *Mary Jane Campbell.*

Family of Benjamin Bartlett.

BENJAMIN BARTLETT married *Miriam Flanders.* They were natives of Connecticut. Settled in Stanstead near Fitch Bay in 1807. He was drowned in crossing Lake Champlain in 1841; she d. in 1852. Their children were Sarah, John, Mehitable, Collins, Amos, Esther, Benjamin, Miriam and Philander.

COLLINS, son of Benjamin Bartlett, was born July 18, 1799. March 23, 1820, m. *Sally Brown*, b. June 21, 1789. They settled near Cassville. She d. April 27, 1861; he d. in 1872.

CHILDREN.

ORVILLE, b. December 11, 1820—m. *Harriet Norcross.*
SEMANTHA, b. March 7, 1822—m. *Gilbert Cass.*
ORANGE, b. July 30, 1824—m. *Florinda McGaffee.*
NELSON, b. April 14, 1826—m, *Maria Morrill.*
JAMES V., b. November 7, 1827—d. April 7, 1832.
SANBORN J., b. March 4, 1829—m. *Jerusha Morrill.*
COLLINS, b. January 4, 1831—m. *Elmina Lee.*

Family of Simeon Cole.

SIMEON COLE married *Elizabeth Sherman.* They were natives of Waterbury, Conn. She was a near relation of Roger Sherman, of revolutionary memory. They settled in Stanstead County in 1798. Two of their sons, Asa and Thomas, settled near Brown's Hill.

ASA COLE, b. in St. Johnsbury, Vt., September 15, 1790, m. *Louisa Dodge,* b. October 14, 1790. They settled on the south part of No. 25, 9th Range of Stanstead. He d. January 26, 1833; she d. August 4, 1851.

CHILDREN.

ASHLEY, b. June 14, 1818—m. *Abba C. Bachelder.*
WILLARD A., b. May 10, 1820—m. 1st, *Hannah Copp ;* 2nd, *Phebe A. Wood.*
LOVISA, b. June 19, 1822—m. *George Shurtliff.*
LUCINDA, b. September 17, 1824—m. *Jonathan Merrill, jun.*
PHILINDA, b. May 25, 1826—m. *Wright Sleeper.*
Two children died young.

Family of Eleazar Clark.

ELEAZAR CLARK, b. in Chester, N.H., June 5, 1779. November 11, 1802, m. *Sarah Brown*, b. in Candia, N.H., March 31, 1782. They settled on No. 24, 10th Range of Stanstead, in 1810. In common with their neighbors, they experienced the inconveniences and privations incident to new settlements, but succeeded in acquiring a competency, and were useful members of the community. He d. May 16, 1830; she d. February 19, 1861.

CHILDREN.

NEHEMIAH, b. in 1803—m. *Irene Tripp.*
SEWELL, b. in 1805—m. *Harriet Dresser.*
NATHANIEL, b. in 1807—m. *Laura Rexford.*
ELEAZAR, b. in 1811—m. *Miranda Haskell.* His career has been a successful one. He sustained the office of High Constable of the District of St. Francis for several years; has been connected with the mining interests of the country, from which he has realized a large property. His eldest daughter married J. Hallowell, Esq.; his second daughter married E. T. Brooks, Esq.
SALLY, b. in 1813—m. *Stephen Reed.*
BELINDA, b. in 1816—m. *Simeon Brown.*
WILLIAM, b. in 1818—drowned in the river St. Francis in 1840.
OSBURN, b. in 1820—m. *Abigail C. Morrill.*
LEWIS, b. in 1822—m. *Harriet Hill.*
SUSAN, b. in 1825—m. *David Ruggles.*
One child died in infancy.

Family of Thomas Cole.

THOMAS COLE, son of Simeon Cole, b. in St. Johnsbury, Vt., March 5, 1787. Settled on the north part of No. 25, 9th Range of Stanstead, in 1818. January 6, 1811, m. *Sally Davis*, b. May 8, 1791. He d. April 9, 1836.

FAMILY OF RUFUS KIMPTON.

CHILDREN.

JOHN S., b. May 3, 1815—m. *Evelina Brown.*
ALVIN, b. August 7, 1818—m. *Mary Small.*
LYMAN, b. March 8, 1821—m. *Emily Cummings.*
AARON H., b. November 23, 1823—m. *Louisa E. Shurtliff.*
PHINEAS, b. March 8, 1826—m. *Irene Small.*
PHILO B., b. August 7, 1828—m. *Adelaide Davis.*
SALLY, b. January 11, 1833—m. *Phineas Davis.*
THOMAS, b. May, 22, 1835—m. *Harriet M. Shurtliff.*

Family of Rufus Kimpton.

RUFUS KIMPTON, b. in Croydon, N.H., September 2, 1762—m. Abigail Brick, b. in Roxbury, Mass., April 23, 1761. They settled near the place now known as The Narrows, in Stanstead, in 1802. The place was then a dense forest. Theirs was the first beginning in that neighborhood.

CHILDREN.

SARAH, b. April 3, 1785—m. *James Martin.*
ABIGAIL, b. September 29, 1786.
RUFUS, b. May 4, 1789—m. *Betsey Wait.*
SUSAN, b. January, 22, 1792—m. *Israel Blake.*
JUDITH, b. June 14, 1794.
ESTHER, b. January 27, 1796—m. *Josiah Gustin, Esq.*
ALPHEUS, b. March 17, 1798—m. *Lillette Laney.*
MAHALA, b. December 27, 1800—m. *Ichabod Shurtliff.*
HANNAH, b. April 10, 1803—m. a *Mr. Remich.*

RUFUS KIMPTON, JUN., b. in Croydon, N.H., May 4, 1789, m. Betsey Wait, b. in Beverly, Mass. They settled in the vicinity of the Narrows Bridge. He d. Sept. 10, 1841.

CHILDREN.

RICHARD, b. Nov. 14, 1809—m. *Rosetta Austin.*
RUFUS, b. Aug. 12, 1811—m. *Abigail Ball.*
JOHN, b. Jan. 12, 1813—m. *Elizabeth Fowler.*
ALPHEUS, b. Feb. 15, 1815—m. *Lovisa Drew.*
NANCY, b. Dec. 27, 1818—m. *Andrew Gardyer.*
GEORGE, b. Feb. 11, 1824—m. *Arvilla Verback.*
MARY, b. Oct. 21, 1827—m. *Chancey Blake.*
BETSEY, b. Dec. 7, 1829—m. *Collins Merrill.*

LILLECTA, b. July 7, 1832—m. *Rev. David H. Merrill.*
AYLMER, b. July 4, 1835—m. *Rosina Laney.*

Family of Benjamin Varnum.

BENJAMIN VARNUM, b. in Dracut, Mass., May 7, 1786, m. *Candace Collins*, b. Dec. 20, 1802. They settled near Harvey's Landing in Stanstead.

CHILDREN.

MOSES, b. Sept. 27, 1821—d. Sept. 8, 1839.
FERRIS, b. Dec. 24, 1823—m. *Laura A. Cunningham*
EVELINA, b. May 14, 1825—d. Feb, 15, 1833.
LAURA A., b. April 21, 1827—m. *Philip Verback.*
FRANKLIN, b. June 13, 1831.
ELIZA ANN, b. March 30, 1838—m. *John Phelan*

Family of Ichabod Collins.

ICHABOD COLLINS m. *Ruth Martin.* They settled in the vicinity of Harvey's Landing in Stanstead in 1804. He d. in 1816; she d. in 1836.

CHILDREN.

EPHRAIM, b. Dec. 15, 1776—m. *Olive Martin.*
RICHARD, b. in 1778—m. *Betsey Martin.*
MOSES, b. in 1780—m. *Olive Putnam.*
MARY, b. in 1782—m. *John McIntyre.*
WILLIAM, b. in 1784—m. *Betsey Merrill.*
CLARISSA, b. in 1786—d. in 1838.
SAMUEL, b. Jan. 26, 1790—m. *Thankful Verback.*
ICHABOD, b. in 1792—m. *Amy Allen.*
ANNA, b. Jan. 6, 1797—m. *Kendrick Blake.*
EPHRAIM COLLINS, b. in Bradford, Vt., Dec. 15, 1776, m. *Olive Martin*, b. June 11, 1775. Settled near Harvey's Landing.

CHILDREN.

CANDACE, b. Dec. 20, 1802—m. *Benjamin Varnum.*
AMANDA, b. Oct. 25, 1808—m. *Richard Camber.*

SAMUEL COLLINS, b. in Bradford, Vt., Jan. 26, 1790, m. *Thankful Verback.* She was b. Oct. 11, 1790. They settled near Harvey's Landing.

CHILDREN.

Samuel, b. Oct. 11, 1812—d. April 5, 1816.
Emeline, b. May 1, 1814—m. *Benjamin Morey.*
Anna, b. June 25, 1816—m. *Franklin Huse.*
Benjamin, b. Aug. 28, 1818—m. *Almira Beebe.*
Arad, b. Nov. 25, 1820—m. *Eleanor Blake.*
Harriet, b. March 6, 1824—d. Feb. 8, 1860.
Betsey, b, May 28, 1826—m. *Willard Nicholls.*
Samuel, 2nd b. July 8, 1832—m. *Nancy Elder.*
One child d. in infancy.

Family of Isaac Rogers.

Isaac Rogers, b. in Chichester, N.H., in 1780—m. *Sarah Brainerd*, b. in Campton, N.H., in 1777. They settled in Stanstead, in 1801. He d. in 1824. She d. in 1856.

CHILDREN.

Almira, b. in 1801—m. *Joseph Foss.*
Sarah W., b. in Sept., 1802—m. *William Jones.*
Susan, b. in Oct., 1804—m. *Nathaniel Lyford.*
Rhoda, b. in Nov., 1806—m. *Benjamin Flanders.*
Louisa, b. in Nov., 1808—m. *Samuel G. Wallingford.*
Caroline, b. in Jan., 1811—m. *John Howlet.*
Mary, b. in April, 1813—m. *William Flanders.*
David, b. in April, 1816—m. *Adeline L. Felch.*

Family of William Rogers.

William Rogers, b. in Portsmouth, N.H., in 1765—m. *Dorcas Bachelder*, b. in Loudon, N.H., in 1769. They began on No. 10, 10th Range of Stanstead, in 1798, but afterwards removed to No. 8, 9th Range. He d. in 1859; she d. in 1845. They were consistent and exemplary members of the Methodist Church.

CHILDREN.

Mary, b. July 6, 1786—m. *Dudley Norris.*
Jonathan, b. April 7, 1788—m. *Rebecca Ruiter.*
David, b. June 9, 1790—deceased.
Lydia, b. March 17, 1792—m. *Phineas Weeks.*
Susan, b. May 19, 1895—m. *Ebenezer Dodge.*

SARAH, b. May 24, 1798—m. *Caleb Carpenter.*
WILLIAM, b. July 3, 1804—lost at sea.
BENJAMIN M., b. Nov. 14, 1809—d. March 23, 1844.

The Davis Families.

These families are of English descent, and are scattered widely over the United States and Canada. Those that settled in Stanstead County were mostly emigrants from New Hampshire. They were generally industrious and useful members of the community.

Family of Capt. Dudley Davis.

DUDLEY DAVIS, b. in Barrington, N.H., May 20, 1770—m. *Dorothy Bachelder*, b. in Loudon N.H., in 1774. They settled on No. 9, 9th Range of Stanstead, in 1800. His wife d. Dec. 20, 1805. In 1806, he m. *Susanna Chamberlin*. He was early appointed captain of militia, was a consistent and exemplary member of the Wesleyan Church. He d. Oct. 8, 1852.

CHILDREN BY 1st MARRIAGE.

MARY, b. Dec. 5, 1794—m. *Joseph Mooney.*
DANIEL, b. July 8, 1796—m. *Hannah Blount.*
SARAH, b. March 4, 1797—m. *Harris Moulton.*
DUDLEY, b. Dec. 5, 1799—m. *Emily Bliss.*
LOIS, b. March 4, 1802—m. *Ira Stevens.*

CHILDREN BY 2nd MARRIAGE.

HEMAN, b. in Aug., 1807. In the Wesleyan Ministry.
HIRAM, b. in Aug., 1809—m. 1st, *Sarah Ann Cobb;* 2nd, *Betsey Mansur.*
LAVINIA, b. Nov. 9, 1812—m. *Erasmus D. Whitcher.*
DOROTHY, b. Feb. 22, 1815—m. 1st, *Silas W. Mack;* 2nd, *George Gale.*
LAURA ANN, b. May 29, 1817—m. *Charles Hatch.*
LEWIS, b. April 6, 1820—m. *Aurelia Day.*
ASENATH, b. April 19, 1822—m. *Elias Lee, jun.*
LEONARD, b. Dec. 31, 1827—m. *Philura Glidden.*
THADDEUS O., b. Feb. 2, 1830—m. *Luvia Lee.*
ELLEN MARIA, b. in Feb., 1832—d. in 1835.

DUDLEY DAVIS, jun., b. Dec. 5, 1799—m. *Emily Bliss.* They settled on part of No. 7, 9th Range of Stanstead ; are members of the Methodist Church. Mr. Davis is a wealthy farmer, has held various offices in the township, and has been employed in public affairs. 2 children—Dudley M., his eldest son, was for some time engaged in mercantile business at Coaticook. Carlos P., the youngest son, resides with his parents upon the family homestead.

Family of Moses Davis.

MOSES DAVIS, b. in Barrington, N.H., March 21, 1786. He came to St. Armand, P.Q., in 1810, and March 20, 1811—m. *Rosamond Basford,* b. in Essex, Vt., May 29, 1787. They came to Stanstead, in 1814, and settled on No. 13, 4th Range. She d. June 20, 1861.

CHILDREN.

SYRENA, b. Jan. 7, 1812—d. Nov. 7, 1818.
ALMIRA, b. May 24, 1813—m. *Moses Libby.*
NANCY, b. Feb. 2, 1815—m. *Andrew Libby.*
MOSES, b. March 6, 1817—d. Nov. 24, 1818.
MARY, b. May 14, 1821—m. *Squire Church.*
DUDLEY, b. Dec. 11, 1822—m. *Matilda Ball.*
MOSES N., b. Sept. 12, 1824—m. *Hannah J. Watson.*
SALLY, b. Dec. 6, 1830—m. *Niles P. Church.*

Family of Nathan Davis.

NATHAN DAVIS, b. in Loudon, N.H., Nov. 22, 1772—m. *Sally Boynton,* b. in Salem, Mass., June 6, 1778. They came to Stanstead in 1819, and settled on No. 24, 12th Range. He d. May 10, 1851.

CHILDREN.

SALLY, b. June 24, 1797—m. *John Roberts.*
RICHARD, b. Jan. 3, 1800.
SUSAN, b. Jan. 7, 1802—m. *Manasseh Fairbanks.*
JOHN, b. Jan. 26, 1804—m. *Jane Lee.*
WILLIAM, b. April 5, 1806—m. *Lydia Boynton.*
EBENEZER, b. May 3, 1808—m. *Harriet Sleeper.*
DAVID B., b. June 18, 1810—m. *Lydia Emory.*
NATHAN H., b. Aug. 14, 1812—m. *Sarah Maxdel.*
LEMUEL F., b. Nov. 22, 1821—d. in Jan., 1854.

Family of Silas Davis.

SILAS DAVIS, b. in Woodstock, Vt., Feb. 20, 1780—m. Phebe Bennett, b. Oct. 5, 1784. They settled near Fitch Bay in 1807. She d. in 1828. He subsequently married a 2nd wife and left the country.

CHILDREN.

IRENE, b. Feb. 5, 1805—m. *Blake Wallace.*
SILAS A., b. Jan. 26 1807—m. *Salome Moulton.*
PHEBE E., twin, b. Jan. 26—m. *Daniel Drew.*
SALINA, b. Nov. 9, 1808—m. *Isaac Ives.*
WILLIAM B., b. Nov. 21, 1810—m. *Martha E. Haywood.*
JAMES E., b. Feb. 13, 1813—m. *Sophia Judkins.*
ROXANA, b. Jan. 9, 1815—m. *Harvey Merriman.*
KINSMAN R., b. Dec. 8, 1816—m. *Sarah A. Brooks,*
ISAAC G., b. March 18, 1819—m. *Almira Bullock.*
ROSAMOND, b. March 2, 1821—m. *Allen W. Hansford.*
POLLY L., b. July 17, 1823—m. *John Packard.*
PHILENDA, b. May 5, 1826—m. *William H. Baker.*

Family of Simeon Davis.

SIMEON DAVIS settled in Woodstock, Vt. Two of his sons, Sampson and Phineas, settled in Stanstead. The family of Sampson Davis left the country as early as 1820. The children of Phineas Davis were Betsey, m. John Bancroft; Sally, m. Thomas Cole; Susan, m. John Taplin; Artemas, m. Sabrina Frisbee; Aaron, m. Roxelana Brainerd; William, m. Betsey Brown; and Phineas, jun., who m. Betsey Pool.

The children of Artemas Davis were Sabrina, m. George Latham, Phineas, Cynthia, Artemas B., Titus and Miriam.

The children of William Davis were Lucina, m. Hiram Foss; Lestina, m. Colby Cass; Spencer, Lucia, Chester and Vincent.

The children of Phineas Davis, jun., were Phineas, 3rd, m. Sally Cole; Adelaide, m. Philo Cole; Lucena and Lawson.

Family of Abraham Martin.

ABRAHAM MARTIN m. *Candace Chapin.* They settled in Stanstead in 1811. He built the Mills known as Judd's Mills. Their children were Daniel, Orrin, Malinda, Jane, Amasa T., Chapin,

Allen, Amarilla, Olive and Foster. Amasa T., m. Elizabeth Kinsman. They settled in Clifton, P.Q., where he has for many years been postmaster. Olive, m. Thomas Pierce, Esq., of Clifton, P.Q. Amarilla, m. a Mr. Houghton. Others have died or left the country. Allen Martin is living on Stanstead Plain.

Family of Capt. John Ruiter.

CAPT. JOHN RUITER, b. in Hoosac, N.Y., June 16, 1769. His father, Col. Henry Ruiter, had served in the British Army during the French War. Being a firm loyalist, he left his country at the time of the American Revolution, and came to Canada, where he was afterwards employed as an officer in the British Service, Capt. John Ruiter, the subject of this notice, married *Sarah Fyler*, b. Nov. 5, 1769. They came to Stanstead in 1800, and settled at the place called by their name, "*Ruiter Corner.*" He was in the British Service as captain in the war of 1812, 1815. He d. Aug. 8, 1853. Sarah his wife d. April 10, 1842.

CHILDREN.

REBECCA, b. Jan. 2, 1789—m. *Jonathan Rogers*.
HENRY, b. May 3, 1791—m. *Phebe Stoddard*.
THOMAS, b. May 30, 1793—m. *Sarah Pinkham*.
JOHN, b. Oct. 5, 1795—m. *Sarah Smith*.
SAMUEL F., b. March 3, 1800—m. *Susanna Pool*.
NANCY, b. May 11, 1802—d. March 11, 1813.
MIRANDA, b. Nov. 20, 1807—m. *Thomas P. Jenkins*.

Family of Asa May.

ASA MAY married *Alzina Bishop*. They were natives of New Hampshire, came to Stanstead in 1805, and settled on No. 7, 9th Range, which they afterwards sold to Dudley Davis. He d. Feb. 26, 1812; she d. June 12, 1843. Their children were Phila, m. *John Sutton*; Sally, m. *Dean Haseltine*; Daniel, m. *Louisa Mix*; James, m. *Almira Boynton*; Harvey, m. *Mary Ann White*; and Calvin, who m. *Eliza McConnell*.

Family of Comfort Carpenter.

COMFORT CARPENTER married *Thankful Canfield*. They settled in Stanstead near the place now known as Smith's Mills, in 1800. Mr. Carpenter built a saw mill that year, the first erected in the town. He d. in 1806; she d. in 1851. Their children were

Theodosia, m. *Samuel Pinkham;* Thankful, m. *John Merrill;* Caleb, m. *Sarah Rogers;* Charles, m. *Eliza Eaton;* Persis, m. *Benjamin Tilton;* Harvey, m. *Esther Wright;* and Harriet, who m. *Ebenezer Barry.*

Family of John Barry.

JOHN BARRY, b. in Chester, N.H., July 21, 1776—m. *Lydia Worth,* b. in Hampton, N.H., in 1775. They settled on No. 8, 9th Range of Stanstead, in 1803. He d. in 1851; she d. in 1858. Their children were Lydia, Simeon, Daniel, John, Mary, Ebenezer, m. *Harriet Carpenter;* and David, who m. *Marietta Brown.*

Family of Hezekiah May.

HEZEKIAH MAY, b. in Strafford, Vt., March 3, 1775—m. *Sally Ham,* b. March 22, 1784. They settled on the west part of No. 7, 9th Range of Stanstead, in 1806. He d. Aug. 21, 1857; she d. in 1871.

CHILDREN.

ELECTA, b. July 19, 1806—m. *William Clarke, jun.*
SYLVESTER, b. April 17, 1808—m. *Elmeda Marsh.*
HANNAH, b. April 13, 1810—m. *Allen Martin.*
WILLARD, b. Nov. 14, 1813—m. *Mary A. Baldwin.*
LYMAN, b. April, 16, 1815—m. *Electa Hathaway.*
LORENZO, b. Sept. 9, 1818—m. *Emeline D. Mears.*
RUBY, b. May 19, 1820—m. *Dean Sutton.*
LOUISA, b. Jan. 30, 1823—d. July 21, 1838.
JAMES, b. March 4, 1825—m. *Amy Whitcomb.*
MARY ANN, b. June 18, 1827—d. Nov. 3, 1850.
MARIA A., b. May 30, 1830—m. *Dean Sutton,* 2nd wife.

Family of William Clark.

WILLIAM CLARK, b. in Andover, Mass., Feb. 14, 1771—m. *Betsey Danforth,* b. in Hollis, May 10, 1774. They settled on No. 9, 10th Range of Stanstead, in 1797. He d. March 28, 1846; she d. Feb. 14, 1843.

CHILDREN.

WILLIAM, b. Dec. 16, 1795—m. *Electa May.*
BALLARD, b. Aug. 31, 1797—m. *Hannah Rogers;* 2nd, *Marietta Whitcher.*

FAMILY OF CALVIN WILCOX.

LEONARD, b. July 14, 1799—m. *Wealthy Remich.*
BETSEY, b. June 2, 1801—d. May 31, 1826.
HANNAH, b. Sept 24, 1803—m. *Capt. Daniel Manseur.*
RUFUS, b. Nov. 14, 1805—m. *Miriam Worth.*
CUSHMAN, b. Aug, 12, 1807—m. *Betsey Rogers.*

Family of Jonathan Gordon.

JONATHAN GORDON, a native of Salem, Mass., m. *Esther Saunders.* Their ancestors emigrated from Scotland and settled in New Hampshire. They settled on No. 1, 12th Range of Stanstead, in 1800. He d. in 1812; she d. in 1834. Their children were *David, Phineas, Jonathan, Peaslee, Abigail, Betsey, Alexander, Jeremiah, Isaac, Esther, John,* and *Polly.* Isaac, m. *Mary Ann Bates.* He d. Nov. 25, 1854. His descendants are settled in Hatley.

Family of Nathan Stearns.

NATHAN STEARNS married *Mary Holmes.* Settled in Stanstead in 1804. Their children were Nathan, Mary, m. *Nicholas Fowler;* Nancy, m. *Samuel Bachelder;* Aliva, m. *Quartus Pomroy;* Cynthia, m. *Elijah Smith;* Horatio, Lucien, and Christopher. The family are mostly dead or have left the country.

Family of Samuel Stearns.

SAMUEL STEARNS, b. in Hollis, Mass., Nov. 30, 1761. June 2, 1800, m. *Sally Holmes,* b. in Campton, N.H., April 27, 1776. They settled in Stanstead in 1803. He d. May 2, 1858. Their children were *Samuel, John, Sally, Mary, Harry, Erastus, Almira, Lucy, Charles, Alice, Nathan,* and *Louisa.*

Family of Calvin Wilcox.

CALVIN WILCOX b. in Killingworth, Conn., April 27, 1781—m. *Clarissa Pope,* b. in Deering, N.H., March 18, 1789. They settled originally in Morgan, Vt., removed to Stanstead in 1817, and located on the east part of No. 5, 11th Range. They were members of the Wesleyan Church. He d. in 1868; she d. July 18, 1853.

CHILDREN.

RUTH, b. Dec. 30, 1811—d. Aug. 6, 1814.
PARDON B., b. Nov. 30, 1813—m. *Judith Allen* of Craftsbury Vt.

CALVIN, b. Dec. 25, 1815—m. 1845 *Charlotte M. Smith.* 3 children, none living.

LUTHER, b. Jan. 11, 1818—m. *Seraph Glidden;* 2nd, *Mary A. Rix.* Lives in Etna, Minn., 2 children.

ABEL A., b. Feb. 8, 1820—d. Sept. 3, 1830.

MARK P., b. March 7, 1822—m. *Margaret Robinson.* Lives in Holland, Vt.

LYDIA, b. March 6, 1825—m. *Thomas Clark.* 2 children. Lives on the homestead.

RICHARD P., b. March 31, 1827—m. *Sarah E. Edson.* Has 3 children.

CLARISSA, b. Dec. 18, 1830—d. Dec. 7, 1833.

The Peaslee Families.

These families were the descendants of *Paul Peaslee,* who came from England near the close of the 17th century and settled in Plaistow, N.H.

SILAS PEASLEE, b. in Plaistow, N.H., came to Stanstead in 1797, began on No. 10, 10th Range, sold out and settled near the Lake Shore upon a lot which he drew as an Associate. Some of his descendants are settled in that vicinity. Philip Peaslee, his son, was among the men that surveyed the township.

JEDEDIAH PEASLEE, b. in Plaistow, N.H.—m. *Judith Hunt.* They settled originally in Danville, Vt., came to Stanstead in 1803, and began on No. 9, 10th Range, sold out, and removed to the West in 1808. Their children were *Mary, James, Samuel, Hannah, Betsey, Sally, Nancy,* and *William.*

James Peaslee.

JAMES PEASLEE, son of Jedediah Peaslee, b: in Plaistow, N.H. Sept. 22, 1783. Came to Stanstead with his father in 1803: In 1807, m: *Priscilla Glidden,* b. in Sandwich, N.H., June 29, 1787. Settled on No. 9, 12th Range.

CHILDREN.

ALDEN S., b. Nov. 13, 1808—m. *Clara J. Burns.*
CHARLES, b. Sept. 23, 1810—m. *Susan Sargent.*
HULDAH, b. July 13, 1812—m. *John Manseur.*
JUDITH, b. July 17, 1814—m. *Alonzo Lee.*

FAMILY OF DANIEL BACHELDER. 209

Lois, b. Sept. 24, 1816.
Joseph, b. Dec. 29, 1818.
Orrin, b. Jan. 5, 1821.
Nancy, b. Feb. 7, 1823—m. C. T. Whitcher.

Family of John Sarles.

John Sarles, b. in 1782—m. *Sibyl Rose.* They settled on No. 7, 14th Range of Stanstead, in 1801. He d. June 17, 1858; she d. Oct. 12, 1849.

CHILDREN.

Edward, b. Sept. 1, 1805.
Cyrus, b. Feb. 22, 1808—m. *Roxana Cass.*
Luthera, b. April 8, 1812—m. *Tristram Rollins.*
Sibyl, b. April 22, 1810—m. *Joel Abbott.*
Almon, b. April 11, 1814—m. *Roxana Danforth.*
Horace, b. Nov. 9, 1816—m. *Marcella Durgan.*
Harry, b. in Nov., 1818—m. *Maria Smith.*
Praxo, b. in 1820—m. *John C. Kennison.*
Hiram, b. April 8, 1824.
Mary Ann, b. in Nov., 1826—m. *Orange Sprague.*
Gilman, b. July 6, 1829.

The Bachelder Families.

These families are the descendants of Jethro Bachelder who emigrated from England and settled in Loudon, N.H., in the 18th century.

Family of Daniel Bachelder.

Daniel Bachelder, b. in Loudon, N.H., m. *Judith Jedkins*, who was b. in Hopkinton, N.H. They settled on No. 9, 12th Range of Stanstead, in 1800. Judith, his wife, d. in 1796. He afterwards m. *Zeruiah Morrill.* She d. in 1853. He d. Feb. 17, 1832. 12 children, Jonathan, Dorothy, Hannah, Anna, Judith, Polly, Jethro, Abigail, Samuel, Nathaniel, Silas and Daniel.

Jonathan Bachelder.

Jonathan Bachelder, b. in Loudon, N.H., Oct. 9, 1796, began on No. 10, 9th Range of Stanstead, in 1800. In 1801—m. *Betsey Pinkham*, b. May 22, 1784. He d. Feb. 22, 1842.

CHILDREN.

JUDITH, b. Dec. 30, 1801—m. *Robert Kelsey.*
DANIEL, b. May 29, 1804—m. *Sally Chadwick.*
DAVID, b. June 12, 1806—m. *Amanda Kellum.*
ABIGAIL, b. April 11, 1808—d. in 1810.
ELECTA, b. April 8, 1810—m. *Israel Hoitt.*
SAMUEL P., b. May 23, 1812—m. *Mary Ann Hunt.*
AHATA, b. March 27, 1816—m. *Stephen Smith.*
JAMES W., b. Feb. 18, 1814—m. *Mary Ann Ingalls.*
MARTHA, b. Jan. 28, 1818—m. *Hollis Phipps.*
LASURA, b. Sept. 28, 1819—m. *David Houghton.*
ELIZA JANE, b. Nov. 2, 1821—m. *Joshua Little.*
SOPHRONIA, b. March 22, 1822—m. *David Hill.*
EMILY, b. Feb. 10, 1824—m. *Jonas Kent.*

Nathaniel Bachelder.

NATHANIEL BACHELDER, b. in Danville, Vt., Feb. 12, 1792. March 12, 1815—m. *Mary Wadleigh*, b. in Sutton, N.H., Dec. 20, 1797. They settled on No. 9, 12th Range of Stanstead. He d. in 1870; she d. in 1873.

CHILDREN.

SALLY, b. Feb. 28, 1816—m. 1st, *C. S. Knight;* 2nd, *Isaac Libbee.*
LAURA, b. May 30, 1817—m. *Daniel Colby.*
MARY, b. Aug. 17, 1822.
GEORGE, b. June 11, 1825—m. a *Miss King.*
ALICE, b. Nov. 27, 1839.

Jacob Bachelder.

JACOB BACHELDER, b. in Loudon, N.H., 1792—m. *Mehitable Blake,* b. in Epsom, N.H., Jan. 25, 1797. They settled on No. 12, 13th Range of Stanstead, in 1827. He d. Dec. 18, 1862. She d. Sept. 25, 1866.

CHILDREN.

FLORINDA, b. July 15, 1820—m. *Joshua S. Woodman.*
CAROLINE, b. May 1, 1822—m. *Truman Maxfield.*
JOHN L., b. May 9, 1829—m. *Harriet G. Small.*

Family of Capt. John Brown.

JOHN BROWN, b. in Epsom, N.H., Aug. 27, 1780. Nov. 25, 1802, m. *Hepzibah Wallace*, b. Aug. 15, 1781. They settled on No. 17, 9th Range of Stanstead in 1805. He was early appointed captain of militia, and held the office of deacon in the Congregational Church of Stanstead. He d. Feb. 4, 1843; she d. March 21st of the same year.

CHILDREN.

BETSEY P., b. Oct. 25, 1803—m. *William H. Davis.*
OZIAS G., b. March, 27, 1806—m. 1st, *Margaret Foss;* 2nd, *Mrs. H. Shurtliff.*
JOHN, b. July 17, 1810—d. Sept. 12, 1812.
LESTINA, b. Feb. 3, 1815—m. *Stephen Cass.*
CHESTER W., b. Dec. 11, 1828—m. *Nancy Shurtliff.*

Family of John Brown.

JOHN BROWN, brother of Theophilus Brown, was b. in Candia, N.H., Oct. 17, 1774—m. *Mehitable Robie*, b. May 2, 1775. They settled near Brown's Hill, in 1818. He d. September 10, 1856; she d. April 7, 1842.

CHILDREN.

SHERBURN S., b. in 1803—m. 1st, *Hannah Dustan;* 2nd, *Sylvia Richardson.*
JONATHAN R., b. April 12, 1806—m. *Sarah Rollins.*
ROBIE, b. September 22, 1809—m. *Flavilla Hopkins.*
Four other children died young.

Family of Israel Brainerd.

ISRAEL BRAINERD, b. in Campton, N.H., April 15, 1779. August 25, 1803—m. *Roxelana Houghton,* b. in Springfield, Vt., January 7, 1784. They settled on No. 17, 9th Range of Stanstead, in 1804. They were worthy members of the Congregational Church. Both deceased.

CHILDREN.

ROXELANA, b. August 4, 1804—m. *Aaron Davis.*
ISRAEL, b. February 12, 1807—m. *Rosamond Brown.*

ELICENA, b. March 9, 1809—d. in September, 1848.
DEBORAH, b. May 22, 1811—d. December 1, 1837.
JOB, b. July 26, 1813—d. March 2, 1818.
MIRIAM, b. September 5, 1815—d. March 16, 1818.
LYDIA, b. December 1, 1817—m. *Joshua R. Davis.*
TIMOTHY D., b. September 16, 1823—m. *Sophronia Cass.*
CHAUNCEY, b. September 27, 1825.

Family of Samuel Pinkham.

SAMUEL PINKHAM, b. in Durham, N.H., May 11, 1760. In 1783, m. *Dorothea Redway*, a native of Amesbury, Mass. They settled in Loudon, N.H., and in 1788 removed to Danville, Vt., whence they removed to No. 11, 9th Range of Stanstead, in 1800. He d. in May, 1830; she d. August 10. 1850.

CHILDREN.

BETSEY, b. May 22, 1784—m. *Jonathan Bachelder.*
DEBORAH, b. September 2, 1785—m. *Thomas Williams.*
SAMUEL, b. August 5, 1787—deceased.
SARAH, b. April 20, 1789—m. *Thomas Ruiter.*
MARY, b. May 20, 1791—m. *Ede Lee.*
JAMES, b. February 4, 1793—d. May 5, 1813.
JOSEPH, b. February 18, 1795—m. *Sarah Moulton.*
MARTHA, b. December 18, 1796—m. *Nathaniel Bartlett.*
DOROTHY, b. December 16, 1798—m. *Manda T. Cushing, Esq.*
ABIJAH, b. March 5, 1802—m. *Hannah Sleeper.*

The House Families.

The earliest account we can give of these families is that FRANCIS HOUSE married a *Miss Hammond*. They were natives of England, whence they came to America and settled in Salem, Mass. They afterwards removed to Fairlee, Vt., where, by a somewhat singular coincidence, they died of Spotted Fever within a few hours of each other. Their children were Francis, William, Esther, Sally, Hannah, John, Frederick, Benjamin and Grace. These all married and had families, who with scarcely an exception have been respected and valuable members of the communities in which they have lived; and many of them have occupied prominent positions in public life. Three only of the number settled in Cannda. Francis, Esther, who m. *Thomas Beebe*, and Grace, who m. *William Moulton.*

Family of Francis House.

FRANCIS HOUSE, b. in Fairlee, Vt. Settled in the vicinity of Beebe Plain, in 1800. The children were Hiram, Harry, Francis, Alvin, George and Lyman J.

HIRAM, eldest son of Francis House, was born in Stanstead, August 26, 1802—m. *Hannah Norris.* Settled near Beebe Plain in Derby, Vt. She d. in 1852. In 1859—m. *Nancy House.*

CHILDREN BY FIRST MARRIAGE.

HORACE, (adopted) b. February 19, 1828—m. *Ellen,* dau. of *David White.*
FRANCIS, b. March 9, 1830.
EMELINE, b. May 21, 1832—m. *Charles Boynton.*
JANE, b. February 11, 1834.
ELLEN, b. September 17, 1837.
CARLOS, b. January 31, 1845.

FRANCIS HOUSE, JUN., b. in Stanstead, December 30, 1805—m. *Lucinda,* dau. of *John Bragg,* b. September 18, 1812. They settled near Beebe Plain. He is a farmer.

CHILDREN.

EVELINA, b. September 18, 1832—d. in infancy.
HARRISON F., b. October 25, 1833—m. *Harriet Channell.*
SARAH A., b. May 19, 1836—d. in infancy.
LUTHER J., b. May 19, 1837.
MALVINA L., b. September 13, 1839.
EDWIN L., b. September 23, 1841.
MARY E., b. July 6, 1844.
ALBERT C., b. August 22, 1846.
CHARLES E., b. November 14, 1849.
JOSEPH B., b. December 27, 1851.
WILLIAM H., b. November 16, 1855—d. in infancy.

ALVIN HOUSE, third son of Francis House, was born in Stanstead, October 9, 1803. His opportunities of early education were limited to the common schools of the settlement, but he succeeded in acquiring a knowledge of the branches of a thorough English education, and was a successful teacher. He m. *Sally,* dau. of *Elisha Miller.* She d. in 1861. In 1865 he m. *Dimmis Smith,* b. April 23, 1802.

CHILDREN BY FIRST MARRIAGE

ROYAL S., b. September 27, 1827—m. *Isabella Ward*
SELON J., b. September 14, 1829.
ROANA, b. November 15, 1831—m. *Quimby Loveland.*
ALONZO A., b. February 27, 1834—m. *Susan Sager.*
ESTELLE V., b. August 17, 1839—m. *Edward House.*
EMMA F., b. February 4, 1845—m. *C. G. Boynton.*

GEORGE HOUSE, fourth son of Francis House, was b. in Stanstead, August 27, 1807. In 1833—m. *Lucy,* dau. of *Henry Lee.* They settled near the family homestead. She d. December 5, 1845. In 1846 he m. *Persis Kittredge,* b. December 9, 1805. She d. March 20, 1870. One child by first marriage; one child by second marriage.

HARRY HOUSE, 5th son of Francis House, was b. in Stanstead, in 1809—m. *Pamelia,* dau. of *James Porter.* They settled near Beebe Plain.

CHILDREN.

JAMES W., b. February 9, 1833—m. *Lavinia Harvey*—d. in 1857. In 1860 he m. *Mary Bull.*
LYDIA, b. July 13, 1836—m. *Thomas Jenkins.*
AMELIA L., b. November 26, 1846—m. *M. Dixon, Esq.*

JOHN L. HOUSE, 6th son of Francis House, was b. in Stanstead, July 16, 1811—m. *Mary Ann,* dau. of *Dexter White.* Settled at Beebe Plain, where Mr. H. is extensively engaged in mercantile business, and holds the office of Postmaster.

CHILDREN.

DENISON L., b. October 12, 1841; is engaged in mercantile business, and holds the appointment of Postmaster.
MILO D., b. November 24, 1843.
MARY C., b. August 1, 1848.
GEORGE H., b. June 2, 1857.

The Stewart Families.

The earliest record we can find of these families is that JOHN STEWART came from Scotland to America about the middle of the past century; that during his passage he made the acquaintance of *Anne Newton,* whom he afterwards married. They settled in Brattleboro', Vt. Families of this name are found in England,

Scotland and Ireland, and are widely scattered over the United States and Canada; but all who spell their names Stuart or Stewart, could probably be traced to the same source; as far back, at least, as to the time of James the First, King of England.

Two of the sons of John Stewart above mentioned, settled in Derby, Vt. Rufus was a prominent man in the settlement, and took an active part in the management of public affairs; received the appointment of Major in the Militia; was one of the founders of Lively Stone Lodge. In early life he married *Jane Fraser.* She d. October, 1840; he d. June 29, 1846, aged 71 years. Their children were Harriet, who m. *George Robinson;* Maria, who m. *Jacob Bates;* Horace, m. *Catherine Hinman;* Nancy, m. *Aaron Hinman, Esq.;* Emory, m. *Julia Daggett,* and Jane, m. *Martin Newcomb.* Of these, Horace, only, settled in Canada.

John Stewart, brother of Rufus, settled in Derby, but after some 20 years, removed to the South. His children and their descendants reside mostly in the Southern States.

Family of Horace Stewart, Esq.

HORACE STEWART was born in Derby, Vt., September 25, 1804. He married *Catherine,* dau. of *Hon. Timothy Hinman,* b. October 26, 1806. They settled at Beebe Plain, in 1826. In early life he engaged in mercantile business, and was eminently successful. He was a careful financier, and riches seemed to flow into his hands almost spontaneously. He is now one of the wealthiest men in the county. Had he been ambitious of public distinctions he could, probably, have attained to any position of honor he might have wished, but he wisely chose the enjoyments of home and domestic life. To the interests of the village where he resides he has been a liberal contributor.

CHILDREN.

MARTHA M., b. April 28, 1831—m. *Carlos F. Haskell.* He was for many years engaged in an extensive mercantile business at Rock Island, P.Q. He d. July 2, 1865.

RUFUS R., b. January 19, 1836—m. *Annie S. Brown.* Is a successful business man, and bids fair to sustain a prominent position in the community.

HARRIET L., b. September 28, 1838—d. October 21, 1858.

HOEL S., b, July 19, 1842—d. August 22, 1868.

The Steele Families.

The first persons known in America by this name were two brothers, James and Stephen Steele, who emigrated from England about 1640. They were both Congregational Ministers of the Puritan stamp. One settled in Tolland, and the other in Ellington, Conn. In later years, various families of the name have emigrated from Scotland and Ireland, but these omit the final *e*, in the orthography of their name,

Family of Zadok Steele.

ZADOK STEELE, a grandson of James Steele, above mentioned, was b. in Tolland, Conn., Dec. 17, 1758. At the age of 16 he enlisted into the American Army as waiter to his father, who held a commission in the Continental Service, in the time of the Revolution. He remained in the army nearly three years; and at the close of the term of his enlistment, commenced a settlement in the town of Randolph, Vt., then an almost unbroken wilderness. Here he was captured by a company of Indians who were on their return from the burning of Royalton—a town lying 10 miles south from Randolph. He was taken by the Indians to Canada; and, after passing through a captivity of two years, in which he experienced almost unparalleled hardships and suffering, succeeded in making his escape, and returned to the place he had previously purchased in Randolph. He published a narrative of his captivity and sufferings, to which the reader is referred. Feb. 10, 1785, he m. *Hannah*, dau. of *Mr. William Shurtliff*, of Ellington, Conn. In 1815, he came to Stanstead, and purchased the lots, Nos. 1 and 2, 7th Range, comprising the site of the village of Beebe Plain, and moved his family in, the following year. In 1825, he divided his property between his two youngest sons, Solomon and Sanford. He d. March 28, 1845, in the 87th year of his age. His wife d. Sept. 25, of the same year. "They were lovely in their lives, and in their death, they were not (long) divided." They were consistent and exemplary members of the Congregational Church.

CHILDREN.

ABIGAIL, b. in Randolph, Vt., May 24, 1787—m. *E. Smith, Esq.* He d. in 1842.

HIRAM, b. in Randolph, Vt., Feb. 1, 1789. In 1812—m. *Abigail Keenan.* They settled at Sackett's Harbor, N.Y., where he sustained the office of Judge for the county in which he lived; and held other important offices. He d. in 1838.

HORACE, b. in Randolph, Vt., March 1, 1791. Studied law, and was admitted to the bar, at Montpelier, in 1820. His taste for literary pursuits induced him to relinquish, measurably, the duties of his profession, and for many years he sustained the editorial department of different newspapers in Vermont, New York and Ohio. He is now living with his 3rd wife, in Ohio.

ZADOK, JUN., b. in Randolph, Vt., Jan. 11, 1793. In 1822, m. *Theda*, dau. of *Mr. Lemuel Wright*, of Stanstead. They settled in Watertown, N.Y.

JAMES, b. in Brookfield, Vt., Jan. 25, 1795. Studied law at the Guildhall, Vt., and was admitted to the bar, in 1829. Commenced practice at Canaan, Vt., but subsequently returned to Guildhall, where he continued a lucrative business until 1851, when, from the failure of his health, he retired. He d. Dec. 6, 1857.

ROSWELL, b. in Brookfield, Vt., April 14, 1797. A successful merchant; was engaged in trade several years at Salina, N.Y. He d. of cholera, Aug. 12, 1834.

SOLOMON, b. in Brookfield, Vt., Aug. 20, 1799. Came to Stanstead with his parents in 1816. In 1832, he m. *Eliza*, dau. of *Dr. Joseph Whyte* of Banff, Scotland. His early years were spent in teaching. From 1836 to 1857, he held the successive appointments of commissioner for the summary trial of small causes and magistrate. He was a practical farmer, and had brought his farm of 280 acres into a state of high cultivation, but in the fall of 1856, his house, barns and out-buildings were destroyed by fire. He sold out in 1857, and removed to Derby, Vt. His 3rd son is a graduate of the Medical College of Philadelphia, and is a successful practitioner.

SOPHRONIA, b. in Brookfield, Vt., April 13, 1802—m. *Harvey W. Carpenter, Esq.* She d. in 1859; he d. in 1849.

SANFORD, b. in Brookfield, Vt., April 13, 1804. Settled upon the farm adjoining that of his brother Solomon. Dec. 14, 1835, he m. *Mary*, dau. of *Benjamin Hinman, Esq.*, of Derby, Vt. He d. Sept. 4, 1856. Benjamin H. Steele, his eldest son, graduated at Dartmouth. Studied law, and became eminently distinguished in his profession, received the appointment of Judge of the Orleans County Court. He d. in 1872.

Hiram, the second son, served as captain in the army of the late

218 FORESTS AND CLEARINGS.

American Rebellion. Sanford Steele was a model farmer, a kind husband and father, and an exemplary christian.

HANNAH, b. in Brookfield, Vt., April 10, 1807—m. *Henry B. Perkins.* She d. June 26, 1842.

Family of Israel Williams.

ISRAEL WILLIAMS, b. August 27, 1760—m. *Mary Collins,* b. September 6, 1767. They were natives of Guilford, Vt.; came to Stanstead in 1809, and located on No. 3, 6th Range, near Glines' Corner. He d. in 1817; she d. in 1857.

CHILDREN.

DANIEL, b. November 5, 1794—m. *Sarah Wilson.*
JOEL, b. December 17, 1796—m. *Almira Wilson.*
MARY, b. in 1799—d. in 1811.
JOHN, b. in 1801—m. *Miriam Abbey.*
HANNAH, b. in 1803—m. *Charles Carpenter.*
CHESTER, b. in 1805—m. *Lucy Collins.*
JEFFERSON, b. in 1807—m. *Maria Starks.*
WARREN, b. in 1809.
LYMAN, b. in 1811—m. *Julia Todd.*

Family of James Porter.

JAMES PORTER, b, in Oxford, Conn., August 28, 1772—m. *Margaret Tilton,* b. August 28, 1774, and settled in Stanstead near the Lake Shore, in 1800. He d. in 1860; she d. in 1852.

CHILDREN.

FREDERICK, b. September 29, 1795—m. *Anne Hamilton.*
ZACHARIAH, b. July 22, 1797—m. *Mary Kingsbury.*
Ira, b. July 23, 1799—d. in 1811.
MATILDA, b. November 16, 1801—m. *Squire Wood.*
WILLIAM, b. February 16, 1804—m. *Ruth Hunt.*
JANE, b. March 23, 1806—d. in 1811.
LOUISA, b. April 24, 1808—m. *Charles Gardner.*
PAMELA, b. March 17, 1810—m. *Harry House.*
HANNAH, b. February 16, 1814.
JAMES, b. April 10, 1816—d. in 1820.

Family of John Bragg.

JOHN BRAGG, b. in Springfield, Vt., April 16, 1781—m. *Sally Gilman,* b. in Northfield, Vt., December 2, 1785. They resided in

Montreal about 8 years, and afterwards settled in Stanstead. He died in 1825. She subsequently married *Jonathan Magoon.* Children by her first marriage, Lucinda, who m. *Francis House;* Sarah, m. *Andrew Bodwell;* Samuel G., m. *Lorinda Beebe;* Joseph W., Mary Jane, m. *Gardner Blount;* and Elizabeth, who .m. *Joseph Frischl.*

Family of John Moir.

JOHN MOIR, b. in 1796—m. *Mary Morrison,* b. in 1795 They were natives of Scotland. She d. in 1829. In 1831, he m. *Sophia Nicol,* b. in Banff, Scotland, in 1807. They emigrated to Canada with three children of the previous marriage, two of whom died on their passage. Mr. M. and his family settled on No. 3, 5th Range of Stanstead.

CHILDREN BY FIRST MARRIAGE.

WILLIAM, b. in 1823—m. *Jane Ball;* settled in Iowa.

CHILDREN BY SECOND MARRIAGE

MARY, b. March 15, 1832—m. a *Mr. Cleaveland;* d. in 1856.
JOHN, b. May 25, 1835.
GEORGE, b. April 12, 1837.
DAVID, b. July 18, 1842.
SOPHIA, b. June 24, 1845.

The Gilman Families.

We cannot find any authentic account of the early history of these families. They are of English extraction, and their ancestors must have been among the early colonists of America, as families of this name are scattered widely over the United States and Canada.

Family of Capt. Samuel T. Gilman.

CAPT. SAMUEL T. GILMAN m. *Sally Hurd.* They were natives of Exeter, N.H.; settled originally in Northfield, Vt.; removed to Stanstead in 1804, and located on No. 6, 7th Range. He d. in 1840; she d. in 1855. Their children were Lucy, Betsey, Sally, Polly, John, Nathaniel, and Samuel. Two children died in infancy.

JOHN, eldest son of Capt. S. T. Gilman, was born in Northfield, Vt., September 23, 1791—m. *Lydia,* dau. of *John Gustin, Esq.*

They settled near Griffin Corner. He was a wealthy farmer, an influential man in the community; received the appointment of Captain of Cavalry in 1837, and was in the service during the time of the Rebellion. He was one of the Directors of the Conn. and Pass. Railroad. He d. in 1866.

CHILDREN.

JOHN G., b. May 3, 1816; engaged in mercantile business at Rock Island several years. He d. October 29, 1850.

LUCY, b. September 4, 1818—d. in infancy.

MARY ANN, b. May 27, 1821—m. *Daniel W. Mack.*

LYDIA, b. February 2, 1824—m. *Charles Weston.* D. in 1857.

JAMES K., b. October 24, 1828—m. *Cynthia*, dau. of *L. K. Benton, Esq.* Sustains the office of Captain of Infantry; is otherwise engaged in public affairs.

SARAH H., b. December 27, 1830—m. *Austin T. Foster, Esq.* He is extensively engaged in mercantile business.

NATHANIEL, b. June 7, 1833.

CHARLOTTE RUTH, b. February 5, 1836—m. *Benjamin F. Knight.*

SAMUEL, youngest son of S. T. Gilman, came with his parents to Stanstead in 1804, when a mere lad. He married *Fanny*, dau. of *Abijah Mack.* They settled at Beebe Plain. He was for some time engaged in mercantile business, and otherwise employed in public affairs, and during the time of the Rebellion served as Captain of Cavalry.

Family of Capt. Eliphalet Bodwell, Sen.

ELIPHALET BODWELL, SEN., b. in Methuen, Mass., July 21, 1767. Nov. 13, 1794—m. *Betsey Currier*, b. in Unity, N.H., Sept. 30, 1773. Settled at Griffin Corner, 1800. Received the appointment of Captain of Militia in 1814. He d. Feb., 1847; she d. in 1871.

CHILDREN.

ARNOLD, b. July 22, 1795—d. Feb. 19, 1798.

ELIPHALET, b. March 1, 1797—m. *Matilda*, dau. of *Col. C. Kilborn.*

BETSEY, b. Sept. 4, 1799—m. *Elisha Gustin, Esq.*

HANNAH, b. Feb. 10, 1802—m. *Roswell Verback.*

ANDREW, b. April 18, 1804—m. 1st, *Ruth Gustin;* 2nd, *Sarah Bragg.*

FAMILY OF CALEB WHITE.

HORACE, b. Feb. 1, 1809—m. *Lurany Mack.*
PAMELA, b. July 12, 1806—m. *Cephas Gardner.*
LORENZO, b. June 13, 1810—d. Dec. 19, 1820.
EMELINE, b. Dec. 2, 1813—d. Feb. 21, 1821.
Wellington, b. July 31, 1816—m. *Mary Ann Cobb.*

James Bodwell,

Brother of Capt. Eliphalet Bodwell, sen., married Maria Glidden. They settled at the place now called Mack's Mills. He built a Grist Mill, sold to Ephraim Hopping and left the country.

Joab Bodwell,

Brother of Capt. Eliphalet Bodwell, sen., married *Hannah Glidden.* They settled at Griffin Corner in 1801. He d. in 1843; she d. in 1860. Joseph, their youngest son, married Chestina Rollins.

Family of Capt. Eliphalet Bodwell, jun.

CAPT. ELIPHALET BODWELL, JUN., b. in Unity, N.H., March 1, 1797. April 23, 1822—m. *Matilda,* dau. of *Col. Charles Kilborn,* b. in Stanstead Nov. 1, 1802. They settled near "The Narrows." He has for many years sustained the office of Captain of Militia.

CHILDREN.

BETSEY E., b. March 20, 1823—m. *Anson Beebe.*
EDWARD F. G., b. Dec. 24, 1824—m. *Adelia Pearsol.*
JULIA ANN, b. June 10, 1828—d. Feb. 19, 1847.
HARRIET C., b. July 8, 1830—m. *W. C. Copp.*
CHARLES W., b. March 2, 1834—d. March 25, 1861.
Mary E., b. Feb. 10, 1836—d. Jan. 16, 1841.
MARGARET E., b. Oct. 21, 1841—d. Oct. 29, 1864.

Family of Caleb White.

CALEB WHITE, b. in Sutton, Mass., in 1777—m. *Martha Henderson.* Settled on No. 9, 5th Range of Stanstead, in 1801, afterwards removed to Griffin Corner. Both deceased.

CHILDREN.

ROSWELL, b. in 1800—m. *Emily Comstock.*
HENRY, b. in 1804—m. *Martha A. Lambkin.*

MEHITABLE, b. in 1806—m. *Orrin Hunt.*
ERASTUS, b. in 1808—m. *Mary Comstock.*
LUCY H., b. in 1810—m. *Luther Verback.*
CLARINDA, b. in 1813—m. 1st, *Jefferson Boody;* 2nd, *Stephen Comstock.*
NANCY, b. in 1815—m. *Henry Morrill.*
PHILENA, b. in 1819.

Family of Dexter White.

DEXTER WHITE was born in Sutton, Mass., in 1785—m. *Mary Glidden,* b. in Unity, N.H., April 27, 1788. Settled near Griffin Corner, and died in 1838. She afterwards m. *Jonathan Richardson.*

CHILDREN.

HOSEA, b. Jan. 3, 1807—m *Maria Morgan.*
HELEN M., b. March 27, 1811—m. *Harry Comstock.*
OSWALD, b. June 10, 1813—m. *Betsey Clute.*
ANDREW, b. Dec. 16, 1815—m. *Emily Tilton.*
MARY ANN, b. Jan. 3, 1818—m. *John L. House, Esq.*
ELIZA J., b. Feb. 16, 1829—d. in 1839.

Family of Hosea White.

HOSEA WHITE married *Grata Wright.* They settled near Griffin Corner, in Stanstead. Their children were Lewis, Elisha G., Rufus L., Lemuel W., Hosea J., Semantha, Charles, Harriet, and Edwin, Hosea White, sen., d. in 1856 ; his wife d. in 1846.

Family of Philip Verback.

PHILIP VERBACK, b. in Framingham, Mass., March 22, 1760—m, *Sarah Martin,* b. in Bradford, Vt., March 15, 1766. Settled on No. 2, 4th Range of Stanstead, in 1806. He d. Dec. 30, 1856; She d. July 16, 1852.

CHILDREN.

NATHANIEL, b. March 5, 1786—m. *Miriam Tilton.*
LOIS, b. March 23, 1788—m. *Morrill Magoon.*
THANKFUL, b. Feb. 11, 1790—m *Samuel Collins.*
WILLIAM, b. April 28, 1792—m. *Sarah Colby.* He sustained the offices of deacon in the Congregational Church of Derby for many years. D. in 1867.

BENJAMIN, b. Aug. 20, 1794—d. in 1815.
CALVIN, b. Sept. 20, 1796—m. *Judith Small.*
ROSWELL, b. April 19, 1799—m. *Hannah Bodwell.*
JEREMIAH, b. Feb. 18, 1801—m. *Damaris Morey.*
JEHIEL, b. May 26, 1804—m. *Betsey Morey.*
LUTHER, b. Oct. 1, 1808—m. *Lucy White.*

Family of Osmyn Smith.

OSMYN SMITH, b. in Unity, N.H., Aug. 19, 1806. April 8, 1834, m. *Sarah Magoon*, b. in Stanstead, April 5, 1809. She d. Oct. 8, 1839. May 5, 1842, m. *Martha J. Magoon.* She d. April 25, 1862.

CHILDREN BY 1ST MARRIAGE.

OSMYN F., b. April 17, 1835.
LEWIS N., b. June 18, 1838.

Family of Luther Comstock.

LUTHER COMSTOCK, b. in Newport, N.H., June 8, 1781—m. *Celia Wilmoth*, b. in Attleborough, Mass., Oct. 29, 1780. They settled in Stanstead in 1815. He d. in 1860; she d. 1862.

CHILDREN.

WILLARD, b. Nov. 15, 1804—d. Nov. 24, 1835.
HARRY, b. Sept. 30, 1806—m. *Helen M. White.*
MARTIN, b. June 11, 1809—has buried his 2nd wife.
STEPHEN, b. Jan. 24, 1811—m. *Clarinda White.*
ELIZABETH, b. Aug. 1, 1816—m. *D. W. Mack, Esq.*
CHARLES, b. Oct. 14, 1819—m. *Annis Peaslee.*
MARY, b. May 7, 1823—m. *Erastus White.*

Family of Edward Worth.

EDWARD WORTH, b. in Corinth, Vt., July 28, 1778—m. *Nancy Merrill.* They settled on No. 3, 8th Range of Stanstead. His wife d. in 1855. In 1857, he m. *Isabel Merrill.* She d. in 1862; he d. in 1868. 12 children, *Nancy, Edward, Charles, Betsey, Harriet, George, Lewis, Galusha, Emily, Simon, Jacob,* and *Lydia.*

Family of Joel Smith.

JOEL SMITH, b. in Winchendon, Mass., April 22, 1773—m. *Polly Nourse*, b. Dec. 10, 1779. Engaged in mercantile business for some time in Unity, N.H., where his wife d. In 1807, he removed to Stanstead and settled on No. 7, 9th Range. In 1814—m. *Clarissa Carpenter*, b. Aug. 10, 1790 ; d. April 25, 1857. Mr. Smith d. Aug. 15, 1867, aged, 94 years.

CHILDREN BY 1ST MARRIAGE.

PHILIP N., b. Feb. 8, 1800—m. *Ethelinda Mack.*
JOEL, JUN., b. May 29, 1802—m. *Harriet Drew.*
PERMELIA, b. July 5, 1804—d. in 1812.
OSMYN, b. Aug. 19, 1806—m. *Sarah Magoon.*

CHILDREN BY 2ND MARRIAGE.

CHAUNCEY W., b. June 9, 1815.
SCHYLER S., b. Jan. 1, 1819.

Philip N. Smith.

PHILIP N. SMITH, b. Feb. 8, 1800—m. *Ethelinda*, dau. of *Silas Mack*. They settled at Smith's Mills. Their children were Charlotte, who m. *Calvin Wilcox, jun.* ; Delphine, m. *Wm. P. Mack* ; and Polly N.

Joel Smith, jun.

JOEL SMITH, JUN., b. in Unity, N.H., May 29, 1802—m. *Harriet Drew*, b. in Goshen, Vt., Oct., 11, 1806. She d. Nov. 11, 1845. July 14, 1847—m. *Abigail Skinner.* She d. Oct. 21, 1852. May 23, 1854—m. *Fanny Parker.*

CHILDREN.

JOEL E., b. Feb. 26, 1827.
WILLIAM D., b. May 2, 1829—d. Jan. 8, 1856.
ETHELINDA, b. July 20, 1831.
SCHUYLER, b. July, 1835.
HARRIET M., b. Oct. 1, 1843.

Family of John Gustin, jun.

JOHN GUSTIN, JUN., b. in Lyme, Conn., Sept. 27, 1768—m. *Esther Way*, b. Aug. 26, 1771. She d. April 14, 1837 ; he d. Nov. 26, 1841.

CHILDREN.

ELISHA, b. May 9, 1791.
LYDIA, b. June 11, 1793—m. *Capt. John Gilman.*

FAMILY OF JOSIAH GUSTIN, JUN.

LEONARD, b. Oct. 16, 1796—d. Dec. 19, 1864.
ETHELINDA, b. Sept. 2, 1798—d. Jan. 20, 1820.
POLLY, b. Oct. 5, 1800—m. *Franklin Mack, Esq.*
RUTH, b. March 9, 1809—m. *Andrew Bodwell.*
ESTHER, b. June 11, 1810—m. *Willard Miller;* 2nd, *John Taylor.*
ELISHA GUSTIN, b. May 9, 1791—m. *Betsey Bodwell.* He ,d. March 28, 1868.

CHILDREN.

CHRISTOPHER O., b. July 26, 1819—was appointed Magistrate in 1864.
EMELINE, b. Feb. 23, 1821—d. Sept. 12, 1822.
ELIPHALET B., b. June 9, 1826—m. *Mary Bean.*
ETHELINDA, (adopted,) b. April 11, 1834.

Family of Josiah Gustin.

JOSIAH GUSTIN, b. in Lyme, Conn., in 1749—m. *Margaret Wardner,* a native of New York. They settled originally in Marlow, N.H. In 1806, located on No. 17, 6th Range of Stanstead. He d. in 1810. She survived him many years, and died at the advanced age of 97 years. Their children were Samuel, Philip, Josiah, Aaron, Levi, Catherine, Lydia, Margaret, Mary, and Sarah. These all married and had families. Some of their descendants settled in Stanstead.

Family of Josiah Gustin, jun.

JOSIAH GUSTIN, JUN., b. in Marlow, N.H., April 25, 1788. March 31, 1814, m. *Esther Kimpton,* b. June 17, 1796. They settled in the vicinity of Fitch Bay. He sustained the office of Major of Militia.

CHILDREN.

LORIAN, b. June 29, 1817—m. *Abigail Wood.*
ABIGAIL, b. May 31, 1819—m. *John Brown.*
JOSIAH, b. Oct. 22, 1821—m. *Lucy Clefford.*
NORMAN, b. March 22, 1829—m. *Mary Cathy.*
WILLIAM, b. July 18, 1832—m. *Caroline Buzzell.*
JOHN, b. July 27, 1834—m. *Phedora Gage.*
ESTHER, b. March 14, 1837—m. *Gilbert Blake.*

Family of Aaron Gustin.

AARON GUSTIN, b. in Marlow, N. H., April 5, 1793—m. *Miriam Flanders*, b. in Chelsea, Vt., Nov. 9, 1799. They settled in the vicinity of Fitch Bay, in 1806.

CHILDREN.

LYMAN, b. March 15, 1818—m. *Mary Brown.*
LAURA, b. Oct. 22, 1819—m. *Samuel Mix.*
EMILY, b. Feb. 7, 1822—m. *John Huckins.*
LEVI, b. April 10, 1824—m. *Sarah Small.*
JOHN, b. April 12, 1826—m. *Emily Walker.*
AMOS, b. March 6, 1828—m. *Harriet Robinson.*
MARSHALL, b. March 7, 1834—m. *Mary Ann Osman.*
SEMANTHA, b. Sept. 6, 1836—m. *Ephraim Hanson.*
MARY, b. July 22, 1838—d. June 8, 1853.
LAVINIA, b. Feb 15, 1841.
JULIA ANN, b. Oct. 3, 1845.
Two other children died young.

Family of Abijah Mack.

ABIJAH MACK, b. in Lyme, Conn.,Jan. 7, 1769—m. *Lurany Gustin*, b. Sept. 23, 1770. They were among the pioneers of the Marlow settlement in 1801.

CHILDREN.

PHEBE, b. Oct. 18, 1788—m. *Peter Rowe.*
CLARISSA, b. May 17, 1791—d. March 17, 1813.
SEBRE, b. Nov. 13, 1792—d. Aug. 9, 1799.
WILLARD, b. Nov. 4, 1794—d. Oct. 9, 1822.
FANNY, b. Aug. 18, 1796—m. *Capt. Samuel Gilman.*
SEBRE, 2nd, b. May 4, 1798—m. *Nancy Wright.*
LYDIA, b. April 20, 1801—m. *Harlow Drew.*
ZOPHAR, b. March 17, 1803—m. *Betsey Mansur.*
ABIJAH, b. March 17, 1805—d. Dec. 8, 1808.
LUCRETIA, b. May 26, 1807—m. *Calvin Verback.*
LURANY, b. Feb. 22, 1809.—m. *Horace Bodwell.*
One child died young.

Family of Silas Mack.

SILAS MACK, b. in Marlow, N.H., Sept 8, 1778. Jan. 7, 1802—

FAMILY OF FRANKLIN MACK. 227

m. *Ethelinda Way*, b. in Lyme, Conn., Aug. 2, 1780. They settled on No. 9, 7th Range of Stanstead, in 1816. She d. July 10, 1848. He d. May 13, 1853.

CHILDREN.

CHARLOTTE, b. Jan. 9, 1803—m. *Asa Masten.*
ETHELINDA, b. April 6, 1805—m. *Philip N. Smith.*
SILAS W., b. April 29, 1807—m. *Dorothy Davis.*
DANIEL W., ESQ., b. June 15, 1812—m. 1st, *Elizabeth Comstock;* 2nd, *Mary Harvey;* 3rd, *Mary Ann Gilman.* He sustained the office of magistrate, and was otherwise employed in public affairs.
MARY ANN, b. Dec. 24, 1819—m. *Martin Comstock.*

Family of Asa Mack.

ASA MACK, b. in Marlow, N.H., Feb. 18, 1791—m. *Sally Atwood,* b. Dec. 8, 1792. They settled on the east half of No. 13, 4th Range of Stanstead, in 1822; afterwards removed to Cabot, Vt.

CHILDREN.

BETSEY B., b. March 16, 1815—m. *Ezra Magoon.*
POLLY M., b. Nov. 15, 1818—m. *Rufus Miller.*
JOHN A., b. Oct. 23, 1820—m. *Cordelia A. Stevens.*
CLARISSA G., b. June 23, 1824—m. *Jesse Morse.*
SALLY L., b. March 8, 1826—m. *Luther Dutton.*
ASA B., b. April 5, 1828—m. a *Miss Kenuston.*

Family of Franklin Mack, Esq.

FRANKLIN MACK, b. in Marlow, N.H., March 26, 1795. The early years of his life were spent in teaching. He settled on the east half of No. 13, 4th Range of Stanstead, in 1822. Was for many years one of the managers of the Elementary Schools of the Township, sustained the office of magistrate, and successively that of Mayor of the Township and County Councils. He m. *Polly,* dau. of *John Gustin, jun.*

CHILDREN.

ORVILLE, b. in 1831.
WILLIAM P., b. Oct. 2, 1833—m. *Delphine L. Smith.*

Family of Jasper Ball.

JASPER BALL, b. in Strafford, Vt., Sept. 26, 1797—m. *Polly Mack*, b. Nov. 13, 1798. They settled in Stanstead, but afterwards removed to Iowa.

CHILDREN.

LOREN, b. May 24, 1824—d. Sept. 24, 1845.
OSCAR F., b. Sept 7, 1826—m. *Mary Hunt.*
MARY M., b. April 26, 1829—m. *S. S. Pinkham.*
OLIVE J., b. May 28, 1831—m. *William J. Moir.*
LUCY, b. April 20, 1834—d. young.
HARRIET E., b. Oct. 10, 1841—m. *Richard F. Ripley.*

Family of Lemuel Wright.

LEMUEL WRIGHT m. *Deborah Erskine.* They were natives of Connecticut and Massachusetts. They settled near Griffin Corner, Stanstead, in 1800. He d. in 1846. She d. in 1843. Their children were Malinda, who m., 1st, *Wm. Lanphire;* 2nd, *Warren Burr;* Grata, Philena, m. *Barach Burpee;* Seraph, m. *Alanson Ball;* Theda, m. *Zadock Steele, jr.,* Nancy, m. *Sebre Mack*, Sally, Lemuel Betsey and Ira.

Family of William Lanphire.

WILLIAM LANPHIRE, b. Dec. 15, 1781—m. *Malinda Wright.* They settled in the Marlow neighborhood. He d. July 3, 1813. She subsequently m. *Warren Burr.*

CHILDREN.

WILLIAM, b. Feb. 28, 1805.
BETSEY, b. Jan. 16, 1807—m. *John Tibbets.*
MATILDA, b. Dec. 13. 1810—m. *Gardner Ayer.*
2 children d. in infancy.

Family of Warren Burr.

WARREN BURR m. *Malinda,* widow of *William Lanphire.* They settled on the Lanphire homestead.

FAMILY OF HUGH ELDER.

CHILDREN.

SAREPTA, b. May 6, 1816—m. *Stimson Drew.*
LUCINDA, b. May, 29, 1821.
MARY, b. Aug. 15, 1825.
NANCY, b. April 10, 1827.
CHESTINA, b. May 14, 1829.

Family of Moses Blount.

MOSES BLOUNT, b. Dec. 6, 1793—m. *Lydia Boynton,* b. Aug. 15, 1791. They were among the early settlers of Stanstead. He d. Sept. 12, 1834.

CHILDREN.

MOSES, b. Jan. 18, 1811—d. Feb. 17, 1813.
SOPHRONIA, b. March 30, 1814—d. Aug. 11, 1822.
EMILY, b. June 21, 1817—d. Aug. 13, 1822.
HARRIET, b. May 5, 1821—d. Aug. 25, 1822.
GARDNER, b. Aug. 11, 1823.
MOSES, 2d., b. Nov. 8, 1828.
6 children d. in infancy.

Family of Asa Blount.

ASA BLOUNT m. *Nancy Boynton.* They settled in the Marlow neighborhood. In 1819 he was killed by a fall from a load of hay. She afterwards m. *Heman Lindsey.* Mr. Blount left two children, Orpheus and Asa. Mr. Lindsey d. about 1855. 2 children, Osmond and Clarissa.

Family of Hugh Elder.

HUGH ELDER, b. in Lanarkshire, Scotland, Aug. 2, 1798. Graduated at the University of Edinburgh in 1822. Had been educated in view of the Ministry, but preferring the occupation of teaching, he engaged in it and was very successful. May 25, 1829, he m. *Margaret Thompson,* of Lanarkshire. They came to Canada, in 1830, and we find them successively in Montreal, Ottawa City and Stanstead. He was for some time Principal of Stanstead Seminary, and subsequently taught several years in other parts of the Township. He has sustained a prominent place in the management of the educational affairs of the Township, and has been distinguished for his efforts in the Temperance Reformation.

CHILDREN.

JESSIE ANN, b. March 29, 1830—m. *John Buchanan, M.D.*
AGNES H., b. April 22, 1832—m. *Samuel Collins.*
HUGH W., b. May 18, 1834—m. *Susan Watson.*
DAVID T., b. May 28, 1836—m. *Philinda Tilton.*
JOHN G., b. Aug. 20, 1841—m. *Sarah Bryant.*

The Drew Families.

The earliest record we can find of these families is that John Drew, who was born May 20, 1724, m. *Mary Northcops;* that June 24, 1760, he m. *Joanna Thorps*, and that Dec. 4, 1787, he m. *Joanna Lacy.* He d. March 1, 1819, aged 95 years. Three of his sons, Noah, Samuel and Abel, settled in Stanstead.

CHILDREN.

WILLIAM, b. July 28, 1746.
JOHN, b. Dec. 16, 1749.
ISAAC, b. June 17, 1752.
PETER b. April 22, 1754.
MARY, b. March 29, 1758.
HANNAH, b. Feb. 9, 1760.
SARAH, b. May 12, 1762.
DANIEL, b. April 24, 1764.
ANNA, b. Oct. 30, 1765.
NOAH, b. Aug. 8, 1768.
SAMUEL, b. March 21, 1770.
ABEL, b. March 20, 1773.
ASAHEL, b. Aug. 29, 1776.

Family of Samuel Drew.

SAMUEL DREW, b. March 21, 1770. Feb. 26, 1792—m. *Ruth McDuffee*, b. Nov. 25, 1769. They settled on No. 14, 4th Range of Stanstead, in 1800.

CHILDREN.

JOANNA, b. Oct. 14, 1793—d. Aug. 30, 1819.
JOHN, b. July 4, 1796—d. Nov. 6, 1803.
DANIEL, b. Dec. 11, 1798—m. *Morilla Thompson.*

MARY, b. April 1, 1801—m. *Alexander Young.*
SALLY, b. March 15, 1804—m. *Simon Stone.*
SAMUEL, b. July 14, 1806.
JOHN, b. Oct. 26, 1808.
LOUISA, b. May 7, 1812—m. *Alpheus Kimpton.*

Family of Abel Drew.

ABEL DREW, b. March 20, 1773—m. *Beulah Stimson.* They settled on No. 15, 5th Range of Stanstead, in 1800. He d. March 3, 1825. She d. Oct. 12, 1819. Their children were Harlow, who m. *Lydia Mack;* Abel, m. *Abigail Blake;* Stimson, who m. *Sarepta Burr;* Cynthia, m. *Jesse Bullock;* Clarissa, m. *Heman Lindsey;* and Laura who m. *Julius Ives.*

Family of Harlow Drew.

HARLOW DREW, b. Feb. 2, 1795—m. *Lydia Mack.* He d. in 1865.

CHILDREN.

ROSANNA, b. July 25, 1826—d. May 24, 1855.
HARRY S., b. June 15, 1828—d. Feb. 16, 1851.
CYNTHIA, b. Aug. 14, 1830—m. *Alonzo Brooks.*
LYDIA A., b. Sept. 2, 1837—d. March 30, 1855.
SAMUEL, b. June 6, 1839—m. Helen Watson.
ABEL, b. Nov. 8, 1841.

Family of Abel Drew, jun.

ABEL DREW, JUN., b. Oct. 27, 1796 May. 13, 1820—m. *Abigail Blake,* b. Aug. 17, 1799.

CHILDREN.

CHARLES E., b. Sept. 27, 1821—m. *a Miss Brown.*
ADELINE, b. April 14, 1823—m. *Willard Atkinson.*
GEORGE A., b. Oct. 10, 1825—m. *Louisa Gregg,*
HENRY S., b. March 7, 1831.
CAROLINE, b. June 23, 1833.
EMELINE, b. Jan. 23, 1837—m. *John G. Christie, Esq.*

Family of Daniel Miller.

DANIEL MILLER, b. in Marlow, N.H., May 15, 1781—m. *Rebecca Royce,* b. Oct. 30, 1786. Settled on No. 7, 4th Range of Stanstead, in 1804. He d. Oct. 9, 1855.

CHILDREN.

GILBERT, b. Sept. 20, 1810—m. *Mary Moore.*
LOOMIS, b. March 5, 1812—m. *Louisa Dodge.*
SELDEN, b. March 24, 1816—d. Sept. 10, 1820.
DANIEL, b. Jan. 25, 1819—m. *Eliza Moore.*

Family of Elisha Miller, jun.

ELISHA MILLER, jun., b. Nov. 20, 1799—m *Sabrina Harvey*, b. June 9, 1800. She d. March 21, 1843. Nov. 30, 1843—m. *Lianthe Stone.*

CHILDREN BY 1ST MARRIAGE.

REYNOLD, b. June 13, 1822—d. Oct. 4, 1862.
CAROLINE, b. Dec. 28, 1825—m. *Stewart Magoon.*
SALLY, b, Feb. 4, 1829—m. *John Garvin.*
ERASTUS, b. Oct. 29, 1839.

CHILDREN BY 2ND MARRIAGE.

SABRINA, b. Aug. 21, 1844.
DELPHINE, b. Nov. 30, 1853.

Family of Ira Miller.

IRA MILLER, b. in Marlow, N.H., Oct. 1, 1771—m. *Sally Way*, b. in Lyme, Conn., April 22, 1778. They settled on No. 7, 4th Range of Stanstead, in 1803. He d. in Nov. 1841. She d. March 27, 1859.

CHILDREN.

WILLARD, b. Oct. 16, 1800—m. *Esther Gustin.*
RUFUS, b. June 16, 1803—m. *Elmira Shaw;* 2d, *Polly Mack.*
LAURA, b. May 16, 1807.

Family of Elisha Miller.

ELISHA MILLER, one of the three pioneers of the Marlow Settlement, was b. in Marlow, N.H., June 4, 1773. He m. *Sally Way.* She d. in 1812. In 1813, he m. his 2nd wife, *Betsey Hall.* He d. June 16, 1848.

CHILDREN BY FIRST MARRIAGE.

ELISHA, b. Nov. 25, 1799—m. *Sabrina Harvey.*
PATRICK C., b. in Sept., 1801—m. *Huldah Cowie.*

FAMILY OF MOSES COPP, JUN.

REYNOLD, b. in 1805.
SALLY, b. June 5, 1807—m. *Alvin House.*
FREEMAN, b. April 6, 1811—m. *Roxana Sias.*
IRENE, b. May 25, 1809—m. *Israel Blake.*

CHILDREN BY 2nd MARRIAGE.

JOHN H., b. Dec. 23, 1813.—m. *Lucena Gale.*
ARLEY, b. Feb. 15, 1822.

Family of Capt. Moses Copp.

MOSES COPP, b. in Hampstead, Mass., in 1760—m. *Anna Mills,* b. in 1761. She d. in 1833. He d. in 1845.

CHILDREN.

RICHARD, b. in 1786—m. 1st, *Mary Welch;* 2nd, *Agnes Wood.*
JOSHUA, b. in 1791—m. 1st, *Hannah Blake;* 2nd, *Annis Peaslee.*
MOSES, b. in 1794—m. *Mary Oliver.*
GEORGE F., b. in 1796—m. 1st. *Betsey Rexford;* 2nd, *Susan Burr.*
CYNTHIA, b. in 1799—m. *David Merrill, jun.*
SALLY, b. in 1802—m. *Ira Putney.*
BETSEY, b. in 1804—m. *James Brown.*

Family of Capt. Richard Copp.

RICHARD COPP, b. in Warren, N.H., in 1786—m. *Mary Welch,* and settled on the family homestead. She d. in 1851. In 1853, he m. *Agnes,* widow of *Ephraim Wood.* She d. in 1865; he d. in 1867.

CHILDREN.

MOSES W., b. in 1809.
MARY, b. in 1811—m. *Hollis Packard.*
ANNA, b. in 1819—m. *Chester B. Packard.*
HANNAH, b. in 1826,—m. *Willard A. Cole.*
WRIGHT, b. in 1829—killed on the G. T. Railway.

Family of Moses Copp, jun.

MOSES COPP, JUN., b. in 1794—m. *Mary Oliver,* b. in 1798. Their children were Cynthia, William, Richard, Sewell, who m. Susanna Williamson; Turton, and Louisa, who m. Jeremiah Morrill.

Family of George F. Copp.

GEORGE F. COPP, the *first* child born in Stanstead, was b. in 1797, m. 1st, *Betsey Rexford;* 2nd, *Susan Burr.* The children by the 2nd marriage were Stillman, Charlotte, Lucinda, Maria, and Edwin.

Family of Capt. Moses W. Copp.

CAPT. MOSES W. COPP, b. in Stanstead in 1809—m. *Susan Remich.* She d. in 1841. In 1842, m. *Emeline Locke.* Mr. Copp was engaged in mercantile business for many years, and carried on an extensive machine factory at Magog Outlet; was variously employed in public affairs.

CHILDREN BY 1ST MARRIAGE.

FLORENCE, who m. *A. M. Bullock ;* ERNEST, who d. in 1867.

CHILDREN BY 2ND MARRIAGE.

JOSHUA W., b. June 6, 1843.
RICHARD J., b. March 4, 1845.
EMELINE L., b. July 1, 1847.
CHARLES F., b. May 24, 1853.
WILLARD W., b. Jan. 15, 1856.
ELLA J., b. March 22, 1861.
1 child d. young.

Family of Richard Packard.

RICHARD PACKARD, b. in Providence, R.I., April 7, 1765. March 29, 1787, m. *Sally Coats,* a native of the same town. They settled on No. 27, 2nd Range at Georgeville, in 1798. He was a prominent member of the Methodist Church. Was the first class leader appointed in the town. He d. in 1840 ; she d. in 1854.

CHILDREN.

JOHN A., b. March 27, 1788—m. *Miriam Bullock.* He was for many years a local Methodist preacher.
SALLY, b. Oct. 8, 1789—m. *Lent H. Perkins.*
MARY, b. Dec. 4, 1791—m. *Wm. Bullock, jun.*
MERCY, b. Dec. 8, 1793—m. *Whiting Rexford.*

LAURA, b. July 13, 1797—m. *Samuel Doloff.*
DANIEL, b. July 22, 1799—m. *Mary Moore.*
MOSES, b. May 24, 1802—m. 1st, *Rhoda A. Lilly;* 2nd, *Harriet Reynolds.*
ARTEMISIA, b. in Jan., 1804—m. *Peletiah Morrill.*
HOLLIS, b. Sept. 16, 1806—m. 1st, *Mary Copp;* 2nd, *Mary Geer.*
CHESTER B., b. Aug. 2, 1808—m. *Anna Copp.*
ERASTUS, b. April 4, 1810—m. *Lucinda R. Russell.*
WALES E., b. Aug. 9, 1812—m. *Almira Milligan.*

Family of Samuel S. Kendall, M.D.

SAMUEL S. KENDALL, b. in Windsor, Vt., Jan. 14, 1799. Came to Derby, Vt., with the family in 1810. Studied medicine successively with Drs. M. F. Colby and F. W. Adams. Received diplomas from the Medical Departments of Vermont and Dartmouth Universities. Commenced practice at Coventry, Vt., but subsequently removed to Georgeville.

The character of Dr. Kendall was one of peculiar interest. With the most unassuming but sincere piety were combined all the qualities which constitute the real gentleman. His medical attainments were of the very first order, and he ranked high in his profession. His career though short was eminently useful, and he will be long remembered by many in Coventry and Georgeville.

In 1825, he m. *Emily,* dau. of *S. Colby,* of Derby, Vt. She d. April 13, 1843. Sept. 17, 1843—m. *Sarah Abigail,* dau. of *Dr. P. Redfield,* of Coventry, Vt. Dr. Kendall d. Feb. 4, 1854.

CHILDREN BY 1ST MARRIAGE.

SAMUEL C., b. March 23, 1827.
LAURA C., b. Sept. 29, 1829.
EMILY, b. June 24, 1832—d. Jan. 31, 1838.
SARAH L., b. March 15, 1835—d. May 14, 1856.
KATHERINE W., b. Sept. 13, 1837—d. March 28, 1842.
NATHANIEL, T., b. Oct. 19, 1841.

CHILDREN BY 2ND MARRIAGE.

FLETCHER R., b. July 13, 1844.
HANNAH P., b. May 31, 1846.
PELEG R., b. Nov. 24, 1848.

Family of Timothy K. Hill.

TIMOTHY K. HILL, b. in Brookfield, Mass., March 19, 1780. Came to Stanstead in 1806. In 1808—m. *Kezia Welch.* They settled on No. 27, 3rd Range, near Georgeville. He d. Feb. 5, 1871.

CHILDREN.

THOMAS K., b. April 18, 1810—m. *Dulcina Kneeland.*
ARCHELAUS W., b. June 11, 1813—m. *Lucia Curtis.*
MARY, b. June 15, 1816—d. in 1834.
SUSAN B., b. Nov. 4, 1819.
BETSEY A., b. Oct. 3, 1822—m. *J. B. Osgood.*
ANNA M., b. Oct. 11, 1825—d. in 1842.
SARAH A., b. March 1, 1828—m. *Horace S. Ingalls.*
RICHARD C., b. March 8, 1831—m. *Sarah J. Welch.*
DULCINA, b. Feb. 25, 1836.
Two children died young.

Joseph Foord, M.D.

We are not able to trace the origin and history of Dr. Foord. He was a well educated and successful physician. Had an extensive practice in Georgeville and the surrounding neighborhoods for years.

Nelson Cheney, M.D.

Was born in Barton, April 17, 1830. His early opportunities had been limited to the Common Schools of the town, but he acquired a good English education, and was for some years engaged in teaching. Having a predilection for the profession of medicine, he pursued his preparatory studies under the instructions of Dr. J. B. Mastee, of Barton, Vt., improving his leisure time while engaged in teaching. In 1859, he received his diploma from the Physico-Medical College of Medicine and Surgery at Cincinnati, Ohio. He commenced practice in Glover, Vt., afterwards removed to Georgeville, and subsequently to Beebe Plain.

Family of William Bullock, Esq.

WILLIAM BULLOCK, ESQ., was born in Guilford, Vt., in 1770—m. *Artemisia Wellman.* They settled on Nos. 27 and 28, 2nd Range of Stanstead, near Georgeville, in 1801. Being among the very earliest settlers, they experienced the fortunes that attended the labor of our fathers in making for themselves homes in the wilderness. He early took an active part in the management of public affairs, having received a magistrate's commission and other offices of trust from the Provincial Government. With hardly an exception, his family have all been active and useful members of the community. He d. in 1828. His wife d. in 1836. Their children were *William, Miriam, Biel, Thaddeus, Chauncey, Rectina, Samuel, Jesse, Artemisia, Increase, Noble,* and *Harriet.* These all married and had families, and their descendants are widely scattered over Canada and the United States.

The progenitors of William Bullock, the subject of this notice, can be distinctly traced back to the time of the Norman Conquest in 1066, and some 300 years before the time of the introduction of surnames into England. We find the name and coat of arms of the family in English Heraldry. The insignia upon the shield are *Three Bulls' Heads,* and above the shield, a crest of five battle axes with the motto, "*nil conscire sibi.*" In 1635, three brothers, Henry, Edward, and Richard Bullock, emigrated from England and settled in Salem, Mass. Richard Bullock removed to Rehoboth, Mass., in 1647, and from him, William Bullock was a descendant in the fifth generation.

Family of Chauncey Bullock, Esq.

CHAUNCEY BULLOCK, b. in Guilford, Vt., Sept. 21, 1796. Commenced mercantile business in Georgeville in 1817, and continued for several years. Was the first postmaster appointed at Georgeville; was actively employed in public affairs, having held several offices of high responsibility and trust; his last appointment was Collector of Customs for the Port of Stanstead. In 1818, he m. *Betsey Ives*—she d. April 8, 1841. In 1842, he m. *Mary Ives,* who d. Feb. 16, 1843. In 1844, he m. *Jerusha Ives ;* she d. May 28, 1861. In 1862, he m. *Annis Abbott,* widow of Noble Bullock. His family were members of the Wesleyan Church. He d. in 1870.

CHILDREN BY 1ST MARRIAGE.

CLARISSA, b. March 17, 1819—m. *Hon. Amasa T. Merriman.*
EMILY, b. Dec. 18, 1823—d. May 14, 1846.
BETSEY L., b. March 11, 1825—d. Nov. 17, 1834.
CHAUNCEY H., b. Jan. 18, 1829—d. Aug. 24, 1848.
HELEN A., b. Dec. 7, 1831—m. *Isaac Butters.* She d. Dec. 2, 1858.

WILLIAM E., b. Oct. 25, 1836. An Advocate in Montreal.
MARY L., b. April 29, 1840—d. young.

ONE CHILD BY 2ND MARRIAGE.

MARY IVES, b. Jan. 28, 1843.

Family of Increase Bullock, Esq.

INCREASE BULLOCK, b. in Stanstead, Oct. 22, 1808. Feb. 16, 1830, m. *Harriet Cross*, b. in Sutton, P.Q., Jan. 17, 1809; she d. April 20, 1858. July 11, 1860, he m. *Mary Jane Bryant*, b. July 12, 1835. Mr. Bullock early received the appointment of magistrate; has held important and responsible offices in the town and county, and been extensively employed in public affairs.

CHILDREN BY 1ST MARRIAGE.

ALFRED M., b. Jan 6, 1831—m. *Florence Copp.*
EDWIN C., b. Jan. 30, 1836—m. *Arvilla Austin.*
CHARLES C., b. July 17, 1837—m. *Betsey Burnham.*
HAZEN J., b. Jan. 30, 1841.
DON ALBERT, b. Sept. 22, 1848.

CHILDREN BY 2ND MARRIAGE.

CLARA E., b. June 24, 1861.
GEORGIANA, b. Oct. 5, 1864.

Family of Noble Bullock.

NOBLE BULLOCK, b. in Stanstead, Jan. 6, 1810—m. *Annis Abbott*, b. May 12, 1812. They settled at Magog, and afterwards removed to Georgeville. He d. Oct. 29, 1858. She afterwards m. Chauncey Bullock, Esq.

CHILDREN.

ANNIS A. W., b. Jan. 22, 1831—m. *Wesley Blake.*
TALBOT J., b. Oct. 15, 1832.
NOBLE T., b. Aug. 14, 1834—d. Feb. 22, 1836.
AUGUSTUS F., b. June 14, 1837.
FRANCIS F., b. Sept. 24, 1839.

Family of William Bullock, jun.

WILLIAM BULLOCK, JUN., b. Oct. 17, 1791. Nov. 10, 1811, m. *Mary Packard*, b. Nov. 8, 1791. They settled in the vicinity of

FAMILY OF EZRA B. RIDER.

Georgeville. She d. Oct. 11, 1834. Aug. 5, 1835, he m. *Roxana Kenaston.* He d. June 21, 1849. She d. in June, 1851.

CHILDREN BY 1ST MARRIAGE.

SARAH, b. July 2, 1812—m. *Jesse Willey.*
BETSEY, b. Nov. 22, 1813—d. July 8, 1826.
CHAUNCEY, b. Nov. 5, 1815—d. Nov. 15, 1821.
WILLIAM, b. Sept. 1, 1817—m. a *Miss Drake.*
ALANSON G., b. Jan. 5, 1822—d. March 22, 1844.
JOSEPH F., b. Dec. 12, 1826.
IRA, b. Oct. 8, 1829.
Four children died young.

CHILDREN BY 2ND MARRIAGE.

SEALY, b. May 4, 1837.
JAMES J., b. Sept. 25, 1839.
MARY R., b. Jan. 13, 1844.

Family of Ezra B. Rider.

EZRA B. RIDER, b. June 10, 1798—m. *Fanny Chandler,* b. March 3, 1801. She d. March 19, 1843. He afterwards m. *Dorothy A. Lee.* She was b. Jan. 4, 1824. He died Nov. 1, 1862.

CHILDREN BY 1ST MARRIAGE.

CARLOS A., b. April 6, 1820—m. *Emily Foss.*
BENJAMIN F., b. Aug. 10, 1821.
SARAH D. F., b. Oct. 29, 1822—d. Sept. 12, 1823.
WELLINGTON, b. Feb. 5, 1826.
SARAH B., b. March 3, 1824—d. Aug. 4, 1826.
CYNTHIA W., b. May 29, 1827—m. *George Chase.*
GUSTAVUS A., b. Nov. 4, 1831—m. *Betsey Lee.*
EZRA B., b. Sept. 13, 1842.

CHILDREN BY 2ND MARRIAGE.

TIMOTHY B., b. Jan. 8, 1848—m. *Mary L. Shaw.*
HAMILTON M., b. Dec. 14, 1850.
HELEN D., b. Aug. 25, 1857.
DORA A., b. May 4, 1863.

FORESTS AND CLEARINGS.

The Magoon Families.

These families are of Scotch extraction—were emigrants from Newhampshire.

Family of Jonathan Magoon.

JONATHAN MAGOON, b. in Exeter, N. H.—m. *Betsey Smith.* They came to Stanstead in 1796, settled on No. 1, 4th Range, in 1816, removed to Magoon Point. He died in 1826, she d. in 1857. Their children were Jonathan, Betsey, Simeon, John, Daniel, Jeremiah, David and Polly.

JONATHAN MAGOON, jun., born in Exeter, N.H., April 16, 1786, —m. *Prudence Abbott*, b. April 8, 1786. She d. September 30, 1836. He afterwards m. *Sally Gilman*, widow of John Bragg. His residence was the Point first taken up by Caples and Abels.

CHILDREN.

FANNY, b. Feb. 8, 1806—m. *Hiram Lilly.*
WILLARD, b. May 7, 1809—m. *Adeline Blake.*
WILDER, b. May 20, 1811—m. *Electa Blake.*
HANNAH, b. April 6, 1813—m. *Harrison Smith.*
AURELIA, b. Feb. 20, 1815—m. *Nason Peaslee.*
ERASTUS, b. June 5, 1817—m. *Mary Miller.*
CHARLES, b. Feb. 28, 1820—m. *Caroline Miller.*
RILEY, b. Feb. 20, 1822—m. *Lydia Smith.*
LEVI, b. July 19, 1824—m. *Biel Blake.*
ASA, b. Sept. 25, 1826—m. *Eliza Smith.*
HIRAM, b. March 3, 1829—m. *Betsey Blake.*

Family of Alexander Magoon.

Alexander Magoon married Jemima Leavitt, she d. in 1804. He afterwards m. Hannah Hall. Children, James, Dudley, Alexander, Joseph and Sally.

Dudley Magoon married Nancy Smith. They settled on No. 3, 4th Range, in 1800. Children, Dudley, Roxana, and Hannah.

Simeon Magoon married Martha Briggs. They were among the settlers of Magoon Point. Children, Simeon, Roxana, and Sophronia.

John Magoon married *Electa Beebe.* Children, Ezra, Stewart, Orrin, Plummer, Rhoda, and Jesse.

Daniel Magoon married *Melita Briggs.* Children, Guilford, Betsey, Hannah, and Plummer.

David Magoon married *Hannah Elliott.* Children, John, Dennis, Chester, and George.

MORRILL MAGOON married *Lois,* daughter of *Philip Verback.* They settled in Stanstead about 1806.

CHILDREN.

JOSEPH F., b. May 2, 1807—m. *Eleanora Henderson.*
SALLY, b. April 5, 1809—m. *Osmyn Smith.*
WILLIAM V., b. Aug. 24, 1813—m. *Sarah A. Crooker.*
DOROTHY, b. Feb. 18, 1816—m. *Simeon Fletcher.*
MARTHA, b. Feb. 16, 1818—m. *Osmyn Smith.* His 2d wife. She d. April 25, 1862.
LOUISA, b. Aug. 18, 1822—m. *Bartlett Bryant.*

Family of Dea. John Christie.

DEA. JOHN CHRISTIE, b. Nov. 22, 1795, married *Magdalen Lumsden,* b. May 26, 1793. They were natives of Banffshire, Scotland, where they originally settled. They emigrated to America in 1830, and after residing several years in Derby, Vt., removed, and settled at Magoon Point. Mr. Christie was killed in the summer of 1864, in attempting to secure an infuriated bull. A further account of him will be found in connection with that of the Congregational Church of Stanstead.

CHILDREN.

ALEXANDER, b. Dec. 19, 1821—d. Feb. 3, 1865.
CATHERINE, b. Feb. 28, 1823—m. *Robert H. Trumbull.*
JOHN G., b. Oct., 1, 1824—m. *Emma Drew.*
ROBINA, b. Aug. 5, 1828.
ANNA G., b. June 22, 1830—m. *Adams W. Boynton.*
PENELOPE, b. Sept. 29, 1832—m. *Henry Roedell.*
MARGARET D., b. Nov. 8, 1834, d. Sept. 4, 1859.
GEORGE, b. July 14, 1836—d. Sept. 4, 1839.

Family of James Geddes.

JAMES GEDDES married *Robina Lumsden*. They were natives of Banffshire, Scotland. They were of the number who followed the Rev. Joseph Gibb, in 1831. They settled near Glines' Corner. Both deceased. 4 children: Catherine, who m. *James Fraser*, Magdalen, Robina, and James.

Family of John Badenoch.

JOHN BADENOCH, a native of Aberdeenshire, Scotland, settled in Stanstead in 1832. 4 children: Andrew, James, Margaret, and Mary Jane.

Family of James Fraser.

JAMES FRASER and his wife, Jeanette Fraser, were natives of Inverness, Scotland. They came to Stanstead in 1831, and located near Beebe Plain. He d. Oct. 14, 1846, aged 6; she d. March 9, 1861, aged 75.

CHILDREN.

GEORGE, b. March 15, 1822—d. April 11, 1838.

JAMES, b. Sept. 23, 1823.

JOHN, b. June 26, 1826, entered the Congregational College at Toronto, Ont., in 1847, and, after completing the required course of study, was ordained pastor of the Congregational Church in Brockville, Ont., in 1856; he removed to Derby, Vt., and supplied the Congregational Church of that place for several years. In 1859, he married *Ruth M.*, dau. of *Col. L. B. Child*. He was for some time a missionary in Australia. Is now preaching with much acceptance and usefulness in Montreal.

Family of John Fraser.

JOHN FRASER, b. in Inverness, Scotland, in 1774, m. *Isabella Forbes*, b. in Aberdeenshire, Scotland, in 1786. They settled near Beebe Plain in 1831. He died in 1856.

CHILDREN.

AGNES, b. May 19, 1806—m. *Timothy Winn*.

WILLIAM, b. Feb. 4, 1808—d. in Scotland

JOHN, b. Sept. 20, 1810—m. *Isabella Warren*, a native of London, Eng., where Mr. F. was for some time engaged in business as a merchant tailor. They came to Stanstead in 1857, and subsequently removed to Montreal.

JANE, b. July 6, 1813—d. in 1834.

JAMES, b. July 17, 1822—m. *Catherine Geddes.*

Family of John Lorimer.

JOHN LORIMER, b. Feb. 5, 1779—m. *Isabella Brodie*, b. May 25, 1795. Natives of Scotland, where, for many years, he was engaged in mercantile business. They came with their family to Canada in 1830, and settled at Beebe Plain. He d. Feb. 27, 1841; she d. in 1869.

CHILDREN.

JOHN, b. Aug. 28, 1817—m. *Semantha*, dau of *W. Frost, Esq.*

WILLIAM, b. Jan. 12, 1819—m. *Sarah*, dau. of *L. Martin, Esq.*

JAMES B., b. May 30, 1820—m. *Mary C.*, dau. of *C. Monro.*

ALEXANDER, b. Oct. 20, 1821—m. *Ruth Haines.* He is pastor of a large and flourishing Baptist Church in Toronto, Ont.

MARY ANN, b. Aug. 10, 1826—m. *Rev. Joseph Chandler.*

ISABELLA, b. May 1, 1828—m. *Lyman Martin.*

BETSEY, b. June 1, 1831—m. *William Doloff.*

JOSEPH, b. Feb. 4, 1833—m. *Almira Hale.* He is pastor of the Baptist Church in Derby, Vt.

PETER, b. Oct. 22, 1835—m. *Mary Morrison.*

JANET, b. Oct. 25, 1836—m. *Rev. James Hay.* Mr. Hay was pastor of the Congregational Church of Stanstead two years. Was a missionary in Van Dieman's Land for several years.

BENJAMIN, b. Oct. 23, 1838—m. *Lucretia Holmes.* She d. in 1872. In 1874, m. *Ella Cummings.*

Family of Donald Simpson.

DONALD SIMPSON, b. Nov. 20, 1795. In 1831, m. *Ellen Rea.* They were natives of Ross-shire, Scotland,—emigrated to Canada in 1832, and settled near Beebe Plain.

CHILDREN.

JAMES, b. Jan. 4, 1832.

ALEXANDER, b. Feb. 14, 1833.

Daniel, b. Oct. 18, 1840.

Family of Colin Monro.

Colin Monro, b. Sept. 2, 1789—m. *Isabella Webster*, b. March 3, 1794. They were natives of Banffshire, Scotland. She d. in May, 1824. May 20, 1827, he m. *Jennet Mustard*. They emigrated to Stanstead in 1830, and settled on part of No. 1, 6th Range. Jennet, his 2nd wife, d. Aug. 26, 1864.

CHILDREN BY 1ST MARRIAGE.

Joseph, b. Oct. 30, 1819—m. *Mary F. Packard*.
Isabella, b. May 26, 1821—m. *James Grant*.
John and George W., twins, b. May 10, 1823. John m. *Jessie, Davidson ;* George W. m. *Emeline Packard*.

CHILDREN BY 2nd MARRIAGE.

Alexander, b. March 28, 1828—m. *Sarah A. Adams*.
Mary P., b. Jan. 12, 1830—m. *James B. Lorimer*.
David G., b. June 10, 1832—d. June 5, 1857.

Family of George Monro.

George Monro, b. July 20, 1802—m. *Christina Yarrow*, b. June 22, 1812. They were natives of Scotland. Came to Stanstead in 1832, and settled near the Lake Shore. He d. Sept. 19, 1865.

CHILDREN.

John, b. July 16, 1833—m. *Kate Simonds*.
William A., b., May 14, 1837.
George J., b. Oct., 16, 1839—m. *J. M. Vanriper*.
James A., b. Jan. 2, 1842.
Mary A., b. July 30, 1844.
Charles A., b. April 20, 1849—d. April 20, 1851.
Emma A., b. Nov. 9, 1853.

Family of Alexander Brodie.

Alexander Brodie, b. Oct. 20, 1788—m. *Janet Coull*, b. July 15, 1789. They were natives of Banffshire, Scotland, and settled near the Lake Shore in Stanstead in 1832.

CHILDREN.

James, b. May 13, 1816—m. *Mary Farnham*.
Janet, b. Aug. 27, 1817—m. *John Webb*.

FAMILY OF BARACH BURPEE.

ELIZABETH, b. May 22, 1819—m. *James French.*
ALEXANDER, b. Sept. 11, 1823—d. Sept. 10, 1847.
MARGARET, b. July 25, 1825—m. *A. B. Cleary.*
GEORGE, b. March 20, 1827—m. *Caroline Beebe.*
WILLIAM, b. Nov. 8, 1828.
JOHN, b. Dec. 29, 1830.
MARY, b. Sept. 14, 1832
DAVID, b. Sept. 19, 1834.

Family of James Glines.

JAMES GLINES, b. in Canterbury, N.H., m. *Mary Dow,* b. in Methuen, Mass. In 1805, they settled at the place that bears their name, Glines' Corner. He d. Jan. 11, 1843. She d. Feb. 19, 1845.

CHILDREN.

MARY, b. in Aug., 1791—m. *T. S. Bangs.*
NANCY, b. June 20, 1793—m. *Greeley Dow.*
HANNAH, b. July 10, 1795—m. *Zebulon Hunt.*
SAMUEL, b. in 1797—d. in 1812.
STEPHEN, b. in 1799—m. *Sarah Sinclair.*
LOUISA, b. in 1803—d. in 1820.
MOSES, b. Aug. 14, 1806—m. *Emily Abbott.*
IRA, b. in 1811—d. in 1813.

Moses Glines, M.D.,

Son of James Glines, was b. in Stanstead, Aug. 14, 1806. He studied medicine under the supervision of M. F. Colby, M.D., in Stanstead. In 1838, he spent some months in the Marine Hospital at Quebec, and after examination was admitted as a licentiate. He was afterwards elected a member of the College of Physicians and Surgeons of Canada, and subsequently elected one of the Governors of the same College, and received his honorary diploma. In the meantime, he spent several months at the University of New York. Dr. Glines stood deservedly high in his profession. He had acquired an extensive and lucrative practice in Compton and the neighboring towns, but was cut down in the prime of life and usefulness. He d. in 1863.

Family of Barach Burpee.

BARACH BURPEE, b. in Sterling, Mass., July 4, 1797. Came to Stanstead in 1819. Aug. 4, 1823, m. *Philena Wright.* They settled

R

in the vicinity of the Lake Shore. She d. Feb. 6, 1825. Feb. 6, 1826, he m. *Lucinda Royce.* One child living, William M., b. May 16, 1838—m. *Lucinda Collins.*

Family of Ellson Fowler.

ELLISON FOWLER m. *Betsey Gilman.* They settled in Stanstead, in 1806. He d. in 1840. She afterwards m. *David Moe, Esq.*, of Sherbrooke, P.Q. Both deceased. 3 children by 1st marriage, John, Elisabeth, who m. *John Kimpton*, and Lucy who m. *Sewell Moe.*

Family of Capt. Henry Blake.

CAPT. HENRY BLAKE was b. Epping, N.H., in 1764—m. *Abigail Tilton*, b. in the same place in 1765. They resided in Sanbornton, N.H., until 1806, when they came to Stanstead and settled on No. 23, 2nd Range. He d. in 1848; she d. in 1846.

Their children were Abraham, Mary, Dolly, Hendrick, Betsey, Noble, and Hannah.

Abraham Blake.

ABRAHAM BLAKE, son of Capt. Henry Blake, was b. in Sanbornton, N.H., in 1787. He m. *Biel*, dau. of *William Bullock, Esq.*, of Georgeville. Received the appointment of Captain of Militia, about 1835. Biel, his wife, d. in 1843.

Family of David Harvey.

DAVID HARVEY, b. in Dracut, Mass., in 1757—m. *Abigail Elliott*, b. in Portsmouth, N.H., in 1770. They settled on No. 9, 3rd Range upon the Lake Shore in Stanstead, in 1805. He d. in Aug., 1830 She d. in April, 1853.

Their children were Lavinia, Samuel, William, Asa, and Sabrina.

HATLEY AND MAGOG.

The Hovey Family.

We have no authentic account of the origin of this family. Tradition says that their ancestors emigrated from England and were among the early colonists of Connecticut.

Family of Capt. Ebenezer Hovey.

EBENEZER HOVEY m. *Rebecca Simmons*. They were natives of Connecticut, were the earliest of the pioneers of the settlement of Hatley. He sustained the office of Captain of Militia for many years, and was actively employed in public affairs. He d. April 24, 1836. His wife d. in October, 1829.

CHILDREN.

POLLY, b. Feb. 21, 1776—m. *David Chamberlin*.
CHESTER, b. Jan. 20, 1778.
ROXANA, b. Dec. 5, 1779—m. 1st, *T. McConnell;* 2nd, *P. Flanders*.
CLARISSA, b. Feb. 16, 1782—m. *Abraham Rexford*.
EBENEZER, b. Feb. 1, 1784—m. *Mary Cox*.
JOHN, b. April 16, 1786—m. 1st, *Ruth Kezar;* 2nd, *Ann McLean*.
PIERCY, b. Aug. 15, 1788—m. *Simon Kezar*.
CHAUNCEY, b. Aug. 20, 1790.
SALLY, b. Dec. 20, 1792—m. *John Wadleigh*.
LAURA, b. July 29, 1795—m. 1st, *Z. Johnson ;* 2nd, *W. Cox*.
HORACE, b. Dec. 21, 1798—m. *Pamelia Wadleigh*.

Chester Hovey.

CHESTER HOVEY, b. Jan. 20, 1778—m. *Olive Rexford*. She d. Aug. 21, 1833. He afterwards m. *Achsah Kimball*. He d. Feb. 10, 1853. His children by 1st marriage were Malinda, who m. Capt. Taylor Wadleigh; Mary, m. Seth Huntingdon, Esq.; Elmira, who d. at the age of 28 ; Lucy, m. Charles Wallace ; Sophronia, m. Nathaniel Hawes ; Olive, m. Russell Rexford, Caroline, m. Simon Bean, Esq., Chester, who d. when about 30 years old; Alonzo, m. Emily A. Willard, and Hester M., m. George Oliver. No children by 2nd marriage.

Family of Seth Huntingdon, Esq.

This family are the descendants of the eighth generation in the regular line from Simeon and Margaret Huntingdon, who emigrated from England to America in 1633. For a more particular account of their ancestors, the reader is referred to a Historical and Genealogical Memoir of the Huntingdon Family, lately published in Connecticut.

SETH HUNTINGDON, Esq., was born in Roxbury, Vt., June 13, 1796. April 3, 1825, m. *Mary*, dau. of *Capt. Chester Hovey.*

CHILDREN.

LUCIUS S., b. May 26, 1827—m. *Miriam Wood.* Studied law; has a good practice in Shefford County, P.Q.; has served in the Provincial Parliament of Quebec, and in the New Domion Parliament at Ottawa, Ontario. His political career has been an eminently successful one.

CAROLINE, b. May 20, 1829—m. *Oscar Woodward.*
CLARISSA, b. May 20, 1829—m. *Jesse Kezar.*
THOMAS F., b. April 6, 1831—d. in March, 1832.
FREDERICK A., b. Sept. 29, 1836—d. when about 25 years old.
ELMIRA, b. June 7, 1838—m. *Benjamin Le Baron.*
EMELINE, b. April 24, 1842—m. *Henry Pennoyer.*

Family of John Hovey.

JOHN HOVEY, b. April 16, 1786—m. *Ruth Kezar,* b. Nov. 16, 1785. She d. in 1854. He afterwards m. *Ann McLean.* No children.

Family of Horace Hovey.

HORACE HOVEY, youngest son of Capt. Ebenezer Hovey, was b. in Hatley, P.Q., Dec. 21, 1798—m. *Pamelia Wadleigh.* She d. in 1844. He subsequently m. *Mary Flanders,* b. June 13, 1819.

CHILDREN.

WRIGHT, b. July 23, 1833—m. *Lois Hitchcock.*
ALICE J., b. Nov. 24, 1836—m. 1st, *Horace Taylor;* 2nd, *Wm. Attwood.*
HORACE M., b. Dec. 15, 1840. Studied law; has a good practice in Stanstead.
LESLIE P., b. Oct. 29, 1842.

The Le Baron Family.

This family are of French origin. Their ancestors were among the early emigrants to the New England colonies, and their descendants are scattered widely over the United States and Canada.

Family of Japheth Le Baron.

JAPHETH LE BARON, b. Nov. 30, 1769. June 9, 1792, m. *Betsey Prouty*, b. Feb. 1, 1777. Settled on the Lake Shore in 1795, and subsequently removed to the east part of Hatley. She d. Aug. 16, 1811. He afterwards m. *Polly Huntingdon*, b. Nov. 21, 1774. He d. Feb. 10, 1845; she d. July 6, 1850.

CHILDREN BY 1ST MARRIAGE.

RHODA, b. Feb. 14, 1795.
RICHARD, b. Aug. 21, 1797.
JAMES, b. Oct. 6, 1800.
CHAUNCEY, b. Feb. 14, 1803.
ORRIN, b. Sept. 22, 1804.
HORACE, b. July 14, 1807.
BETSEY, b. Aug. 6, 1811—m. *Lowell Simonds*.

CHILDREN BY 2ND MARRIAGE.

ELIJAH H., b. Dec. 6, 1814.
JAPHETH B., b. May 14, 1817.

Family of Joseph Sampson.

JOSEPH SAMPSON m. *Rhoda Le Baron*. He d. Aug. 10, 1843. She d. April 15, 1853. Their children were *Diana, Lovina, Charles, Jane, Mary* and *Betsey*.

Family of Richard Le Baron.

RICHARD LE BARON, b. Aug. 21, 1797—m. *Lavinia Simonds*, b. Jan. 2, 1806. They settled on the west shore of Massawippi Lake, but afterwards removed to No. 20, 2nd Range of Hatley. She d. March 21, 1861.

CHILDREN.

EMELINE, b. Dec. 25, 1824—m. *Gilbert Wallingford*—d. July 21, 1845.
HORACE, b. Nov. 3, 1829—m. *Henrietta Wallace*.
EVELINA, b. May 28, 1835—m. *Alonzo Colby*. She d. Oct. 3, 1853.

Family of James Le Baron.

JAMES LE BARON, b. Oct. 6, 1800—m. *Cynthia A. Bowen*. She was b. April 26, 1802. They settled in Barnston.

CHILDREN.

ORRIN, b. Aug. 28, 1826—m. *Adeline Morell.*
MARY, b. Jan. 28, 1828—d. Oct. 17, 1850.
CYNTHIA, b. Aug. 25, 1829—d. Dec. 12, 1853.
ELLEN, b. Jan. 19, 1831—m. *Luther Abbott, Esq.*
ELSIE, b. Nov. 8, 1832—d. Jan. 11, 1853.
CATHERINE, b. Sept. 2, 1833—d. Aug. 6, 1852.
LOUISA S., b. Feb. 22, 1835—m. *George Ayer.*
RUSSELL A., b. Dec. 31, 1838.
NELSON J., b. Jan. 4, 1840.
EMILY C., b. March 30, 1842.
GILBERT C., b. Feb. 4, 1844.
HARRIET, b. Dec. 23, 1845.
FRANCIS W., b. April 15, 1848.

Family of Chauncey Le Baron.

CHAUNCEY LE BARON, b. Feb. 4, 1803—m. *Cordelia Hitchcock*, b. April 27, 1810. They settled on No. 23, 4th Range of Hatley.

CHILDREN.

LESTINA, b. June 1, 1831—m. *Samuel Bean.*
BENJAMIN, b. Nov. 23, 1832, is engaged in trade, and is postmaster at North Hatley—m. *Almira Huntingdon.*
ALEXANDER, b. Nov. 14, 1834—m. *Caroline Jackson.*
FEDORA, b. Feb. 1, 1837—m. *Ozro Pool.*
HIRAM N., b. Jan. 13, 1839.
MELVIN, b. Oct. 23, 1842.
CHARLES W., b. Dec. 21, 1845—d. Nov. 7, 1849.
MARY P., b. May 6, 1847—d. April 25, 1864.
BETSEY J., b. April 20, 1849.
HOLLIS W., b. Nov. 21, 1851.
ALBERT G., b. May 26, 1854.
WILLFORD, b. March 28, 1857.

Family of Orrin Le Baron.

ORRIN LE BARON, b. Sept. 22, 1804. He m. 1st, *Ruth Colbe;* 2nd, *Mary Ann Digby.* He d. in 1864.

FAMILY OF JAPHETH B. LE BARON.   251

CHILDREN BY 1ST MARRIAGE.

Sarah, b. in 1831. Burt, b. in 1833. Taylor, b. in 1835. Ai, b. in 1838. Solon and Sylvia, twins, b. in 1840. Llewellyn, b. in 1844, and Aylmer, b. in 1846. One child d. in infancy.

CHILDREN BY 2ND MARRIAGE.

Utheria, b. in 1853; Edson Y., b. in 1856, and Burt, 2nd, b. in 1860.

Family of Horace Le Baron.

HORACE LE BARON, b. July 15, 1807—m. *Charlotte Kenaston.* She was b. Nov. 16, 1815. They settled in West Hatley. He d. March 11, 1863.

CHILDREN.

CHARLES O., b. May 13, 1839—m. *Nancy R. Demary.*
LOUISA J., b. May 2, 1840—m. *Henry Hunting.*
CHARLOTTE H., b. Sept. 1, 1849.

Family of Elijah H. Le Baron, Esq.

ELIJAH H. LE BARON, b. Dec. 26, 1814. March 16, 1843—m. *Maria,* dau. of *Sherburn Brown,* b. Aug. 2, 1818. They settled in Massawippi Village. He has sustained several offices of responsibility and trust, has been actively employed in public affairs and has rendered valuable assistance to the compiler of this book, particularly in furnishing much of the material connected with the history of Hatley.

CHILDREN.

PAMELIA A., b., Feb. 27, 1844.
EMELINE, b. Oct. 4, 1845.
HERVEY H., b. May 20, 1847.
JAMES M., b. March 7, 1849—d. Jan. 7, 1850.
WILLIE S., b. Feb. 27, 1855.

Family of Japheth B. Le Baron.

JAPHETH B. LE BARON, b. May 14, 1817—m. *Lucy Wadleigh,* b. May 9, 1823. He has for many years sustained the office of magistrate, and has been variously employed in public affairs. The family reside in Charleston Village, East Hatley.

CHILDREN.

MATTHEW W., b. June 9, 1852.
MARY L., b. July 17, 1854.
CHARLES S., b. April 8, 1856—d. in infancy.

Family of Lowell Simonds.

LOWELL SIMONDS m. *Betsey Le Baron.* Their children were Amelia, who m. *Levi Partridge;* Mary, m. *Joseph Sampson;* Elizabeth, m. *Carlos Williams;* Ellen, Flora, and Ella.

Family of Charles O. Le Baron.

CHARLES O. LE BARON, b. May 13, 1839. May 17, 1863, m. *Nancy B. Demary,* b. Aug. 17, 1840. They settled in West Hatley.

CHILDREN.

SARAH O., b. July, 1864.
ALICE L., b. June 20, 1866.

Family of Bond Little.

BOND LITTLE m. *Ruth Atwood.* They were natives of New Hampshire, and settled on No. 15, 1st Range of Hatley, in 1798. They experienced the privations and hardships incident to new settlements, but soon made themselves a comfortable home, and lived to see their children mostly settled in good circumstances, and some of them wealthy. He d. in 1813; she d. in 1815. Their children were Taylor, Alice, Abijah, Ezekiel, Ruth, Bond, and Thomas.

Family of Dea. Taylor Little.

DEA. TAYLOR LITTLE, son of Bond Little, m. *Polly Marsh.* She d. some years afterwards, and he m. *Sally White.* He was "a good man"—was for many years a pillar in the Free-Will Baptist Church of Hatley. To that Church his death was a very serious, if not an irreparable, loss. He made a liberal bequest at his death for the support of the officiating ministers in the church, which was to be paid in yearly stipends. His donations to the schools and other institutions of the township are a permanent benefit to the community. He d. Feb. 5, 1854.

Family of Abijah Little.

ABIJAH LITTLE m. *Elizabeth Bean.* They were natives of New Hampshire. They settled on No. 15, 1st Range of Hatley, with his father, Bond Little, in 1800. He sustained his parents during the remainder of their lives, and lived on the same farm until the time of his death, which was Dec. 19, 1860. His wife d. Jan. 30, 1866. Their children all married and had families.

CHILDREN.

SARAH, b. Aug. 1, 1801—m. *Amasa Marsh.*
MARY, b. in 1803—m. *Joel Shurtliff.*
THOMAS, b. Aug. 7, 1805—m. *Ruth Little.*
ELIZA, b. in 1807—m. *Thomas Reed.*
ABIJAH, b. in 1809—m. *Helen Norton.*
BOND, b. May 20; 1811—m. *Sarah Furrington.*
ARMINA, b. in 1814—m. *Thomas Drew.*
CHARLOTTE, b. in 1816—m. *Henry Putney.*
JANE, b. in 1818—m. *Amos Ball.*
JOHN, b. in 1820—m. *Mary Morey.*

Thomas Little.

THOMAS LITTLE, b. Aug. 7, 1805—m. *Ruth Little.* She was b. May 9, 1811. They settled on No. 14, 1st Range of Hatley. Mr. L. is among the most wealthy men of the town.

CHILDREN.

CELIA M., b. Sept. 19, 1836—m. *Michael Mullin.*
THOMAS, b. June 1, 1841—m. *Annis J. Thwaits.*
SARAH, b. March 30, 1849.

Family of Ezekiel Little.

EZEKIEL LITTLE married *Judith Nelson.* They were natives of New Hampshire. Settled on No. 16, 1st Range of Hatley, in 1800. Sold out and left the country in 1812. Of their children, one only settled in Hatley, Jonathan Little.

JONATHAN LITTLE, b. May 14, 1812—m. *Lavinia Colby*, b. Aug. 7, 1812. They settled in Hatley. She d. June 4, 1855. He subsequently m. *Sarah E. Ball*, b. Jan. 10, 1823.

254   FORESTS AND CLEARINGS.

ONE CHILD BY 1ST MARRIAGE.

MELISSA A., b. March 29, 1836—m. *Francis Shurtliff.*

ONE CHILD BY 2ND MARRIAGE.

ERASTUS, b. July 20, 1864.

Family of Moses Bean.

MOSES BEAN, b. in Sutton, N.H., July 21, 1774. Settled on No. 13, 2nd Range of Hatley, in 1798. In 1802, he m. *Betsey,* dau. of *Capt. Simon Kezar.* He d. Oct. 19, 1826. She d. Oct. 25, 1830.

CHILDREN.

SIMON, b. Oct. 16, 1804.
MARK, b. Jan. 17, 1806—m. *Roxana Gordon.*
LORA, b. Feb. 19, 1807—m. *Augustus Abbott.*
BETSEY, b. Feb. 15, 1808—m. *Hiram Abbott.*
VENEN, b. June 15, 1810—m. *Lydia Abbott.*
LUKE, b. March, 15, 1813—m. *Eliza Ordway.*
Two children d. in infancy.

Family of Simon Bean, Esq.

SIMON BEAN, eldest son of Moses Bean, was born in Hatley, Oct. 16, 1804. Was administrator of his father's estate. Settled with the other heirs, took the family homestead, and sustained his mother during the remainder of her life. In 1831, he m. Sarah, dau. of Bond Little. She d. Feb. 11, 1858. Oct. 2, 1862, he m. *Caroline,* dau. of *Chester Hovey, Esq.,* b. Dec. 12, 1813. He has sustained the office of Captain of Militia and magistrate for many years, and has been actively employed in public affairs.

CHILDREN.

LORA, b. Dec. 24, 1832—m. *John Ives.*
WILLIAM, b. Dec. 24, 1834—d. in 1837.
MARY, b. May 30, 1836—m. *E. B. Gustin.*
JOSEPHINE, b. April, 1840—m. *Edwin Bean.*
LUCINDA, b. April, 1842—m. *Edwin Woodward.*
SIMON W., b. Nov. 22, 1844.
One child d. in infancy.

Family of Capt. Simon Kezar.

CAPT. SIMON KEZAR, b. in Sutton, N.H., July 21, 1672—m. Piercy Hovey, b. Aug. 15, 1788. They were among the most enterprising of the settlers of Hatley. He d. Jan. 10, 1833.

CHILDREN.

SHERBURN, b. Sept. 29, 1807—d. July 5, 1813.
PRAXANA, b. July 22, 1809—m. *Amos Lawrence.*
SIMON, b. May 16, 1811—m. *Mary Wadleigh.*
SHERBURN, 2d, b. Feb. 15, 1813—m. *Amanda Remick.*
LUCINDA, b. Feb. 6, 1817—m. *William Little.*
HOLLIS, b. Nov. 29, 1822—m. and settled at the south.
MARIA, b. May 5, 1825—m. *Hale Johnson.*
HELEN, b. April 5, 1826—m. *Burton Harvey.*

Family of Amos Kezar.

AMOS KEZAR married *Dorcas Lowell.* Settled on Nos. 11 and 12, 4th Range of Hatley, in 1802. Their children were Samuel who m. *Betsey Hutchins;* Chauncey, m. *Roxana Wadleigh;* Mehitable, m. *Edward Hitchcock;* John, m. *Eliza Griffin;* Dorothy, m. *B. F. Brown,* Amos, m. *Emily J. Colby;* Clarissa, m. a *Mr. Huntingdon,* and Albert, who died young.

AMOS KEZAR, JUN., b. in Hatley, June 12, 1819—m. *Emily J. Colby,* who was b. in Coventry, Vt., May 10, 1823. They settled on the homestead of his father, in Hatley.

CHILDREN.

LOVISA, J., b. Aug. 10, 1844—d. Aug. 18, 1864.
JONATHAN, b. Oct. 3, 1846.
HOLLIS, b. June 3, 1851—d. July 29, 1853.
ALBERT H., b. Sept. 9, 1854.
IDA M., b. Dec. 26, 1856.
HOLLIS, 2d, b. Oct. 9, 1862—d. Aug. 19, 1864.

Family of Joseph Kezar.

JOSEPH KEZAR, b. in Sutton, N.H., Nov. 28, 1780—m. *Polly Fletcher,* b. in Groton, Mass., Aug. 17, 1787. They settled in Hatley, in 1812. He d. in February, 1847.

CHILDREN.

JOSEPH, b. Aug. 28, 1811— m. *Celina Leavitt.*
MARY, b. June 5, 1814—m. *Anson Ellworth.*
EMILY, b. May 22, 1824—m. *Charles L. Percival.*
ELEANOR, b. March 15, 1827—d. Oct., 1833.

The Harvey Families.

These families were among the early settlers of Hatley. They were generally active, enterprising, and intelligent. We have not been able to get their genealogical record.

Family of Joseph Fish.

JOSEPH FISH, b. in Pepperell, Mass., April 17, 1770—m. *Sarah Spear,* b. in Walpole, N.H., March 24, 1770. He d. April 32, 1859. She d. Oct. 12, 1858.

CHILDREN.

LEMUEL, b. Aug. 16, 1794—m. *Mary Rowell.*
JOSEPH, b. Aug. 28, 1795—d. Aug. 28, 1812.
CHAMPION, b. Sept. 6, 1797—m. *Polly Wells.*
HORACE, b. Jan. 6, 1800—m. *Hannah Leavitt.*

Family of Lemuel Fish.

LEMUEL FISH, b. in Walpole, N.H., Aug. 16, 1794—m. *Mary Rowell,* b. in Fishersfield, N.H., Oct. 20, 1799. They settled on No. 9, 1st Range of Hatley.

CHILDREN.

SALLY, b. Feb. 20, 1818—m. *Nathan Emory.*
JOSEPH, b. June 6, 1820—m. *Elizabeth Paradis.*
LEONARD, b. Feb. 4, 1824—m. *Cynthia Elliott.*
LYDIA, b. April 7, 1827.
THOMAS, b. July 1, 1829—d. April 8, 1832.
THOMAS, 2nd, b. June 19, 1833—m. *Ida Bachelder.*
NATHAN, b. May 26, 1836—m. *Mary Sheldon.*
KENDRICK, b. April 12, 1841—m. *Lizzie Morse.*

Family of Champion Fish.

CHAMPION FISH, b. Sept. 6, 1797—m. Polly Wells. They settled in Hatley.

CHILDREN.

ELEANOR, b. Oct. 27, 1819—m. *Abial Abbott.*
BETSEY, b. April 8, 1821—m. *Asa Foster.*
Mary Ann, b. in May, 1823—m. *Josiah Osgood.*

The Hitchcock Families.

These families are of English origin. Their ancestors were among the New England Colonists of the 17th century.

Family of Ephraim Hitchcock.

EPHRAIM HITCHCOCK and his wife were natives of Reading, Vt. Settled on No. 6, 4th Range of Hatley, in 1796, but afterwards sold out and removed to the West. Their children were Ephraim, who m. *Esther Johnson*; Artemas, m. *Mary Tilden*; Polly, m. a *Mr. Hart*, and Hannah, who m. a *Mr. Bajeau.*

Family of Paul Hitchcock.

PAUL HITCHCOCK, b. in Reading, Vt., Nov. 22, 1772—m. *Hannah Pease*, b. in Weathersfield, Vt., Nov. 30, 1774. They settled in Hatley. He d. May 15, 1845. She d. Jan. 14, 1851.

CHILDREN.

LOIS, b. June 28, 1804—m. *Appleton Plumley.*
EDWARD, b. in May, 1806.
SUMNER, b. April 27, 1809.
BEAMOND, b. in Feb. 1811—m. *Rebecca Lord.*
PAUL, b. June 29, 1814.

PAUL HITCHCOCK, b. June 29, 1814—m. *Emeline Woodward*, b. April 30, 1816. He was engaged in mercantile business several years in Massawippi Village.

CHILDREN.

HOLLIS J., b. Feb. 24, 1838.
AMANDA M., b. Feb. 19, 1840—d. Aug. 24, 1846.
OLIVE M., b. March 14, 1846.
SANFORD C., b. Nov. 5, 1848.
GILBERT P., b. Jan. 16, 1851.
IDA W., twin, b. June 26, 1856—d. Oct. 14, 1856.
ADA F., twin, b. June 26, 1856.

EDWARD HITCHCOCK, b. in August, 1806—m. *Mehitable Kezar.* Their children were Caroline, who m. *Roscoe Woodward;* Lois, who m. *Wright Hovey;* Melissa, and Teresa.

SUMNER HITCHCOCK, b. April 27, 1809—m. *Prudence Barber*, b. March 23, 1813. They settled in West Hatley.

CHILDREN.

ANGELINE, b. May 23, 1834—m. *William Utten.*
PORTUS H., b. June 22, 1841.
MARY A., b. Sept. 19, 1852.

Family of Appleton Plumley.

APPLETON PLUMLEY, b. in Bristol, Vt., in 1783—m. Lois Hitchcock, b. June 28, 1804. They settled in Hatley in 1815. He d. Jan. 30, 1859.

CHILDREN.

ALDEN, b. May 5, 1823—m. *Julia A. McConnell.*
HANNAH, b. Oct. 1, 1824—m. *H. Chilson.*
APPLETON, b. Aug. 8, 1832—m. *Eliza A. Hitchcock.*
HORATIO, b. Sept. 16, 1835—m. *Sarah J. Leet.*
ANNA, b. June 16, 1837—m. *Samuel Vorney.*
HOMER, b. June 30, 1839.
EMMA J., b. Nov. 16, 1841—m. *Lyman Duslin.*
BENJAMIN, b. March 16, 1844—m. *Matilda Sias.*
HORACE, b. Sept. 9, 1846—m. *Martha Curtis.*
DARWIN, b. Sept. 16, 1849.

The Judd Family.

Branches of this family are found in different parts of New England and Canada. Their ancestors were among the early

FAMILY OF EPHRAIM WADLEIGH.

emigrants from England to the New England colony. The earliest record we find is that Ebenezer Judd married *Mary Hawkin*, and settled in Watertown, Conn.

Family of Hawkins Judd.

HAWKINS JUDD, son of Ebenezer Judd, was b. in Watertown, Conn., Oct. 22, 1765. In 1790, he m. *Annis Butler*, a native of Claremont, N.H. They were among the earliest settlers of Hatley. She d. Dec. 3, 1807. In 1814, he m. Mary Marsh. He died in April, 1856.

CHILDREN OF 1ST MARRIAGE.

LAURA, b. May 3, 1791—m. *Augustus Abbott*.
FRANCIS, b. Aug. 12, 1792.
ANNIS, b. Dec. 21, 1796—m. *James C. Peaslee, Esq*.
HAWKINS, b. Oct. 26, 1799. Settled in Illinois.
ELVIRA, b. Oct. 22, 1804—m. *Wm. G. Cook, Esq*.

The children by the 2nd marriage were Bedar, who m. a *Miss Abbott*, Osburn, Marsh, and Mary.

The Wadleigh Families.

These families are among the most numerous in Hatley. They are of English origin, and their ancestors were among the early colonists of New England.

Family of Ephraim Wadleigh.

EPHRAIM WADLEIGH, b. in Hampstead, N.H., March 8, 1770—m. *Alice Little*, b. in Sutton, N.H., May 2, 1773, and settled on No. 10, 2nd Range of Hatley, in 1801. He d. Jan. 30, 1852. She d. Feb. 21, of the same year.

CHILDREN.

SAMUEL, b. Jan. 17, 1794—m. 1st, *Polly Marsh;* 2nd, *Mary Evans*.
BETSEY, b. Oct. 7, 1796—m. *Moses Coburn*.
MARY, b. Dec. 20, 1798—m. *Nathaniel Bachelder*.
TAYLOR, b. Dec. 8, 1799—m. *Malinda Hovey*.

THOMAS, b. April 15, 1802—m. *Hannah Little.*
RUTH, b. Sept. 13, 1805—m. 1st, *Thomas Paradis;* 2nd, *John Bellows.*
ROXANA, b. May, 16, 1808—m. *Chancey Kezar.*
LUKE, b. Aug. 10, 1810—m. *Phebe Rowell.*

Family of Capt. Taylor Wadleigh.

TAYLOR WADLEIGH, b. in Fishersfield, N.H., Dec. 8, 1799. Was about three years old when his parents settled in Hatley. His early opportunities of education had been limited to the defective schools of the settlement, but his native good sense, shrewdness, and general observation enabled him to overcome in a great measure the defects of his early school training. Such was the clearness of his perception, that he seemed to grasp intuitively almost any subject presented to him, and in private discussion and in public debate, he was excelled by very few. He was a first rate farmer, ever ready to adopt improvements and to infuse a spirit of enterprise among his neighbors.

He early took an active interest in the politics of the country, and associated himself with the Radical Reform Party, and was active in the agitation which resulted in the Rebellion of 1837-1839. In the fall of 1837 he was arrested on a charge of high treason, and confined for a few weeks in Montreal Jail. On examination no evidence was adduced against him and he was set at liberty. He lived, however, to see the principles he advocated at least in part acknowledged, and the Government administered in accordance with his views of justice and right. In early life, he m. *Malinda Hovey.* She d. July 26, 1864. He d. November 29, 1866.

CHILDREN.

HORATIO, b. in Feb., 1820—m. *Matilda Gould.*
MALINDA, b. Aug. 19, 1822—m. *Edward Hawes.*
ALICE C., b. June 7, 1830.
EVERETT F., b. Aug. 23, 1832—m. *Addie,* dau. of *George W. Brooks, Esq.*
ELLEN, b. Aug. 19, 1844.

Family of John Wadleigh.

JOHN WADLEIGH m. *Judith Emory.* They settled on No. 8, 1st Range of Hatley. He d. April 25, 1843. She d. in 1859. Their children were Amasa, who m. Z. P. Jones, and Lydia, who m. 1st,

Joseph Fletcher; 2nd, Samuel Kezar.

Amasa Wadleigh.

AMASA WADLEIGH, b. July 27, 1809—m. *Zilphia P. Jones.* They settled on the family homestead.

CHILDREN.

VIOLA, b. Dec. 31, 1838—m. *Bradley Jones.*
JOHN R., b. April 26, 1841—enlisted in the United States' Army, Was dangerously wounded, and d. at the Hospital in Brattleboro', Vt., June 23, 1864.

The Abbott Families.

The earliest account we have of these families is that Deacon Abial Abbott and wife removed from Charlotte, Vt., in 1794, and settled in Magog. Two or three sons and one daughter settled in Canada.

Family of Abial Abbott, jun.

ABIAL, son of Dea. Abial Abbott, was b. Aug. 15, 1778. Came to Canada with his parents at an early age. Located in Hatley, and, Dec. 11, 1800, m. *Grace Hitchcock*, b. in Reading, Vt., Dec. 21, 1778. She came to Hatley at the age of 22 years, and d. in 1866, at the advanced age of 89 years. He d. March 6, 1841.

CHILDREN.

STEPHEN, b. Oct. 15, 1791—d. May 24, 1803.
ELECTA, b. Nov. 5, 1803—m. *Joel Tilden.*
AUGUSTUS, 2nd, b. Nov. 24, 1805—m. *Lora Bean.*
JAMES, b. May 21, 1808—d. March 28, 1814.
STEPHEN, 2nd, b. March 11, 1810—d. March 21, 1814.
LUCINDA, b. Jan. 21, 1812—d. March 2, 1814.
ABIAL S., b. June 7, 1814—m. *Eleanor Fish!*
PHILIP J., b. Feb. 17, 1816—m. *Caroline Hovey.*
LUTHER, b. April 16, 1818—d. April 18, 1819.
LUTHER, 2nd, b. Nov. 12, 1821—m. *Ellen LeBaron.*

Luther Abbott.

LUTHER ABBOTT, b. in Hatley, P.Q., Nov. 11, 1821. July 26, 1849, he m. *Ellen*, dau. of *James LeBaron.* He is a successful merchant has sustained the office of Mayor of the Township Corporation 4 years, and been otherwise actively employed in public affairs and received the appointment of postmaster in 1855. One child, Ella G., b. Nov. 16, 1853.

Family of Colbe Abbott.

COLBE ABBOTT, son of Dea. Abial Abbott, was born in Tolland, Conn., May 21, 1783. Came to Hatley with his father when 13 years old. He settled on No. 11, 13th Range of Hatley. Married *Esther Oliver*, b. March 4, 1792. She d. Feb. 11, 1866. He d. in 1866.

CHILDREN.

ESTHER, b. April 12, 1808—m. *Wm. Chamberlin.*
CALVIN, b. in December, 1810—m. *Sylvia Chamberlin.*
LUTHER, b. Nov. 8, 1813—d. Feb. 5, 1814.
COLBE, b. July 7, 1816—m. *Rectina Rexford.*
GEORGE, b. Jan. 24, 1818—m. *Betsey Merry.*
JOSEPH, b. Oct. 13, 1819—m. *Sarah Amy.*
LUCINDA, b. May 30, 1824—m. *Rice Rexford, jun.*

COLBE ABBOTT, JUN., b. July 7, 1816—m. *Rectina Rexford*, b. Oct. 3, 1815: They reside on the family homestead. No children.

CALVIN ABBOTT, b. in December, 1810—m. *Sylvia Chamberlin.* Commenced mercantile business in Magog, in 1844; has been successful. Was appointed Postmaster in 1850, and has been otherwise employed in public affairs. Was one of the founders of the present village of Magog. No children.

GEORGE ABBOTT, b. Jan. 24, 1818— m. *Betsey Merry*, b. Aug. 5, 1821. Is employed in public affairs; is Secretary-Treasurer of the Corporation of Magog.

CHILDREN.

ARTHUR, J., b. May 4, 1845.
ARINA, b. July 23, 1849.

JOSEPH ABBOTT, b. Oct. 30, 1819—m. *Sarah Amy*, b. May 6, 1827. Settled on No. 12, 14th Range of Hatley, now Magog.

CHILDREN.

ELLERY P., b. Sept. 14, 1851.
VIOLA A., b. July 19, 1854—d. June 30, 1857.
OLIVE A., b. May 6, 1857.
WARREN F., b. April 14, 1860.
ESTHER V., b. Jan. 4, 1866.

The Merry Families.

Ralph Merry, 1st, the earliest of these families of whom we have any record, was a native of London, England, whence he emigrated to Massachusetts, then a British Colony, in the latter part of the 17th century. He sold the vessel of which he was the owner and master, and settled in Lynn, Mass., where he m. a Miss Rhodes, and had one son named Ralph. This son married, and his descendants are scattered over the Northern and Southern States. One of this family, Ralph Merry, 3rd, settled in Canada. He was b. in Lynn, Mass.—m. Sarah Sylvester. Settled on No. 6, 17th Range of Bolton, now Magog, in 1798. He subsequently purchased several other lots in the vicinity, and became proprietor of the entire tract which comprises the present village of Magog. He built the first grist mill and saw mill at the Outlet, and started an iron foundry, and was a practical farmer. He d. in 1825. His wife d. in 1814. Their children were Daniel, who m. *Lucinda Young;* Sarah, m. *Solomon Reeve;* John S., m. *Olive Chamberlin;* Polly, m. *Nason Hoyt;* Ralph 4th, m. *Ruth Whitcomb;* Benjamin was lost in the woods at the age of 10 years, and never found; Lucy, m. *Samuel Hoyt, Esq.;* Joseph d. at the age of 17 years, and Benjamin, 2nd, who m. *Lorena Nelson.*

Family of John S. Merry.

JOHN S. MERRY, b. in Providence, R. I., in 1783—m. *Olive Chamberlin,* b. in Charlotte, Vt., in 1793. They settled in Bolton, P.Q. He d. 1855; she d. in 1857.

CHILDREN.

RALPH 5, b. Nov. 6, 1809.
OLIVE, b. Feb. 5, 1811—d. in 1814.
LAVINIA, b. Feb. 16, 1813.
OLIVE 2ND, b. Aug. 15, 1814—m: *Lyman Willey.*

Polly, b. April 23, 1816—m. *Orrisson Bullard.*
John S., b. March 2, 1819—d. Feb. 2, 1857.
Betsey, b. Aug. 15, 1821—m. *George Abbott, Esq.*
Julia A., b. June 27, 1823—d. July 5, 1836.
Maria, b. Dec. 11, 1824—m. *Orrisson Bullard,* his 2nd wife.
Arina, b. Sept. 14, 1826—d. March 20, 1848.
Matilda, b. Aug. 13, 1828—m. *Elisha Jenne, Esq.*
Horace H., b. July 22, 1830—d. April 5, 1849.
D. Lewis, b. Feb. 24, 1832.
Emily, b. Nov. 5, 1834—d. Jan. 29, 1848.

Ralph Merry 5th, b. in Bolton, now Magog, Nov. 6, 1809—m. *Susan Rexford,* b. in Bolton Sept. 11, 1817. He has been engaged in mercantile business for many years, has been successful and has been actively employed in public affairs.

CHILDREN.

Julia A., b. March 13, 1838—m. *A. H. Moore, Esq.,* who is engaged in mercantile business at Magog.
Lestina A., b. Oct. 5, 1840.
Florence L., b. June 5, 1843—m. *Geo. O. Somers, M.D.,* his 2nd wife.
Horace R., b. Feb. 10, 1850.

Family of Joseph Merry.

Joseph Merry, son of Daniel Merry, was b. June 25, 1811—m. *Sarah Buzzell,* b. March 19, 1814. They settled on No. 5, 12th Range of Bolton, now Magog

CHILDREN.

Lestina, b. Sept. 18, 1847,

Elwin J. } twins, b. Jan. 5, 1850.
Elena

Lucy A., b. Aug. 2, 1839.
John W., b. April 2, 1843.

Family of Benjamin Rexford.

Benjamin Rexford m. *Catherine Rice.* They were natives of Connecticut, and settled on No. 4, 16th Range of Hatley, in

FAMILY OF ABRAHAM REXFORD. 265

1795. He afterwards received a grant of this lot as an Associate. He d. May 19, 1845; she d. Aug. 13, 1835. Their children were Benijah, who m. 1st *Suviah Squire;* 2nd, *Roxana Ayer;* Abraham, m. *Clarissa Hovey;* Olive, m. *Chester Hovey;* Joanna, m. *Dr. Robert Boyes;* Rice, m. *Marcia Nelson;* and Sally who died young.

RICE REXFORD, b. in Meriden, Conn., Dec. 12, 1790—m. *Marcia Nelson*, b. in Springfield, Mass., June 21, 1796. They settled on the homestead of his father, Benjamin Rexford.

CHILDREN.

RECTINA, b. Oct. 3, 1815—m. *Colbe Abbott.*
SUSAN, b. Sept. 11, 1817—m. *Ralph Merry, 5th.*
FANNY, b. April 11, 1819—m. *Joshua Chamberlin.*
MIRANDA, b. Sept. 11, 1821—m. *Luke Bullard.*
RICE, b. Feb. 14, 1825—m. 1st, *Lorinda Abbott;* 2nd, *Ann Chamberlin.*
RUSSELL, b. Oct. 19, 1827.
MARTHA, b. Aug. 11, 1839—m. *Samuel Randall.*

RUSSELL REXFORD, youngest son of Rice Rexford was born Oct. 19, 1827—m. *Lavinia A. Bryant*, b. Sept. 25, 1829.

CHILDREN.

MARY, b. March 25, 1852—d. Oct. 6, 1858.
SUSAN, b. April 13, 1861.

Family of Abraham Rexford.

ABRAHAM REXFORD m. *Clarissa Hovey.* Their children were Laura, who m. *David Jewett;* Myron, m. *Martha Boynton;* Sarah, m. *Joseph Cass;* Chester, m. *Asenath Moore;* George, m. *Sophia Taylor;* Clara, m. *James Howe;* and Jane, who m. *Squire W. Taylor.*

When quite a young man, Abraham Rexford was attacked in the woods by a she-bear with three cubs. His father and brothers, who were near, ran to his assistance. After a desperate encounter, the old bear succeeded in making her escape. They killed the cubs, which were fat, and furnished a good supply of meat for the family. The wild game from the forest and the fish from the lake formed an important part of the support of the early settlers.

Family of Isaac Rexford.

ISAAC REXFORD m. *Lucretia Besey.* They settled in Hatley in 1794. Their children were LUCY, who m. *Elam Hall;* Whiting, m. *Mercy Packard;* POLLY, m. *Elam Hall;* (his 2d wife); ORRIN, m. *Lydia Mansfield;* ISAAC, m. a *Miss Fuller;* and HORACE, who m. a *Miss Mansfield.* These are mostly dead or have left the country.

Family of Samuel Rexford, jun.

SAMUEL REXFORD, jun., b. in Hatley, Dec. 18, 1808—m. Joanna Taplin, b. in Stanstead, May 2, 1814. They settled on Nos. 14 and 15, 16th Range of Hatley.

CHILDREN.

JOHN M., b. Sept. 21, 1836—m. *Eliza Barber.*
LAWSON, b. Feb. 5, 1838—d. Aug. 31, 1848.
ELLEN, b. Feb. 15, 1846.
MANSON, b. June 15, 1848.

Family of William Oliver, M.D.

WILLIAM OLIVER, M.D., m. *Elizabeth Kinston.* They were natives of Massachusetts, and settled on No. 15, 14th Range of Hatley, in 1807. He d. Aug. 19, 1819; she d. Oct. 29, 1829. Their children were ESTHER, who m. *Colbe Abbott, sen.;* WILLIAM, m. *Polly Remich;* EBENEZER, m. *Nancy Call;* POLLY, m. *Moses Copp, jun.;* GEORGE, m. *Marilla Chamberlin;* and JOHN, who m. *Lydia Buzzell.* These families are settled mostly in Magog and the neighboring towns.

WILLIAM OLIVER, jun., b. in Were, N.H., Oct. 27, 1793—m. *Polly Remich,* b. in Dunbarton, N.H., Aug. 19, 1798. She d. Dec. 1, 1848. Mr. Oliver sustained the office of Captain of Militia nearly 40 years.

CHILDREN.

EDWARD, b. May 22, 1818.
MARION B., b. June 14, 1819—m. *Joshua Perry.*
WILLIAM W., b. Oct. 14, 1821.

EDWARD OLIVER, b. May 22, 1818—m. *Mary Foss,* b. Jan. 22, 1818, and settled near Oliver Corner in Magog.

FAMILY OF EDWARD REMICH.

CHILDREN.

AVA, b. July 19, 1843—d. Oct. 16, 1853
JAMES R., b. July 6, 1845.
IDA M., b. Sept. 9, 1847.
MARION B., b. May 16, 1850.
ADAMS P., b. June 18, 1852.
WILLIAM W., b. March 7, 1858.
WILLIAM W. OLIVER, b. Oct. 14, 1821—m. *Sarah Perry*, b. March 9, 1821. They reside on the homestead. He has been variously employed in public affairs.

CHILDREN.

MARY R., b. Aug. 14, 1851—d. Sept. 16, 1865.
MINNIE, b. Dec. 25, 1860.

Family of Daniel Merry.

DANIEL MERRY, Son of Ralph Merry, 4th—m. *Lucinda Young.* Their children were Lucy, HIRAM, who m. *Esther Willey*; JOHN S. m. *Dorothy Ward*; JOSEPH, m. *Sarah Buzell*, and Electa, who m. *Calvin Bruce*. Daniel Merry d. in 1816; his wife d. in 1835.

Family of Edward Remich.

EDWARD REMICH, b. in Haverhill, Mass., Aug. 8, 1775—m. *Polly Hogg*, b. in Dunbarton, N.H., March 31, 1779. They were m. Aug. 17, 1797. Settled originally in New Hampshire. Came to Canada in 1799, and located on No. 9, 15th Range of Hatley, now Magog. He d. April 10, 1850.

CHILDREN.

POLLY, b. Aug. 19, 1798—m. *William Oliver.*
EDWARD, JUN., b. Sept. 17, 1801.
PAIGE, b. July 24, 1803—m. *Laura Ward.*
BETSEY, b. Feb. 8, 1808—m. *A. A. Adams, Esq.*
SUSAN, b. March 11, 1810—m. *Captain M. W. Copp.*
AMANDA, b. Dec. 3, 1814—m. *Sherburn Kezar.*
ELSIE D., b. May 31, 1817—m. *Abel C. Geer.*
SEWELL S., b. July 20, 1819—m. *Susan Oliver.*

2 CHILDREN DIED YOUNG.

EDWARD REMICH, JUN., b. Sept. 17, 1801—m. *Lydia H. Mooney*, b. Sept. 6, 1807. They reside on No. 10, 14th Range, in Magog. He has for many years been employed in public affairs.

CHILDREN.

ROBERT B., b. March 31, 1826.
ANDREW M., b. July 14, 1834—m. *Myrtilla Collins*.
DON C., b. May 11, 1836.
ALVAREZ, b. March 31, 1844—d. in 1847.
LUCINDA L., b. July 10, 1846.
BURNHAM, b. June 26, 1850.

Family of David Remich.

DAVID REMICH m. *Lydia Austin*. Their children were DANIEL, who m. *Polly Kilborn*; LYDIA, m. *Erastus White*; WEALTHY, m. *Leonard Clark*, and POLLY, who m. a *Mr. Davis*.

Family of Jonathan Cox.

JONATHAN COX m. *Naomi Smith*. They were natives of New Hampshire—were among the early settlers of Hatley. Their children were WEALTHY, who m. *Abraham F. J. Channell*; JONATHAN, m. *Comfort Martin*; SALLY, m. *Joseph Srew*; WARREN, m. *Sarah Bacon*, HARRIET, m. *Amasa Ramsdell*, and POLLY, who m. *Ebenezer Hovey, jun.*

The children of Jonathan Cox, jun., were SOPHRONIA, who m. *Guilford Magoon*; ERASTUS, m. *Elsie Magoon*; JOSEPH, m. *Margaret Mitchell*; CHARLES, m. *Sarah Randall*; WEALTHY, m. *Ira Abbey*, and LUCIUS, who m. *Sophia Mitchell*. The children of Warren Cox were Nelson, Orson, Carlos, and Ai.

Family of Nicholas Austin, jun.

NICHOLAS AUSTIN, jun., b. in 1783—m. *Lavinia Harvey*. They settled in Bolton. She d. Jan. 25, 1851.

CHILDREN.

ABIGAIL, b. Oct. 28, 1819—m. *Wm. Sargeant*.
SOPHRONIA, b. April 26, 1821—m. *Harvey Hammond*.
CLARISSA, b. Oct. 19, 1823.

SABRINA, b. June 20, 1827.
EMILY, b. Aug. 27, 1834.
WILLIAM H., b. Feb. 26, 1837.

Family of Moses Austin.

MOSES AUSTIN was b. in Wolfeborough, N.H., June 24, 1780. Came to Canada with his father in 1794, m. *Temperance Glidden*, and settled on No. 24, 12th Range of Bolton. He d. in 1852. She d. in 1855.

CHILDREN.

SARAH, b. 1813—m. *Isaiah Clough*.
DANIEL, b. June 17, 1815.
LUCETTA, b. Dec. 17, 1817—m. *Richard Kimpton*.
BRITANIA, b. in Feb., 1820—m. *George Mansergh*.
BETSEY, b. in May, 1822.
SOPHRONIA, b. in Sept., 1825—m. *Alpheus Kimpton*.
GEORGE, b. in 1827—m. *Emily Heath*.

DANIEL AUSTIN, b. June 17, 1815—m. *Harriet Bachelder*, b. in Rougemont, C.E., in 1823. They settled on No. 24, 2nd Range of Stanstead.

CHILDREN.

DANIEL, JUN., b. April 21, 1851.
MOSES, b. Nov. 24, 1854.
SOPHRONIA, b. Feb. 14, 1859.
PHEBE, b. Oct. 3, 1860.
GEORGE, b. Dec. 20, 1862.
HARRIET, b. Feb. 8, 1863—d. in Aug., 1864.

Family of Isaac H. Merriman.

ISAAC H. MERRIMAN, eldest son of Amasa Merriman, was born in Meriden, Conn., in 1793. Came to Canada when a child. He married *Rectina*, dau. of *Wm. Bullock, Esq.*, born in 1798. They settled near the present village of Georgeville, in 1818. He d. in 1858.

CHILDREN.

AMASA J., b. Dec. 1, 1818—engaged as clerk in mercantile business with Chancey Bullock, Esq., in 1836, and subsequently married his daughter, *Clarissa J. Bullock*. In 1842 he began business in his own name, at Bloomington, Illinois, where he has been for many years a successful merchant. Was for several years mayor of the city, and in 1855, received the appointment of Judge of Probate,

HARRY P.,—m. *Mary Thomas.*
ANNIS, m. *John Lovell.*
ARTEMISIA, m. *Henry Lovell.*
LORENA, m. *Luman Sutton.*
OLIVE, m. *Walter Lovell.*
CHARLES, d. at the age of 21.
4 children d. young.

Family of Amasa Merriman.

AMASA MERRIMAN, b. in Meriden, Conn., June 7, 1767—m. *Anna Hall*, b. in Enfield, Conn., in 1777. They settled on No. 1, 17th Range of Hatley, (now Magog,) in 1794. The neighborhood was then a dense forest. He and his wife were among the number that formed the Baptist Church of Hatley and Stanstead, at its first organization. He d. June 6, 1843; she d. in 1853. Their children were Sally, who d. at the age of 18; Isaac, who m. *Rectina Bullock;* Amasa, who d. when about 15 years old; Joseph, m. *Nancy Mooney;* Harvey, m. *Clarissa Ives;* Betsey, m. *Samuel Bullock;* Nathaniel, drowned at an early age; Titus, who d. young; Lewis, m. *Harriet Bullock;* Charles, m. and settled in Illinois; Sally, 2nd, m. *Amos Nott;* Nancy A., m. a *Mr. Frost;* and Ira, who m. *Belinda Webster.*

Family of Joseph Merriman.

JOSEPH MERRIMAN, 3rd son of Amasa Merriman, was b. in Hatley, April 4, 1798— m. *Nancy Mooney*, b. in Alton, N.H., March 8, 1801. They settled on the family homestead.

CHILDREN.

TITUS M., b. April 23, 1822—m. *Zeviah Blanchard.*
SARAH ANN, b. Aug. 25, 1826—m. *Wm. Oliver.*
IRA, b. Feb. 18, 1829.
LUCIUS T., b. March 20, 1831—m. *Pamelia D. Buzzell.*
MARY L., b. Jan. 4, 1834—m. *Jonathan Converse.*
FRANCIS G., b. April 3, 1836—m. *Betsey Archilles.*
NATHANIEL D., b. June 25, 1838—d. March 25, 1839.

The Ives Families.

These families settled in different parts of Stanstead County, are all the descendants of Joseph and Joel Ives. They were natives of Connecticut and came to Canada in 1793. We have no authentic account of their ancestry, but tradition says that they were among the early emigrants to the New England Colonies. Joseph and Joel Ives were men of energy, and their posterity, with hardly an exception, have been intelligent and useful members of the community, some of whom have occupied prominent positions in public life. We find them generally identified with the different branches of the Christian Church.

Family of Joel Ives.

JOEL IVES, b. in Meriden, Conn., in 1770—m. *Lucy Hart*, b. in the same town in 1780. He d. Oct. 11, 1833. She d. April 30, 1843.

CHILDREN.

ELI, b. Feb. 11, 1799.
JULIUS, b. Sept. 13, 1800—m. *Laura Drew*.
JOEL, JUN., b. Sept. 1, 1804.
JERUSHA, b. Dec. 21, 1807—m. *A. B. Potter;* 2nd, *Chauncey Bullock*.
ESTHER, b. Feb. 21, 1810—m. *Gladden Farewell*.
JOHN, b. Sept. 1, 1812—m. *Elizabeth Appleton*.
HART, b. Dec. 27, 1814.
LUCY, b. March 1, 1817—m. *Rev. A. Gillies*.
ERASTUS, b. Sept. 14, 1822—m. *Harriet Green*.

ELI IVES m. *Artemisia Bullock.* Their children were Harriet, who m. *Rev. John Armstrong;* Frances, who m. *Isaac Butters;* Adelaide, Eli, William, and Thaddeus.

JULIUS IVES m. *Laura Drew.* Their children were Julius, b. Sept. 19, 1824; Cornelius, b. Dec. 18, 1827; Laura B., b. Feb. 18, 1833; Joel H., b. April 1, 1836, and Wolfred N., b. Aug, 18, 1838.

BENJAMIN H. IVES m. *Lucretia Rexford.* Their children were Homer, b. Oct. 8, 1848; Emily, b. July 12, 1851; Caroline L., b. Dec. 8, 1855, and Ann E., b. Dec. 25, 1857.

Family of Joseph Ives, sen.

JOSEPH IVES, SEN, m. *Clarissa Hall*. Their children were Harley, Joseph, Isaac, Titus, and Avery.

ISAAC IVES, b. in Hartley, Oct. 28, 1801—m. *Celina Davis*. They settled in Hatley, subsequently removed to Stanstead. She d. Sept. 14, 1837. March 10, 1839, he m. *Lucy Patch*.

CHILDREN BY 1st MARRIAGE.

MARION, b. Aug. 27, 1835—m. *James C. Kerr*.
3 children died young.

CHILDREN BY 2ND MARRIAGE.

ELLEN, b. Feb. 17, 1840,
BETSEY, b. Oct. 10, 1841—m. *Joel H. Ives*.

HARLEY IVES, b. Aug. 20—m. *Martha Sleeper*, b. Aug. 17, 1797. They settled on parts of Nos. 4 and 5, 1st Range of Hatley. Their children were Joseph, Ozro, Alfred, Emily C., Mary, and Riley—Riley m. Maria Little.

JOSEPH IVES, JUN., b. Dec. 12, 1796. In 1826, he m. *Alzada Kimball*. Settled on Nos. 4 and 5, 1st Range of Hatley, with his brother Harley Ives. In 1849, his buildings and their contents were destroyed by fire.

CHILDREN.

CLARISSA, b. Aug. 26, 1827—d. Oct. 27, 1848.
JOHN, b. July 27, 1829—m. *Lora Bean*.
AVERY, b. May 15, 1831—m, *Eleanor Pool*.
BETSEY, b. March 4, 1833—m. *G. A. Kennedy*.
CELINA, b. March 29, 1835—m. *Fletcher Boynton*.
SARAH M., b. Sept. 13, 1837—m. *Henry Pool*.
EMILY P., b. Nov. 4, 1839—m. *Charles Lawton*.
JAMES, b. Oct. 14, 1843.

The McConnell Family.

THOMAS MCCONNELL, a native of Ireland, m. *Anna Garvin*, b in England. They emigrated to America early in the 18th century. Settled originally in New Hampshire, but removed to Johnson, Vt., where they died. Their children were *Moses*,

Jonathan, Thomas, Lemuel, David, Mary, Betsey, Sarah, and *Anna.* Four of these, only, settled in Canada.

Family of Thomas McConnell, jun.

THOMAS MCCONNELL, JUN., a native of New Hampshire, began on No. 16, 2nd Range of Hatley, in 1796, removed subsequently to No. 6, 1st Range. He m. *Roxana Hovey.* He afterwards left the country. She married C. Flanders, survived him, and lived to the age of more than 90 years. The compiler received many interesting reminiscences from her. The children of Thomas McConnell, jun., were *John,* who m. *Alice Wadleigh* ; *Mary,* m. *Jonathan Ayer, Minerva,* m. *True Worthen, James,* who died at New Orleans; *Orange* m. *Augusta Worthen,* and *George,* who lives at Honolulu, S. I.

Family of Col. John McConnell.

JOHN MCCONNELL, b. in Hatley, May 20, 1799. His early training, like that of the other young pioneers, had been limited to the very defective schools of the settlement, but, possessing a clear and discriminating mind, he acquired a good amount of knowledge, and was well acquainted with jurisprudence and the politics of our country. In 1844 he was elected to represent Stanstead county in the Provincial Parliament, and in 1847 was returned by acclammation. His political career was a prosperous one. He has sustained the office of magistrate for many years, has filled successively, the offices of sergeant, ensign, lieutenant, captain, major, and lieut-colonel, in the militia, and has been active in the municipal and educational interests of the township and county. At the age of 21 he m. *Alice,* dau. of *Jesse Wadleigh.*

CHILDREN.

JULIA A., b. April 1, 1821.—m. *Alden Plumley.*
OSCAR F., b. April 21, 1823—m. *Rossilla Leavitt.*
MARIETTA, b. July 26, 1827—d. July 1, 1832.
JOHN, b. April 30, 1832—d. April 24, 1842.
JESSE W., b. July 9, 1836—m. *Mary J. Woodward.*

The Johnson Families.

The name of Johnson, like that of Smith and Brown, appears to be ubiquitous. The name was probably formed by the affix *son* to the christian name, *John*. Of the various families of this name scattered widely over Europe and America, few are probably able to trace their origin to the same source.

Family of Jonathan Johnson.

JONATHAN JOHNSON was a native of England, came to America in the early part of the 18th century, settled in Amherst, Mass., where he m. *Sarah Bates*, a native of that town. Their children were *David*, who was a soldier in the American army and was killed in the battle of West Point; Delilah, m. a *Mr. Jameson;* Jonathan, m. *Susanna Hale*, and Sarah, who m. a *Mr. Proctor*.

JONATHAN JOHNSON, jun., m. and settled in Westfield, Mass. His children were *David, Loammi*, and *Jonathan*. He subsequently married his 2nd wife, Susanna Hale. Their children were *Zacheus, Esther, Arthur, Eliza*, and *Abel B*. Jonathan Johnson, jun., settled in Hatley, in 1802. He d. in 1830; his wife d. in 1834. A part of their descendants, only, settled in Canada.

ABEL B., youngest son of Jonathan Johnson, jun., was born in Hatley, March 16, 1803—m. *Polly Chamberlin*, b. in Hatley, Jan. 20, 1799. They resided in Hatley until 1832, when they settled in Magog village. He sustained the office of magistrate many years, and took an active interest in the municipal and educational affairs of the town. He d. in 1867. The family are connected with the Adventists.

CHILDREN.

SARAH A., b. March 5, 1824—m. *George O. Somers, M.D.*

JOSEPHINE, b. June 22, 1829—m. *Rev. J. M. Orrock*.

ELLEN M., b. Oct. 27, 1834. She was a woman of good talents and devoted piety. Among her literary productions were a volume of poems and contributions to different periodicals. She d. March 13, 1862.

EDWIN R., b. April 24, 1840. Graduated at McGill College, Montreal. Studied law, has a good practice at Stanstead Plain where he m. *Harriet Clark*.

George O. Somers, M.D.,

Was b. in Barnet, Vt., Jan. 15, 1819. Studied medicine under the charge of J. F. Skinner, M.D., of Brownington, Vt. Graduated at the Medical Department of Dartmouth College. Commenced practice in Magog Village in 1846. He has an extensive and lucrative practice and stands high in his profession. He has been employed in public affairs, and has sustained several offices of trust and responsibility. He m. 1st, *Sarah A. Johnson;* 2nd, *Florence L. Merry.*

Family of Zacheus Johnson.

ZACHEUS JOHNSON, b. in Charlestown, N.H., July 9, 1793—m. *Laura Hovey,* whose birth was the first that occurred in Hatley, July 9, 1795. They settled on No. 10, 3rd Range of Hatley. He d. Sept. 24, 1834.

CHILDREN.

ZACHEUS H., b. Jan. 15, 1818—m. *Maria L. Kezar,* d. in July, 1847.
LAURA J., b. July 8, 1819—m. *Squire Colby,* d. Aug. 4, 1859.
SARAH A., b. Feb. 26, 1823—d. March 12, 1824.
REBECCA, b. Jan. 20, 1825—m. *Solon Shurtliff, M.D.*
JONATHAN, b. Dec. 30, 1827—m. *Harriet Sweet.*
WILLIAM E., b. April 24, 1831—m. *Elizabeth Saddler.*
JOHN H., b. Aug. 6, 1834—m. 1st, *Elena Kezar;* 2nd, *Celina Sterling.*

Family of David Chamberlin.

DAVID CHAMBERLIN m. *Polly Hovey.* They were natives of Connecticut, and settled on the Lake Shore about two miles above the Outlet in Hatley, in 1794. He d. in 1847; she d. in 1836. Their children were Olive, who m. *John S. Merry;* Ira, m. *Mary Erwin;* David, m. *Thankful Whitcomb;* Polly, m. *A. B. Johnson, Esq.;* Arvilla, m. *George Oliver;* Matilda, m. *Arthur Johnson;* William, m. *Esther Abbott;* Fanny, m. *John Emory;* Lucy, m. *Lyman Rexford;* Sylvia, m. *Calvin Abbott;* Sarah, m. *John Sweeney;* and Aaron, who m. and settled at the West. These have generally large families, and are settled mostly in Canada.

The Hoyt Families.

The ancestors of these families were among the early colonists of New England. The orthography of the name has in some instances been changed, but all the different families have probably sprung from the same origin.

Family of Joseph Hoyt.

JOSEPH HOYT and wife settled originally in Grafton, N.H., where their children were born. They removed to No. 5, 16th Range of Bolton, now Magog, in 1798. Their children were Samuel, who m. *Lucy Merry;* John, m. *Martha Call;* Amherst, m. *Sally Chapman;* Nason, m. *Polly Merry;* Joseph, Chandler, Benjamin, Ebenezer, Moses, and Asa.

SAMUEL HOYT m. *Lucy Merry.* They settled on the homestead, then removed to No. 2, 16th Range of Bolton. He was drowned in the Lake in 1862. Their children were Samuel, who m. *Judith Sampson;* Sylvester, m. *Polly Currier;* Ralph, m. *Sally Hoyt;* Charles, m. a *Miss Whittaker;* Lucy. m. *Daniel Merry;* Irene, Sophronia, and Lavinia.

SAMUEL HOYT, b. in Bolton, P.Q., Jan. 16, 1815—m. *Judith Sampson,* b. in Medford, Mass., July 4, 1813, and settled on Nos. 2 and 3, 16th Range of Bolton. He has been variously employed in public affairs. Has for many years been captain of militia, and has sustained the offices of magistrate, mayor of the Township of Magog, and warden of the County Council.

CHILDREN.

EDWARD, b. Nov. 29, 1838—deceased.
EDWARD, 2d, b. Oct. 4, 1840.
WARREN, b. Sept. 27, 1842—deceased.
WARREN, 2d, b. Feb. 27, 1844.
ALBERT, b. July 5, 1847.
ALPHONSO, b. June 7, 1849.

ALONZO HOYT m. *Sally C. Currier.* She was b. Feb. 9, 1810 Their children were:
ELECTA B., b. Aug. 7, 1833—m. *E. H. Oliver.*
MARY A., b. Jan. 28, 1835—m. *Leonard Morse.*
MANNING, b. Sept. 25, 1836.

JOSEPH HOYT, m. *Susan Currier.* She was b. Oct. 13, 1821. Their children were:
WALLACE N., b. Dec. 30, 1842.
ALWILDA, b. June 24, 1845.

FAMILY OF HENRY CURRIER.

ARRATHRA, b. April 14, 1847.
ALFRITA, b. Nov. 18, 1849.
ADRIAN, b. Nov. 7, 1862.
SYLVESTER HOYT m. *Polly S. Currier.* He d. May 4, 1866. Their children were Melvin, b. May 7, 1850; Ella M., b. Sept. 5, 1858.

Family of Sherburn Blake.

SHERBURN BLAKE m. *Nancy Currrier.* Their children were Sophia, Loella, and Harvard.

Family of Elisha Smith.

ELISHA SMITH m. *Martha Kinston.* They were natives of Massachusetts. They settled on the Lake Shore, about two miles south of Georgeville, in 1810. He d. in 1822; she d. in 1858. Their children were Jesse, who m. *Parthenia Collins*; Hiram, m. *Sophia Whiting*; Mehitable, m. *Emerson Libbee*; Nancy, m. *Charles Turner*; Catherine, m *Chester Cook*; Abigail, m. *Christopher Blake*; Belinda, m. *Manly Nelson*, Richard, m. *Corilla Godfrey*; Shubel, David, and Parthenia. These settled mostly in Canada.

Family of Henry Currier.

HENRY CURRIER, b. Jan. 18, 1780. July 18, 1806, m. *Sally Morse,* b. July 6, 1786. They were natives of New Hampshire, and among the early settlers of Bolton, now Magog.

CHILDREN.

BENJAMIN, b. Feb. 12, 1807.
NATHAN M., b. Sept. 5, 1808.
SALLY C., b. Feb. 8, 1810.
NATHANIEL, b. Jan. 26, 1814.
LYMAN, b. Aug. 14, 1816.
HANNAH, b. Dec. 29, 1819.
SUSAN, b. Oct. 13, 1821.
POLLY, b. May 31, 1825.
NANCY, b. Dec. 21, 1826.

BENJAMIN CURRIER, b. Feb. 12, 1807. In 1830, m. *Nancy Hoyt,* b. March 12, 1808. They settled in Magog. She d. Nov. 26, 1855.

CHILDREN.

HENRY, b. April 21, 1831—m. *Sarah Embury.*
DAVID, b. July 6, 1832—m. *Electa Moses.*
HIRAM, b. Feb. 11, 1834—m. *Hannah Gould.*
CLARK M., b. in 1837.
JOHN, b. in 1839.
BETSEY, b. in 1842—d. Feb. 8, 1861.
ESTHER, b. in 1844—m. *John Randall.*
GARDNER, in 1849.

NATHAN M. CURRIER, b. Sept. 5, 1808—m. *Jane M. Adams.* She d. July, 1848. March 1, 1852, m. *Dulcena Fuller.* One child by 1st marriage, *Aluvia,* b. Nov. 3, 1839, m. *Levi Rexford.*

CHILDREN BY 2ND MARRIAGE.

AMOS N., b. Dec. 4, 1853.
AMANDA F., b. June 25, 1855.
ERNEST N., b. Dec. 9, 1860.

NATHANIEL CURRIER, b. Jan. 26, 1814—m. *Sally S. Merry.*

CHILDREN.

CYNTHIA A., b. May 18, 1840—m. *Carlos Chamberlin.*
NANCY, b. May 30, 1845—m. *Richard C. Tilson.*
EZRA N., b. June 25, 1853.
VICTOR M., b. June 15, 1860.

LYMAN CURRIER, b. Aug. 14, 1816—m. *Lorina Hoyt.* He died in April, 1843. Their children were *Sally and Lyman.*

Family of E. W. Goff.

E. W. GOFF, b. in Richford, Vt., Oct. 7, 1803. Sept. 28, 1823, m. *Sarah Jones,* b. in Brandon, Vt., Aug. 25, 1804. They settled in Magog Village in 1828. Mr. Goff was manager of the woollen factory at the Outlet for many years.

CHILDREN.

NELSON O., b. Feb. 2, 1825—d. Sept. 27, 1827.
LEMUEL R., b. Nov. 24, 1826.
GEORGE N., b. Jan. 29, 1829—m. *Mary F. Merrill.*
MALINDA, b. Oct. 12, 1830—d. March 12, 1853.
CELINDA, b. April 10, 1833—m. *E. G. Scribner.*
SARAH A., b. May 14, 1838—m. *Bernard McGivern.*
EUGENE W., b. March 27, 1842—d. Sept. 23, 1845.
MARY and MARTHA, twins, b. Oct. 23, 1845.

The Turner Families.

Jesse and David Turner settled on the Lake Shore in Bolton, in 1800. Jesse Turner d. in 1850; his wife d. in 1821.

Family of Jesse Turner.

JESSE TURNER m. *Anna Ramsay*. Their children were CHARLES, SOPHIA, m. *Sherburn Blake*; JESSE, m. *Sally Hoyt*; SUSAN, m. *John C. Call*; LAURA, m. *Newton Knowlton*, and MELISSA, who m. *Moses Foss*.

CHARLES TURNER, b. in Bolton, P.Q., Oct. 30, 1802—m. *Nancy Smith*, b. March 21, 1809. They settled in Magog Village, where he has acquired a large property, and has been variously employed in public affairs.

CHILDREN.

ANN, b. Jan. 14, 1831—m. *Charles Rogers*.
WRIGHT, b. Aug. 21, 1832—d. May 18, 1865.
JUST, b. Dec. 16, 1833—d. July 14, 1865.
JANE, b. March 1, 1835—m. *Andrew Lindsey*.
MARY O., b. Nov. 18, 1836.

Family of David Turner.

DAVID TURNER m. *Elizabeth Rider*, and settled in Bolton, in 1800. Their children were ORRIS, who m. *Mary Ann Hoyt;* ORRIN, m. *Polly Call;* HARRIET, m. *Robert Harvey;* HIRAM, m. *a Miss Cass;* MARTHA, m. *Gilman Cass;* ELIZABETH, m. *Albert Dustin;* DAVID, ABEL, and CARLTON. Of these, the families of Orris, Orrin, Martha and Elizabeth, form the settlement of Turner Town, in Hatley. Daniel and Timothy Turner, cousins to the above-named families, settled in the vicinity of the Lake, about 1810.

Family of Stephen Lord.

STEPHEN LORD m. *Rebecca Lowell*. They were natives of New Hampshire, and among the earliest settlers of Hatley. Their children were REBECCA, who m. *Bemond Hitchcock;* ELIZA, who d. young; STEPHEN O., m. *Eliza Lord*, his cousin; WILLIAM, m. *Sarah Wheeler;* MARIA, m. *Elisha Aldrick;* RACHEL, m. *Solomon Fisk;* BETSEY, d. young; CHARLES, m. *Cynthia Emery;* RUTH, m. *J. T. Wetherell;* SARAH, m. *Moses Griffin;* and MARK, who d. young.

Family of Isaac Lord.

ISAAC LORD m. *Eunice Farnham.* They were natives of New Hampshire. Settled in Hatley about the same time with his brother Stephen. Their children were STEPHEN, who m. *Julia Wells;* DOROTHY, m. *Orrin Cook;* ELIZA, m. *Clark Lord;* ISAAC, m. *Rebecca Bowen;* PAMELIA, m. *John Bowen;* SYLVIA, m. *Calvin Magoon,* and CHARLOTTE.

Family of John Lord.

JOHN LORD, b. in Lebanon, N.H., Sept. 30, 1797—m. *Mary Lowell,* b. in Warner, N.H., April 29, 1798. They settled on No. 12, 3rd Range in Hatley.

CHILDREN.

JOHN, JUN., b. Feb. 19, 1821.
MARY M., b. Feb. 14, 1823.
NANCY, b. Feb. 28, 1826—d. May 22, 1829.
LUCINDA, b. Aug. 9, 1828.
NANCY, 2nd, b. March 1, 1833.
GEORGE P., b. June 5, 1836—m. *Hannah Lord.*
WILLIAM, b. March 12, 1841.

Family of Christopher Flanders.

CHRISTOPHER FLANDERS, m. *Sarah Smith.* They were natives of New Hampshire. Settled on No. 13, 1st Range of Hatley, in 1801. They were prominent members of the Free Will Baptist Church. He d. Dec. 31, 1833; she d. some years before. Their children were David; Sarah, m. *Asa Barnes*; Polly, m. *David Smith;* and Philip.

PHILIP FLANDERS m. *Lydia Hall,* and settled in Hatley. Their children were Craig, m. *Maria Little;* Seth, m. *Lucina Wood;* Mary, m. *Horace Hovey;* Hiram, m. *Mary Alexander;* Amanda, m. *Alonzo Hovey,* and George, who settled at the West.

DAVID FLANDERS m. *Rachel Kent,* and settled in Hatley. Their children were David S., Philip, m. *Mary Elliott,* Rufus, for many years a successful preacher in connection with the Canada Wesleyan Conference, laboring with acceptance and usefulness on different circuits, and d. in 1865. Their other children were Alvin, Lewis and Jackson.

DAVID S. FLANDERS, b. in Hatley, Oct. 3, 1812—m. *Sally Leavitt,* b. in Compton, P.Q., Sept. 23, 1812. They belong to the Methodist Church.

FAMILY OF JOSEPH PUTNEY, SEN.

CHILDREN.

JEREMIAH, b. Jan. 22, 1836—m. *Elizabeth Stater.*
CAROLINE, b. Oct. 31, 1838—m. *Benjamin Fletcher.*
RUFUS, b. Dec. 18, 1843.
DAVID, b. Nov. 10, 1845.
ELVIRA, b. Oct. 10, 1847.
MARY, b. Sept. 12, 1849.

2 CHILDREN DIED YOUNG.

Family of Squire Woodward.

SQUIRE WOODWARD m. *Lucy Hawes.* They were natives of New Hampshire. Settled on No. 8, 2d Range of Hatley, in 1800. He d. in 1846. She d. the same year, aged 92. Their children were ABIATHAR, who m. *Hannah Hadlock;* JOHN, m. *Mary Webster;* WILLIAM, m. *Jane Harvey;* and Christopher. The children of Abiathar Woodward were Squire, Lucinda, Amos, William, Dolly, Elvira, Eliza, Lucy, John, Hiram, and Mary Jane. The children of John Woodward were Hannah, John, Polly, Chester, and Emeline. The children of William Woodward were Lucy, Judith, Diana, Eliza, Sally, Mary A., Phebe, Melissa, Fanny, and Elizabeth.

CHRISTOPHER, youngest son of Squire Woodward, was b. in Wendell, N.H., Dec. 19, 1792. Came to Hatley with his father, m. *Judith Harvey.* They settled on No. 9, 2d Range of Hatley. She d. Dec. 17, 1864.

CHILDREN.

LEMUEL, b. Oct. 18, 1818—m. *Mary Carlton.*
IRENE, b. Aug. 8, 1820—m. *Joseph Stone.*
ELVIRA, b. Feb. 15, 1823—m. *Cyrus Whitcomb.*
HIRAM, b. April 14, 1825—m. *Abigail Wood.*
JOHN, b. April 6, 1827—m. *Clara Gerry.*
EDWIN, b. April 27, 1830—m. 1st *Lucy Whitcomb;* 2nd, *Lucinda Bean.*
HARRIET, b. Oct. 8, 1832—m. *Albert C. Perkins.*

Family of Joseph Putney, sen.

JOSEPH PUTNEY, sen., m. *Hannah Blaisdell.* They were natives of New Hampshire—were among the earliest settlers of Hatley, located on No. 8, 4th Range. Their children were Joseph; Bernard, m. *Betsey Cole ;* Molly, m. *Moses Hall*; Hannah, m. *Samuel Brown*, and Henry, who m. *Charlotte Little.*

JOSEPH PUTNEY, jun., b. in Hopkinton, N.H., June 5, 1785—m. *Roxana Hall*, b. in Hanover, N.H., Jan. 7, 1794. They settled on the homestead in Hatley.

CHILDREN.

MOSES S., b. Nov. 18, 1815.
SARAH M., b. May 2, 1817—m. *S. F. Emory.*
NICHOLAS B, b. Sept. 28, 1822.
HIRAM H., b. Dec. 14, 1828.
WILLIAM J., b. June 14, 1830.

Family of Nathaniel Hawes.

NATHANIEL HAWES, m. *Sarah Dodge*. They were natives of New Hampshire. Settled on the south-east part of No. 16, 2d Range of Hatley. He d. in 1841. She d. in 1851. Their children were William, who m. *Eliza Johnson;* Nathan, m. *Abigail Harvey*, and Nathaniel.

NATHANIEL HAWES, jun., b. April 20, 1802—m. *Sophronia Hovey.* They settled on the Sloam Place in Hatley.

CHILDREN.

SARAH, b. in 1804—m. *Holland Stevens.*
PERKINS, b. in 1806—m. *Lydia Bean.*
SQUIRE, b. in 1808—m. *Mary Wells.*
TABITHA, b. in 1810—m. *James Moulton.*
LYDIA, b. in 1812—m. *Hoel Moulton.*
OBADIAH, b. in 1814—m. *Diana Sampson.*
HEPZIBAH, b. in 1816—m. *Philip Bean.*
EDWARD, b. in 1818—m. *Malinda Wadleigh.*

Family of William Taylor.

WILLIAM TAYLOR m. *Thankful Fish.* They settled in Hatley in 1795. Their children were Nathan, who m. *Mary Lovejoy*, (see narrative of Mrs. Taylor); David, m. *Huldah Kent*; Polly, m. *John Parnell;* Sally, m. *George Robinson*, and Maria, m. *Gershom Ellsworth.*

Family of Jeremiah Lovejoy.

JEREMIAH LOVEJOY m. *Hannah Johnson.* They were natives of Andover, Mass., settled in Hatley in 1797. He d. July 17, 1810; she d. March 2, 1809.

CHILDREN.

JOSIAH, b. March 6, 1785.
JERRY, b. Jan. 17, 1787, practised medicine in Barnston many years. He d. in 1862.
HANNAH, b. June 2, 1789—m. *Dan. Lyman.*
LYDIA, b. Aug. 29, 1791.
MARY, b. July 2, 1793—m. *Nathan Taylor.*
OBADIAH, b. Nov. 20, 1795.
JOHN, b. April 8, 1798.
DOLLY, b. June 20, 1802.
SALLY, b. Dec. 23, 1805—m. *George Willard.*

Family of Charles L. Percival.

CHARLES L. PERCIVAL, b. in Norwich, Vt., July 20, 1820—m. *Emily Kezar,* who was b. May 24, 1824. They settled in West Hatley.

CHILDREN.

LODEMA, b. June 11, 1843.
MARY E., b. April 24, 1845—d. in infancy.
OSCEOLA, b. Nov. 22, 1854.
JAMES L., b. Sept. 17, 1858—d. Jan. 14, 1864.
MARY A., b. May 16, 1861.

Family of Thomas Rowell.

THOMAS ROWELL, b. in Goffstown, N.H., Dec. 13, 1765—m. *Lydia Hawes,* b. in Fishersfield, N.H., Nov. 12, 1769. They settled in Hatley, in 1802. He d. Dec. 20, 1833; she d. Oct. 15, 1856.

CHILDREN.

BETSEY, b. April 10, 1789—m. *Joseph Bean.*
LYDIA, b. July 30, 1791—m. *William Harvey.*
POLLY, b. Jan. 26, 1794—d.

THOMAS, JUN., b. May 20, 1796—m. *Lydia Leavitt.*
MARY, b. Oct. 20, 1798—m. *Lemuel Fish.*
NATHAN, b. March, 4, 1801—m. *Anna Leavitt.*
LUCY, b. Aug. 15, 1803—m. *John Leavitt.*
KENDRICK, b. Nov. 12, 1806— m. *Sarah Hawes;* 2nd, *Pluma Rowell.*
PHEBE, b. March 4, 1809—m. *Luke Wadleigh.*

Family of William Emery.

WILLIAM EMERY m. *Polly Simmons.* They were natives of New Hampshire, were among the earliest settlers of Hatley. She d. Feb. 3, 1843 ; he d. May 23, 1860. Their children were John, who m. *Fanny Chamberlin*; Judith, m. *Charles Hovey*; Hannah, m. *James Hensley*; Simon, m. *Pamelia Stearns,* 2nd *Sarah Putney*; Sally, m. *Morris Neal*; Nathan; William, m. *Betsey Weare*; Rachel, m. *James Archles*; Polly, m. *Henry DuBois*; and Moses, who m. *Mary Glidden.*

NATHAN EMERY, son of Wm. Emery, was b. Aug. 18, 1815—m. *Sally Fish.* They settled on No. 9, 1st Range, in Hatley. Are Free-Will Baptists.

CHILDREN.

MARY E., b. Jan. 25, 1838—m. *Gilbert Emery.*
LEMUEL F., b. July 9, 1840—m. *Martha A. Kent.*
ALONZO A., b. July 23, 1848.
LYDIA E., b. Nov. 28, 1851.

Family of Col. Henry Cull.

COL. HENRY CULL was b. in Dorsetshire, England, in 1753. He m. *Elizabeth McMillan,* a widow. She d. Dec. 12, 1814 ; he d. Jan. 8, 1833. They and their family were Episcopalians. For a more particular account of Col. Cull, see sketches of the settlement of Hatley.

CHILDREN.

REV. ALEXANDER H., b. Jan. 14, 1803— m. *Catherine,* dau. of *Samuel Hubbard, Esq.,* of Franklin, Vt., where he was for several years a clergyman of the Episcopal Church.
JOHN C., b. Nov. 1, 1804—was drowned at the age of 25 years.

SARAH ANN, b. Jan. 23, 1807—m. *Hon. J. H. Hubbard.*
GEORGE, b. Nov. 2, 1809—d. Aug. 11, 1860.
RICHARD, b. March, 21, 1811—m. *Frances Stevens.*
CAROLINE, b. June 20, 1813—d. March 30, 1831.

Family of Jethro Bachelder.

JETHRO BACHELDER, b. in Danville, Vt., Dec. 20, 1784—m. *Betsey Moore* of Stanstead. She d. May 14, 1813. He afterwards m. *Esther Smith.* She d. June 23, 1844. Oct. 17, 1848, he m. *Charlotte Bachelder.* She d. Aug. 1, 1849. In 1854, he m. *Mary Sloane.* The family were among the early settlers of Hatley; are connected with the Methodist Church. He d. in Aug., 1866.

CHILDREN BY 1st MARRIAGE.

JANE, b. Feb. 25, 1807—m. *William Henry.*
NARCISSA, b. Oct. 10, 1810—m. *Joseph Henry.*
SIAS, b. May 5, 1813—d. Feb. 26, 1842.

CHILDREN BY SECOND MARRIAGE.

SMITH E., b. Feb. 19, 1815—m. *Sally Dresser.*
HANNAH, b. July 9, 1817—m. 1st, *James Walker;* 2nd, *Benj. Heath.*
MILTON J., b. Sept. 8, 1824—m. *Hannah L. Rogers.*
BETSEY, b. Oct. 9, 1821—m. *David W. Moulton.*

SMITH E. BACHELDER, b. Feb. 9, 1815—m. *Sally Dresser.* They settled in Hatley.

CHILDREN.

SIAS, b. in Feb., 1842—m. *Alvesta Buckland;* 2nd, *Diana Shongo.*
FLORINE, b. July, 23, 1851.

MILTON J. BACHELDER, b. Sept. 8, 1824—m. *Hannah L. Rogers.* They reside on the family homestead in Hatley.

CHILDREN.

ELLA R., b. July 28, 1852.
LOUISA M., b. April 14, 1854.
JULIA A., b. Feb. 5, 1856—d. in infancy.

Family of John Weston, M. D.

JOHN WESTON, M.D., was descended in direct line and in the 6th generation from John Weston, who was born in Buckinghamshire, England, in 1631, and emigrated to America in 1644.

The subject of this notice was born in Rockingham, Vt., Sept. 20, 1780. He graduated at Dartmouth, and, after pursuing the regular course of medical and surgical studies at Keene and Hanover, N.H., received an honorary diploma from the Medical College at Burlington, Vt. He came to Hatley in 1810, and was soon after licensed by the Medical Board at Quebec. His practice rapidly increased, and for many years he was the only practical surgeon within the present limits of Stanstead county. He was successful in his practice, but the hardships and fatigue which he endured in his frequent long journeys, made often to the distance of 20 miles through the woods by almost impassable roads, would have broken down the constitutions of stronger men of later days. He was distinguished for his benevolence, often visiting the poor and supplying medicines without any prospect of compensation, but was cut down in the prime of strength and usefulness. His death, which was caused by a kick from his horse, occurred July 16, 1832. He was a consistent and exemplary member of the Episcopal Church, and his memory will be cherished by many with respect and esteem. Oct. 30, 1812, he m. *Jane*, dau. of *Capt. N. Snow*, of Compton, P.Q., b. Sept. 9, 1789.

CHILDREN.

CHARLOTTE, b. Oct. 16, 1813—m. *Capt. Alonzo Wood.*
GEORGE, b. Sept. 1, 1815.
CAROLINE, b. Dec. 18, 1817—d. July 13, 1835.
CHARLES, b. Nov. 28, 1819—m. *Lydia J. Gilman.*
SARAH, b. Nov. 23, 1823—m. *Wm. Brooke, Esq.*
MIRIAM, b. Dec. 28, 1825.

Family of Robert Vincent, Esq.

ROBERT VINCENT, ESQ., (date of birth not found,) m. *Caroline Snow*, in 1815. She was b. Feb. 16, 1794. Mr. Vincent was engaged in mercantile business in Hatley, more than 20 years, during which time he sustained the offices of postmaster and magistrate. Was collector of customs at Hereford, P.Q., for several years. He d. Aug. 6, 1858; his wife d. in Oct., 1862 They were Episcopalians.

CHILDREN.

JANE A., b. Feb. 28, 1818—m. *Lucius Marsh.*
LILIA, b. April 3, 1820—d. March 7, 1832.

ELIZA, b. Aug. 15, 1823.
CHARLES, b. Dec. 25, 1825.
CAROLINE, b. in Oct., 1832—m. *L. D. Robertson, M.D.*

Family of Major John Jones.

MAJOR JOHN JONES, a native of Wales, and born Jan. 11, 1790, settled in Charleston Village, Hatley, in 1817. Oct. 14, 1820—m. *Sarah Snow*, b. March 19, 1798. Mr. Jones was engaged in mercantile business several years in Hatley. Sustained successively, the offices of captain and major of the militia, and magistrate, and was employed in the Frontier service during the Rebellion of 1837–1839. He d. Nov. 20, 1862. The family are Episcopalians.

CHILDREN.

JOHN M., b. Jan. 19, 1822—m. *Caroline Rhodes.*
SOPHIA, b. March 25, 1826.

Family of Lathrop Shurtliff, M.D.

LATHROP SHURTLIFF, M.D., a native of Vermont, was born Dec. 7, 1797. Dec. 22, 1819, m. *Ruth Little*, b. Sept. 24, 1797. He studied medicine, and his life was devoted mostly to the practice of that profession. He d. March 16, 1862.

CHILDREN.

HELEN R., b. April 6, 1822—m. *De Witt Forman.*
SOLON, b. May 24, 1824—m. *Rebecca Johnson.*
LUCIA S., b. April 18, 1826—m. *T. H. M. Hyndman.*
MARY J., b. Sept. 26, 1828—d. June 1, 1832.
THOMAS, b. June 24, 1830—m. *Mariette Little.*
ASAPH, b. April 22, 1832—m. 1st, *Katie Crockett*; 2nd, *Louise De Witt.*
JOHN, b. May 13, 1835—d. in 1855.
AMOS, b. April 28, 1837.
MATTHEW S., b. Aug. 12, 1839—m. *Marilla Marston.*
ALICE J., b. July 5, 1841—m. *Robert Forman.*
MARY E., b. Dec. 26, 1843—m. *Ludo M. Little.*

SOLON SHURTLIFF, b. May 24, 1824. Studied medicine, graduated at the Geneva Medical College, N.Y. Commenced practice at Massawippi Village in Hatley in 1853, was successful and was variously employed in public affairs. Sept. 26, 1848, he m. *Rebecca Johnson*, b. Jan. 20, 1825.

CHILDREN.

AMOS J., b. July 13, 1849.
LAURA H., b. Aug. 22, 1859.
FREMONT E., b. Aug. 5, 1861.
THOMAS SHURTLIFF, b. June 24, 1830. Jan. 28, 1850, m. *Mariette Little*, who was b. in 1828. Mr. S. has for many years been engaged in teaching.

CHILDREN.

WILLIAM, b. July 9, 1853.
JOHN, b. June 7, 1857.
FLORA, b. April 18, 1859.
CLARISSA, b. March 22, 1861.
RILLA, b. July 17, 1863.

Family of Thomas McCoy.

THOMAS MCCOY m. *Sarah Merrill*. They were natives of New Hampshire, settled on No. 3, 1st Range of Hatley, in 1805. Their children were Sarah, who m. *Rufus Pool, 2nd*; Thomas; John, m. *Lucretia Parker*; Margaret, Eliza, Alexander, and Merrill.

THOMAS MCCOY, JUN., b. May 14, 1805—m. *Lucy Flint*, b. July 15, 1817. They settled on the homestead.

CHILDREN.

AYLMER, b. Dec. 3, 1837—m. *Eliza Johnson*.
WILLIAM, b. March 12, 1840.
NELSON, b. July 21, 1842—m. *Electa Edwards*.
ELLEN, b. Dec. 10, 1844—m. *Harvey Gould*.
LUVIA, b. Oct. 29, 1847.

Family of William G. Cook, Esq.

The earliest record we can find of this family is that Nathaniel Cook, b. in Norton, Mass., Jan. 9, 1779, m. *Margaret Grannis*, b. June 15, 1778; that they settled in Claremont, N.H., and had

FAMILY OF ELIAS WHITCOMB.

three sons, one of whom, the subject of this notice, only, settled in Canada. WILLIAM G. COOK, ESQ., was b. in Claremont, N.H., Nov. 18, 1803. March 24, 1827, he m. *Elvira Judd*, b. Sept. 22, 1805. She d. Jan. 29, 1849. Feb. 5, 1850, he m. *Clara Stimson*, b. March 10, 1825. Mr. Cook began his career as clerk in 1823, commenced business for himself in Hatley a few years afterwards, and has been eminently successful. He served as lieutenant in the regular forces, during the Rebellion of 1837-1839, has sustained the offices of postmaster, captain of militia and magistrate; has been for many years an active manager of Charleston Academy. The family are members of the Episcopal Church.

CHILDREN BY 1ST MARRIAGE.

FRANCES W., b. Nov. 5, 1828—d. May 22, 1832.
JANE G., b. May 28, 1833—m. *Alpheus Boynton*.
WILHELMINE, b. May 10, 1839—m. *George Wood, M.D.*

ONE CHILD BY 2ND MARRIAGE.

GEORGE W., b. Dec. 17, 1854.

Family of William Boynton.

WILLIAM BOYNTON, b. in Wheelock, Vt., Jan. 18, 1800. Jan. 23, 1822—m. *Harriet Curtis*, b. Feb. 14, 1806. They settled in Hatley, where he d. in 1837.

CHILDREN.

EMILY, b. Oct. 3, 1822—m. *Joseph W. Young*.
LUCENA, b. Aug. 26, 1823—d. Aug. 22, 1825.
GEORGE W., b. Dec. 3, 1824—m. *Mary J. Young*.
JOHN W., b. Nov. 29, 1826—m. *Rebecca Gilson*.
ALPHEUS S., b. Feb. 22, 1828—m. *Jane G. Caok*.
HENRY R., b. Aug. 29, 1829.
ALVA F., b. Aug. 30, 1831—m. *Celina Ives*.
ALONZO F., b. Nov. 29, 1833—d. July 2, 1842.
CHARLES M., b. April 25, 1836.

Family of Elias Whitcomb.

ELIAS WHITCOMB m. *Betsey Webster*. They were natives of New Hampshire, and among the early settlers of Hatley. Their children were Zenas, who m. *Sally Fletcher*; Polly, m. *Joseph*

Fletcher; Joseph, m. *Sarah A. Jackson*; Cyrus, Louisa, m. a *Mr. Hanson*; Lucy, m. *Edwin Woodward;* and Sarah, who d. when about 26 years old.

CYRUS WHITCOMB, b. May 31, 1821—m. *Elvira Woodward*, b. Feb. 15, 1823. They settled in East Hatley.

CHILDREN.

WRIGHT, b. March 13, 1847.
ALICE E., b. June 26, 1853.
ELIZABETH G., b. Nov. 14, 1862.
4 children died young.

Family of Francis D. Gilbert, M.D.

This family are of Norman extraction, their ancestors having come over to England, in the time of William, the Conqueror. The original name was *Guilbert*, but in most instances, the orthography has been changed.

FRANCIS D. GILBERT was born in Flintshire, Wales, March 4, 1820. Graduated at Eton College, Eng., spent five years in training with a distinguished surgeon of the Royal House, at Windsor, and subsequently served three years in the London Hospital—the last year, as surgeon in that institution. He came to Canada in 1843, and was soon after admitted a licentiate of medicine, and elected governor of the College of Physicians and Surgeons of Canada. His practice has been successful, and he stands high in his profession. In 1841 he married *Elizabeth Philips*, b. April 6, 1822. They settled originally in Hatley, but afterwards removed to Sherbrooke, P. Q.

CHILDREN.

CATHERINE, b. Jan. 30, 1843.
ELLEN M., b. July 24, 1845.
ANNA L., b. Sept. 7, 1847—d. Aug. 5, 1851.
MARY W., b. June 2, 1849.
HENRY L., b. Dec. 19, 1854.
One child d. in infancy.

Family of John H. Burland, M.D.

JOHN H. BURLAND, b. at St. Johns, P.Q., March 28, 1838. Studied medicine and surgery at the Medical Department of McGill College, in Montreal, from which he received his diploma—commenced practice in Hatley in connection with Dr. Gilbert, in 1863. He has thus far been successful, and bids fair to become distinguished in his profession. In 1859 he m. *Amy M. Hornby*, b. in Montreal, May 15, 1840.

CHILDREN.

ARTHUR E., b. Sept. 10, 1862.
ANNA G., b. Nov. 16, 1864.

The Moore Families.

These families are found in various parts of Britain and America, with merely a change in the orthography. The name having been written, More, Moore, Moor and Moir by different families. The ancestors of John Moore, the subject of the following sketch, were among the early colonists of New England.

Family of John Moore.

JOHN MOORE m. *Abigail Noyce.* Were natives of New Hampshire, and settled in Stanstead in 1804, but afterwards removed to No. 8, 9th Range of Hatley.

CHILDREN.

JOHN, b. Oct. 6, 1781.
HANNAH, b. Nov. 1, 1784.
RODNEY, b. Oct. 6, 1786.
THOMAS, b. Dec. 5, 1788—m. *Margaret Dickey.*
JAMES B., b. March 29, 1790.
WASHINGTON, b. March 29, 1793.
JACOB G., b. Feb. 23, 1796.
ISAAC, b. May 24, 1797.
EPHRAIM, b. July 4, 1800.
NANCY, b. March 8, 1802.

Family of Thomas Moore.

THOMAS MOORE, b. in Concord, N.H., Dec. 5, 1788—m. *Margaret Dickey*, b. in Epsom, N.H., in 1795. They settled on No. 8, 9th Range of Hatley.

CHILDREN.

MARY ANN, b. Oct. 15, 1814—m. *William Robinson.*
LOUISA, b. July 29, 1816—m. *Rev. T. P. Moulton.*

ASENATH, b. June 22, 1818—m. *Chester Rexford.*
JOHN, b. May 3, 1820—m. *Ruth Abbott.*
ROSINA, b. July 12, 1822—m. *Robert Spendlove.*
GEORGE W., b. May 21, 1824.
BETSEY, b. Feb. 21, 1826.
THOMAS, b. March 20, 1830—d. June 19, 1865.
MARGARET, b. Aug. 4, 1828—m. *George J. Woodward.*
ALVIN, b. April 20, 1836—m. *Julia A. Merry.*
GILES, b. Feb. 21, 1838.

Family of Joel Parker.

JOEL PARKER was born in Westminster, Vt., Oct. 9, 1802. His lineage is connected with a family of the name who were among the early colonists of New England. He m. *Lucy Wyman*, a native of the Province of Ontario, b. Sept. 28, 1807. They settled in Hatley in 1827.

CHILDREN.

ADALINE L., b. March 1, 1829—m. *Asahel Parker.*
LEVI E., b. Aug. 5, 1830—engaged in mercantile business, and variously employed in public affairs:
AMANDA, b. June 23, 1836.
EDWIN W., b. March 13, 1842.
ALVA W., b. June 18, 1845.
ORVILLE H., b. June 1, 1848.
ALICE F., b. May 29, 1854.

Family of Gershom Ellsworth.

GERSHOM ELLSWORTH, b. in Bakersfield, Vt., Oct. 26, 1812. Settled on No: 3, 5th Range of Hatley, and m. *Maria Kezar.* She d. in 1842. In 1843, m. *Maria Taylor.* She d. in 1853. In 1854, he m. *Almira Jackson.* Mr. Ellsworth is a farmer.

CHILDREN.

PROSPER H., b. Aug. 12, 1834.
HOLLIS, b. Sept. 20, 1836.

The Pool Families.

The ancestors of these families were among the early emigrants from England to Massachusetts. Of their descendants, two families, viz., those of Theodore C. and Rufus Pool were among the earliest settlers of Stanstead. The following is the only record we can find of these families:

THEODORE C. POOL m. *Sarah Lee.* Their children were HENRY L., who m. *Zelinda Osgood;* RUFUS, m. *Sarah McCoy;* BETSEY, m. *Phineas Davis;* and Jonathan L., m. *Mary Evans.* THEODORE C. POOL subsequently m. *Betsey Lee.* One son, WHITTAKER, who m. *Sophronia Bartlett.*

RUFUS POOL (brother of Theodore C. Pool) settled in Stanstead in 1802. We are not able to give a full account of their family. The following particulars have been supplied by G. F. A. Pool, a relative of the family, who resides in Barford, P.Q.

The children of Rufus Pool are WALTER K., who m., 1st, a *Miss Gates,* 2nd a *Miss Kimball;* SUSANNA, m. *Samuel Ruiter;* MARY, m. a *Mr. Fuller;* POLLY, m. *Richard Bailey;* CAROLINE, m. *Peter Locke;* WILLIAM and ESTHER.

The Osgood Family.

DAVID OSGOOD was among the earliest settlers of Hatley. His children were David, Samuel, John, Alexander, James and Thomas The children of ALEXANDER OSGOOD were WILLIAM A., who m. *Caroline Pierce;* LUVIN, m. *R. D. Morkill, Esq.;* LUCIUS, m. *Harriet O'Connor;* NELSON, m. *Marcia F. Weston,* and THOMAS who d. when about 21 years old.

Family of Henry L. Pool.

HENRY L. POOL, eldest son of Theodore C. Pool, was born in Stanstead, P.Q., Aug. 17, 1801—m. *Zelinda Osgood,* b. March 12, 1806. They settled on No. 1, 1st Range of Hatley—are connected with the Episcopal Church.

CHILDREN.

OZRO, b. June 3, 1829—m. *Fedora Le Baron.*
HENRY, b. May 12, 1831—m. *Sarah A. Ives.*
HORACE L., b. July 19, 1833—m. *Emma J Harding.*
CHARLES C., b. June 10, 1840.

Family of George Perkins.

GEORGE PERKINS, a native of Bridgewater, Mass., and b. in 1762 —m. *Hannah Knight,* b. in Norwich, Conn., 1767. They settled in Hatley in 1805. Were members of the Free-Will Baptist Church.

U

CHILDREN.

SILAS, b. Sept. 25, 1793—m. *Ruth Redway.*
LOIS, b. July 25, 1798.
HANNAH, b. April 20, 1803—m. *Calvin Woodman.*
RUBY, b. Sept. 8, 1806—d. Jan. 4, 1866.
JOHN, b. March 16, 1809.
MARY, b. Aug. 29, 1811—m. *Eliphalet Strong.*

Family of Silas Perkins.

SILAS PERKINS, b. in Plainfield, N.H., Sept. 23, 1793. Came to Hatley with his parents in 1805. He was almost " blind from his birth," but succeeded in acquiring a good English education, including the higher branches of mathematics. He taught school a few years, but, after a time, became entirely blind. At the age of about 30, he married *Ruth Redway*, who, though " tender eyed," was not entirely blind, and while their sphere was comparatively humble, their moral worth and industry secured the confidence and sympathy of the community. They ever cherished a strong feeling of independence, and by their united efforts succeeded in sustaining respectably a large family, some of whom survive, and are useful members of society. He d. June 18, 1860 ; she d. Sept. 6, 1856.

CHILDREN.

LUCY, b. March 12, 1828—d. June 18, 1847.
LAURA, b. May 16, 1830.
ELIZA, b. Jan. 12, 1832.
PLUMA, b. Nov. 5, 1834. Perished in the burning of her father's house, Oct. 30, 1845.
HANNAH, b. July 31, 1839.

JOHN PERKINS, b. March 16, 1809—m. *Maria Colby*, b. March 27, 1812. They settled on parts of Nos. 10 and 11, 4th Range of Hatley.

CHILDREN.

ISAAC N., b. Sept. 16, 1834—d. Aug. 10, 1854.
GEORGE W., b. June 2, 1837.
EMILY J., b. Jan. 25, 1841.
JOHN, b. June 30, 1845.
LUVIN, b. Sept. 1, 1849.
DELPHINE, b. Dec. 4, 1851.

Family of Calvin Woodman.

CALVIN WOODMAN, b. in New Grantham, N.H., May 4, 1804—m. Hannah Perkins, b. April 20, 1803. They settled on No. 4, 2nd Range of Hatley.

CHILDREN.

JOHN C., b. Jan. 28, 1833—m. Mary Dibble.
LOIS A., b. Dec. 15, 1834—m. William Spendlove.
RUBY M., b. July 30, 1836—m. Asa Dutton.
HIRAM, b. Nov. 17, 1840—m. Helen Forsyth.

Family of Joshua S. Woodman.

JOSHUA S. WOODMAN, b. in Franklin, N.H., in 1790—m. Polly Sturtevant, b. in Barton, Vt., Jan. 10, 1786. They settled on No. 5, 2nd Range of Hatley, in 1819. His wife d. March 15, 1849. He afterwards m. Arethusa Bucknell. She d. June 27, 1854; he d. March 10, 1865.

CHILDREN.

MARY M., b. Oct. 3, 1813—m. George Walker.
JOSHUA S., b. Oct. 25, 1815—m.
ELIZA J., b. April 3, 1821—m. Isaac Gordon.
CALEB T., b. Aug. 3, 1823—m. Eunice Blodget.
ALBERT A., b. July 19, 1825—m. Mary Sanborn.
SARAH, b. July 27, 1828—m. Levi Parker.
JOSHUA S. WOODMAN, JUN., b. Oct. 25, 1815—m. Florinda Bachelder. He is a practitioner of the Thompsonian System of Medicine.

CHILDREN.

ELVIRA E., b. Sept. 15, 1844—m. Alonzo Chapman.
MARIA J., b. Jan. 15, 1848.
JOHN L., b. Oct. 11, 1849.

Family of Hazen Haseltine.

HAZEN HASELTINE, b. in Fryeburg, Maine, Aug. 19, 1800—m. Sarah Sias, b. in Danville, Vt., Nov. 25, 1807. They were among the early settlers of Hatley. He is a blacksmith. They are members of the Wesleyan Church, and both highly esteemed in the community.

Family of Benjamin Colby.

BENJAMIN COLBY, b. Dec. 3, 1821— m. *Emma Brunning.* They settled on Nos. 19, 1st and 2nd Ranges of Hatley.

CHILDREN.

CHARLES A., b. May 20, 1851.
MARY E., b. July 24, 1857.

Family of John Colby.

JOHN COLBY, m. *Hannah Clough.* They settled in Hatley in 1831. Their children were Maria, who m. *John Perkins;* Squire, m. *Laura J. Johnson;* Joseph, m. *Louisa Wadleigh;* Benjamin, m. *Emma Brunning;* Emily, m. *Amos Kezar;* George, m. *Lucy Wadleigh;* Alonzo, m. *Eveline Le Baron* ; and Albert, ¡who was killed by a kick from a horse when about 19 years old.

Family of Isaac Fletcher.

ISAAC FLETCHER and wife settled in Hatley in 1799. Their children were Ruth, who m. *John Hall;* Polly, m. *Joseph Kezar;* Charlotte, m. *L. P. Harvey;* Gardner, 'm. *Mary A. Gilson;* Eliza, m. *Wm. Thomas;* Sophia, m. a *Mr. Breaden;* Nancy, m. *Hiram Harvey;* Joseph, m., 1st, *Polly Whitcomb,* 2nd, *Lydia Wadleigh;* and Sally.

The Bacon Families.

DANIEL BACON m. *Esther Jones.* They settled on No. 1, 2nd Range of Hatley, in 1800. Their children where Sarah, Moses, Fanny, Daniel, Nancy, Esther, Mary, Betsey, John, Levi, Denison, and Lucretia. The children of Daniel Bacon, jun., were Esther, Moses, Daniel 3d, Kezia, Ebenezer, and Sarah. These all married and had families, and several of their descendants are` settled in Hatley, Barnston, and Barford.

BARNSTON, COATICOOK, AND BARFORD.

Family of Capt. Joseph Bartlett.

CAPT. JOSEPH BARTLETT m. *Lucretia Hamilton.* They were natives of Massachusetts, settled in Barnston in 1796, at the place now known as Bickford Corner. He early received the appointment of captain of militia. She d. Feb. 16, 1840; he d. in March, 1840. Their children were Judith, who m. *Joshua Parker;* Sally, m. *Samuel Hill;* Joseph, m. *Mary Whitney;* Willard, m. *Lois Mosher;* Lavinia, m. *Lemuel White:* Fraser, m. *Caroline Brown;* Ira, m. *Susan Huntingdon;* Lucy, m. *Samuel Willard;* Betsey, m. *Cyrus Young;* Alden, who d. in the British Army in the war of 1812-1815, and Wyman, who m. *Ruth Willey.* Of these families, two only settled in Barnston—those of Judith and Sally.

Family of Levi Baldwin.

LEVI BALDWIN m. *Experience Goff.* They were natives of Connecticut, settled on No. 15, 6th Range of Barnston, in 1799. She d. in 1815. He afterwards m. Abigail Mills. He d. in 1843. She d. in 1830. The children by the 1st marriage were Huldah, who m. *Augustus Taplin;* Lotes, m. *Sarah Lamb;* Richard, m. *Betsey Drew;* Deborah, m. *John Lamb;* and Patience, who m. *Joseph Drew.* The children by the 2nd marriage were Elizabeth, who m. *Horace Cutting,; Esq.* Percival, m. *Jenett Baker;* and Huldah, who m. *Amos K. Fox, Esq.*

Family of Lotes Baldwin.

LOTES BALDWIN, b. in Westminster, Vt., in 1783—m. *Sarah Lamb,* a native of Vermont. They settled in Barnston, where he succeeded in acquiring a good property, and lived to see his children well settled in life. He d. Jan. 1, 1858. His wife d. Jan. 26, 1841.

CHILDREN.

HULDAH, b. Jan. 23, 1806—d. May 4, 1807.
IRA, b. Feb. 14, 1807—m. *Susan Glover.*
SARAH, b. Jan. 19, 1809—m. *Wm. Cleaveland.*
ZILPHINA, b. Nov. 23, 1811—m. *Levi Cleaveland.*

298   FORESTS AND CLEARINGS.

LOTES, b. March 11, 1813.
LUCINDA, b. July 14, 1815—m. *Samuel Page.*
PHILA, b. May 14, 1817—m. *Samuel Page, his 2nd wife.*
FANNY, b. Jan. 28, 1819—m. *Samuel Cleaveland.*
FRANCIS, b. Jan. 12, 1824—m. *Sarah H. Taylor.*
GEORGE W., b. April 22, 1826—m. *Orissa Drew.*
LUCY, b. June 3, 1829—m. *John Thornton, Esq.*

Family of Lotes Baldwin, jun.

LOTES BALDWIN, JUN., b. March 11, 1813 — m. *Matilda McKeech*, b. Jan. 20, 1819. They settled on No. 16, 6th Range of Barnston.

CHILDREN.

WILLIAM W., b: July 10, 1841—m. *Sarah Davis.*
VICTOR M., b. June 28, 1843—m. *Loren G. Ladd.*
EDWIN R., b. Nov. 21, 1846.
GEORGE P., b. April 25, 1850.
DELPHINE, b. Dec. 15, 1851.
LOVELL L., b. Jan. 16, 1853.
IRA BALDWIN, b. in Barnston, P.Q., Feb. 14, 1807—m. *Susan Glover.* They settled on No. 15, 8th Range of Barford, in 1829. The family are mostly connected with the Methodists.

CHILDREN.

SALLY, b. in 1832—d. in 1851.
LOTES, b. in 1834—d. in 1855.
OZRO, b. in 1836—m. *Nancy Piper.*
ISRAEL, b. in 1838—m. *Almira Chaffee.*
EVELYN, b. in 1840—m. *Moses Ham.*
BRUCE, b. in 1842—m. *Armandilla Humphrey.*
JOHN, b. in 1844—m. *Clara Fuller.*
FLORENCE, b. in 1846—m. *Orrin Terrill.*
EMMA, b. in 1848.

Family of Richard Baldwin, sen.

RICHARD BALDWIN, SEN., b. May 30, 1785—m. *Betsey Drew,* b. Sept. 18, 1797. They settled on Nos. 16 and 17, 9th Range of Barford. He d. April 23, 1863; she d. April 8, 1856. Their chil-

FAMILY OF RICHARD BALDWIN, JUN. 299

dren were Richard, Betsey, m. *Parker Tabor;* Isaac, m. *Lucretia Glover* Levi, Huldah, m. *Thomas Tabor;* Lewis, m. *Mary Thomas;* Mary, m. *Willard May;* Ezra; Walter, m. *Abby Stoddard;* Rufus, m. and settled in Wisconsin; Elvira, m. *Jesse Heath;* Oscar who m. *Ruby May.*

RICHARD BALDWIN, JUN., b. in Barnston, March 5, 1808—m. *Sophia Chesley,* b. in Plymouth, N.H., in 1807. They settled on what is now known as Child Street, in Coaticook. She d. Nov. 25, 1845. He subsequently m. *Mary Ann Wright,* b. in Barton, Vt., March 1, 1829, and d. April 9, 1864. Mr. Baldwin was the pioneer of the settlement of the present village of Coaticook. As an active and thorough business man, he is not surpassed by any in the county. He is the owner of several buildings and building lots in Coaticook, and valuable mills in Barford, and other localities.

CHILDREN BY 1ST MARRIAGE.

JUSTUS, b. March 15, 1833—d. March 15, 1843.
CLARA A., b. March 10, 1835—m. *Dudley Davis,* 3rd.
ELIZABETH, b. May 19, 1837—m. *A. F. Adams.*
AMANDA, b. April 6, 1839—m. *Uriah J. Rugg.*
SOPHIA, b. Dec. 8, 1840—d. May 8, 1841.
DUSTIN P., b. April 12, 1842.
THOMAS J., b. Jan. 10, 1844.
RICHARD C., b. Nov. 5, 1845.

CHILDREN BY 2ND MARRIAGE.

STUART A., b. May 12, 1849.
FRITZ W., b. Jan. 7, 1851.
MARY A., b. May 25, 1852—d. June 14, 1854.
EMMA G., b. April 24, 1854.
LESLEY, b. July 4, 1857—d. Dec. 4, 1857.
LILLIAN, b. May 1, 1861.

LEVI BALDWIN, b. April 22, 1811—m. *Lydia Converse,* b. March 24, 1819. They settled near Pinnacle Pond in Barnston, but subsequently removed to Water Street, Coaticook.

CHILDREN.

NORMAN, b. Dec. 4, 1839—m. *Ellen Wright.*
PARKER, b. Aug. 9, 1841—d. July 8, 1844.
ELVIRA, b. June 9, 1843—m. *John Buckland.*

ADELAIDE, b. May 7, 1848.
DELPHINE, b. June 4, 1860.
ISAAC BALDWIN, b. Feb. 17, 1815—m. *Catherine Chesley.* She d. in Nov., 1839. Jan. 5, 1842, m. *Lucretia Glover.* They settled in Barford ; are members of the Wesleyan Church.

CHILDREN BY 1ST MARRIAGE.

ISRAEL, } twins, b. Nov. 16,1839. Israel, m. *Chestina Buckland.*
ISAAC, } Isaac, m. *Loella Buckland.*

CHILDREN BY 2ND MARRIAGE.

ELLEN, b. March 6, 1843—m. *Harlow H. Thomas.*
PARKER F., b. Sept. 3, 1845.
MARY E., b. Oct. 14, 1846.
CLARA A., b. Jan. 2, 1850.
CLAUDE, b. Feb. 6, 1858.
CHARLES E., b. April 17, 1861.

EZRA BALDWIN, b. in Barnston, Sept. 15, 1831—m. *Valina A. Shoff*, b. Sept. 24, 1838. They settled in Barford, are members of the Wesleyan Church.

CHILDREN.

CLARA E., b. Jan. 3, 1858.
IDA G., b. Jan. 15, 1865.

Family of John Percival Baldwin.

JOHN PERCIVAL BALDWIN was b. Oct. 28, 1822—m. *Jenett Baker*, b. Feb. 5, 1828. They settled near the outlet of Pinnacle Pond, where he is the proprietor of one of the best mills in the county, and is doing an extensive business in sawing lumber and in various wood manufactures.

CHILDREN.

EDSON, b. Oct. 31, 1848.
EUGENE, b. May 14, 1843.
LESLIE, b. March 14, 1855.
WILLIE, b. March 17, 1857.

Family of Walter Baldwin.

WALTER BALDWIN, b. May 12, 1823—m. *Sarah Locke.* She d.

FAMILY OF GEORGE J. BALDWIN. 301

Jan. 15, 1855. He afterwards m. *Abby A. Stoddard*, b. Sept. 15, 1834. They settled in Coaticook.

CHILDREN BY 2ND MARRIAGE.

SARAH A., b. Aug. 5, 1857.
WRIGHT A., b. June 29, 1860.
HIRAM W., b. Aug. 8, 1862.

Family of Lewis Baldwin.

LEWIS BALDWIN, b. April 24, 1813—m. *Mary Thomas*, b. Jan. 16, 1821. They settled on Nos. 16 and 17, 8th Range of Barford.

CHILDREN.

JAMES L., b. July 30, 1843.
JUDSON R., b. Dec. 13, 1852.
MERRY E., b. July 11, 1858.

Family of Willard May.

WILLARD MAY, b. in Stanstead, P.Q., Nov. 14, 1812—m. *Mary A. Baldwin*, b. Oct. 25, 1826. They settled on the north half of No. 16, 8th Range of Barford. Mr. May has been employed in the municipal and educational affairs of the town.

CHILDREN.

ALICE E., b. April 16, 1853.
ELVIRA W., b. Jan. 30, 1857.
JENNIE, b. Feb. 26, 1860.
ADDIE E., b. April 28, 1863.
ZILLAH E., b. Sept. 17, 1865.

Ozro Baldwin.

OZRO BALDWIN, son of Ira Baldwin—m. *Nancy Piper*. Family record not supplied.

Bruce Baldwin.

BRUCE BALDWIN, son of Isaac Baldwin, m. *Armadilla Humphrey*. Record not supplied.

Family of George J. Baldwin.

GEORGE J. BALDWIN, son of Rev. Jonathan Baldwin, was b. in Westminster, Vt., July 17, 1819. He m. *Mary Huntoon*, b. Feb. 14, 1819. They settled on No. 15, 7th Range of Barford, in 1854. They belong to the Baptist Church.

CHILDREN.

SOPHIA F., b. Nov. 26, 1843—m. *Lewis Wright.*
CHARLES A., b. April 4, 1845.
ANGELINE, b. Dec. 18, 1847.
ELMORE, b. March 3, 1851.
NANCY J., b. Aug. 12, 1853.
CARLOS W., b. Nov. 19, 1857.
One child d. in infancy.

The Converse Families.

JUDE CONVERSE m. *Lydia Bemis.* They were natives of Massachusetts, and settled in Barnston in 1798. Capt. Joseph Bartlett was their only neighbor nearer than Stanstead Plain. They suffered severely for a time from the privations incident to new settlements in the wilderness, but the forests gave way gradually to their industry and perseverance, and they soon found themselves in the possession of a comfortable home and a good property. She d. in 1808. He spent his last days in the vicinity of Portland, Maine. Their children were Relief, who m. *Vester Cleaveland;* Reuben, m. *Achsah Lyman;* Jonathan, m. *Sarah Dresser;* Ruth, m. *David Sanborn;* Luke, m. *Susan Bean;* Asaph, m. *Lydia Hanson;* and Royal, who d. young.

Family of Jonathan Converse.

JONATHAN CONVERSE, b. in Spencer, Mass., Sept. 5, 1788—m. *Sarah Dresser*, b. in Royalton, Vt., June 1, 1795. They settled on No. 15, 4th Range of Barnston. Were consistent and exemplary members of the Wesleyan Church.

CHILDREN.

MARY, b. Feb. 16, 1812—m. *Moses McDuffee.*
JUDE, b. April 23, 1813—m. *Laura Henry.*
LYDIA, b. March 24, 1819—m. *Levi Baldwin.*

CLARISSA, b. Oct. 17, 1824—m. *Lucard W. Cutting.*
JOHN, b. Aug. 4, 1828—m. *Persis A. Buckland.*
JAMES, b. May 25, 1834—m. *Adeline Buckland.*

Family of Asaph Converse.

ASAPH CONVERSE, b. in Lyndon, Vt, Nov. 5, 1797—m. *Lydia Hanson*, b. June 13, 1794. They settled on No. 17 and 18, 1st Range of Barnston. Were members of the Methodist Church.

CHILDREN.

JONATHAN, b. June 17, 1828—m. *Mary L. Merriman.*
One child d. in infancy.

The Cleaveland Families.

The ancestors of these families came from England, and were among the early colonists of New England.

Family of Vester Cleaveland.

VESTER CLEAVELAND, b. in Canterbury, Conn., Aug. 1, 1780. Came to Barnston in 1801, and soon after m. *Relief Converse*, b. in Spencer, Mass., Feb. 22, 1783. They settled on No. 15, 15th Range. He d. in April, 1855; she d. in Aug., 1853. The families of their descendants are generally in good circumstances, and some of them wealthy. They are mostly connected with the Wesleyan Church.

CHILDREN.

SAMUEL, b. Nov. 7, 1802.
LYDIA, b. May 10, 1804—m. *Lewis Hanson.*
WILLIAM, b. Feb. 22, 1806.
RUTH, b. Dec. 18, 1808—d. Nov. 16, 1829.
CYNTHIA, b. Dec. 2, 1810—m. *Micajah Hanson, jun.*
HULDAH, b. March 5, 1812—m. *Albert Wheeler.*
LEVI, b. Feb. 8, 1814—m. 1st *Zilphia Baldwin;* 2nd, *Elizabeth Davis.*
EZRA, b. May 19, 1816.
ASAPH, b. Aug. 28, 1818.
MEHITABLE, b. Aug. 29, 1820—m. *Charles Wheeler.*
ABIGAIL, b. March 5, 1825—m. *George Adams.*

Family of William Cleaveland.

WILLIAM, 2nd son of Vester Cleaveland, was b. in Barnston, P.Q., Feb. 22, 1806. He m. *Sarah Baldwin*, b. Jan. 19, 1809. They settled in Barnston. Belong to the Methodist Church.

CHILDREN.

RUTH, b. Dec. 31, 1831—m. *James Bryan.*
CHESTER, b. July 11, 1835—m. *Mary A. Herron.*
ELSIE D., b. Oct. 19, 1837—d. in 1846.
CHARLES, b. March 12, 1842—d. in 1855.
ALMA L., b. Sept. 19, 1844.
GEORGE A., b. March 17, 1846.
AGNES A., b. July 5, 1848.
ALICE D., b. Nov. 28, 1854—d. in 1856.

Family of Ezra Cleaveland.

EZRA, 3rd son of Vester Cleaveland, was b. in Barnston, P.Q., May 19, 1816— m. *Nancy Child*, b. in Barnston, P.Q., Dec. 25. They settled near Barnston Corner; are members of the Methodist Church.

Record of children mislaid or lost.

Family of Norman Cleaveland, M.D.

NORMAN CLEAVELAND, a descendant from a different branch of the original Cleaveland family, was b. in Royalton, Vt., Oct. 12, 1801. Studied medicine with Dr. A. Page, of Bethel, Vt. Graduated at the Medical Department of the University of Vermont; practised several years in Vermont; removed to Barnston in 1837. Has a good practice, and stands fair in his profession. He m. *Alice Tucker*, b. in 1808.

CHILDREN.

WILLIAM RUSH, b. in February, 1845—m. *Henrietta Quimby.* Studied medicine, has a good practice in Barnston.
J. TRACY, b. Jan. 1, 1848.
6 children d. young.

The Parker Families.

The ancestors of these families emigrated from England, in the latter part of the 17th century, and settled in Massachusetts.

Family of Joshua Parker.

JOSHUA PARKER, b. in New Marlborough, Mass., March 9, 1775—m. *Judith Bartlett*, b. in Brookfield, Mass., Dec. 10, 1778, and settled on No. 17, 3rd Range of Barnston. They experienced the hardships and privations incident to new settlements in the forest, and, like the other pioneers, had to winter their stock of cattle mostly upon browse. In the winter of 1821, one of their sons, a promising young man of 19 years of age, was killed when falling trees for that purpose. They succeeded, however, in acquiring a good property. She d. Dec. 16, 1864; he d. in 1867. Their family were members of the Baptist Church.

CHILDREN.

JUDITH, b. Jan. 28, 1798—m. *Samuel Elliott*—d. April 29, 1834.
JOHN, b. June 9, 1800—d. Sept. 17, 1803.
SALLY, b. Dec. 29, 1801—m. *Samuel Elliott*, his 2d wife.
ALVIN, b. March 29, 1804—d. March 5, 1821.
HARVEY, b. Aug. 15, 1806.
ALPHEUS, b. Nov. 10, 1808.
JOSHUA, b. March 8, 1811—m. *Mary Wingate.*
ZERUIAH, b. March 14, 1813—m. *Joseph Gammon.*
LUCRETIA, b. May 13, 1817—m. *John McCoy.*
EDWARD W., b. June 28, 1819—m. *Harriett Merrill.*
ALFRED, b. Dec. 7, 1823—m. *Eunice Clefford.*

HARVEY PARKER, b. in Barnston, P.Q., Aug. 15, 1806—m. *Margaret Humphrey*, b. Feb. 6, 1811, and settled on No. 12, 5th Range of Barford. Are members of the Baptist Church.

CHILDREN.

ALVIN, b. Dec. 18, 1827.
MARGARET, b. Jan. 17, 1830—m. *Moses Drew.*
LUCRETIA, b. Sept. 13, 1834—m. *Luther Bean.*
JASPER, b. Sept. 20, 1838—m. *Emma Simonds.*

Family of Rev. Alvin Parker.

ALVIN PARKER, son of Harvey Parker, was b. Dec. 18, 1827—m. *Margaret Pollard*, b. Oct. 11, 1833. See account of the Baptist Church in Barnston and Barford.

CHILDREN.

JOSEPH A., b. Feb. 26, 1852.
JAMES P., b. Sept. 5, 1854.
ALLISON J., b. July 7, 1858.
LAURA A., b. June 16, 1861.
ARCHIBALD G., b. Feb. 13, 1864—d. young.

ALPHEUS PARKER, b. in Barnston, Nov. 10, 1808—m. *Susan K. Crooker*, b. in Woodstock, Vt., July 2, 1808. They settled on the homestead. Are members of the Baptist Church.

CHILDREN.

ORPHA, b. Feb. 15, 1834—m. *Curtis Willey*.
PROSPER P., b. Oct. 26, 1835—settled in Maine.
HENRY, b. May 31, 1838—m. *Maria Haseltine*.
JOSHUA J., b. Aug. 15, 1840—m. *Elvira Hurd*.
FRANCIS, b. April 28, 1843.
ZERNIAH, b. July 1, 1846.
JAMES A., b. Oct. 6, 1848.
JOSIAH, b. July 13, 1851.

Family of Josiah Crooker.

JOSIAH CROOKER, b. in Pembroke, Mass., Nov. 13, 1777—m. *Joanna Churchill*, a native of the same town, b. Oct. 20, 1779. They resided in Woodstock, Vt., several years, removed to Barford in 1832. In 1848 removed to Wisconsin. They were Baptists. He d. in 1860. She d. in 1862.

CHILDREN.

EDWARD, b. Sept. 11, 1798—m. *Sally Clement*.
HEMAN, b. April 2, 1801—m. *Sarah Bartlett*.
JOSIAH J., b. July 3, 1805—m. *Sylvia Wheeler*.
SUSAN R., b. July 2, 1808—m. *Alpheus Parker*.
JULIA A., b. May 4, 1812—m. *William Glover*.
FRANCIS E., b. Sept. 11, 1817—m. *Judith Drew*.
HENRY A., b. March 15, 1820—m. *Alice Ide*.
QUINCY, b. Jan. 9, 1827.

Family of Samuel Hill.

SAMUEL HILL m. *Patience Meader*. They were natives of Portsmouth, N.H. Settled in Barnston in 1799. Their children were

FAMILY OF JOHN HORN.

Silas, who m. *Sarah Holmes;* Joseph, m. *Hannah Scruten ;* Patience, m. *Philip Peaslee;* Samuel, m. *Sally Bartlett;* Anna, m. a *Mr. Belden;* Levi, m. *Polly Locke ;* Martha, m. *Isaac Hinman;* Hannah, m. *Gideon Davis,* and Aaron, who m. *Deborah Williams.*

Family of Isaac Hill.

ISAAC HILL, son of Silas Hill, was b. in Barrington, N.H., Sept. 18, 1788—m. *Huldah Marsh,* b. in Wheelock, Vt., June 6, 1793. They settled on No. 15, 9th Range of Barnston. She d. in 1836. His 2nd wife was *Julia Harford.* She d. April 25, 1852.

CHILDREN.

BETSEY, b. Feb. 20, 1833—d. young.
AMASA, b. May 29, 1816—m. *Betsey Ham.*
ISAAC, b. Oct. 6, 1818—m. *Abby Gilman.*
HAWLEY, b. Jan. 28, 1820—m. *Lydia Horn.*
NELLY, b. Jan. 28, 1822—m. *Lewis Keeler.*
WILDER, b. Nov. 19, 1824—m. *Mary Currier.*
RUFUS, b. March 18, 1827—m. *Abigail Child.*
HULDAH, b. Oct. 16, 1829—d. in 1847.
EDWARD, b. Nov. 19, 1831—m. *Abby Buckland.*

Family of Samuel Hill, 3rd.

SAMUEL HILL, 3RD, b. Oct. 20, 1800—m. *Mary Heath,* who was b. Oct. 8, 1809. They settled on No. 9, 8th Range of Barnston. Their children were MINERVA, who m. *Lewis F. Hanson;* ARVILLA m. *George Smith ;* MARTHA, m. *Ezra Aldrich,* 2nd; ALVIN, JOSHUA, PATIENCE, LUCY, CARLOS, SYLVESTER, and SAMUEL.

Family of John Horn.

JOHN HORN, son of Paul Horn, was b. May 10, 1800—m. *Lucy Heath.* They settled on No. 15th Range of Barnston. He d. Oct. 22, 1851. She afterwards m. *Peter Embury.*

CHILDREN.

FRANCIS, b. Feb. 19, 1827—m. *Lydia Hinman.*
MARY, b. Jan. 27, 1826—m. *Thomas Ewens,* 2nd *Charles Stevens.*
SUSANNA, b. Oct. 26, 1829—m. *Jonathan Godfrey.*
MARGARET, b. Oct. 23, 1831—m. *Amos Harford.*
LAVINIA, b. Aug. 31, 1833—m. *Beazar Aldrich.*

Ozro, b. Oct. 2, 1855—m. *Sarah Hall.*
Norman, b. March 17, 1837—m. *Loella Kinney.*
Rosina, b. Feb. 10, 1838—m. *Charles Fletcher.*
Persis R., b. March 28, 1840—m. *George Kinney.*
Nancy, b. Feb. 17, 1845—m. *Orrin Pratt.*
John M., b. Feb. 21, 1848.
George E., b. Dec. 7, 1849.
Three children d. in early youth.

The Child Families.

These families are numerous, and are scattered widely over the Northern States and Canada.

Of the Barnston Branch, we have no record farther back than to the middle of the eighteenth century. Samuel Child married Elizabeth Wells. They were natives of Woodstock, Conn., and settled in Vermont. Their children were Harba, Waldo, Ezra, Azubah, Lucinda, Belinda, Roxana, Sally, and Joanna. One of these only settled in Barnston, Harba Child.

Family of Harba Child.

Harba Child, eldest son of Samuel Child, was b. in Woodstock, Vt., in 1764. He m. *Molly Lee,* b. in Strafford, Conn., in 1767. They settled on No. 15, 9th Range of Barnston, in 1805. Their eldest children had been favored with better opportunities of education than most of the other pioneers, and they were employed in teaching the early schools of the town. Mr. Child d. in June, 1814. She d. in September of the same year.

CHILDREN.

Samuel, b. Feb. 12, 1787—m. *Nancy Drew.*
Sally, b. in 1791—m. *Jonathan Waterman.*
Lucy, b. in 1796—m. *Reuel Taylor.*
Charles, b. in 1798.
Stephen, b. in 1800—m. *Hannah Lyman.*
Betsey, b. in 1802.
Seth, b. April 12, 1812—m. *Juliet Wood.*

Samuel, eldest son of Harba Child, was b. in Hartland, Vt., Feb. 12, 1787—m. *Nancy Drew,* b. June 26, 1785. They settled on the family homestead, No. 15, 9th Range of Barnston.

CHILDREN.

MARY, b. April 30, 1815.
HARBA, b. June 26, 1816.
NANCY, b. Dec. 25, 1817—m. *Ezra Cleaveland.*
SAMUEL, b. June 9, 1819—m. *Ulissa E. Eastman.*
MARCUS, b. Sept. 6, 1821.
BETSEY, b. Jan. 10, 1824—a successful teacher.
IRENE, b. Oct. 4, 1826. Settled in one of the Western States.
ABIGAIL M., b. June 12, 1830—m. *Rufus Hill.*

Harba Child,

Eldest son of Samuel Child, was b. in Barnston, June 26, 1815. He m. *Adeline Bowley.* They settled on the south part of No. 14, 7th Range of Barford. He afterwards purchased the south half of No. 13, of the same Range. His wife d. Sept. 6, 1852. June 12, 1864, he m. *Jane Emerson,* b. in Alexandria, N.H. He has sustained various offices of trust and responsibility, and has been actively employed in public affairs. Received the appointment of magistrate. One child by the 1st marriage d. in infancy.

MARCUS, 3rd son of Samuel Child, was b. in Barnston, P.Q., Sept. 6, 1821. He m. *Rosetta Straw,* b. in Barford, Aug. 15, 1836. They settled on the south half of Nos. 13 and 14, 4th Range of Barford. He was for many years a successful teacher, is now actively employed in the municipal affairs of the town and sustains the offices of magistrate and postmaster.

CHILDREN.

MARCUS L., b Nov. 4, 1857—d. Aug. 21, 1862.
HARBA W., b. July 15, 1862.
IVA J., b. Nov. 17, 1863.

The Drew Families.

For an account of the origin of these families, see sketch of the Drew Families of Stanstead.

Family of Isaac Drew.

ISAAC DREW m. *Priscilla Lord.* They were natives of Maine, and settled in Barnston in 1799. He m. his 2nd wife, *Martha Davis.* She d. in 1812 ; he d. in 1821. The children by the 1st marriage were James, Joseph, Nancy, m. *Samuel Child;* Polly, Betsey, and Abigail. The children by the 2nd marriage were Isaac, Ezra, m. *Lois Wood;* Priscilla, m. *Harry Buckland;* and Martha, who m. *James Cobb:*

JAMES DREW m. *Betsey Bliss.* They settled on No. 14, 5th Range of Barford, in 1834. He d. Feb. 17, 1859. She d. Oct. 5, 1861.

CHILDREN.

BETSEY, b. Nov. 19, 1816—m. *Chase Straw.*
ORVILLE, b. Nov. 8, 1821—m. *Abigail Crooker.*
JOSEPH DREW m. *Patience Lamb.* They settled within the limits of the present village of Coaticook in 1802. He cleared away the forest where the present Railway Station is, and afterwards sold out and left the country. Their children were Huldah, Hiram, Cynthia, Patience, Lauren, Joseph, Hollis, and Elvira.

ISAAC DREW, JUN., m. *Ada Young,* widow of *Silas Corlis.* She d. in 1830. In 1832, he m. *Henrietta Flanders.* He d. about 1854. Children by 1st marriage, Isaac, Martha, and Dorcas. One child by 2nd marriage, Hiram Drew.

Family of Samuel Burbank.

SAMUEL BURBANK, b. in Boscawen, N.H., March 25, 1777. His wife (name not given) was b. March 1, 1782. They settled at the place called New Boston, in Barnston, in 1808. He d. in 1846, She d. in 1843.

CHILDREN.

CYRUS, b. Nov. 11, 1801—m. *Betsey Clifford.*
SAMUEL, b. Aug. 17, 1806.
SUBMIT, b. Aug. 17, 1810—m. *John Mosher.*
MARY, b. Jan. 18, 1813—m. *Mark Morden.*
JOSEPH, b. Feb. 1, 1816.
JESSE, b. Aug. 27, 1818.
ROYAL, b. Sept. 24, 1822.

Family of Francis Cooper.

FRANCIS COOPER, b. in Cavan County, Ireland, Dec. 17, 1814—m. *Sybil Aldrich,* b. in Barnston, Nov. 10, 1816. They settled at South Barnston, where he is postmaster.

CHILDREN.

CHARLES F., b. May 22, 1839.
GEORGE T., b. June 16, 1842.
JOHN T., b. June 11, 1843.
OLIVE R., b. April 18, 1847.
ALBERT E., b. Feb. 14, 1855.

Family of Capt. John Heath.

CAPT. JOHN HEATH, b. in Plymouth, N.H., April 15, 1771—m. *Margaret Mosher*, b. in Middlebury, Conn., Jan. 20, 1771, and settled on No. 8, 8th Range of Barnston. He early received the office of Captain of Militia, and was a prominent man in public affairs. He d. Jan. 20, 1846; his wife d. Jan. 20, 1857.

CHILDREN.

DANIEL, b. Nov. 22, 1791.
ELIZABETH, b. in August, 1793—m. 1st, *Harvey Colby;* 2nd, *N. Sanborn.*
RUTH, b. in Jan. 1795—m. *Capt. Wm. Boroughs.*
DOROTHY, b. in 1796—m. *Daniel Sprague.*
JOHN, b. in 1798—m. 1st, *Sarah Flanders;* 2nd, *Marinda Bean.*
PERRIS, b. in 1802—m. *Joseph Clifford.*
CLARISSA, b. in 1804—m. *Wm. Buckland.*
ZILPHIA, }   Zilphia m. *John Ewens.*
MICHAEL, } twins b. in 1811.
HIRAM, b. Oct. 7, 1813.

DANIEL HEATH, b. in Bridgewater, N.H., Nov. 22, 1791. In 1817 he m. *Jemima Clement*, b. July 10, 1797. They settled on No. 6, 8th Range of Barnston. He was distinguished in early life for energy and perseverance, and these qualities secured to him a good position in society.

CHILDREN.

JESSE W., b. Jan. 2, 1820—m. 1st, *Elvira Baldwin;* 2nd, *Betsey E. Taplin.*
MICHAEL, b. Dec. 7, 1824—m. *Susan Buckland.*
GEORGE L., b. Aug. 27, 1827—m. *Mary L McKeech.*
EMERSON, b. Feb. 6, 1830—d. Aug. 15, 1845.
ISAAC W., b. Aug. 4, 1832—m. *Alina A. Sanborn.*
ALMEDA, b. Aug. 5, 1835—d. March 21, 1853.
MATILDA E., b. June 15, 1833—m. *Richard C. Packard*

HIRAM HEATH, b. in Barnston, Oct., 7, 1813—m. *Sarah Ewens,* b. in Moultonborough, N.H., March 27, 1813. They settled on No. 7, 8th range of Barnston.

CHILDREN.

GEORGE H., b. Aug. 21, 1838.
WILLIAM W., b. June 6, 1842.
LUCY M., b. July 18, 1846—m. *Cyrus Sarles.*

Family of Thomas Locke.

THOMAS LOCKE, b. in Bridgewater, N. H., April 14, 1751—m. Martha Worthen a native of the same town, and b. in 1745. They settled on No. 12, 7th Range of Barnston, in 1800, but afterwards removed to No. 5, 8th Range. He d. April 14, 1816. She d. March 17, 1826. Their children were Moses, who m. *Margaret Durgan;* Abigail, m. *Obadiah Belknap;* Levi, and Polly, who m. *Levi Hill.*

LEVI, son of Thomas Locke, was b. in Bridgewater, N.H., Dec. 22, 1780. Sept. 30, 1804, he m. *Sally Clement,* b in Fishersfield, N.H., Feb. 28, 1787. They settled on No. 8, 5th Range of Barnston, where they sustained his parents during the remainder of their lives. In common with many others of the early settlers he had for a time indulged in the intemperate use of " strong drink ;" but was early led to see his danger and with that firmness for which he was distinguished, at once adopted the motto, "touch not, taste not, handle not." In after years, we find him among the ablest advocates of the Temperance Reformation. His opportunities of education had been limited, but he had acquired an amount of knowledge from reading and general observation, that was highly respectable. He sustained the office of magistrate for many years, and his memory will be long cherished with respect by the community in which he lived.

CHILDREN.

BETSEY, b. Nov. 23, 1805—m. *John Mosher.* She d. Dec. 24, 1831.
LEVI, b. Jan. 19, 1814—d. unm.
CHLOE, b. Jan. 16, 1816—m. *Guy Aldrich.*
LOUISA, b. Nov. 8, 1819—m. *Wm. Boroughs, jun.*
AMANDA, b. Feb. 13, 1822—m. *Thomas Cooper.*
THOMAS, b. June 16, 1824.

SALLY, b. April 20, 1826—m. *Walter B. Baldwin.*
LUCY, b. May 27, 1829—m. *John Sheerar.*
THOMAS, son of Levi Locke, was born in Barnston, P.Q., June 16, 1824—m. *Lydia E. Howard,* b. in Lisbon, N.H., Feb. 22, 1825. They settled on the homestead in Barnston. He has for many years sustained the office of magistrate ; was elected to the House of Commons for the Province of Quebec, for the County of Stanstead, in 1867, and re-elected by acclamation. His political career has, thus far, been a successful one.

CHILDREN.

CLARA E., b. Oct. 1, 1847.
SARAH E., } twins, b. Sept. 14, 1856.
ELLEN,
LIZZIE E., b. Nov. 30, 1859.
LEVI FRED., b. July 27, 1864.

Family of Timothy Clement.

Timothy Clement married Jemima Chandler. They were natives of Dracut, Mass. In early life he served in the British Army, during the French war, in which he experienced hardships and hair-breadth escapes, the recital of which would fill several pages. He was a soldier in the American army, during the war of the Revolution, and lived to see the result of the British and American war of 1812-15. He and his wife spent the latter part of their lives with their son Timothy Clement, jun., in Barnston. He d. in 1819. She d. in 1811. He was a well-educated man.

TIMOTHY CLEMENT, JUN., m. *Abigail Fellows.* They settled near Mosher Corner in 1800. He d. in 1821 ; she d. in 1824.

CHILDREN.

LUCY, b. Jan. 9, 1777—m. *David Austin.*
TIMOTHY 3rd, b. Nov. 28, 1779—m. *Nancy Bellows.*
ISAAC 2nd, b. in 1781—m. *Polly Eastman.*
MARY, b. April 22, 1783—m. *Thomas Knapp.*
SARAH, b. Feb. 28, 1787—m. *Levi Hill.*
ABIGAIL, b. June 3, 1789—m. *George Aldrich.*
SEWELL, b. Nov. 27, 1791—m. *Asenath Bean.*
ELLEN, b. Dec. 14, 1793—m. *Stephen Wood.*
JEMIMA, b. July 10, 1797—m. *Daniel Heath.*

ISAAC, son of Timothy Clement, sen., m. *Dorothy McHorn.* They settled in Barnston in 1800, afterwards removed to Holland, Vt., where they died. Among their children were Jemima, who m. *Daniel Mosher ;* Dolly, m. *William Armstrong*, and Polly, m· *Joseph Wood.*

Family of Michael Mosher.

MICHAEL MOSHER, b. June 5, 1732, m. *Zilphia Pierce,* b. June 19, 1746. They were natives of Middlebury, Conn. They settled at the place that bears their name, (Mosher Corner,) in Barnston, in 1805. He d. Sept. 25, 1823; she d. March 4, 1830.

CHILDREN.

MARGARET, b. June 20, 1771—m. *Capt. John Heath.*
RICHARD, b. June 29, 1772.
DANIEL, b. July 24, 1774—m. *Jemima Clement.*
ZADOK, b. Sept., 1776, m. *Bethiah Brown.*
MARY, b. July 7, 1779—m. *Samuel Bean.*
ZILPHIA, b. Feb., 13, 1782—m. *Thomas Haines.*
BETSEY, b. Jan. 4, 1784—m. *Levi Cass.*
LOIS, b. Sept. 7, 1787—m. *Willard Bartlett.*
MICHAEL, b. June 24, 1789—d. at Quebec.

RICHARD, eldest son of Michael Mosher, was b. June 29, 1772—m. *Jane Craig,* b. Dec. 15, 1774. They settled at Mosher Corner. He was a blacksmith. He d. April 28, 1843; she d. June 24, 1847.

CHILDREN.

MARGARET, b. June 2, 1798—m. *William McMachin.*
JANE, b. Jan. 31, 1800—m. *Samuel Stevens.*
MARY, b. April 28, 1801—m. *Nathan Weston.*
JOHN M., b. Nov. 19, 1802—m. 1st, *Betsey Locke;* 2nd, *S. Burbank.*
BETSEY, b. Oct. 2, 1804—m. *Michael Hatch.*
CHARLOTTE, b. May 9, 1806—m. *Mitchell Belknap.*
MICHAEL, b. March 11, 1812—m. *Mary A. Miles.*
ALEXANDER, b. Feb. 29, 1814—m. *Ellen Standish.*
FRANCES, b. June 2, 1818—m. *Heman Durkee.*

Family of Josiah Boroughs.

JOSIAH BOROUGHS, m. *Sarah Knowlton.* They were m. April 15, 1768, no record of places and dates of birth. They settled near Bickford Corner in Barnston, in 1803. The family were

FAMILY OF MICAJAH HANSON.   315

Methodists, and their house was for many years a stopping place for the Circuit preachers from the South, and the place where they held their meetings. He d. Jan. 6, 1835, aged 105 years. She d. Nov. 4, 1834, aged 87 years.

CHILDREN.

ASA, b. Nov. 18, 1768.
BENJAMIN, b. Jan. 1, 1770—m. *Amy Marshall.*
JOSIAH, b. Oct. 28, 1773.
DAVID, b. Jan. 3, 1777.
SALLY, b. July 4, 1779—m. *Israel Smith.*
JOHN, b. Aug 8, 1781—m. *Susan Stearns.*
MARTHA, b. Aug. 1, 1783—m. *John Rix.*
WILLIAM, b. Aug. 6, 1795—m. *Ruth Heath.*
3 children died in early youth.

WILLIAM, 6th son of Josiah Boroughs, was b. in Topsham, Vt., Aug. 7, 1795—m. *Ruth Heath*, b. in 1795. They settled near Bickford Corner in Barnston. He was among the youngest volunteers in the British and American War of 1812-1815. He commanded a company of volunteers during the Rebellion of 1837-1839, and was in command of a company of volunteers to be employed in the invasion of the Fenians from the United States. The children of Capt Boroughs were Elizabeth, who m. *Ezra B. Aldrich;* Horace, m. *Mehitable Renal;* William, m. *Louisa Locke;* Sarah, m. *Leonard Pevey;* Lydia, m. *Levi Gates;* Melissa, m. *George Simonds;* Hiram, m. *Mary Shumway;* and David.

Family of Micajah Hanson.

MICAJAH HANSON, b. in Dover, N.H., May 7, 1763—m. *Nancy Rogers*, b. in Rochester, N.H., March 25, 1782. They settled in Barnston in 1808. Their children were Stephen, who m. *Susan Colborne;* Lydia, m. *Asaph Converse;* Mary, m. *Wm. Lovell;* Lewis, Elijah, m. *Lydia Humphrey;* Micajah, m. *Cynthia Cleveland;* Walter, m. *Matilda Norton;* Ivory, m. a *Miss Gorman;* and Hiram. These had large families, and settled mostly in Barnston and the neighboring towns.

LEWIS, son of Micajah Hanson, was b. in Alton, N.H., March 1, 1798. He m. *Charity Wheeler*, b. in Barnston, July 10, 1804. She d. Aug. 11, 1826. He subsequently m. *Lydia Cleaveland*, b. May 10, 1814. They settled in Barnston.

CHILDREN BY 1ST MARRIAGE.

CALVIN W., b. July 29, 1826.
Two children died young.

CHILDREN BY 2ND MARRIAGE.

FRANCIS C., b. June 3, 1828.
GEORGE C., b. June 1, 1830.
RUFUS K., b. March 12, 1832.
ALBERT C., b. Aug. 28, 1834.
LAURA A., b. Jan. 26, 1837—d. Oct. 27, 1856.
WALTER C., b. July 20, 1839.
WILDER A., b. Feb. 28, 1842.
Two children died young.

Family of Charles Hanson.

CHARLES HANSON m. *Dorcas Mills.* They settled in Barnston in 1809. She d. in 1811. He d. in 1830. They had 12 children of whom one son and three daughters only settled in Barnston. Benjamin, Mahala, m. *Daniel Brown;* Dorcas, m. *Joseph Clay;* and Sarah, m. *Elisha Aldrich.*

BENJAMIN, son of Charles Hanson, was b. in Bartlett, N.H. Oct. 29, 1795. He m. *Patience Wood.* They settled on parts of No. 6, 7th Range, and No. 6, 9th Range of Barnston. He Feb. 24, 1843.

CHILDREN.

LEWIS F., b. Oct. 31, 1818—m. 1st, *Minerva Hill;* 2nd, *Mary Armstrong.*
DORCAS M., b. Dec. 25, 1819—m. *John Groves.*
CHARLES, b. July 11, 1821—m. *Mary Copp.*
JOSEPH R., b. Jan. 24, 1823—m. *Martha Warren.*
MARY, b. March 13, 1824—m. *George Worth.*
BENJAMIN H., b. Sept. 8, 1826.
LORENZO G., b. Jan. 27, 1828—m. *Adeline Spencer.*
HARRIET M., b. Nov. 19, 1829—m. *Newton Weeks.*
CORDELIA P., b. May 25, 1831—d. May 13, 1855.
GEORGE, b. March 5, 1833—m. *Emma Evans;* 2nd, *Phœbe Boston.*

HIRAM, b. Aug. 24, 1834—m. *Almira Bean* ; 2nd, *Emeline Danforth*.
JOHN B., b. Nov. 20, 1836.
ELVIRA, b. Feb. 23, 1838.
WILLIAM J., b. July 16, 1840—m. *Lucinda Hall*.

Family of Ezra Ball, Esq.

EZRA BALL, ESQ., a native of Connecticut, m. *Fanny Bricknell*. One child, Sylvester Ball, who m. *Sally Green ;*. He subsequently m. *Susan Pinney*. She d. in 1811. Their children were Betsey, who m. *Frederick Sprague ;* and Cynthia, who m. *Benjamin Dresser*. He afterwards m. *Deborah Boynton*, widow of Gardner Green, Esq.

Mr. Ball was among the earliest settlers of Barnston. He settled near Mosher Corner in 1805, was soon after appointed magistrate, and sustained a prominent part in the management of public affairs ; was one of the founders of Golden Rule Lodge. He was a well educated man. His correspondence with individuals in the pioneer settlements and elsewhere, some scraps of which have been preserved, show a clear and discriminating mind and a highly cultivated intellect. His family are mostly dead, or have left the country. He d. in 1828.

Family of Benjamin Dresser.

BENJAMIN DRESSER, b. April 26, 1800—m. *Cynthia Ball*. They settled on No. 7, 5th Range of Barnston.

CHILDREN.

ALMON, b. Feb. 25, 1820—m. *Electa Fairchild*.
SUSAN, b. Sept. 18, 1822—m. *Charles Dresser*.
LEWIS, b. Sept. 10, 1824—m. *Sarah Davis*.
MARY, b. Feb. 19, 1827—m. *Benjamin Smith*.
EZRA, b. Jan. 22, 1829—m. *Nancy Davis*.
HARRIET, b. March 10, 1831—m. *Hiram Howe*.
WILLIAM, b. July 31, 1833—m. *Eliza Goodwin;* 2nd, *Maria Pyer*.
WILBUR, b. July 6, 1835.
MASON, b. July 5, 1837.
BETSEY, b. Jan. 30, 1840.
SALLY, b. July 17, 1841—m. *Loren Bean*.
CHARLES, b. June 12, 1843—d. Feb. 6, 1864.
CHESTER, b. Dec. 30, 1845.

Family of John Dresser.

JOHN DRESSER m. *Mary Boynton.* They were among the earliest settlers of Barnston. Their children were John, who m. *Lucy Wheeler;* Sally, m. *Jonathan Converse;* William, m. *Mehitable Converse;* and Benjamin, m. *Cynthia Ball.*

Family of Levi Aldrich.

LEVI ALDRICH m. *Sibyl Merrill.* They were natives of Westmoreland, N.H. He settled in Barnston in 1800, having previously buried his wife. He subsequently m. (name not given.) He was for many years an officer in Golden Rule Lodge. He d. in 1832. His wife d. in 1862. Children, George, Sibyl, Azubah, Corinne, and Guy.

GEORGE, son of Levi Aldrich, was b. in Westmoreland, N.H., Dec. 25, 1789—m. *Abigail Clement,* b. June 3, 1789. They settled near Mosher Corner. He was for several years lieutenant of militia. He d. April 10, 1866. Abigail, his wife, d. April 10, 1856.

CHILDREN.

GEORGE, b. Aug. 19, 1809—m. *Mary Howard.*
EZRA B., b. Feb. 10, 1813.
OLIVE, b. Sept. 29, 1814—m. *James Wilson.*
SIBYL, b. Nov. 10, 1816—m. *Francis Cooper.*
IRA, b. March 25, 1819.
DIANTHE, b. June 3, 1821—m. *Harry Sarles.*
One child d. young.

GUY, son of Levi Aldrich by 2nd marriage, was b. in Barnston, Aug. 30, 1813—m. *Chloe Locke,* was b. Jan. 16, 1816. They settled near Mosher Corner. Are members of the Methodist Church.

CHILDREN.

BEAZAR, b. Dec. 19, 1833—m. *Lavinia Horn.*
BETSEY, b. June 21, 1835—m. *John Corliss.*
MARY B., b. March 17, 1837—m. *Rufus H. Paine.*
THOMAS, b. Dec. 19, 1839—m. *Emma Kane.*
LEVI L., b. Jan. 6, 1841—m. *Anna Lewis.*
TIMOTHY C., b. Feb. 19, 1843.
LESTER A., b. Oct. 21, 1848.
NORMAN E., b. Nov. 11, 1853.
GUY E., b. Oct. 4, 1854.

FAMILY OF SAMUEL CLEFFORD.

EZRA B., son of George Aldrich, was b. Feb. 10, 1813—m. *Elizabeth Boroughs*, b. Feb. 14, 1816. They settled near Mosher Corner.

CHILDREN.

ASA, b. Dec. 20, 1835.
RUTH R., b. Oct. 4, 1837—m. *Abel Heath.*
LYDIA M., b. June 2, 1839.
EZRA W., b. Dec. 7, 1840—m. *Emma A. Whitman.*
ELIZABETH, b. May 17, 1842.
CLEMENTINE J., b. May 17, 1845—m. *Charles Knight,* d. Sept. 15, 1874.
EMMA, b. Oct. 6, 1848.

IRA, son of George Aldrich, was b. March 25, 1819—m. *Anna Blake,* b. March 21, 1833. They settled on No. 13, 8th Range of Barnston.

CHILDREN.

ABBY C., b. Dec. 18, 1863.
ALFRED M., b. Sept. 9, 1864.
MINNIE A., b. June 1, 1866.

The Clefford Families.

For an account of the ancestry of these families the reader is referred to the sketches of the Clefford Families of Stanstead.

Family of Samuel Clefford.

SAMUEL CLEFFORD m. *Sarah Riddell.* They were natives of New Hampshire, settled on No. 9, 4th Range of Barnston in 1806. He d. in 1845. She d. in 1842. Their children were Samuel, who m. *Deborah Kilborn;* Huldah, m. *Josiah Kilborn;* James, m. *Mary Beaman;* Jacob, Joseph, Sarah, m. *Joshua Sutton;* Philander, m. *Louisa McDuffee;* Mary, m. *Rufus Kinney;* Betsey, m. *Cyrus Burbank;* Nancy, m. *James Wyman;* and Deborah.

JACOB CLEFFORD, b. Oct. 31, 1795—m. *Nancy McDuffee,* b. June 19, 1801. They settled in Barnston.

CHILDREN.

BETSEY, b. Dec. 18, 1822—d. young.
CLARINDA, b. April 27, 1824.
FRANCIS, b. March 26, 1826—m. *Delia Way.*

CELESTIA, b. Sept. 9, 1830—m. *John Walker.*
NANCY D., b. Aug. 30, 1832—m. *Arthur Cummings.*
SARAH R., b. Oct. 10, 1837.
JOSEPH CLEFFORD, m. *Persis Heath.* Their children were Semira, who m. Horace Taplin; Charles m. Luthera Clefford; Hiram, Burton, Persis, James O., and Gardner.

Family of Daniel McDuffee.

DANIEL McDUFFEE was b. in Rochester, N.H., April 3, 1770. He was a descendant in the 3rd generation from Daniel McDuffee, a Presbyterian clergyman of Scotland who emigrated to America in the latter part of the 17th century, and settled in Dover, N.H., where he died. The subject of this notice m. *Margaret Lucas*, b. in Wolfsborough, N.H., Sept. 3, 1776. They settled on No. 16, 4th Range of Barnston, in 1807, and subsequently removed to No. 5, 6th Range. He d. June 3, 1860. She d. Nov. 2, 1864.

CHILDREN.

ANDREW, b. in 1798—m. *Sally Taylor.*
DANIEL, b. in 1800—m. *Caroline Clark.*
NANCY, b. Jan. 19, 1801—m. *Joseph Clefford.*
MARY, b. July 5, 1803—m. *Simeon Clark.*
MOSES, b. Jan. 16, 1807—m. *Polly Converse.*
LOUISA, b. in July, 1811—m. *Philander Clefford.*
JAMES, b. March 24, 1814.
HANNAH, b. Aug. 14, 1818.
One child died young.

Family of Philander Clefford.

PHILANDER CLEFFORD m. *Louisa McDuffee.* Their children were Harriet, who m. *Jackson Corkins;* and Margaret, who m. *A. F. Colborn.*

Family of Capt. Ebenezer Kilborn.

EBENEZER KILBORN, a descendant in the 7th generation from Thomas Kilborn who emigrated from England to America in 1635, was a native of Connecticut. He m. *Eunice White*, a native of Gilsum, N.H. They were among the early settlers of Barnston. He sustained the office of captain of militia several years, d. in 1851. Children, Josiah, who m. *Sally Clefford;* Deborah, who m. *Samuel Clefford* ; Eunice, who m. *Col. Amos Fox;* Ebenezer and Otis. These two last married and settled in Barnston. All these families were useful and respected members of the community.

Family of Squire Howe.

SQUIRE HOWE, son of Caleb and Jemima Howe, was b. in Dummerston, Vt., Nov. 2, 1852, (see sketch of his captivity by the Indians.) He m. *Phœbe Paine,* b. Jan. 13, 1760. They settled on No. 9, 5th Range of Barnston, in 1804; He d. in 1834. She d. in 1849.

CHILDREN.

ANSON, b. March 28, 1782—m. *Anna Buckland.*
CLARISSA, b. July 28, 1784—m. *Beniah Barney.*
SARAH, b. July 12, 1787—m. *Elias Wheeler.*
MARTHA, b. Nov, 15, 1789—m. a *Mr. Taggard.*
EUNICE, b. April 1, 1791—m. *Joseph Clefford.*
PHŒBE, b. April 14, 1794—m. *Lewis Smith.*
JONAS, b. Feb. 22, 1797.
SQUIRE, b. July 13, 1800—m. *Lucina Humphrey.*

JONAS, 2nd, son of Squire Howe, was b. Feb. 22, 1797—m. *Prudence Hollister,* b. Feb. 12, 1807. They settled on No 9, 5th Range of Barnston. He d. April 4, 1855.

CHILDREN.

WARREN, b. Dec. 25, 1829—m. *Harriet Dresser.*
JUSTIS, b. Sept. 9, 1831.
JULIA, b. May 7, 1833—m. *George C. Hanson.*
JENETT, b. Feb. 22, 1835—d. May 14, 1856.
JANE C., b. May 6, 1837.
LAURA, b. April 29, 1839—d. July 31, 1857.
EDWIN, b. Aug. 31, 1841.
MARIA, b. March 28, 1843.
EBER, b. Jan. 31, 1845.

Family of Nathaniel Hollister.

NATHANIEL HOLLISTER m. *Prudence Strickland.* They settled in the vicinity of Way's Mills in Barnston in 1808, afterwards removed to Compton, P.Q., where he built the mills known as Hollister's Mills. They subsequently returned to Barnston, where he d. in 1838 ; she d. April 15, 1843.

CHILDREN.

ARNOLD, b. in 1793—d. June 29, 1820.
AURELIA, b. in 1794—m. *John Chandler.*
PERCY, b. in 1796—m. a *Miss Clark.*
ASA, b. in 1798—m. *Almira Hall.*
ELIZA, b. May 14, 1800—m. *Ebenezer Kilborn,* 3rd.
HARRY, b. March 24, 1802—m. *Mary Ann Yemons.*
PRUDENCE, b. Feb. 12, 1807—m. *Jonas Howe.*

Family of Elisha Bartholomew.

ELISHA BARTHOLOMEW m. *Lois Hall.* They settled on No. 19, 4th Range of Barnston, in 1806. He received the appointment of magistrate in 1808, left the country in 1814. Their children were George, Franklin, Elizabeth, and Charity.

Family of Edmund Davis.

EDMUND DAVIS, b. in 1787—m. *Elizabeth Smith.* They were natives of New Hampshire, settled on No. 19, 4th Range of Barnston, previously owned by Elisha Bartholomew. He d. July 10, 1855. She d. Dec. 19, 1861.

CHILDREN.

CHARLES W., b. Aug. 22, 1816—d. April 12, 1846.
EDMUND S., b. Dec. 2, 1818—m. *Emeline Woodman.*
ELIZABETH, b. July 30, 1820—m *Levi Cleaveland.*
HENRY H., b. May 9, 1822—m. *Laura Goldsmith*
HARRIET, b. May 9, 1822—d. Nov. 8, 1849.
MARY A., b. June 19, 1824.
ISAAC F., b. April 13, 1826 – m. *Minerva Green*
SUSAN M., b. Aug 12, 1828.
AMANDA C., b. April 27, 1830—d. April 1, 1846.
STEPHEN, b. Oct. 13, 1833—m. *Helen M. Ayer.*
ADELINE F., b. Oct. 3, 1835—m. *Lucius Kilborn.*

Family of Jasper Grisim.

JASPER GRISIM m. *Ann Campbell.* They were natives of Ireland. They settled on the south half of No. 13, 1st Range of Barnston, in 1817. He d. June 24, 1842.

CHILDREN.

MARY JANE, b. June 4, 1815—m. *Albert Wheeler.*
JAMES, b. Jan. 19, 1818—m. *Olivia Bickford*
ELIZA, b. Feb. 13, 1821—d. in 1848.
ANN, b. Sept. 7, 1823—m. *Roswell Bent.*
ELLEN, b. Oct. 18, 1826—m. *Samuel Amy.*
JOHN, b. Feb. 26, 1828—m. *Sarah Sutton.*
CAMPBELL, b. Sept. 10, 1830—m. *Roxana Morgan.*
LETITIA, b. March 10, 1833—m. *Samuel A. Amy.*

Family of Josiah Wheeler.

JOSIAH WHEELER m. *Hannah Howe.* They were natives of Plainfield, Conn. They settled in Royalton, Vt., where most of their children were born, removed to Canada in 1803, and located on No. 15, 5th Range of Barnston. He d. April 11, 1827. She d. Sept. 6, 1846.

Mr. Wheeler had been among the early settlers of Royalton, and resided there when the town was burned by the Indians in 1780. The Indians had arrived in sight of the place before the alarm was given. He gathered up his family, placed his wife and babe on one horse, his sister and eldest son on another, and he following on foot, they succeeded with hair's breadth escape in reaching the Connecticut River settlements in safety. Their property escaped the general conflagration of the town.

The children of Josiah Wheeler were Howe, who m. *Amy Parkhurst;* Weston, m. *Sarah Fuller;* Phila, m. *Philo Barke;* Elias, m. *Sarah Howe;* Squire, d. when about 24 years old; Sylvester, Sarah, m. *Parley Wheeler;* Abigail, who d. at 22; Lucy, m. *Leverett Buckland;* and Charity who m. *Lewis Hanson.* Three or four of these families, only, settled in Canada.

SYLVESTER WHEELER, b. in Royalton, Vt., Jan. 20, 1795—m. *Patience Hill,* b. March 25, 1801. They settled on No. 16, 5th Range of Barnston. She d. April 2, 1843. Oct. 23, 1843, he m.

Martha Webster, b. Sept. 23, 1808. The family belong to the Wesleyan Church.

CHILDREN BY 1ST MARRIAGE.

HORACE, b. Oct. 8, 1818—d. April 16, 1850.
CHARLES, b. March 21. 1821—m. *Mehitable Cleaveland.*
LUCY, b. Sept. 5, 1822—m. *Hiram O. Wood.*
LEWIS, b. Aug. 18, 1824—m, *Abby Harford.*
LUCIA, b. July 15, 1826—m. *Thomas Marsh.*
NORMAN, b. Nov. 5, 1828—m. *Sarah Harford.*
GEORGE, b Jan. 6, 1831—m. *Martha Welch.*
SHERMAN, b. Feb. 19, 1834—m. *Jane Osburn.*
JOSIAH, b. May 25, 1837—m, *Martha Whipple.*
ORANGE, b. Dec. 14, 1839—m. *Luthera Sarles.*
PATIENCE, b. March 9, 1843—m. *Harvey Colby.*

CHILDREN BY SECOND MARRIAGE.

SYLVESTER, b. June 13, 1845.
RUTHANNA, b. Dec. 18, 1846—m. *Cassius Remich.*
ALBERT, b. May 29, 1848—d. young.

Family of Augustus Taplin.

AUGUSTUS TAPLIN, a native of Montpelier, Vt., married *Mary Drew*, b. in Corinth, Vt. They settled in Barnston in 1800. He d. in 1861. She died in 1852.

CHILDREN.

FREDERICK A., b. in 1807—m. *Chloe Humphrey.*
MARY, b. in 1809—m. *James Cass.*
HULDAH, b in 1812—m. *Jeremiah Horn.*
SARAH, b. in 1815—m. *Walter Taplin.*
HIRAM, b. in 1818—m. *Lucina Clefford.*
RELIEF, b. in 1824.
BETSY E., b. in 1826—m. *Jesse W. Heath.*
WALTER G., b. in 1831—m. *Harriet Belknap.*
One child died in early youth.

Family of Walter Buckland.

WALTER BUCKLAND m. *Elizabeth Drew.* They were natives of Connecticut and Vermont, and settled at Barnston Corner in 1806. He was an industrious and useful mechanic, and supplied the early settlers of Barnston and Stanstead with the good old-fashioned chairs, tables and spinning-wheels of by-gone days. He d. in 1840; she d. in 1855. Their children were Epaphras, who m. a Miss Mosely; Polly and Betsey, twins. Polly m. Elias Parkhurst, Betsey m. Michael Martin, Ann m. Cyrus Mosely, Leverett m. Lucy Wheeler, Walter, Alexander m. Aris Fletcher, Henry m. Priscilla Drew, Sarah m. Robert Sutton, Erastus m. Phebe Bailey, William m. Clarissa Heath, John m. a Miss Avery, and Parley, who d. young.

WALTER BUCKLAND, jun., b. Feb. 15, 1798—m. *Jane Morrison*, b. in 1800. She d. in 1844.

CHILDREN.

AMANDA F., b. Dec. 4, 1826—m. *John Humphrey, Esq.*
LEVERETT, b. Dec. 7, 1828.
GILMAN, b. April 12, 1833—m. *Marion Gardyn.*
EPAPHRAS, b. April 8, 1835—m. *Nancy Howe.*
ORANGE, b. in 1837.
CLARISSA, b. June 28, 1839—m. *Charles Griffin.*
LUCIUS L., b. in Oct., 1841—m. *Lizzie Shields.*
JOHN BUCKLAND, b. in Barnston, Feb. 13, 1829—m. *Elvira Baldwin.* They settled in Barford, where Mr Buckland has been variously employed in public affairs. They are members of the Free-Will Baptist Church.

CHILDREN.

ALICE G., b. March 12, 1863.
CLARA A, b. Aug. 7, 1864.

Family of Manda T. Cushing.

DEA. MANDA T. CUSHING, b. in Putney, Vt., Nov. 10, 1798—came to Stanstead Plain in 1820. Carried on the saddle and harness making business until 1830, and then moved to Barnston Corner. In 1823, he m. *Sally Haseltine.* She d. in 1829. In 1830 m. *Dorothy Pinkham.* She d. in 1843. He afterwards m. *Martha E. Abbott.* He has for many years been employed in public affairs in connection with the municipal and educational departments of the town. He is a deacon in the Baptist Church.

CHILDREN BY 1ST MARRIAGE.

GEORGE S., b. in 1825—m. *Elizabeth Clay.*
JOHN H., b. in 1827—m. *Mary Eastman.*
ADISON, b. in 1828—m. *Electa Martin.*

W

CHILDREN BY 2ND MARRIAGE.

SARAH E., b. in 1832—m. *Mr. Haseltine.*
MARY, b. in 1835—m. *John N. Pierce.*
SOPHRONIA P., b. in 1837—m. *Sylvender B. Humphrey.*

Family of John Sanborn.

JOHN SANBORN m. the Widow *Blanchard.* They settled in Barnston in 1808.

CHILDREN.

ELIZA, b. June 20, 1808—m. *Cyrus Burbank,* his first wife.
NANCY, b. Sept. 6, 1810—m. *Hiram Aldrich.*
JOHN, b. Aug. 6, 1812—m. *Phebe Daniels.*
GEORGE, b. June 9, 1814—m. *Euphrata McKeech.*
CARLISLE, b. Aug. 13—m. *Nancy Hoeg.*

Family of Obadiah Belknap.

OBADIAH BELKNAP, b. in Lisbon, N.H., in 1774—m. *Abigail Locke,* b. in Bristol Vt., in 1779. They settled on No. 12, 8th Range of Barnston, in 1807. He d. in 1834. She d. April 3, 1861.

CHILDREN.

MITCHELL, b. Jan. 21, 1800.
SALLY, b. Dec. 21, 1801—m. *Nicholas Davis.*
THOMAS, b. Aug. 10, 1803—m. *Sallie Dearborn.*
WILLIAM, b. Sept 20, 1805—m. *Roxana Taylor.*
MARTHA, b. in April, 1806—m. *James Telden.*
HANNAH, b. in 1810— m. *Joseph Bailey.*
MITCHELL BELKNAP, b. Jan. 21, 1800—m. *Elsie C. Mosher.* They settled in Barnston.

CHILDREN.

ELSIE, b. Nov. 17, 1823—m. *Simon Cass.*
EUNICE, b. March 10, 1825—m. *Samuel Plummer.*
MITCHELL, b. June 20, 1826.
LYDIA, b. Dec. 12, 1827—m. *R Wilson.*
AMANDA, b. March 23, 1829—d. Aug. 19, 1865.
WILLIAM, b. Sept. 21, 1830.
MARGARET, b. March 13, 1832—m. *O. S. Davis.*
HANNAH, b. Oct. 17, 1833—m. *George Smith.*
JOSHUA, b. May 7, 1835—d. in infancy.

MARY, b. Sept. 22, 1836.
LEVI L., b. July 13, 1838—m. *Abbey Perkins.*
LABAN, b. Nov. 27, 1839.
LEWIS R., b. Sept. 27, 1841—d. April 6, 1861.
WRIGHT, b. Jan. 3, 1853.
CURTIS, b. Nov. 28, 1854.
AUSTIN, b. Nov. 19, 1856.
NELSON, b. Jan. 12, 1859—d. Jan. 21, 1860.
POTTER, b. Sept. 3, 1861.

Nathaniel Jenks, M.D.

NATHANIEL JENKS was born in Burke, Vt., Oct. 14, 1818. He received his preparatory training at Lyndon Academy, Vt., pursued the study of medicine under the charge of Drs. S. Newell and B. Sanborn of that place, followed the regular course at the Vermont Medical College at Woodstock, and received his diploma. In 1846, he located at Barnston Corner. In 1847, he married *Lucy*, dau. of *John Thornton, sen.* He has had a successful and lucrative practice, and in addition to the duties of his profession, has been employed in the municipal and educational interests of the township.

Family of Thomas Chapman, M.D.

THOMAS CHAPMAN, was born in Stafford, Conn., Sept. 17, 1776. Studied medicine, and received his diploma from the Medical Department of Yale College. He m. *Betsey Wood*, b. April 12, 1781. Commenced practice in his native town, removed to Brownington, Vt., and in 1808, settled in Barnston. He soon acquired an extensive practice, but his labor during the time of the spotted fever in 1811–1813, was so excessive that his constitution broke down under it. He died of bilious fever, Jan. 12, 1814, in the prime of life and usefulness. His wife subsequently married *Issachar Norton, jun.*

CHILDREN.

LUCIUS, b. March 2, 1809—m. *Lydia Leavitt.*
ELIZABETH W., b. Sept. 5, 1810.
THOMAS, b. March 16, 1814—d. Feb. 17, 1833.

Family of John Bellows, Esq.

JOHN BELLOWS, b. in Dalton, Mass., Aug. 31, 1784—m. *Sarah Sutton*, and settled near Barnston Corner, in 1806. She died in

1843. In 1844, he m. *Ruth Wadleigh*, widow of Thomas Paradis. He was early appointed magistrate, was actively employed in public affairs, was a prominent leader in the Baptist Church, and a distinguished advocate of the Temperance Reformation. One child by 2nd marriage, Sarah, b. Sept. 24, 1844—m. *Henry C. Buckland.*

Family of Thomas Paradis.

THOMAS PARADIS, b. in Quebec, Dec. 22, 1804. Sept. 8, 1826—m. *Ruth Wadleigh*, b. Sept. 13, 1805. They settled in Hatley. He d. May 21, 1827. In Jan. 1844, she m. John Bellows, Esq., of Barnston. One child by 1st marriage, Elizabeth, b. July 25, 1827—m. Joseph Fish.

Family of Aaron Adams, Esq.

AARON A. ADAMS, was b. in Henniker, N.H., Sept. 2, 1816. The early part of his life was spent upon the farm of his father in Bolton, P.Q. He commenced mercantile business at Georgeville in 1831, afterwards removed to Barnston, where he continued several years in trade, and held the office of Postmaster. He subsequently removed to Coaticook, and after a few years retired from trade and received the appointment of magistrate. He has been identified with the movements connected with the rise and progress of the village of Coaticook, and has otherwise been a prominent man in public affairs. Feb. 27, 1832, he m. *Betsey*, dau. of *Edward Remich*, b. Feb. 18, 1808.

CHILDREN.

AARON F., b. Aug. 7, 1834—m. *Elizabeth Baldwin.*
VICTOR S., b. March 23, 1836—m. *S. J. Pomroy, Esq.*
ELSIE D., b. May 21, 1840—m. *Robert H. Baker.*
AGNES, b. Feb. 6, 1842—d. Sept. 17, 1860.
GEORGE E., b. Feb. 6, 1842.
One child d. in infancy.

Family of John Thornton, Esq.

The ancestors of this family emigrated from England and settled in Grafton County, N.H., in the 17th century.

JOHN THORNTON was born in Derby, Vt., April 3, 1823. In 1844, commenced mercantile business at Barnston Corner in company with Samuel Cleaveland. He subsequently bought out, and continued the business in successive partnerships and in his own name. He received the appointment of magistrate in 1863, and has for several years been actively employed in public affairs. In 1847 he m. *Lucy*, dau. of *Lotes Baldwin*, b. June 3, 1821. He now has a residence and business in Coaticook.

CHILDREN.

JOHN L., b. Aug. 1, 1848.
CHARLES P., b. July 12, 1854.
JENNIE E., b. July 19, 1866.

Family of Capt. Amos K. Fox.

CAPT. AMOS K. Fox, son of Col. Amos Fox, was born in Stanstead, P.Q., Aug. 13, 1824. He began his mercantile career as clerk for J. W. Boody and Marcus Child, Esq., at Stanstead Plain, and afterwards engaged successively in partnerships with Mr. Child and with Horace Cutting, Esq., at Coaticook. He has sustained the office of captain of militia, and has been actively employed in the municipal operations of Coaticook. He m. *Huldah*, daughter of *Levi Baldwin*, sen., b. in Barnston, July 18, 1830.

CHILDREN.

ELLEN M., b. Feb. 26, 1851.
ALICE J., b. Sept. 19, 1853.
CHARLES A., b. April 7, 1856.
LAURA E., b. May 22, 1858—d. Jan. 1, 1865.
HATTIE A., b. July 21, 1861.
ALBERT E., b. March 16, 1863.

Family of Joel Shurtliff, jun.

JOEL SHURTLIFF, jun., b. in Barre, Vt., Dec. 31, 1798. In 1823 he m. *Mary Little*, b. in Hatley, P.Q., Aug. 8, 1803. They resided some 20 years at Charleston village. He was a carpenter and house joiner, and afterwards removed to different places for the convenience of his trade, and is now settled at Coaticook.

CHILDREN.

LYMAN, b. Feb. 27, 1824—m. *Caroline Rockwood;* 2nd, *Ruth Lewis.*
JULIA E., b. Feb. 17, 1826—m. *Stephen Impey.*

EMILY, b. Jan. 16, 1828—m. *Bradley Fisher.*
JOEL ED., b. June 2, 1830—m. *Clara Penwell.*
ROSCOE G., b. June 24, 1832—m. *Annis Lewis*; 2nd, *Frances Williams.*
FRANCIS, b. April 14, 1835—m. *Ann Little.*
THOMAS F., b. June 4, 1837—m. *Mary A. Webster.*
ALBERT, b. Jan. 21, 1841.
OTIS, b. Oct. 14, 1843—m. *Lucy Wood.*
Albert and Otis are engaged in mercantile business at Coaticook—are employed variously in public affairs.

The Damon Families.

Isaac, Aaron, Benjamin, John, Charles, and Albert Damon, brothers, natives of Massachusetts and Vermont, settled in Barnston about 1830. Benjamin was a physician, and practised in Barnston and the neighboring towns with good success—commenced the business of drugs and medicines at Coaticook about 1860. The others were mostly farmers. Benjamin, m Anne Watkins; Isaac, m Angelina Watkins; Aaron, m Charlotte Sutton; John, m. Jane Baldwin; Albert, m. Anna Fenton. The different families have generally been useful members of the community.

Family of Zadok Cutting.

Zadok Cutting married Abigail Waters. They settled in Hebron, Conn., where two children, Jonathan and Zadok, were born. They settled on No. 21, 4th Range of Barnston, in 1808. He d. Aug. 21, 1832. His wife d. some years previously. Zadok Cutting, jun., remained unmarried—was sustained in his later years by his brother, Jonathan Cutting.

Family of Jonathan Cutting.

Of this family we have no authentic record. Jonathan Cutting settled the affairs of his father's estate, and afterwards purchased several valuable lots of land in Barnston and Barford. These lots form one of the most valuable tracts of land in the country. His children were Lucard, b. March 2, 1817, Horace, b. Feb. 26, 1818, Aris, b. Oct. 3, 1853, Alice C., b. Dec. 14, 1856, and Mary E., b. Jan. 30, 1859. Lucard Cutting m. Clarissa Converse, b. Oct. 17, 1824. They settled in Barnston.

FAMILY OF EPHRAIM HUMPHREY. 331

HORACE CUTTING was b. in Barnston, P.Q., Feb. 26, 1818. He remained with his father's family until about 23 years of age. Commenced in mercantile business as clerk for M. Child, Esq., at Stanstead Plain, and afterwards, without any pecuniary assistance from his father, began in trade by bringing in small supplies of goods from Boston and other markets, which he sold at good profits. In 1842, he built a small shop near the centre of the present village of Coaticook. There were then but two dwelling houses in the settlement. Here, Mr. Cutting began business with Mr. Child. Some three years afterwards, they built a new store which Mr. Child took at the time of their separation in 1847. Mr. Cutting again built, and in 1852, took in Amos K. Fox, as a partner. In 1857, Mr. Cutting built the store on Pleasant Street now occupied by Cutting & Fox. He is a a *self made* man, and has succeeded in acquiring a large property; is the proprietor of several valuable buildings and building lots in Coaticook. He received the appointment of postmaster in 1844, and has been variously employed in public affairs. He m. *Elizabeth*, dau. of *Levi Baldwin*. His family are members of the Episcopal Church.

CHILDREN.

ARTHUR H., b. May 24, 1845
LAURA E., b. Nov. 24, 1846—m. *Rev. John Foster.*

The Humphrey Families.

The ancestors of these families emigrated from England in the 17th century, and settled in Rehoboth, Mass.

Family of Ephraim Humphrey.

EPHRAIM HUMPHREY, b. in Rehoboth, Mass., in 1763, m. *Margaret Allen*, a native of the same town. They settled on No. 14, 4th Range of Barnston, in 1821. He d. in 1840. She d. in 1824. Their children were Thomas, Samuel A., m. Clarinda Walker; Timothy, m. Sabrina Cushing; Nancy, m. Dudley Ladd; Lydia, m. Elijah Hanson; John, and Abel. The families of Samuel A., Thomas, Timothy and Lydia, settled in Barnston and its vicinity.

THOMAS HUMPHREY, m. *Susan Olmstead.* Their children were Thomas who m. Mary Bowen; Margaret, m. Harvey Parker, and

Curtis A., m. Violetta Jenkins. There were other children, who married and settled in the United States.

Family of Samuel A. Humphrey.

SAMUEL A. HUMPHREY, b. in Danville, Vt., Dec. 15, 1794—m Clarinda Walker, b. in Peacham, Vt., Oct. 19, 1797. They settled in Barnston in 1821. He has been variously employed in public affairs.

CHILDREN.

FREDERICK A., b. Dec. 15, 1817.
CARLOS D., b. May, 4, 1819—d. Aug. 29, 1823.
SAMUEL, b. Feb. 19, 1821.
JOHN, b. Nov. 13, 1823.
HOLLIS S., b. Jan. 15, 1826.
CHARLES W., b. May 25, 1828.
BENJAMIN F., b. Oct. 28, 1830.
SYLVENDER B., b. Feb. 6, 1833.
LEANDER, b. April 20, 1836—d. Dec. 20, 1842.
FRANCIS E., b. July 29, 1838—d. May 4, 1844.
SAMUEL HUMPHREY, b. Feb. 19, 1821— m. *Adeline Rix.* They settled in Barnston. He d. June 21, 1865.

CHILDREN.

ARMINELLA, b. Jan. 29, 1844—m. *R. B. Baldwin.*
SAMUEL E., b. April 3, 1847.
FLORA, b. May 6, 1849.
HELEN R., b. Dec. 3, 1851.
HOLLIS S. HUMPHREY, b. Jan. 15, 1826 — m. *Diana Buckland.* They settled in Barnston.

CHILDREN.

CLARENCE E., b. July 12, 1848.
AMANDA O., b. June 4, 1850—d. in 1855.

JOHN HUMPHREY was b. in Barnston, P.Q., Nov. 13, 1823. Began his mercantile career as clerk for Francis Judd and A. A. Adams, was subsequently engaged in some three or four partnerships, and afterwards conducted a business in his own name for several years at Barnston Corner. He was appointed postmaster in 1853, and resigned in 1865. He has been variously employed in public affairs, is secretary treasurer of the Township Corporation. He m. *Amanda F. Buckland,* b. Dec. 4, 1826.

CHILDREN.

CLARENCE E., b. July 12, 1845—d. Feb. 13, 1847.
WALTER, b. June 28, 1847—d. March 10, 1852.
CHARLES G., b. Nov. 15, 1849.
ARTHUR E., b. Feb. 12, 1853.
AMANDA JANE, b. May 3, 1859—d. Jan. 14, 1860.

CHARLES W., 6th son of S. A. Humphrey, was b. May 25, 1828— *Shorey*. They settled in Barnston.

CHILDREN.

CLARINDA, b. Dec. 28, 1851.
SARAH F., b. Jan. 10, 1854.
VERTA V., b. July 13, 1856.
MARY A., b. July 25, 1858.
EDNA, b. Jan. 7, 1861.
LILIAS A., b. May 2, 1863.
CORA G., b. Aug. 3, 1865.

BENJAMIN F., 7th son of S. A. Humphrey, was b. Oct. 28, 1830—m. *Mary Ann Lane*. They settled in Barnston.

CHILDREN.

LEANDER F., b. May 7, 1855.
ALBERT E., b. Aug. 23, 1860.

SYLVENDER B., 8th son of S. A. Humphrey, b. Feb. 6, 1833—m. *Sophronia P. Cushing*. They settled in Barnston.

CHILDREN.

CARRIE E., b. Dec. 23, 1855.
DOLLY S., b. April 8, 1859.
ALLEN C., b. May 13, 1863.

Family of Capt. Issachar Norton.

CAPT. ISSACHAR NORTON m. *Lorana Paine*. They settled in Barnston in 1805. He d. in 1825. She d. in 1843. Their children were Seth, Shadrach, Issachar, Samuel, m. *Orpha Heath;*

Eldad, m. *Betsey Heath;* Olive, m. *Roswell Smith;* Laura, m. *John Henry;* Roswell, was drowned in Vermont; Roswell, 2nd, m. a *Miss Lane,* and Elon, who m. *Sarah Corey.* These families settled mostly in Barnston and the neighbouring towns.

SETH NORTON, b. in Bennington, Vt., Dec. 31, 1778—m. *Lydia Sprague,* b. in Methuen, Mass., May 2, 1783. They settled in Barnston in 1803. He was a millwright, and consequently changed his residence frequently. He d. July 8, 1831. She d. in 1849.

CHILDREN.

CLARISSA, b. April 22, 1806.
FRANCES, b. March 21, 1807—d. Nov. 5, 1850.
MATILDA, b. June 9, 1809.
OLIVE, b. Dec. 21, 1810—d. March 20, 1848.
LYDIA, b. Feb. 3, 1813—d. July 9, 1849.
CHARLOTTE, b. Dec. 20, 1815.
ELEANOR, b. March 27, 1818.
MARIA, b. Oct. 20, 1831.
One child d. in early youth.

SHADRACH NORTON, b. in Bennington, Vt., Nov. 20, 1781—m. *Abigail Porter,* b. in Stockbridge, Mass., Sept. 8, 1781. They settled in Barnston, in 1803. He d. June 11, 1838. She d. Feb. 28, 1838.

CHILDREN.

AMELIA, b. Dec. 9, 1803.
ARUNAH, b. Dec. 1, 1805.
MARTIN, b. Feb. 17, 1808.
LORANA, b. Aug. 21, 1810.
PORTER, b. June 30, 1813.
ARTHUR, b. Jan. 20, 1815.
SARAH E., b. Dec. 14, 1819.
JULIA, b. April 7, 1822.
One child d. young.

ISSACHAR NORTON, JUN., b. in Newhaven, Vt., in 1783—m. *Betsey Porter,* a native of Middlebury, Vt. They settled in Barnston in 1803. She d. in 1811. July 11, 1815, he m. *Betsey,* widow of *Dr. J. Chapman.* He d. June 21, 1850. She d. May 23, 1859. One child by 1st marriage, Orissa, b. Sept. 6, 1810—m. George Thomas.

CHILDREN BY 2ND MARRIAGE.

Issachar 3rd, b. June 7, 1816.
Harriet, b. June 19, 1818—m. *Abner Foster.*
Corbin, b. Nov. 15, 1819.
One child d. young.
Arunah Norton, eldest son of Shadrach Norton, was b. Dec. 1, 1805—m. *Fanny Huntoon,* b. in Coventry, Vt., June 28, 1817. They settled in Barnston, removed to Coaticook, where he holds the office of captain of militia.

CHILDREN.

Ernest V., b. Oct. 8, 1839.
Osmond O., b. Feb. 17, 1845.
Annie M., b. July 20, 1847.
James T., b. Sept. 20, 1850.
Three children d. young.

The Sutton Families.

Philpot J. Sutton m. *Susan Hammox.* They were natives of England, emigrated to America, and after a sojourn of eight years in New Hampshire and Vermont, settled on No. 12, 2nd Range of Barnston, in 1805. They were exemplary and useful members of the Baptist Church. He d. Dec. 24, 1813. She d. in 1847. Their children were Sarah, m. John Bellows, Esq.; John, Daniel and Joshua.

Family of Dea. John Sutton.

John Sutton, b. in London, Eng., Jan. 18, 1792. He came to Barnston with his family in 1805. He m. *Sally Smith.* She d. March 13, 1821. Jan. 22, 1822, he m. *Philinda May.* The family were members of the Baptist Church, in which he sustained the office of Deacon.

CHILDREN BY 1ST MARRIAGE.

John P., b. Nov. 22, 1816—m. *Anna Green.*
Susan C., b. Dec. 7, 1818—m. *A. U. Damon.*

CHILDREN BY 2ND MARRIAGE.

CALVIN M., b. July 8, 1824—d. June 30, 1847.
LUMAN G., b. Sept. 22, 1826—m. *Lorany Merriman.*
SARAH, b. Sept. 29, 1828—m. *John Grisim.*
DEAN H., b. July 14, 1831—m. *Maria May.*
GEORGE W., b. Sept. 26, 1835—m. *Rosa Hanson.*

Family of Simeon White.

This family are descendants of the 6th and 7th generations in a direct line from *Elder John White,* who emigrated from England and settled in Hartford, Conn., and whose posterity is scattered widely over the United States and Canada.

SIMEON WHITE was b. in Gilsum, N.H., in 1765. Oct. 25, 1789, m. *Eunice Cressy.* Resided in Tunbridge, Vt., where their children were born, until 1806, when they settled on the north half of No. 15, 7th Range of Barnston. They experienced the hardships and privations incident to new settlements, but succeeded in acquiring a competence. They belonged to the Baptist Church, and were useful and valuable members of the community. He d. Aug., 21, 1825. She d. Aug. 5, 1850.

CHILDREN.

SIMEON, b, July 23, 1790—m. *Lydia Colburn.*
SALLY, b. July 1, 1792—m. *Dea. Taylor Little.*
LENDA, b. May 13, 1794—m. *Nathan Kenaston.*
ELI S., b. April 23, 1802.
Four children d. young.

ELI S., 4th son of Simeon White, sen., was b. April 23, 1802. In 1822, his left leg was crushed by the fall of a tree. He bore the pain of amputation with firmness, and instead of sinking down in despondency, set about making provision for the future. He made a wooden leg for himself, and with the assistance of friends, succeeded in acquiring a good English education. Was for several years a successful teacher in the schools connected with the Royal Institute, was a proficient in music, and taught in that department, spent several years in trade. In 1830, he m. *Caroline Pattee*, of Stanstead. They settled at Barnston Corner, where he was variously employed in public affairs. He d. in 1869.

FAMILY OF SAMUEL SHOREY. 337

CHILDREN.

JOHN, b. March 15, 1832—m. *Elizabeth Smith.*
HELEN, b. Feb. 3, 1834—m. *Waterman Harrington.*
JAMES, b. July 1, 1839.
CHARLES, b. Aug. 8, 1846.
Four children d. young.

Family of Samuel Shorey.

SAMUEL SHOREY m. *Bethiah Lee.* Their children were Samuel E., Lucy m. Oliver Smith; Betsey, m. Thomas R. Dennett; Charlotte, Joseph Davis, and Chloe.

SAMUEL E. SHOREY m. *Fanny Jones.* They were natives of Maine, were among the early settlers of Barnston. He d. Jan. 26, 1842. She afterwards m. *J. W. Fletcher.* She d. April 24, 1856.

CHILDREN.

HOLLIS, b. Dec. 2, 1823.
SAMUEL W., b. Oct. 20, 1825.
SALLY, b. Feb. 7, 1828—m. *Charles W. Humphrey.*
JOHN B., b. Feb. 7, 1832—m. *Ellen Donahue.*
ALANSON J., b. Feb. 17, 1834—m. *Eunice Haines.*
ALONZO C., b. April 23, 1836—m. *L. M. Moulton.*
MARY, b. Feb. 16, 1839—m. *W. Humphrey.*
VIENNA, b. June 15, 1841—d. March 14, 1856.

HOLLIS, eldest son of Samuel E. Shorey, was b. Dec. 2, 1823—m. *Fanny Whaler,* b. in June, 1825. She d. Nov. 8, 1849. Feb. 14, 1851, he m. *Clara Gilson.* For many years, he sustained a prominent part in the management of the municipal and educational affairs of Barnston. He is now engaged in mercantile business in Montreal.

CHILDREN BY 1ST MARRIAGE.

LAURA E., b. May 16, 1846—m. *Edward A. Small.*
SAMUEL O., b. May 23, 1848—m. *Lelia O. Knight.*

CHILDREN BY 2ND MARRIAGE.

CHARLES L., b. Aug. 28, 1854.
MARY L. M., b. Aug. 29, 1863.

Family of Oliver Smith.

OLIVER SMITH m. *Lucy Shorey.* They settled in Stanstead in 1806. Subsequently sold out and left the country.

Family of Thomas R. Dennett.

THOMAS R. DENNETT m. *Betsey Shorey.* They settled in Stanstead in 1808—left the country in 1815. He was a carpenter and house joiner.

Family of Joseph Davis.

JOSEPH DAVIS m. *Charlotte Shorey.* They settled in Barnston in 1807—left the country some ten years afterwards.

Family of Benjamin Jones, jun.

BENJAMIN JONES, JUN., m. *Susanna Butterfield*, widow of Levi Baldwin. They settled in Barnston in 1806. He d. in 1834. She d. in 1825. Their children were *Roxana*, b. Oct. 17, 1775; *Asenath*, b. March 20, 1777; *Benjamin*, b. March 29, 1780; *Anerancy*, b. Aug. 30, 1782; *Annis* b. May 27, 1785; *Sybil*, b. March 18, 1788; *Ruhannah*, b. April 17, 1790; *Griffin*, b. July 6, 1792, and *Rhoda*, b. Jan. 31, 1795.

BENJAMIN JONES, 3rd, b. March 29, 1780—m. *Sally Jones.* They settled in Barnston.

CHILDREN.

FANNY, b. Aug. 19, 1805—m. *Samuel E. Shorey.*
MARY J., b. Feb. 21, 1809—m. *Reuben Heath.*

Family of Leonard Martin, Esq.

LEONARD MARTIN, ESQ., was born in Peacham, Vt., Jan. 5, 1802 —m. *Elizabeth Kellogg*, a native of the same town, and b. Feb. 11, 1801. They settled on No. 14, 6th Range of Barford, in 1823. She d. June 22, 1840. In 1841, he m. *Priscilla Abbott*, b. in Haverhill, N.H., Aug. 29, 1808. He has sustained the offices of captain of militia and magistrate, and has been otherwise employed in public affairs. The family are respected and useful members of the community—belong to the Baptist Church.

FAMILY OF GARDNER BLONDIN.

CHILDREN BY 1ST MARRIAGE.

LYMAN, b. Nov. 5, 1827—m. *Isabella Lorimer.*
ELECTA, b. May 14, 1829—m. *Addison Cushing.*
SARAH, b. Dec. 29, 1831—m. *William Lorimer.*
ELIZABETH, b. Aug, 19, 1833—d. Dec. 5, 1850.
CAROLINE, b. March 19, 1835—d. June 22, 1860.

CHILDREN BY 2ND MARRIAGE.

LAURIN, b. Aug. 27, 1843.
LAURA, b. Nov. 10, 1846.

Family of Chase Straw.

CHASE STRAW, b. in Compton, P.Q., Oct. 23, 1809—m. *Betsey Drew,* b. in Barnston, Nov. 19, 1816. They settled on No. 15, 5th Range of Barford, in 1834.

CHILDREN.

OSCAR B., b. Dec. 7, 1834—d. Dec. 14, 1864.
ROSETTA, b. Aug. 15, 1836—m. *Marcus Child, Esq.*
MELISSA, b. Dec. 27, 1837—m. *Nelson Eagleston.*
ELLEN, b. Sept. 27, 1839—m. *Francis Benoit.*
JAMES S., b. Oct. 17, 1842.
BETSEY P., b. Jan. 30, 1846—m. *George Piper.*
CURTIS A., b. March 27, 1848.

Family of Moses Ham.

MOSES HAM, b. in Barford, P.Q., Jan. 8, 1835—m. *Eveyn Badwin,* b. March 9, 1840. They settled on No. 17, 8th Range of Barford. One child, Adella, b. in Oct., 1859.

Family of Gardner Blondin.

GARDNER BLONDIN b. in Bethlehem, N.H., June 30, 1797—m. *Judith Sartwell,* b. July 9, 1804. They settled on part of No. 15, 8th Range of Barford. Their children were Ann C., who m. Alva T. Weeks; Alice A., m. Frederick Parker; Gilbert U., Flavius J., Faustus; Flavilla, Faustina, Evelyn, and Alva C.

Family of David Young.

DAVID YOUNG, b. in Hollis, Maine, March 22, 1790—m. *Dolly Marsh*, b. in Wheelock, Vt., in 1799. They settled in Barnston in 1808, after some years, they removed to Holland, Vt., where she d. Dec. 27, 1862. A part of their family settled in Barford. Their children were Harriet, who m. Levi Lamb; Daniel, m. Phebe Wheeler; David, m. Freda Pratt; Elvira, m. Lewis Hall; Charles, m. Semira Brown; Amanda, m. Horace Mathews; George, m. Adeline Farewell; Nathan, and Henry.

Family of Ira Daniels.

IRA DANIELS, b. in Wheelock, Vt., Dec. 9, 1811—m. *Sarah A. Bean*, b. in Albany, Vt., Feb. 29, 1818. They settled on No. 16, 1st Range of Barford, in 1843. He has been employed in the municipal and educational affairs of the township.

CHILDREN.

CAROLINE, b. Dec. 19, 1837—m. *Joseph Willis*.
FRANCIS E., b. Oct. 20, 1839.
JAMES W., b. Oct. 20, 1841.
GEORGE P., b. Nov. 28, 1843.
ONIAS H., b. Dec. 26, 1848.
LUCY, b. July 29, 1854.
ELIZABETH, b. Aug. 4, 1856.

Family of Ezra Drew.

EZRA DREW, m. *Lois Wood*. They settled in Barford in 1835, removed to Ontario in 1862. Their children were George, Diana, Isaac, Eunice, Ezra, Moses, Lewis, and Lois.

MOSES DREW, son of Ezra Drew, m. *Margaret Barker*, b. in Barnston, Jan. 17, 1830. They settled in Barford.

Family of William Bliss.

WILLIAM BLISS, b. in Lebanon, Conn., June 30, 1785—m. *Phebe Farmer*, b. in Rutland, Vt., in 1788. They settled in Barnston in 1803, but subsequently left the country. Their children were Nancy, Emily, Caroline, Emerson, and Phila.

Family of John Wright, Esq.

JOHN WRIGHT, b. in Suffolk County, England, Oct. 28, 1814, came to Canada in 1836. Served as a volunteer in Capt. Kilborn's Company in Stanstead during the Rebellion of 1837-1839, settled on No. 15, 3rd Range of Barford. In 1837, he m. *Elizabeth Major*, a native of Suffolk County, Eng., and b. Oct. 18, 1820. They began upon a new farm in the wilderness, and, by industry and economy, have succeeded in acquiring a competence. He sustains the office of magistrate, and has been variously employed in public affairs.

CHILDREN.

WILLIAM, b. July 1, 1838—d. young.
ANN, b. March 16, 1840—m. *Rev. Thomas Gales*.
LEWIS P., b. March 2, 1842—m. *Sophia Baldwin*.
GEORGE, b. Aug. 2, 1850.
JOHN E., b. Sept. 6, 1854.

Family of Elisha Thomas.

ELISHA THOMAS and wife were among the early settlers of Barnston. They were natives of New Hampshire. Their children were George, John, Elisha, Edmund, James, and Nancy.

GEORGE THOMAS, m. *Orissa Norton*. They settled in Barford. Their children were Collostin, who m. *Mary Bush*; Harlow, m. *Ellen Berland*; Norton, m. *Sally Drew*; Newell, m. *Catherine Burns*; Betsey, m. *E. P. McCoy*; Albert, Lorania, Lucy, Julia, and Matilda. George, Thomas and his son, Collostin Thomas, were, for many years, stage proprietors and mail contractors.

Family of Rev. Joseph Chandler.

REV. JOSEPH CHANDLER, b. in Gloucestershire, Eng., Aug. 21, 1812. In 1847—m. *Maria E. Jenkins*. She d. in 1850. He subsequently m. *Mary Jane Lorimer*, of Stanstead, b. Aug 10, 1826. One child by 1st marriage, Hannah M., b. April 11, 1849.

CHILDREN BY 2ND MARRIAGE.

ISABELLA B., b. Oct. 3, 1851.
GEORGE, b. Aug. 22, 1853—d. in 1857.

JOSEPH, b. Aug. 4, 1855.
JAMES, b. July 18, 1857.
JOHN, b. July 15, 1859.
HARRIET, b. March 16, 1861.
PRISCILLA, b. Dec. 12, 1864.

ADDITIONAL FAMILIES.

FIELD.—Moses S. Field m. *Margaret Innes*, dau. of Rev. Joseph Gibb, b. in Banff, Scotland, and has children :
JOSEPH, b. Oct. 20, 1838—lives at home.
ALONZO, b. Sept. 18, 1840—lives in Nashua, N.H.
EDWARD S., b. Feb. 1, 1841—m.,1873, *Phebe Tichworth*. Lives in Kansas.
ELIZABETH, b. Feb. 4, 1845—m. September 16, 1874, Albert Clark of Stanstead.
HELEN M., b. May 5, 1847.
DAVID GIBB, b. Feb. 27, 1849.
MARY ANNA, b. Aug. 6, 1852.

The residence of the family is near the old homestead in Stanstead. Mr. Field has studied and travelled at times in his life, but of late has lived more at home.

McGAFFEY.— Henry McGaffey born in Lyndon, Vt. M. Dec 31, 1846, *Susan*, dau. of Jona Field, and has children :
ANNIE MARIA, b. Feb. 19, 1847.
HERBERT H., b. May 19, 1850—m. Mar. 8, 1871, *Inez Brewer* of Derby, Vt.
IDA ELIZABETH, b. Oct. 5, 1853—d. June 7, 1872. Greatly endeared by excellent and amiable qualities of character, her death was a sad affliction to kindred and friends.
FREDERICK B., b. Nov. 10, 1856—lives at home.
Residence of family, Stanstead.

WILCOX.—Pardon B. Wilcox m. June, 1838, *Judith Allen*, of Craftsbury, Vt., and has children :
CLARA HELEN, b. July 10, 1839—m. *Erastus Buckland* of Barnston, has 2 children :
ELIZA CORILLA, b. June 9, 1845, died same year.
L. ADELLE, b. Sept. 12, 1855—m. Dec. 25, 1872, *Arthur E. Baldwin* of Barnston, and has Arthur P., b. Jan. 1, 1874.

Mr. Wilcox has lived in Barnston, doing business and sharing in public duties, but now resides near the home of his early life in

ADDITIONAL FAMILIES.   343

Stanstead in easy circumstances, but deprived of the society and help of his wife removed by death Sept. 28, 1868.

POMROY.—Selah J., son of Col. Benjamin Pomroy, m. June 30, 1857, Victoria Sofalie, dau. of A. A. Adams, Esq., of Coaticook, and has children:

LIZZIE V., b. May 15, 1858.
MARY AGNES, b. Nov. 2, 1860.
BENJAMIN A., b. July 5, 1861.
ALBERT LEE, b. July 17, 1863.
AARON ALEXANDER, b. July 13, 1865.
LUCY LEE, b. Nov. 7, 1870.
ELSIE B., b. Sept. 13, 1872.

Mr. Pomroy occupies the homestead in Compton, and is largely engaged in farming, sharing liberally in measures for the good of society. His father, Col. Pomroy, has still here a home.

BALL.—Albert Phelps Ball, b. May 16, 1823, in Montreal. M. Feb. 12, 1850, Mary Lee, daughter of Col. Benjamin Pomroy, of Compton, and has children:

WILLIAM LEE, b. Feb. 7, 1851—lives in Coaticook, assistant in bank.
BENJAMIN P., b. May 8, 1854—d. May 3, 1860.
ALBERT LESPNARD, b. Nov. 8, 1855—d. May 10, 1860.
LUCY LEE, b. Nov. 14, 1857—d. May 10, 1860.
BENJAMIN P., b. March 7, 1860.
CHARLES, b. Jan. 27, 1862—d. June, 1863.
ERASTUS PHELPS, b. Aug. 2, 1863.
ALBERT EASTON, b. Sept. 7, 1864.
MARY ELIZA, b. Jan. 7, 1866—d. Sept. 10, of the same year.
JAMES TURNER, b. July 16, 1868.
HENRY TURNER, b. July 18, 1871.

Five of the children were born during the residence of the family in Sherbrooke. Of late they have lived on the place long owned and occupied by Erastus Lee, uncle of Mrs. Ball, enjoying a home of great value and comfort in Stanstead.

SLEEPER.—A family of this name came from England about the year 1700, and settled in New Hampshire. The branch of this family described in this sketch remained loyal to the Government of England during the struggle of the Colonies for independence, and H. Sleeper, then a child, removed early in life to Vermont, where he married Miss H. Batchelder. Not satisfied with the government and laws they came in 1801 to Canada, and settled on

Lot 14 in the 10th Range of Stanstead. Mr. Sleeper was a captain of militia, and took an active part in the war of 1812 in organizing companies to defend the border against invasion.

This couple lived to see their ten children, five girls and five boys, grown up and settled in life,

No one in the community was more esteemed than Mr. Sleeper. He died the 23rd of September, 1849, at the age of 79 years.

His wife lived to see her great great grand-children, and died in Aug., 1871, at the age of 93.

The oldest child, a daughter, married H. Ives, of Hatley, neither of whom is now living. The second, a daughter, married T. Kimball. They removed to Wisconsin, where they both died. The third, a son, married Miss Davis. They moved to Lancaster, N.Y., Both are living. The fourth, a son, married Miss Davis, and settled in Wisconsin, where they now reside. The fifth, a daughter, married A. Pinkham, and lives in Stanstead. The sixth, a son, L. Sleeper, has taken a prominent position in the Province. He went early in life to Quebec for the purpose of obtaining a good education. He next commenced his travels in the United States, and, after visiting nearly all the great cities, spent two years in Oglethorpe University, Georgia. He then returned to Quebec and took an active part in organizing the High School of that city. After his connection with that institution ceased he joined the Quebec and Richmond Railway Co., and having contributed much valuable information to the Board he was appointed Treasurer. Operations being temporarily suspended, he left the Co. and commenced an investigation of the mineral resources of the Province. The love of geological and mineralogical research had developed itself at a very early age, and he now found an opportunity to gratify his tastes. He soon decided that the deposits of gold were of comparatively little value, and turned his whole attention to copper. He organized a mining company in Quebec, purchased a large amount of property on Harvey Hill, directed the operations of the mine for a considerable time with most favorable results, and finally induced the stockholders to sell to an English Co. That being advantageously disposed of he at once undertook without assistance to open and work the Acton mine. The discovery and development of this extraordinary deposit astonished the world, and none less than the Director of the Geological Survey of the Province. This triumphant result after years of toil and almost universal opposition to his theory created a wide-spread excitement.

At this period he saw his opinions, as embodied in numerous reports, verified—his 'energy and perseverance rewarded with ample provision for his family, and, disgusted with the speculations going on around him, disposed of all his interest and retired from the business.

His next step was to follow out a desire to spend the remainder of his life in his native county, and, looking upon Coaticook as a favorable point for the investment of capital, he chose that place as his residence. He has spent a large sum in utilizing the water-power, and has materially contributed to the rapid growth of the village. He has the confidence and respect of all who know him.

The seventh, a daughter, married E. Davis, and went to Missouri, where they both died. The eighth, a daughter, married J. Smith. They took up their residence in Galveston, in Texas, where he died. She subsequently married the Rev. W. C. Somerville, a thoroughly educated gentleman of the Presbyterian Church. They are now in Newport, Vermont. The ninth, a son, W. Sleeper, married Miss Cole, and lives in Coaticook, where he carries on an extensive business in the manufacture of farming implements. His skill and honorable dealing have given him a well-deserved reputation. The tenth, a son, J. Sleeper married Miss Carswell, and removed to Wisconsin where they are now living.

MRS. ABIGAIL CASS.—The following is a synopsis of an account of the sickness and death of Mrs. Abigail Cass, published in the Boston Medical Journal in 1835, by Drs. M. F. Colby and S. Barnard:

Mrs. Cass was 28 years old when Dr. Colby was called to visit her in 1833,—had been five years married, had suffered severely from sickness in which the head had been much affected—stomach weak and irritable. She recovered and enjoyed her usual health until near the close of the year, when she was taken with severe pain in the head attended with delirium, and the power of vision nearly or quite suspended. After the violence of the attack had been subdued, her delirium subsided, she began to have turns of reverie or a state of sleep in which she talked much, composed poetry, prayed, exhorted, sung, etc.

When in her reveries, her eyes were always closed, her limbs had a convulsive movement, her breathing was laborious, and her frequent moanings and gestures indicated intense suffering, yet her conversation was lively and cheerful, often sarcastic and witty. Sometimes she would sing and pray and exhort in the most solemn and affecting manner.

Although she never had the slightest recollection when awake of what passed in her reveries, yet when in them, she remembered what had passed in former ones. She often supposed herself to be writing poetry, and would recite what she supposed she had written. She seemed always to be governed by the strictest regard to the truth, and if she made a promise, was sure to fulfil it. She once took a fancy to give a lecture on quackery, and appointed the time at 6, on the following Monday evening. Before the time appointed she had several paroxysms and intervals. Feeling curious to see if she would keep her appointment, and if she did, to hear her discourse, Dr. Colby visited her that afternoon. They supposed that the watch hanging in her room would be her guide, and determined to have tea before 6. They all left the room, but on returning, they found to their surprise she was concluding her lecture. She appeared to have been speaking some time with animation, and was greatly exhausted with her efforts. On being asked why she had commenced her lecture before the appointed time, she answered that she had not, but that the watch was twenty minutes too slow—which was found to be the case. She always seemed to possess an accurate knowledge of the *true* time when in her reveries, and when different watches were presented to her, would tell when they were out of the way, and how much.

After continuing an indefinite time in a paroxysm, she always awoke suddenly with an instantaneous and peculiar change in her countenance and in her manner of expression—so much so, that t was often remarked by visitors that she seemed to possess two distinct spirits, each in its turn presiding separate and uncontrolled by the other.

After her clairvoyance was established, it did not always appear necessary that her face should be turned towards an object to perceive it. When her head was turned to the back side of the bed in a dark room, she recognized persons the moment they came in and spoke of their dress. Books were handed her to read and to find passages, which she did very readily. The interposing of solid or opaque substances between her eyes and the book so as to render the passing of rays of light from one to the other impossible, seemed to have no effect in obstructing her vision—a hand, a folded cloth, a pillow, or a tea tray, and other objects were at different times held before the book without impeding her when reading, and without her appearing to notice that anything was in the way.

Setting aside her clairvoyance, many of the mental faculties seemed excited to the highest degree and to manifest powers that they were incapable of in a normal state. This was more particularly the case with ideality, wit, time, tune, and language. Wit, raillery, and sarcasm would often abound in her conversation, and her poetical effusions, which were far above what she was supposed to be able to do in her natural state, were chaste and generally of a highly devotional character. In her case, that part of the head where phrenologists have located the organs of these faculties was the seat of intense pain, and the skin over it was so exquisitely tender that the slightest touch would cause her to shrink as from the approach of a hot iron.

Among the remedies proposed, the warm bath at the temperature of 98 d. Fahrenheit was tried. When taken out she was entirely prostrated—so much so, that for a long time it seemed that the taper must expire in the socket; but when the powers of life had rallied, her head and stomach were much relieved, and her respiration was full and free. She soon, however, passed into a reverie when she immediately exclaimed—"I am blind! Before I was put into the bath, I could see very well and read any book, but now I cannot see at all!" From that moment, she lost her clairvoyance, and a gradual improvement took place in her health, but her convalescence was long and tedious. She recovered so far as to be able to attend to her household affairs for a few months, when she began again to decline, and died Oct. 31, 1835, aged 30 years.

BIRTHS.

Names of Parents.	Time.	Place.

Names of Children.	Time.	Place.

MARRIAGES.

Names of Parents.	Time.	Place.

Names of Children.	Time.	Place.

DEATHS.

Names of Parents.	Time.	Place.

Names of Children.	Time.	Place.

NOTES IN BRIEF.

IN MEMORIAM.

Mrs. Mary Pomroy, second wife of Selah Pomroy, Esq., died April 17, 1837, in Stanstead.

At the time of her marriage, Jan. 14, 1823, she was the widow of Dea. Hubbard Lawrence, of St. Johnsbury, Vt., whom she married Feb. 22, 1801, and by whom she had nine children.

She was the daughter of Major Philip Goss, of Winchester, N.H.

Mother was the dear name of the surviving parent, and what is purer, more fixed, and enduring than a mother's love? She speaks only in accents of kindness. Her eye beams with tenderness and solicitude. Her hands minister day and night to the comfort of her offspring. Her kiss is the sweetness of parental affection. Her unceasing anxiety and untiring activity show that the world itself is less a portion to her than even a wayward child. Inestimable is the treasure of her counsels and reproof, her prayers and holy life, her parting blessing and dying testimony. Such was she whose death has been here noticed, such her love, such her life.

" Far, far beyond the reach of mortal ken,
No eye hath seen it, nor hath human pen
Portrayed the glories of that world above,
Whose very atmosphere is holy love.
Oh! 'twill be passing sweet, to meet the friend
We loved on earth, and there together bend
Before the throne eternal, and rehearse
Its untold glories in exalted verse."

" Clarissa Goss Lawrence, the beloved wife of Rev. Lucius Doolittle, minister of St. George's Church, Lennoxville, departed this life April 4, 1848, aged 45 years."

Louisa Lawrence, widow of Zelotes Hosmer, formerly of Boston and Cambridge, Mass., died July 2, 1871, in Hinsdale, Mass., aged 69 years.

Nancy Temple Wakefield, wife of Rev. John Lawrence, died suddenly of pneumonia, Jan. 6, 1871, in Reading, Mass., aged 42 years.

The last fifteen and a half years of her life were passed in the relations of wife and mother.

Such were the sweetness of her disposition and purity of her character, the accomplishments of education and graces of true piety, that she excelled in all that made her home a sanctuary and a delight; while the smile resting on her face in death was evident proof to what regions of light and bliss her spirit had gone.

" There the foot no thorn e'er pierces,
There the heart ne'er heaves a sigh,
There in white we walk with Jesus
All our loved connections by,
And to reach it 'tis a privilege to die."

THE BISHOP'S COLLEGE AT LENNOXVILLE, P.Q.

By a royal charter granted in 1852, this University was established and empowered to confer degrees in divinity, arts, law and medicine.

The Chancellor, Vice-Chancellor, Principal, and Professors of the College, with such persons as have taken certain prescribed degrees compose the Convocation of the University. The calendar for 1873 gives Hon. Edward Hale as Chancellor, and Hon. George Irvine as Vice-Chancellor. The course of study in the Theological department occupies two years, and students who have completed the same can have certificates as Licentiates in Theology.

To students residing in the College the annual expenses are from $180 to $200. Certain scholarships are in the gift of the College for the benefit of students Divinity Exhibitions, also, worth $150 each per annum.

The " Doolittle" scholarships are soon to be established, as provided by the late Rev. Lucius Doolittle, who was actively instrumental in the foundation, and one of the earliest benefactors of the College.

The Junior Department or College School was founded in 1857, and is chiefly preparatory to the course of study in College, though adapted so as to fit boys for any of the business pursuits of life. Board and tutition to be paid in advance.

The library of the College comprises about 5,000 volumes in theology and classical and general literature.

WESLEYAN COLLEGE, STANSTEAD, P. Q.

A museum containing curiosities from various countries, and specimens in Mineralogy, Numismatology, and Natural History, with philosophical instruments, &c., has a place in the main building of the College.

There are three terms in the Academic year. From the first Saturday in Sept. to Dec. 21st, or Michaelmas Term ; from the third Saturday in Jan. to first Saturday in April, or Lent Term ; and Trinity Term, from the first Saturday in April to the last Thursday in June, giving a month's vacation at Christmas, and f two months at midsummer.

The sons of clergymen in the dioceses of Montreal and Quebec, residing in the school boarding-house, are admitted free of charge for tuition.

Prizes are awarded annually to the best students in their respective years, in classics, mathematics, and French, as found at examination in June.

THE WESLEYAN COLLEGE, STANSTEAD.

The *building* is of granite and brick, 142 feet in length by 52 in width, five stories high, with a wing of the same height 37 by 42 feet on the ground, and a central observatory, from which on all sides is afforded the most delightful range of views that can gratify the eye of the observer.

It has a capacity sufficient for the accommodation of the teachers, 200 boarders, and day pupils to the number of 100. The rooms and apartments are all large, well ventilated, and richly furnished.

The courses of study are such as to give a thorough English education, and prepare young persons of both sexes for College, with a special commercial and scientific course and a special norse. Art, studies, &c., optional.

The collegiate department for young ladies offers an English course of three years, also a course of four years, taking in addition the modern languages, or another of same length, taking Latin and Greek in addition to English studies.

Modifications, so as to include any two of the languages pursued, are admissible.

Diplomas are given to the students completing honorably the courses of study in the ladies collegiate, the commercial, normal school, or industrial and scientific departments.

Special attention given to French, both as to reading and conversation.

Board and tuition to be paid in advance. Absence on account of sickness considered, and due allowance made.

A deduction of $12\frac{1}{2}$ per cent. made in favor of the children of ministers of the gospel, also where two or more students attend from the same family, a reduction allowed.

The College year comprises four terms of ten weeks each, and closes June 29th, having holidays from Dec. 23 to Jan. 6, and vacation in summer of two months or more.

Correspondence may be addressed to the Rev. William Hansford, Governor and Secretary.

The location of this College is *unrivalled* for both natural scenery in variety and beauty, and for *healthfulness*. It is also conveniently situated for access, being connected with railways to Sherbrooke, to Montreal, to Boston, and to Springfield and New York.

Rev. WILLIAM HANSFORD, Governor.

FACULTY.

1. Rev. A. LEE HOLMES, M. A., Principal, *Classics and Higher Mathematics.*
2. Rev. Wm. HANSFORD, *Mental and Moral Science and Evidences of Christianity.*
3. G. J. BOMPAS, M. D., K. R. C. P., *Drawing and Painting.*
4. Rev. E. A. HEALY, *Physical Science, Elocution and Hebrew.*
5. Miss H. F. GILES, Mt. Holyoke Seminary, *German, Italian and History.*
6. Miss C. M. SMITH, *French and Belles Lettres.*
7. Miss M. ROSS, McGill Normal School. *Instrumental and Vocal Music.*
8. Mrs. A. L. HOLMES, *Instrumental Music.*
9. Miss MARY L. FLANDERS, *Common English.*

BOARD OF DIRECTORS.

Hon. T. LEE TERRILL, President,
S. FOSTER, Esq., Vice President.
A. P. BALL, Esq., Treasurer.
Rev. WILLIAM HANSFORD, Secretary.

Rev. S. D. Rice, D. D.
Charles W. Pierce, Esq.
Rev. Geo. Douglas, LL. D.
John J. Maclaren, LL. B.
Rev. J. M. Hagar, M. A.
Wm. H. Lee, M. A.
Rev. D. Connolly.
John Young, M. A.

Col. B. Pomroy.
Charles C. Colby, M. P.
A. A. Adams, Esq.
John Meigs, M. D.
Rev. Leroy Hooker.
C. W. Cowles, M. D.
Rev. J. Grenfell.
H. D. Holmes, Esq.

Rev. A. Lee Holmes, M. A.

Price of Board reduced to $2.75 per week. This covers the cost of excellent board, a comfortable and well furnished bedroom and fuel ; light and washing 50 cents per week extra.

Thus the entire cost of Board and Tuition, say in Common English, need not in any case exceed $152 for the year.

The College has been in operation for twenty-five weeks, the attendance being as follows :

Ladies,................................ 71
Gentlemen,..................... 68
Total,................139

Average per half term, 98.

THE BANK OF THE EASTERN TOWNSHIPS.

The year of incorporation of this Bank was 1855. The organization was completed in 1859, and its capital fixed at $400,000.

The officers of the Bank were :

Col. Benj. Pomroy, of Compton, President; Charles Brooks, Esq., of Lennoxville, Vice-President ; William S. Foster, of Sherbrooke, Cashier.

In 1871, an addition of $100,000 was made to the capital of the Bank.

The increase in 1872 carried it to $750,000, and at the present date the Bank has a capital of $1,000,000.

With its central agency at Sherbrooke it has five branches at different places in the Eastern Townships, viz.,

At Waterloo, Wm. G. Parmelee, Manager.
" Stanstead, A. P. Ball, Esq.,   "
" Cowansville, W. I. Briggs,   "
" Coaticook, B. Austin,   "
" Richmond, A. J. Cleaveland,   "

The first incorporated bank established in the Townships, its progress and present prosperity, show both the wisdom and regard for the public welfare of Col. Pomroy and others instrumental in the work, also, the safe and satisfactory manner in which the business has been conducted.

THE MASSAWIPPI VALLEY RAILWAY.

The charter for this railway was obtained through Albert Knight, Esq., for whose services in the Provincial Parliament a vote of thanks was tendered him at the first meeting of the Directors, appointed under the act of incorporation. At the same meeting held June 18, 1862, in Massawippi village, Col. Benjamin Pomroy was chosen President of the Company, D. W. Mack, Esq., Vice-President, and E. H. Le Baron, Esq., Secretary and Treasurer.

C. C. Colby, Esq., was chosen Managing Director. A meeting of shareholders was held June 25, 1863, when nine Directors were elected under the provisions of the charter, of whom Hon. A. T. Galt was chosen President, Col. Benjamin Pomroy, Vice-President; E. H. Le Baron, Secretary, and D. W. Mack, Treasurer.

Albert Knight, C. C. Colby, and Carlos Pierce were appointed the Executive Committee for the management of business, subject to the approval of the Directors of the Company. April 28, 1864, a meeting of Directors was held which re-elected all the officers of the Company with the addition of Charles Brooks, Esq., to the Executive Committee.

In entering upon the business of construction, the line of railway was divided into three sections, the first begining at the Province Line, the last connecting with the Grand Trunk Road at Lennoxville.

The Directors of the Company chosen Oct. 2, 1867, were the Hon. A. T. Galt, Col. Benjamin Pomroy, C. C. Colby, Albert Knight, Ozro Morrill, Charles Brooks, Gen. H. P. Adams, Stephen Foster and Carlos Pierce.

Jan. 14, 1868, Hon. A. T. Galt was re-elected President, and Col. Benj. Pomroy, Vice-President. Profile and map of spur, and report on location of main line to Ayer's Flat, were presented by Mr. Chamberlin.

The Executive Committee appointed at this meeting were instructed to meet a Committee of Directors of the Passumpsic R. R. Company, and negotiate with them upon the construction of the M. V. Railway, the running of the same, and all matters con-

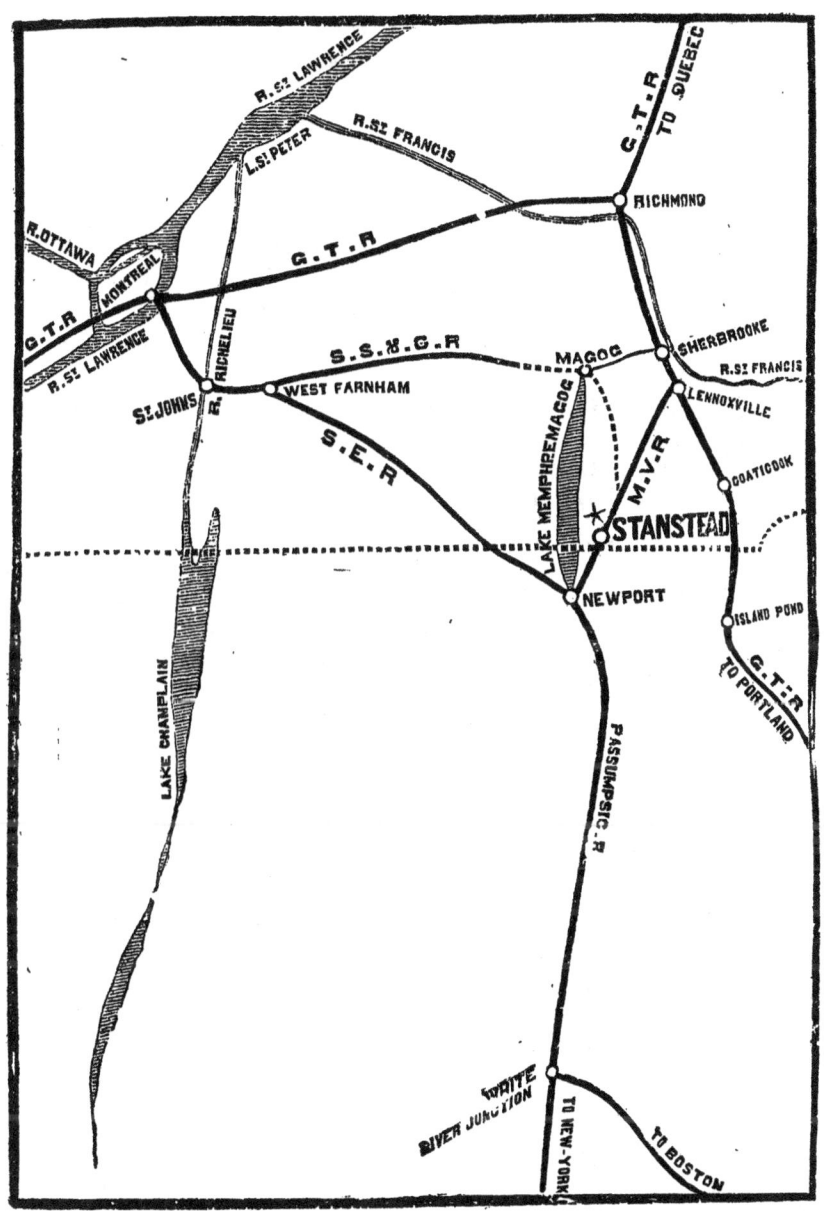

nected therewith, making the necessary provisional agreements—the same to be afterward submitted to the Board for ratification.

June 16, the same year, Carlos Pierce and Albert Knight were appointed to confer with the Directors of Passumpsic R.R., presenting resolutions, and arranging terms for payment of preliminary expenses of M. V. Railway Company.

July 30, 1868, there was submitted to the Directors the draft of a bond for leasing to the Passumpsic R. R. Company the M. V. Railway, also, one of an agreement for the construction, equipment and running of the same, and other matters connected therewith.

Hon. A. T. Galt, Col. Benjamin Pomroy, C. C. Colby, Esq., and Charles Brooks, Esq., were appointed to confer with the Passumpsic R. R. Company on all matters involved in the bond and contract above named.

This Committee subsequently reported the completion of arrangements with the Directors of the Passumpsic Company, which they were willing to accept, which report was received and adopted by the Directors of the M. V. Railway, and entered at length upon their records with the doings of the meeting.

The Vice-President, Col. Pomroy, and E. H. le Baron, Secretary were authorized and instructed to sign the bond and contract between the corporations when executed, and any other documents relating thereto.

The estimated cost of construction, &c., of M. V. Railway, or amount to be paid, was $800,000, viz., $330,000 in cash, $70,000 in stock of Company at par value, and $400,000 in first mortgage bonds.

The sum to be paid annually by the Company leasing the same $24,000 in gold, or its equivalent.

The time fixed for the completion of the M. V. Railway was July 1, 1870.

At a meeting held Sept. 30, 1868, of stockholders, for election of Directors, Hon. A. T. Galt, Col. Benjamin Pomroy, C. C. Colby. M.P.P., A. Knight, Esq., Carlos Pierce, Charles Brooks, Henry Keyes, Emmons Raymond, and B. P. Cheney, were duly chosen, who organized by electing Hon. A. T. Galt, President; Col. Benjamin Pomroy, Vice-President, and A. P. Ball, Esq., Secretary.

THE MASSAWIPPI VALLEY RAILROAD. 359

The Committee on Construction consisted of Henry Keyes, Emmons Raymond, and Col. Benj. Pomroy.

Sept. 29, 1869, the meeting re-elected the officers of the Company with Stephen Foster, Treasurer.

Sept. 7, 1870, a vote of thanks of the stockholders was given to Col. Pomroy, for his gratuitous services, and for the zeal shown by him in behalf of M. V. Railway Company.

A month later, the officers of the Board were re-elected, and Dec. 29, 1870, by vote of Directors, Col. Pomroy, Vice-President, and A. P. Ball, Secretary, were appointed and authorized to sign the contract of the M. V. Railway Company, and deliver the Railway to Conn. & Pass. R. R. Corporation.

The officers of the Company recently elected are Albert Knight, Esq., of Stanstead, President; R. N. Hall, Esq., Sherbrooke, Vice-President; and Stephen Foster, Esq., of Stanstead, Secretary.

The operation and management of the Railway have thus far been quite satisfactory to the public, and its increasing business and prospects are gratifying to those who gave time and money, and strength for its construction.

MAGOG.

The next work of the kind in the county, and greatly needed, is a railway from Ayer's Flat to Magog and beyond, giving access to the unlimited and unfailing water-power at Magog, which, for both quality and quantity, has nothing to compare with it in this section of the country, thus affording opportunity for business which capital and labor would not be slow to improve.

COATICOOK.

All the advantages arising from its location on the G. T. Railway, Coaticook largely enjoys, and that increasingly every year. Other parts of the county are benefited, but Coaticook grows and is taking on new and larger forms of business, erecting more costly and commodious buildings and working up the water-power capital and enterprise of the place more and more, going quite in advance of any other part of the Townships.

A statement of the recent progress and present prospects of this place has been confidently expected in time for publication, but has not been received.

CLOSING WORDS OF THE PUBLISHER.

He is called to express his obligations to Col. Benjamin Pomroy, of Compton, for the pecuniary aid afforded in carrying the History through the press, without which the work could not have been done.

Interested alike in the labors of Mr. Hubbard, and the common advantage of the people of the County, it seemed to him that means should be used to publish the History, and bring it to the families for whose benefit it had been compiled, and it is hoped that something more than what is due Col. Pomroy will be received from the sale of copies published.

It has been the constant desire and aim to reduce as low as possible the cost of publication, and yet afford to subscribers and the public, a book in fair type, well bound, and having desirable embellishments.

The contents will be found quite reliable as to both facts and figures; while there is not, of course, that uniformity in style and language, nor such accuracy in the use of letters, words, and phrases, as mark the writing of certain authors of the age, to those most nearly interested it will, no doubt, be a very acceptable, and highly valuable book.

LONGEVITY.

The instances of persons living to a great age are many, as will be found by any one who looks for them.

They vary from 80 and 85, to 90 and 95, in frequent cases, while some have lived to be 100 years old or 105, and one Mr. A. F. J. Channel, who was born in 1748, and died in 1858, was 110 years old.

CHILDREN.

There is, too, a good proportion of families having a much larger number of children than is common at the present day. Those with 8 and 10 each are numerous. Some with 12 and 15 quite common, and a few with from 15 to 18 by the same parents.

INTERMARRIAGES.

Instances of members of two families intermarrying are quite frequent; no doubt, they were found both convenient and pleasant. So, too, for a man to marry sisters of a first wife, and three daughters of the same family, has not been found impossible.

The readers of this book will not fail to notice the additional interest given to it by the photographic prints or illustrations of Mr. West, of Derby Line, Vt.

Though mostly copied from others, and not taken from life, they are excellent likenesses of the persons whom they represent, and the publisher is happy to commend to the public the skill and success of Mr. West in his business.

THE COUNTY.

The progress, of business and enterprise has plainly depended very much upon the political changes and public improvements going forward.

The steady growth attending the labor on the farm has more than met the advance of work in the mills and shops, hence the farmers are the more hopeful class as to the prospect in the future. With favorable seasons they are sure of a good living and fair profits.

But there is a large field yet open to skill and industry, undeveloped resources and unoccupied privileges abound, and capital and labor have room to do their best.

ADDENDA.

Correction of error of compiler and printer in the family of Joseph Merry, page 264.

CHILDREN.

Lucy A., b. Aug. 2, 1839.
John W., b. April 2, 1843.
Lestina, b. Sept. 18, 1847.
Elwin J., b. Jan. 5, 1850.
Elena, b. Jan. 5, 1850.

On page 309—Errors of compiler—In place of "son of Samuel Child," read "son of Harha Child"—two instances.

The typographical error in numbering pages 160-165 was not discovered in time for correction, but is quite harmless, as are a few others noticed here and there in the book.

INDEX

Every name from the historical sections on pages 1-116 and 347-361 has been indexed. Names in the genealogical section (pages 116-346) have been cross-indexed; thus, if you are looking for the surname Aldrich, look under "ALDRICH, Family" for the main sketch as well as under each given name within that family to find the scattered references. The subject index from the original printing has been incorporated into this index.

ABBEY, Ira 268 Miriam 218 Wealthy 268
ABBOTT, Abial 97 257 Abial Jr 75 Annis 237 238 Augustus 254 259 Betsey 254 264 Calvin 105 275 Colbe 265 Colbe Sr 266 Eleanor 257 Ellen 250 Emily 245 Esther 266 275 Family 261-263 George 264 Grace 74 Hiram 254 Joel 209 Joseph 193 Judith 118 Laura 259 Lora 254 Lorinda 265 Luther 250 Lydia 174 254 Martha E 325 Miss 259 Phebe F 136 Priscilla 338 Prudence 240 Rectina 265 Ruth 97 292 Sarah 193 Sibyl 209 Sylvia 275
ADAMS, 34 A A 55 57 108 125 267 332 343 355 A F 299 Abigail 303 Betsey 267 Electa 118 Elizabeth 299 F W 110 235 Family 328 George 303 H P 356 Jane M 278 Joel 166 L P 95 96 Lucinda 166 Martin 97 Mary 97 Mary A 169 Sarah A 244 Victor 125 Victoria Sofalie 343
ADDITIONAL FAMILIES, 342
ADVENTISTS, 101
AIKIN, Mary 168
AINSWORTH, Clarissa 192
ALBEE, Sally 135

ALDRICH, 55 56 Abigail 313 Beazar 307 Chloe 312 Elisha 316 Elizabeth 315 Ezra 2nd 307 Ezra B 315 Family 186 318 319 George 12 313 Guy 312 Hiram 326 Judith 186 Lavinia 307 Levi 108 Lewis 186 Maria 184 Martha 307 Nancy 326 Sarah 316 Sybil 310 William 184
ALDRICK, Elisha 279 Maria 279
ALEXANDER, Mary 280
ALLEN, A A 83 Amy 200 Deacon 96 Family 145 Judith 207 342 Margaret 331 Stephen 95 W A 89
ALLISON, David 104
AMES, Nancy 183
AMHERST, General 60
AMSDEN, Family 143
AMY, Ellen 323 Family 192 193 Letitia 323 Samuel 323 Samuel A 323 Sarah 262
ANDRE, Major 79
ANDREWS, William 90 91
ANDROS, W R 112
ANTIQUTIES, 60
APPLETON, Elizabeth 271
ARCHILLES, Betsey 270
ARCHLES, James 284 Rachel 284
ARMS, Adelia 106 Family 141 Melissa 145 Wm 92 94 110

ARMSTRONG, Dolly 314 Harriet 271 John 271 Mary 316 William 314
ASHLEY, Cynthia 172 Eunice 120
ATKINSON, Adeline 231 Benjamin 157 Susan M 157 Willard 231
ATTWOOD, Alice J 248 Wm 248
ATWATER, Frances W 121 Isaac 121
ATWOOD, Benjamin 188 Caroline 188 Ruth 252 Sally 227
AUBREY, Laura M 104
AUSTIN, Arvilla 238 B 355 David 313 Family 268 269 Lucy 313 Lydia 268 Nancy 172 Rosetta 199
AVERY, Miss 325
AYER, Betsey 178 Carlton 195 Family 195 196 Gardner 228 George 250 Helen M 322 Jonathan 273 Lavinia 191 Louisa S 250 Mary 273 Matilda 228 Philip 84 Roxana 265 Thomas 36 Willard 36 181
BABBITT, James 101
BACHELDER, Abba C 198 Betsey 167 212 Dorcas 201 Dorothy 202 Electa 177 Family 209 210 285 Florinda 295 Harriet 269 Ida 256 Jonathan 212 Judith 186 Lydia 166 M 111 Mary 259 Nancy 207 Nathaniel 259 Sally 133 Samuel 207
BACON, Daniel 50 76 Ebenezer 49 83 Family 296 Sarah 268
BADENOCH, Family 242
BADWIN, Eveyn 339
BAIL, Amos 253 Jane 253
BAILEY, Hannah 326 Jane 142 173 John 142 173 Joseph 326 Mary Ann 155 Phebe 325 Polly 292 Richard 292
BAIRD, Elijah 44 45 80
BAJEAU, Hannah 257 Mr 257
BAKER, Elsie D 328 Jenett 297 300 Philenda 204 Robert H 328 William H 204
BAKEWELL, W H 88
BALDWIN, 59 89 96 Arminella 332 Arthur E 342 Arthur P 342 Cynthia 142 Elizabeth 328 331

BALDWIN (continued) Elmira 325 Elvira 311 Family 297-302 Francis 173 Huldah 175 329 J 98 Jane 330 L Adelle 342 Levi 54 302 329 331 338 Lotes 329 Lucia 147 Lucy 329 Lydia 302 Mary A 206 301 Mr 193 R B 332 Richard 54 59 Richard Jr 56 57 Sally 313 Sarah 173 193 304 Sophia 341 Susanna 338 Walter B 313 Zilphia 303
BALFOUR, A J 84
BALL, 55 A P 32 108 125 354 355 358 359 Abigail 199 Alanson 228 Arvilla 169 Cynthia 317 Deborah 188 Ezra 109 188 Ezra Jr 188 Family 228 317 343 Jane 219 Lucy 188 Mary Lee 125 Matilda 203 Nancy 174 Sarah 188 Sarah E 253 Seraph 228 Seth F 169 Sylvester 188
BANCROFT, Betsey 204 John 204
BANGS, Achsah 156 Asenath 165 Betsey 172 Dolly 119 Eli 156 159 165 Eliphalet 108 Emma E 167 Esenath 159 Family 117-119 Heman 28 James 27 John E 133 Leonard L 167 Lovisa 133 Lucius J 167 Lucy 116 Lucy C 168 Marcella 180 Mary 131 245 Morrilla 167 Narcissa 174 Oliver 172 Reuben 27 92 94 T S 174 245 Thankful 154 Thankful H 155
BAPTISTS, 96
BARBER, Eliza 266 Prudence 258
BARFORD, 58 Families 338
BARKE, Phila 323 Philo 323
BARKER, Margaret 340
BARLOW, 23
BARNARD, Charlotte 165 S 345
BARNES, Asa 280 Sarah 280
BARNEY, Beniah 321 Clarissa 321
BARNSTON, 51 Academy 105
BARNSTON CORNER, 55
BARNSTON FAMILIES, 297
BARRET, J 102
BARRON, Mary 173 William 173
BARRY, A A 35 Ebenezer 206 Family 206 Harriet 206

BARTHOLOMEW, 55 Family 322
BARTLETT, 96 Benjamin 36
Canborn 160 Collins 186
Family 197 297 Jerusha 160
Joseph 3 12 52-54 302 Judith
305 Lois 314 Lucinda 134
Maria 160 Martha 212 Mary
186 Nathaniel 212 Nelson 160
Olive 118 Ozro 176 Sally 53
307 Sarah 306 Semantha 186
Sophronia 292 Willard 314
BASFORD, Rosamond 203
BATCHELDER, H 343
BATES, 33 Jacob 215 L C 35
Maria 215 Mary Ann 207 Mary
T 104 Sarah 274
BAXTER, Almira Deborah 144
Deborah 144 Family 148 J W
33 James 6 104 P 33 Portus 35
William 132 144
BAYLEY, 55 Enoch 118 Susanna
118
BEACH, Sophia 180
BEAMAN, Mary 319 Rev Mr 94
BEAN, Almira 317 Asenath 313
Betsey 283 Betsy 78 Caroline
247 Elizabeth 253 Family 254
Harriet 186 Hiram 186 Joseph
283 Lestina 250 Lora 261 272
Loren 317 Lucinda 281
Lucretia 305 Luther 305 Lydia
282 Marinda 311 Mary 225 314
Moses 78 Philip 282 Sally 317
Samuel 250 314 Sarah A 340
Simon 64 79 247 Susan 302
BECKETT, Charles G 196 Cordelia L 196
BEEBE, 43 Almira 200 Anson 36
221 Betsey E 221 Calvin 35
Caroline 245 David 35 Electa
241 Esther 212 Lorinda 219
Lurany 42 Mr 81 Plain 35
Thomas 212 Zacchens 42
BELDEN, Anna 307 Mr 307
BELKNAP, Abigail 312 Charlotte
314 Elsie C 186 Family 326
327 Harriet 324 Mitchell 314
Obadiah 312
BELLOWS, 55 Family 327 328
Frances A 104 J 96 John 260
328 Nancy 313 Ruth 328
BEMIS, Lydia 302 Miss 142

BENGHAM, Benjamin 41
BENHAM, Sarah 104
BENNETT, C W 104 Phebe 204
BENOIT, Ellen 339 Francis 339
BENT, Roswell 323
BENTON, Cynthia 220 Family
125 126 L K 129 220 Mary C
129 Sophia A 121 William 121
BERLAND, Ellen 341
BESEY, Lucretia 266
BICKFORD, Olivia 323
BIENVENUE, H 102
BIGELOW, Amos 169 Eliza 176
Levi 28 49 106 131 144 Mary
Ann 169 Samuel 36
BINGHAM, 43 Elizabeth 42
Ripley 42
BISHOP, Alma L 172 Alzina 205
Esseba 135 Hiram 135 Joel
172
BISHOP'S COLLEGE, 352
BLAISDELL, Hannah 281
BLAKE, Abigail 231 277 Adeline
240 Anna 200 319 Anna M 146
Annis A W 238 Betsey 240
Biel 240 Chancey 199 Christopher 277 Eleanor 200 Electa
240 Esther 225 Family 246
Gilbert 225 Horatio C 146 Irene
233 Israel 199 233 Kendrick
200 Mary 199 Mehitable 210
Nancy 277 Patience 192 Sherburn 277 279 Sophia 279 Susan
199 Wesley 238
BLANCHARD, 12 13 Roswell 176
Widow 326 Zeviah 270
BLASDELL, William 56
BLISS, Betsey 310 Ellen 124 Ellen P 124 Emily 202 203
Family 340 Fanny 166 J J 166
Lyman Quartus 124 Olive
Louisa 124 Quartus 124 Sarah
A 124
BLODGET, Eunice 295 Zelia 167
BLODGETT, Alva 192 Sophia 192
BLONDIN, Family 339
BLOUNT, Asa 189 Dorothy 159
Family 229 Gardner 219 Hannah 202 Lydia 189 Mary Jane
219 Moses 189 Nancy 189
BODWELL, A 113 Andrew 113
219 225 Betsey 225 E 113

BODWELL (continued)
 Eliphalet Jr 155 Family 220 221 Hannah 223 Horace 226 Lurany 226 Matilda 155 Ruth 225 Sarah 219
BOMPAS, G J 354
BONAPARTE, Nopoleon 62
BOODY, Clarinda 222 J W 329 Jefferson 222 Joseph 98 99
BOOTH, James 86
BORLAND, John 85 87 88
BOROUGHS, 56 Elizabeth 319 Family 314 315 Josiah 89 Louisa 312 Martha 170 Ruth 311 Stephen 49 72 74 154 Wm 311 Wm Jr 312
BOSTON, Phoebe 316
BOTTEREL, E 90
BOTTERELL, E 91
BOUCHETTE, 22
BOWEN, Cynthia A 249 John 280 Mary 331 Mr 66 Pamelia 280 Rebecca 280
BOWLEY, Adeline 309
BOYES, Joanna 265 Robert 265
BOYINGTON, see BOYNTON
BOYLE, 56
BOYNTON, A W 21 Abigail W 167 Adams W 44 241 Alexander 44 Almira 205 Alpheus 289 Anna G 241 Betsey 188 C G 214 Caroline 188 Catherine 188 Celina 272 Charles 213 Comfort 168 Deborah 188 317 Edmund 188 Edmund Jr 188 Emeline 213 Emma F 214 Ephraim 188 Family 187-190 289 Fletcher 272 Gardner 168 188 Harriet 188 Jane G 289 Jerusha 188 John 165 Lewis 188 Lucinda 196 Lydia 188 203 229 Margaret 188 Martha 265 Mary 318 Nancy 168 188 229 Nathan 188 Sally 203 Sarah 165 Wilder P 167 William 168
BRADFORD, Hunter 18
BRAGG, Family 218 219 John 213 240 Lucinda 213 Sally 240 Sarah 220
BRAINARD, Israel 92

BRAINERD, Family 211 212 Israel Jr 194 Rosamond 194 Roxelana 204 Sarah 201 Sophronia J 194 Timothy D 194
BRANCH, T 84
BRANDALL, Phineas 85
BREADEN, Mr 296 Sophia 296
BREADON, Dr 111
BREWER, Inez 342
BRICK, Abigail 199
BRICKNELL, Fanny 317
BRIGGS, Martha 240 Melita 241 S 85 W I 356
BROCK, James 87 Mr 87
BRODIE, Family 244 245 Isabella 243
BROOKE, Wm 286
BROOKS, Addie 260 Alonzo 231 Charles 355 356 358 Cynthia 231 E T 198 George W 260 Sarah A 204
BROWN, 155 273 Abigail 225 Alonzo 186 Annie S 215 B F 255 Belinda 198 Bethiah 314 Betsey 186 204 Caroline 297 Catherine 196 Chester W 195 Daniel 316 Dorothy 255 Eunice 118 Evelina 199 Family 194 195 211 Francis 97 Hannah 282 Isaac 44 John 36 92 225 Joseph 112 Lesyina 185 Levi 36 Mahala 316 Margaret 197 Maria 251 Marietta 206 Mary 42 226 Miss 231 Mr 103 Nancy 195 Ozias G 197 Rosamond 211 Sally 168 184 197 Samuel 44 282 Sarah 198 Semira 340 Sherborn 36 Sherburn 251 Simeon 176 198 Susan 176 Theophilus 36 Thomas 104 William 168
BROWN'S HILL, 36
BROWNE, J 103
BRUCE, Calvin 267 Electa 267 Elmira 104
BRUNNING, Emma 296
BRYAN, James 304 Ruth 304
BRYANT, Bartlett 241 C 193 G W 108 Lavinia A 265 Louisa 241 Mary E 170 Mary Jane 238 Sarah 230 Sarepta 193

BUCHANAN, Jessie Ann 230 John 230
BUCK, Harriet H 123
BUCKLAND, 55 Abby 307 Adeline 303 Alvesta 285 Amanda F 333 Anna 321 Chestina 300 Clara Helen 342 Clarissa 311 Diana 332 Elvira 299 Erastus 342 Family 324 325 Harry 310 Henry C 328 John 299 Leverett 323 Loella 300 Lucy 323 Persis A 303 Priscilla 310 Sarah 328 Susan 311 Wm 311
BUCKNELL, Arethusa 295
BUELL, Deborah 144
BULLARD, Luke 265 Miranda 265 Orrisson 264 Polly 264
BULLOCK, A M 234 Almira 204 Artemisia 84 271 Betsey 270 Biel 246 Chancey 45 110 269 Chauncey 271 Clarissa J 269 Cynthia 231 Family 236-239 Florence 234 Harriet 270 Hazel I 106 Increase 106 Jerusha 271 Jesse 231 Mary 234 Miriam 84 234 Rectina 269 270 Samuel 270 William 246 Wm 269 Wm Jr 84 234
BUNYAN, 9
BURBANK, Betsey 319 Cyrus 319 326 Eliza 326 Family 310 S 314 Samuel 56 Stephen 50
BURGOYNE, General 42
BURLAND, Family 290 291
BURNHAM, Abigail 148 Betsey 238
BURNS, Catherine 341 Clara J 208 Mary Ann 188 Samuel C 188
BURPEE, Barach 228 Family 245 246 Philena 228
BURR, Family 228 229 Malinda 228 Sarepta 231 Warren 228
BURRAGE, Henry G 82 84
BURT, Betsey 174 Mary 189 R V 131 Susan 131
BUSH, Mary 341
BUSWELL, Sarah 183
BUTIN, Sarah 151
BUTLER, 35 Annis 259 Elder 97
BUTTERFIELD, Abigail 186 J C 139 Louisa B 139 Susanna 338

BUTTERS, Frances 271 Helen A 237 Isaac 31 131 237 271 Martha 131
BUZELL, Sarah 267
BUZZELL, Caroline 225 Lydia 266 Pamelia D 270 Sarah 264
BYINGTON, see BOYNTON
CALKINS, Mary 123
CALL, John C 279 Martha 276 Nancy 266 Polly 279 Susan 279
CAMBER, Amanda 200 Richard 200
CAMERON, Sarah 121
CAMP, Family 169 170 M 131 Rachel 131
CAMPBELL, Ann 323 H T 97 Mary Jane 197 T 86 Thomas 90 91
CANFIELD, Thankful 205
CAOK, Jane G 289
CARLTON, Mary 281
CARPENTER, 35 Caleb 202 Charles 218 Clarissa 224 Family 205 206 Hannah 167 218 Harriet 206 Harvey W 217 Mary 172 Nicholas 167 S C 172 Sarah 172 202 Sophronia 217
CARR, David 127 Eleeta 165 Joel 165 Lois F 127 Nancy 168
CARRINGTON, Cordelia 168 Zenas 168
CARSWELL, Miss 345
CARTER, Almira 118
CASS, 34 98 Abigail 159 345 346 Abraham 37 183 Betsey 180 314 Carlton 184 Clarissa 160 Colby 204 Electa 184 Eliphalet 159 Elsie 326 Emily 193 Family 184-186 Gilbert 197 Gilman 279 James 324 John 183 Joseph 265 Judith 186 Lestina 204 211 Levi 314 Malvina 180 Martha 279 Mary 324 Miss 279 Nancy 183 Polly 183 Roxana 209 Sarah 179 265 Semantha 197 Simon 37 326 Sophia 178 Sophronia 212 Stephen 211 Theophilus 37 178 179
CASSVILLE, 37
CASWELL, 45 Alonzo 176 Family 172 Martha 176

CASWELLBORO, 45
CATHY, Mary 225
CATON, Abigail 180
CHADDOCK, Caroline 193 Mr 193
CHADWICK, Lydia 145 Sally 210
CHAFFEE, Almira 298
CHAMBERLIN, 33 Ann 265 Carlos 278 Cynthia A 278 David 67 247 Esther 262 Family 131 275 Fanny 265 284 Harriet 140 141 J F 85 Jane 120 Joshua 265 Marilla 266 Mr 356 Olive 182 263 Polly 97 247 274 Rachel 119 S 84 W 141 169 Susanna 202 Sylvia 262 W 169 Wm 262 Wright 6 28
CHAMPEAUX, J B 102
CHANDLER, Aurelia 322 Family 341 Fanny 239 Jemima 313 John 322 Joseph 97 243 Mary Ann 243
CHANNEL, A F J 360
CHANNELL, A F G 44 Abraham F J 268 C S 113 Charles E 126 Emily 126 Family 147 148 Harriet 213 Leonard S 126 Mary A 126 Wealthy 268 William E 126
CHAPIN, Candace 204
CHAPMAN, Alonzo 295 Betsey 334 Elvira E 295 Family 327 Henry 44 J 334 Sally 276
CHARLESTON & E HATLEY, 49
CHARLESTON ACADEMY, 105
CHARTIER, J B 103
CHASE, Betsey 192 Gardner 138 George 239 Hortense 138 Laura A 104 Leobens 108
CHENEY, B P 358 Elias 138 Joseph 96 Luman 44 Maria 138 Mary 175 Nelson 236
CHESLEY, Catherine 300 Sophia 299
CHILD, Abigail 307 Family 144 145 308 309 Harba 59 361 Harriet H 153 Hattie H 104 J 153 L B 242 Marcus 6 57 59 110 152 329 339 Nancy 304 310 Rosetta 339 Ruth M 242 Samuel 310 361
CHILDE, see CHILD
CHILSON, H 258 Hannah 258

CHRISTIE, Anna G 189 Deacon 96 Emeline 231 Family 241 John 95 John G 231
CHURCH, Mary 203 Niles P 203 Sally 203 Squire 203
CHURCHILL, Joanna 306 John 146
CLAFLIN, Ephraim 97
CLAPP, G P 129 Mary M 129 Rev Mr 94
CLARK, 56 Abigail C 160 Albert 342 Anna 196 Ballard 119 187 Betsey 187 Caroline 320 Cushman 187 Eleazar 36 Elizabeth 342 Ephraim 92 Esther 170 Family 174 198 206 207 Hannah 171 174 187 Harriet 274 Harvey 96 98 Jenett 173 Leonard 268 Lydia 208 Maria C 171 Marietta 119 Marilla 169 Mary 170 320 Miss 322 Nancy 175 Nellie 124 Osborne 160 Prudence 169 Sarah 168 Simeon 320 Thomas 208 Wealthy 268 William 169
CLARKE, Electa 206 Isaac 3 Leonard 81 William Jr 206
CLAY, Dorcas 316 Elizabeth 325 Joseph 316
CLEARY, A B 245 Margaret 245
CLEAVELAND, 55 59 89 A J 355 Elizabeth 322 Ellen 184 Ezra 309 Family 303 304 Fanny 298 Levi 297 322 Lydia 315 Mary 219 Mehitable 324 Mr 219 Nancy 309 Relief 302 Samuel 298 329 Sarah 297 Vester 302 Wm 297 Zilphina 297
CLEFFORD, 38 Albert 158 Clarinda 158 Deborah 321 Emery O 158 Eunice 305 321 Family 192 319 320 Joseph 320 321 Louisa 320 Lucina 324 Lucy 225 Mary M 158 Mary P 158 Nancy 320 Olive 193 Philander 320 Sally 321 Samuel 321
CLEMENT, 55 56 Abigail 318 Family 313 314 Jemima 311 314 Sally 306 312
CLEMENTS, Hannah 165 Mr 165
CLEVELAND, 57 Cynth 315 N 55

CLIFFORD, Betsey 310 Joseph 311 Perris 311 see also CLEFFORD
CLIPSHAM, J 91
CLOUGH, Hannah 296 Isaiah 269 Sarah 269
CLUTE, Betsey 222
COATICOOK, 56 Academy 106 Families 328
COATS, Sally 234
COBB, James 310 Justus 138 Martha 310 Mary 131 Mary Ann 221 Nancy 155 Sarah Ann 202 Stephen 155 Walter A 131 Walter C 131
COBURN, Betsey 196 259 Hannah 187 Moses 259
COLBE, Ruth 250
COLBORN, A F 320 Margaret 320
COLBORNE, John 14 143 Susan 315
COLBURN, Lydia 336
COLBY, 23 Alonzo 249 C C 6 104 108 356 358 Charles C 355 Daniel 210 Dr 43 Elizabeth 311 Emily 235 Emily J 255 Evelina 249 Family 151-153 296 Harvey 311 324 Irene 133 Laura 210 Laura J 275 Lavinia 253 M F 110 138 235 245 345 346 Maria 294 Mr 133 Nehemiah 33 Patience 324 S 235 Sarah 222 Squire 275 W B 113
COLE, Adelaide 204 Alice 180 Asa 36 Benjamin 91 Betsey 282 Evelina 195 Family 197-199 Hannah 233 Ira 180 Jane 183 John S 195 Miss 345 Philo 204 Sally 204 Simeon 50 76 Thomas 36 204 Willard 183 Willard A 233
COLLINS, Agnes H 230 Candace 200 Family 200 201 Lucinda 246 Lucy 218 Mary 218 Myrtilla 268 Parthenia 277 Samuel 222 230 Thankful 222
COMROY, Azubah 157 George 157
COMSTOCK, Clarinda 222 Elizabeth 227 Emily 221 Family 223 Harry 222 Helen M 222 Martin 227 Mary 222

COMSTOCK (continued)
Mary Ann 227 Stephen 222
CONGREGATIONALISTS, 91
CONNOLLY, D 355
CONNOR, John P 104
CONVERSE, 55 Asaph 315 Clarissa 330 Family 302 303 Jonathan 270 318 Lydia 299 315 Mary L 270 Mehitable 318 Polly 320 Relief 303 Sally 318
COOK, Almira 146 Betsey 175 Catherine 277 Chester 277 Dorothy 280 Elizabeth 149 Elvira 259 Family 288 289 Hortense 189 Orrin 280 Polly 175 Raphael 175 William G 49 55 Wm G 259
COOLEY, Sophia 154
COONEY, Robert 86 87
COOPER, Amanda 312 Family 310 311 Francis 56 318 Sibyl 318 Thomas 312
COPP, Agnes 117 Anna 79 235 C W 179 Emeline 179 Family 233 234 Florence 238 George Fitch 23 81 Hannah 198 Harriet C 221 Joshua 45 80 110 M W 105 267 Mary 235 316 Moses 45 79 181 Moses Jr 266 Polly 266 Richard 12 79 117 Susan 267 W C 221
COREY, Deborah 165 James 165 Sarah 334
CORKINS, Harriet 320 Jackson 320
CORLIS, Ada 310 Silas 310
CORLISS, Betsey 318 John 318
CORNELL, Catherine 172
CORRILL, Dorothy 159 James 159
COTTON, Larona 169
COULL, Janet 244
COWIE, Huldah 232
COWLES, C W 96 108 355 Family 138 139
COX, Family 268 Jonathan 66 Laura 247 Mary 247 W 247 Wealthy 148
CRAIG, Jane 314
CRANE, Margaret 170 Nahum 170
CRAWFORD, Abigail 184 J B 99 J R 84 89

CRESSY, Eunice 336
CROCKETT, Katie 287
CROOKER, Abigail 310 Family 306 Sarah A 241 Susan K 306
CROSS, Harriet 238
CROWN, Sarah 168
CULL, Family 284 285 Henry 2 50 77 78
CUMMINGS, Annette D 126 Arthur 320 Ella 243 Emily 199 Nancy D 320 Olive 146
CUNNINGHAM, Laura A 200
CURRIER, Benjamin 167 Betsey 220 Family 277 278 Judith 180 M F 149 Mary 307 Nancy 277 Polly 134 276 Polly S 277 Sally C 276 Sarah 167 Susan 276
CURRY, Rev Mr 95
CURTIS, Abigail 116 Betsey 154 Elijah 28 Family 168 169 Harriet 189 289 Henry 28 154 Lucia 236 Martha 258 Olive A 189 Phebe 169
CUSHING, Addison 339 Dorothy 212 Electa 339 Family 325 326 M T 55 Manda T 212 Sabrina 331 Sophronia P 333
CUTTING, 55 Clarissa 303 Elizabeth 297 Family 330 331 Horace 56 57 297 329 Lucard W 303
DAGGETT, Julia 215
DAILY, 44
DALY, James 103
DAMON, 55 A U 335 Benjamin 57 Family 330 Susan C 335
DANFORTH, Betsey 206 Emeline 317 Roxana 209
DANIELS, Family 340 Harriet S 172 Lowell 172 Phebe 326
DARNELL, Henry F 82
DAVIDSON, Jessie 244 William 44
DAVIS, 38 55 Aaron 211 Adelaide 199 Asenath 157 Betsey 171 293 Betsey P 211 Celina 272 Charlotte 338 Clara A 299 Dorothy 227 Dudley 205 Dudley 3rd 299 E 345 Elizabeth 303 Family 202-204 322 Gideon 307 Hannah 307 Harris 169

DAVIS (continued)
Helen M 196 Hiram 56 171 John 89-91 Joseph 187 338 Joshua R 212 Judith 187 K R 100 Lavinia 119 Luvia 158 Lydia 42 188 212 Margaret 326 Martha 197 309 Mary 189 Miss 344 Mr 268 Nancy 171 317 Nicholas 326 O S 326 Phineas 199 292 Polly 268 Roxelana 157 211 Sally 160 198 326 Salome 166 Sampson 35 Sarah 156 157 165 192 298 317 Silas A 166 Stephen 196 Susan 189 190 Thaddeus O 158 William 188 William H 211
DAY, Aurelia 202 C D 21 44
DEARBORN, Sallie 326
DEMARY, Nancy B 252 Nancy R 251
DEMICK, 50
DENISON, Mary 156
DENNETT, Betsey 337 338 Thomas E 337 338
DESNOYER, A 103
DEWEY, Ann 193
DEWITT, Louisa 287
DIBBLE, Mary 295 Mary E 120
DICKERSON, Elizabeth 104 Family 150 151 Silas H 17
DICKEY, Elizabeth 177 Helen 177 Isabella 179 Margaret 291
DIGBY, Mary Ann 250
DIXON, Amelia L 214 Elmira 157 Family 142 M 14 214 Matthew 157
DOAK, W R 107
DODGE, Catherine 194 Ebenezer 201 Louisa 197 232 Sarah 282 Susan 201
DODRIDGE, 9
DOLOFF, 38 Betsey 243 Family 191 Laura 235 Samuel 235 William 243
DONAHUE, Ellen 337
DOOLITTLE, Clarissa Goss 351 Lucius 351 352 Rev Mr 82 Sarah 142
DORCHESTER, Lord 2
DOUGLAS, Geo 355
DOUGLASS, Geo 108
DOW, Albert M 149 Fanny 149

DOW (continued)
  Greeley 245 Lydia 189 Mary 245 Nancy 245
DOWNS, 96
DOZIER, Martha P D 125 Sarah A 125 T H 125 William B 125
DRAKE, Miss 239
DRESSER, Benjamin 317 Cynthia 317 Family 317 318 Harriet 198 321 Relief 167 Sally 285 Sarah 302
DREW, 59 Abigail 177 Armina 253 Betsey 297 298 339 C W 35 Clement 3 Daniel 204 Elizabeth 324 Emma 241 Family 230 231 309 310 340 Harlow 226 Harriet 224 Isaac 60 Joseph 297 Judith 306 Laura 271 Lovisa 199 Lydia 226 Margaret 305 Mary 134 324 Moses 305 Nancy 308 Orissa 298 Patience 297 Phebe E 204 Priscilla 325 Sally 341 Sarepta 229 Stimson 229 Thomas 253
DUBOIS, Henry 284 Polly 284
DUFRESNE, A E 103
DUNBAR, Samuel 90
DURGAN, Marcella 209 Margaret 312
DURKEE, Frances 314 Heman 314
DUSLIN, Emma J 258 Lyman 258
DUSTAN, Abigail 143 Eliza 184 Hannah 211 Jonathan 184 Nancy M 147 Ruth 169 Susan 120
DUSTIN, Albert 279 Elizabeth 279
DUTTON, Adoniram 160 Asa 295 Luther 227 Mary Jane 160 Ruby M 295 Sally L 227
DWETTY, A S 193 Hannah 193
EARLY HISTORY, 1
EARLY, J 83
EASTERN TOWNSHIPS BANK, 355
EASTMAN, E 35 Joel 170 Lucretia 170 Mary 325 Polly 313 Rebecca 170 Ruth 170 Seaborn 170 Susan 170 Ulissa E 309
EATON, Eliza 206 Mary 196
EDMONDS, 33

EDSON, Sarah E 208
EDUCATION, 9
EDWARDS, Electa 288 Sarah 136
EGGLESTON, Melissa 339 Nelson 339
ELA, Alex L 172 Mary 172
ELDER, Family 229 230 Hugh 104 Nancy 200
ELKINS, Ralph 13 Salmon 13
ELLIOTT, Abigail 246 Cynthia 256 Hannah 241 Judith 305 Mary 280 Sally 305 Samuel 305
ELLIS, Adelia L 150
ELLSWORTH, Family 292 Gershom 282 Maria 282
ELLWORTH, Anson 256 Mary 256
ELY, Elisha C 172 John F 172 Lydia 172 Mary 172
EMBURY, Lucy 307 Peter 307 Sarah 278
EMERSON, 34 Arabell M 135 Arabella 170 Hiram W 135 Jane 309 Lydia 197 Mary 135 Reuben 197 Samuel E 170
EMERY, Cynthia 279 Family 284
EMORY, Fanny 275 John 275 Judith 260 Lydia 203 Nathan 256 S F 282 Sally 256 Sarah M 282
EPISCOPALIANS, 82
ERSKINE, Deborah 228 Harriet 183
ERWIN, Mary 275
EVANS, Abigail 142 Carrie B 137 D 137 Emma 316 John 91 Mary 259 292
EWENS, John 311 Mary 307 Sarah 312 Thomas 307 Zilphia 311
FACE OF COUNTRY, 24 48 52
FAIRBANKS, Joseph 84 Manasseh 203 Susan 203
FAIRCHILD, Electa 317
FAMILY RECORD, 348
FAREWELL, Adeline 340 Esther 271 Gladden 271 William 101
FARLEY, Amelia 195 Family 172 173 Malvina 160 Mark 195 Sarah 173
FARMER, Phebe 340
FARNHAM, A 140 Eunice 280 Laura 140 Mary 244

FARRINGTON, Sarah 253
FARWELL, Calista 141 Lemuel 141
FELCH, Adeline L 201
FELLOWS, Abigail 313
FELTON, W B 3
FENTON, Anna 330
FERGUSON, J F 97 James F 97 Thomas 3
FIELD, Family 169 342 Jona 342 Lucy M 127 M S 150 Margaret Innes 150 Susan 342
FISH, Eleanor 261 Elizabeth 328 Family 256 257 Joseph 68 75 328 Lemuel 68 284 Lemuel (Mrs) 68 Mary 284 Mr 69 Mrs 69 75 Sally 284 Samuel 70 73 Thankful 282
FISHER, Bradley 330 Emily 330 Susan 121
FISK, Almina 186 Rachel 279 Solomon 279
FITCH BAY, 38
FITCH, George 22 23 39
FITTS, Arba 119 Cynthia 119
FLANDERS, Benjamin 201 C 273 Christopher 99 Family 280 281 Henrietta 310 Lucina 117 Mary 201 248 Mary L 354 Miriam 197 226 P 247 Rhoda 201 Roxana 67 247 273 Sarah 311 Seth H 117 Susan 168 William 201
FLETCHER, Aris 325 Benjamin 281 Charles 308 Dorothy 241 Family 296 Fanny 337 J W 337 Joseph 261 289 290 Lydia 260 261 Polly 255 289 290 Rosina 308 Sally 289 Simeon 241
FLETHER, Caroline 281
FLINT, Lucy 165 288
FOGG, Charles 171 George W 20 Nancy 171
FOLSOM, Catherine 188 Hannah 180 Samuel 188
FOORD, Joseph 236
FORBES, Isabella 242
FORMAN, Alice J 287 DeWitt 287 Helen R 287 Robert 287
FORSYTH, Helen 295 J B 91

FOSS, Almira 201 Emily 239 Family 196 197 Hiram 204 Jonathan 36 Joseph 201 Lucina 204 Margaret 211 Mary 266 Melissa 279 Moses 279
FOSTER, Abner 335 Asa 257 Aurelia 142 Austin 35 Austin T 34 142 220 Betsey 257 Family 137 138 Harriet 335 John 84 331 Laura E 331 S 354 Sarah H 220 Stephen 34 108 356 359 William S 355
FOWLER, Elizabeth 199 Family 246 Mary 207 Nicholas 207
FOX, 45 Almira 119 Amos 321 Amos F 331 Amos K 57 297 Eunice 321 Family 175 176 329 Huldah 297 Lasura 176 M 182 Maria 174 187 Martha 176 Nancy 136 Ogden 174
FRANCE, King of 1
FRASER, Catherine 242 Family 242 243 James 242 Jane 215
FREE-WILL BAPTISTS, 98
FRENCH, 33 Catista 182 David 151 G 182 James 245 Ruth 151 Ruth F 151
FRIOLT, Abraham 3 Thomas 12
FRISBEE, Sabrina 204
FRISCHL, Elizabeth 219 Joseph 219
FROST, Mr 270 Nancy A 270 Semantha 243 W 243
FULLER, Clara 298 Dulcena 278 Mary 292 Miss 266 Mr 292 Sarah 323
FYLER, Sarah 205 Thomas 12
GAGE, Anna B 104 Denison Jr 104 Luthera 191 Phedora 225
GALE, Dorothy 202 George 202 Lucena 233
GALES, Ann 341 Thomas 341
GALT, A T 356 358
GAMMON, Joseph 305
GARDNER, Cephas 221 Charles 218 Louisa 218 Pamela 221
GARDYER, Andrew 199 Nancy 199
GARDYN, Marion 325
GARFIELD, T A 104
GARRETT, Richard 90

GARVIN, Anna 272 John 232 Sally 232
GATES, Family 149 Levi 315 Lydia 315 Martha 170 Miss 292
GAYLORD, 34 Asa 112
GEDDES, Catherine 243 Family 242
GEE, Abigail 42 Ruth 42 Wm 42
GEER, Abel C 267 Elijah 44 Elsie D 267 Family 193 Mary 235
GENDREAU, E P 103
GEORGE III, king of England 1
GEORGE, Judith 184
GEORGEVILLE, 45 High School 106
GERMAINE, E 103
GERRY, Clara 281
GIBB, David 95 104 Family 149 150 Harriet 148 Joseph 94 95 342 Joseph Jr 104 Margaret 342 Margaret I 169 Mr 96
GIBSON, Mary 187
GILBERT, F D 49 Family 290 Louisa 118 Lucretia 104 N P 104
GILES, H F 354 Sarah 104
GILL, Aaron 170 Persis 170
GILLESPIE, Lydia W 120 Robert 120
GILLIES, A 97 271 Lucy 271 Lucy M 106
GILMAN, 35 Abby 307 Betsey 246 Charlotte R 134 Cordelia B 125 Cynthia H 125 Family 219 220 Fanny 226 James K 125 John 14 224 Lydia 224 Lydia J 286 Mary Ann 227 Sally 218 240 Samuel 14 226
GILSON, Clara 337 Mary A 296 Rebecca 289
GLIDDEN, Asenath 183 Hannah 221 Maria 221 Mary 183 222 284 Mary E 160 Miranda 196 Noah 196 Philura 202 Priscilla 208 Ruth 177 Seraph 208 Temperance 269
GLINES, Family 245 James 43 Mary 118
GLOVER, Julia A 306 Lucretia 299 300 Sarah 297 Susan 298

GLOVER (continued) William 306
GODFREY, Corilla 277 Jonathan 307 Susanna 307
GOFF, Experience 297 Family 278
GOLDEN RULE LODGE, 108
GOLDSMITH, 61 Laura 322 Miranda 141 Thomas 141
GOODRICH, Harriet 148
GOODWIN, Eliza 317 Family 181 George L 129 Jacob 27 Julia Ann 129
GORDON, Eliza J 295 Family 207 Isaac 295 Jonathan 28 Roxana 254
GOSS, Mary 351 Mehitable 133 Philip 351
GOULD, Dr 152 Ebenezer 108 Ellen 288 Hannah 278 Harvey 288 Matilda 260
GRAHAM, J 90
GRANNIS, Elizabeth 147 Family 147 John 49 Margaret 289 William 49 Wm 104 147
GRANT, Isabella 244 James 244 Sally 167
GRAVEL, J 103
GRAYDON, Mary 127
GREEN, Anna 335 Columbus 101 Family 188 189 Harriet 271 James 3 97 105 Louisa 123 Louisa P 123 Mary P 123 Minerva 322 Oliver B 123 Olivia P 123 Rebecca 191 Sally 317
GREGG, Louisa 231
GRENFELL, J 355
GRIFFIN, Charles 325 Clarissa 325 Eliza 255 Moses 279 Olive 167 Sarah 279 Sylvanus 167
GRIFFIN'S CORNER, 39
GRISIM, Family 323
GRISIN, John 336 Sarah 336
GRISWOLD, J 96
GROVE, Martin 96
GROVES, Dorcas M 316 John 316
GUILBERT, see GILBERT
GUSTIN, 38 Abigail K 194 Abijah 42 Betsey 220 Clarinda 42 E B 112 113 254 Elisha 41-43 109 111 113 220 Esther 199 232

GUSTIN (continued)
  Family 224-226 Father 113
  John 40 42 101 219 John Jr 39
  42 43 227 John Sr 39 Josiah 39
  42 199 Lurany 42 226 Lydia 42
  219 Lyman 194 Mary 41 194
  254 Past Master 113 Phebe 42
  Polly 227 Ruth 220 Samuel 41
  42 Sebre 42
HACKETT, Mary 172
HADLOCK, 13 Hannah 281
HAGAR, J M 108 355
HAINES, Charles 193 Eliza 178
  Emily 193 Eunice 337 Ruth
  243 Sarah 180 Thomas 314
  Zilphia 314
HALE, Almira 243 Edward 6 352
  Susanna 274
HALL, Almira 322 Anna 270 Betsey 232 Calvin 182 Clarissa
  272 Elam 266 Elvira 340
  Family 150 Hannah 240 Jabez
  49 John 296 Levi 49 Lewis 340
  Lois 322 Lucinda 317 Lucy
  173 266 Luther 49 Lydia 280
  Martha W 167 Mehitable 172
  Missouri 182 Molly 282 Moses
  282 Polly 266 R N 359 R V 95
  Roxana 282 Ruth 296 Sarah 308
  Sylvia 184
HALLETT, Susan 118
HALLOWELL, J 198
HAM, Adella 339 Betsey 307
  Evelyn 298 Eveyn 339 Moses
  298 339 Sally 206
HAMILTON, Anne 218 Lucretia
  297
HAMMOND, Harvey 268 Miss 212
  Pluma 142 Sophronia 268
HAMMOX, Susan 335
HAND, Charles 13
HANEY, Eliza 187
HANSFORD, Allen W 204 Mr 107
  Rosamond 204 William 88 354
  Wm 108 354
HANSON, 56 Charity 323 Cynthia
  303 Elijah 331 Ephraim 226
  Family 315-317 Filey 188
  George C 321 Julia 321 Lewis
  303 323 Lewis F 307 Louisa
  290 Lydia 302 303 331 Micajah
  Jr 303 Minerva 307 Mr 290

HANSON (continued)
  Rosa 336 Semantha 226
HARDING, Emma J 293
HARDY, Molly 182
HARFORD, Abby 324 Amos 307
  Julia 307 Margaret 307 Sarah
  324
HARPER, Adelia 123 Annie 123
  Arthur P 123 Ernestine A 123
  Lewis 123 Louisa A 123 William L 123
HARRINGTON, Helen 337 Waterman 337
HARRIS, Emily 191 Jeremiah 191
HART, Lucy 271 Mr 257 Polly
  257
HARTWELL, 56 Family 174
HARVEY, Abigail 282 Burton 255
  Charlotte 296 Dorcas 180 Elder
  100 Erastus 100 Family 246
  256 Harriet 279 Helen 255
  Hiram 296 J F 157 Jane 167
  281 Judith 281 L P 296 Laura
  Ann 157 Lavinia 214 268 Lydia
  283 Mary 227 Mr 43 Nancy 296
  Robert 279 Sabrina 232 Samuel
  P 50 William 283
HASCALL, S B 85
HASELTINE, C S 110 Dean 205
  Family 295 296 H 49 Maria
  306 Miriam 190 Mr 326 Sally
  205 325 Sarah E 326 Stephen
  111 113 120 Theresa P 120
HASKELL, Carlos F 33 138 215
  Fanny 138 Freeman 33 34 138
  Louisa 138 Martha 138 Martha
  M 215 Miranda 198 Sylvanus C
  33
HATCH, Betsey 314 Charles 202
  Laura Ann 202 Lavinia 186
  Michael 314
HATHAWAY, Electa 206
HATLEY, 46 Families 247
HAVEN, J 141 Miranda 141
HAWES, Edward 260 Family 282
  Lucy 281 Lydia 283 Malinda
  260 Nathaniel 247 Sarah 284
  Sophronia 247
HAWKINS, Mary 259 Mary Jane
  176
HAY, James 95 243 Janet 243
HAYES, Anna 149 Henry 95 149

HAYES (continued)
Julia A 127 R 85
HAYWOOD, Martha E 204
HEALY, E A 354
HEARD, Chester 100
HEATH, 56 Abel 319 Abigail 180 Benj 285 Betsey 334 Betsey E 324 Clarissa 325 Daniel 98 313 Daniel G 187 David 21 Electa 185 Elvira 299 Emily 269 Family 184 311 312 Fanny 159 Hannah 285 Jemima 313 Jesse 299 Jesse W 324 John 12 314 Lucy 307 Margaret 314 Mary 307 Mary J 338 Moses 159 Orpha 333 Persis 320 Reuben 338 Ruth 315 319 Zeruiah 187
HEMMINWAY, Emmons 191 Susan 191
HENDERSON, Eleanora 241 Martha 221
HENRY, Jane 285 John 334 Joseph 285 Laura 302 334 Narcissa 285 Roslin A 178 Sarah 178 William 285
HENSLEY, Hannah 284 James 284
HERBERT, Mary A 131 S M 131
HERRICK, Hortensia 118 Isaac 118
HERRIMAN, Caroline 182
HERRON, Mary A 304
HETHERINGTON, John P 90
HIBBARD, 96 Albert 166 Augustine 28 Elder 97 Family 120 121 Pantha L 166 Phebe 197 Pliny V 92
HICK, John 85 93 94 Mr 86 91
HILDRETH, David 168 Martha 168
HILL, Abigail M 309 Archelaus 169 David 210 Family 236 306 307 Harriet 198 Levi 312 313 Lucia 169 Minerva 316 Patience 323 Polly 312 Rufus 309 Sally 297 Samuel 297 Sarah 143 313 Sophronia 210
HILLS, Amelia 104
HINMAN, Aaron 215 Benj 217 Catherine 215 Isaac 307 Lydia 307 Martha 307 Mary 217 Mr 32 65 66 Tim 26 33 108 215

HITCHCOCK, Bemond 279 Cordelia 250 Edward 255 Eliza A 258 Ephraim 74 75 Family 257 258 Grace 74 261 Lois 248 258 Mehitable 255 Mrs 75 76 Paul 74-76 Prussia 76 Rebecca 279
HOBART, James 92
HODGDEN, Amanda 157 E 157
HOEG, Nancy 326
HOGG, Polly 267
HOIT, Family 177
HOITT, Israel 210
HOLLISTER, 56 Asa 15 Family 321 322 Jerusha A 188 Mr 188 Prudence 321
HOLMES, 33 A L 104 354 A Lee 354 355 Daniel 156 Denison 157 Family 146 155 George R 35 Gertrude J 104 H D 355 Jeremiah 156 Julia G 166 Lucretia 243 Malinda 156 Mary 156 207 Sally 207 Sarah 307 Sarah W 157 W H 34 Wm H 166
HOLT, Moses 3
HOLTON, J H 35
HOOKER, Deacon 94 L 92 Leroy 108 355 Levi 92 144 Levi (Mrs) 92
HOOVER, 38
HOPKINS, Flavilla 211 Harriet 195 Mehitable 136
HOPPING, Ephraim 221
HORN, Family 307 308 Huldah 324 Jeremiah 324 Lavinia 318 Lydia 307
HORNBY, Amy M 291
HORTON, J 128 Mary 128
HOSKINS, Deborah 165
HOSMER, Louisa 351 Zelotes 351
HOUGHTON, Amarilla 205 David 210 Lasura 210 Mr 205 Roxelana 211
HOUSE, 81 A H 96 Alvin 233 Amelia 142 Family 212-214 Francis 219 George 157 Grace 165 Harry 218 John L 36 222 Lucinda 219 Lucy 157 Mary Ann 222 Pamela 218 Sally 233
HOVEY, Alonzo 280 Amanda 280 Capt 69 77 Caroline 254 261 Charles 284 Chester 66 248

HOVEY (continued)
 254 265 Clarissa 265 Ebenezer
 2 12 52 66 67 Ebenezer Jr 268
 Family 246 247 Horace 280
 Horace M 113 Judith 284 Laura
 275 Lois 258 Malinda 259 260
 Mary 196 248 280 Mr 68 Olive
 265 Piercy 255 Polly 268 275
 Roxana 273 Sophronia 282
 Wright 258
HOWARD, Grace 42 Lydia E 313
 Mary 318 R H 104
HOWE, Caleb 59 Clarissa 265 Eli
 175 Family 321 Hannah 323
 Harriet 317 Hiram 317 James
 265 Jonas 322 Mr 60 Mrs 59
 Nancy 325 Polly 175 Prudence
 322 Sarah 323 Squire 59 60
 Wm 110
HOWLET, Caroline 201 John 201
HOYT, Family 275-277 Lorina
 278 Lucy 263 Mary Ann 279
 Nancy 277 Nason 263 Polly
 263 Sally 279 Samuel 62 105
 263 Samuel Sr 62 Sarah 165
HUBBARD, A O 95 Almira 104 B
 F 104 Catherine 92 284 Elmira
 N 158 Family 126-128 Henry
 11 104 106 J H 285 J M 23 169
 Lucy Maria 169 Mary G 190 Mr
 360 Naomi C 106 Phineas 27
 28 95 109 Phineas Jr 95
 Samuel 284 Sarah Ann 285
HUBBELL, Eliza 170 Mary 170
HUCKINS, Emily 226 John 226
HULL, Ann E 149 Lockhart K 149
HUME, William 90
HUMPHREY, Amanda F 325 Armadilla 301 Armandilla 298
 Charles W 337 Chloe 324
 Family 331-333 John 325
 Lucina 321 Lydia 315 Margaret
 305 Mary 337 S B 55 Sally 337
 Sophronia P 326 Sylvender B
 326 W 337
HUNGERFORD, Sophronia 165
HUNT, Almira 192 Hannah 245
 Judith 208 Mary 228 Mary Ann
 210 Mehitable 222 Orrin 222
 Ruth 218 Zebulon 245
HUNTER, Jane 128 W H 31 W S
 128

HUNTING, Henry 251 Louisa J
 251
HUNTINGDON, Almira 250
 Clarissa 255 Family 247 248
 Mary 247 Mr 255 Polly 249
 Seth 247 Susan 297
HUNTINGTON, J 101
HUNTOON, Fanny 335 Mary 302
HURD, Catherine 127 Elvira 306
 Luke 127 Persis S 127 Sally
 219 Samuel A 127
HUSE, Anna 200 Franklin 200
HUTCHINS, Betsey 255
HUTCHINSON, Richard 171
 Valeria 171
HYATT, Lucinda 167
HYNDMAN, Lucia S 287 T H M
 287
IDE, Alice 306 George G 104 Israel 97 John 96
IMPEY, Julia E 329 Stephen 329
IN MEMORIAM, 351
INCORPORATION, 1855 30
INDIAN, Captain Jo 20
INGALLS, E S 91 Edmund S 87
 Horace S 236 Mary Ann 210
 Sarah A 236
INNES, Margaret 342
IRVINE, George 352
ISRAEL, Sarah J 191
IVES, Betsey 237 Celina 289
 Clarissa 270 Family 271 272
 Frances M 104 H 344 Harriet
 104 Isaac 204 Jerusha 237 Joel
 67 Joel H 110 John 254 Joseph
 67 Julius 231 Laura 231 Lora
 254 Mary 237 Salina 204 Sarah
 A 293 William 106
JACKSON, Almira 292 Caroline
 250 Christopher 83 84 Rev Mr
 82 Sarah A 290
JACOBS, Daniel P 104
JAMES, George 35 John Angell 77
JAMES I, king of England 215
JAMESON, Delilah 274 Mr 274
JAMISON, John A 104
JENKERSON, Maria 134
JENKINS, Lydia 214 Maria E 341
 Thomas 214 Thomas P 205
 Violetta 332
JENKS, Family 327 N 55 105
JENNE, Elisha 264 Matilda 264

JEWETT, 45 96 Cynthia 193
  David 44 97 265 Laura 265
JOHNSON, A B 62 105 275 A C
  104 Abigail 116 Arthur 275
  Betsey A 195 Edward 104
  Eliza 282 288 Esther 257
  Family 273-275 Hale 255 Hannah 283 John 11 90 Jonathan Jr
  62 63 Joseph 195 Laura 247
  Laura J 296 M W 185 Maria
  255 Mary W 185 Matilda 275
  Moses M 89 Polly 275
  Rebecca 287 288 Sarah A 275
  Schuyler 116 Thomas 83 Z 247
JONDRO, 34
JONES, 35 45 Bradley 261 Esther
  296 Family 287 338 Fanny 337
  Ira 175 John 49 Mary 184
  Matilda 175 Sarah 278 Sarah W
  201 Viola 261 William 201 Z
  P 260 Zilphia P 261
JUDD, 33 35 Elvira 289 Family
  138 258 259 Francis 55 82 332
JUDKINS, Sophia 204
KANE, Emma 318
KATHAN, C H 34 Clarissa W 116
  Fanny 138 Lovinus 49 116
KEELER, Lewis 307
KEENAN, Abigail 216
KELLOGG, Elizabeth 338
KELLUM, Amanda 210
KELLY, Hannah 174 Lydia 170
KELSEY, Judith 210 Robert 210
KENASTON, Charlotte 251 Nathan
  336 Roxana 239
KENDALL, Emily 151 Family
  235 S S 106 151
KENDRICK, A W 140 150 Anne
  178 Eliza 178 Ellen 140 Laura
  150
KENNEDY, Betsey 272 G A 272 G
  W 49
KENNISON, John C 209 Praxo 209
KENT, Emily 210 Huldah 282
  Jonas 210 Martha A 284
  Rachel 280
KENUSTON, Miss 227
KERR, James C 272 Marion 272
KEYES, Emma Frances 130
  Henry 128 130 358 359 Sarah P
  128

KEZAR, Amanda 267 Amos 296
  Betsey 254 Betsy 78 Chancey
  260 Clarissa 248 Elena 275
  Emily 283 296 Family 255 256
  Jesse 248 Joseph 296 Lydia
  260 261 Maria 292 Maria L 275
  Mehitable 258 Piercy 247
  Polly 296 Roxana 260 Ruth 247
  248 Samuel 261 Sherburn 267
  Simon 12 64 247 254 Simon Jr
  78
KILBON, Charles 3
KILBORN, 89 Adeline 322 Alex
  12 Alexander 14 33 119 144
  Benjamin 12 C 220 C A 14
  Capt 12 13 15 16 341 Charles
  12 28 32 81 108 221 Col 33
  David 90 Deborah 319
  Ebenezer 3rd 322 Eliza 322
  Eunice 175 Family 153-155
  320 321 Huldah 319 Joseph 22
  23 Josiah 319 Lucius 322
  Matilda 220 221 Polly 268
  Thankful H 119
KIMBALL, A 120 Achsah 247 Alzada 272 Amelia B 120 Asa
  137 Maria 137 Miss 292 T 344
KIMPTON, Alpheus 231 269
  Elisabeth 246 Esther 225 John
  246 Louisa 231 Lucretia 269
  Richard 269 Sophronia 269
KING, 56 Howard 166 Lydia 166
  191 Miss 210
KING'S CORNER, 56
KINGSBURY, Mary 218
KINNEY, George 308 Loella 308
  Mary 319 Persis 308 Rufus 319
KINSLEY, Elsie L 166 Hiram 166
KINSMAN, Elizabeth 205
KINSTON, Elizabeth 266 Martha
  277
KITTREDGE, Persis 214
KNAGG, Richard 82
KNAPP, Mary 313 Thomas 313
KNEELAND, Dulcina 236
KNIGHT, 50 A 30 31 358 Albert 6
  136 356 358 359 Benjamin F
  220 C S 210 C S (Mrs) 167
  Charles 319 Charlotte Ruth 220
  Clementine 319 Emily 142
  Family 132-134 Hannah 293

KNIGHT (continued)
  Julia Ann 136 Lelia O 337
  Sally 210
KNOWLAN, James 85 86
KNOWLTON, Harriet 168 Laura
  279 Newton 279 Sarah 314
LABAREE, Hannah 121
LACY, Joanna 230
LADD, 45 Betsey 191 Dudley 331
  Ellen 183 Family 176 Judith
  165 Loren G 298 Martha 172
  175 Nancy 331 Samuel G 175
  William C 191
LAFRANCE, P 102
LAKE SHORE SETTLEMENT, 44
LAKES, 19 46
LAMB, Deborah 297 Harriet 340
  John 297 Levi 340 Patience
  310 Sarah 297
LAMBKIN, Martha A 221
LAMBLY, Osborne M 89
LANE, Mary Ann 333 Miss 334
LANEY, Lillette 199 Rosina 200
LANGDON, J 34 104 137
LANGMADE, Bela 196 Family
  178 Martha J 185 Thomas 185
LANGMAID, John 37
LANGWORTHY, J 12
LANPHIER, Rufus 41 Wm 39
LANPHIRE, Family 228 Malinda
  228 Matilda 196 William 228
  Wm 228
LANTON, H 90 Henry 87
LARABEE, Melinda 151
LAROQUE, Jas 103
LATHAM, George 204 Sabrina 204
LATHROP, Dr 93
LAWRENCE, Amos 255 Clarissa
  Goss 351 E 107 Hubbard 351
  John 351 Louisa 351 Mary 123
  351 Nancy Temple 351
  Praxana 255
LAWTON, Charles 272 Emily P
  272
LEAVITT, Anna 284 Celina 256
  Hannah 256 Jemima 240 John
  284 Lucy 284 Lydia 284 327
  Rossila 273 Sally 280
LEBARON, 50 Benjamin 248 Betsey 97 252 E H 66 195 356 358
  Ellen 261 Elmira 248 Emeline
  182 Eveline 296 Family 248-

LEBARON (continued)
  252 Fedora 293 James 261
  Japheth 49 97 Maria 195 Rhoda
  249
LEE, 38 Achsah 118 Alonzo 208
  Asenath 202 Azubah 123 159
  Bethiah 337 Betsey 239 292
  Daniel 32 160 Deborah 160
  Dorothy A 239 Ede 212 Ede
  2nd 168 Elias 109 165 Elias Jr
  202 Elmina 197 Elmira 142
  Elvira 182 Erastus 32 343
  Family 155-159 Henry 142 214
  J P 104 Jane 203 Jason 104
  Jedediah 32 33 124 167 168
  John P 104 Jonathan 160 165
  Lucy 124 214 Luvia 202
  Malinda 155 Mary 159 160 165
  167 192 212 Molly 308 Orpha
  168 Rhoda 165 Rhoda M 117
  Sarah 146 293 Susan 122 W H
  108 William H 104 Wm H 355
LEET, Sarah J 258
LELAND, Luther 92 Mr 93
LESTER, Robert 3
LEVERETT, Sarah M 104
LEWIS, Anna 318 Annis 330 Jane
  194 Martha 134 Ruth 329
LIBBEE, Abraham 37 David 35
  Ellen 183 Emerson 277 Family
  167 177 178 Isaac 210
  Mehitable 277 Pearson 185
  Sally 210
LIBBEY, 45
LIBBY, Almira 203 Andrew 203
  Moses 203 Nancy 203
LILLY, Fanny 240 Hiram 240
  Rhoda A 235
LIMOGES, A D 103 Mr 102
LINCOLN, Family 176
LINDSEY, Andrew 279 Clarissa
  231 Heman 229 231 Jane 279
  Nancy 229
LITCH, Josiah 101
LITTLE, Alice 259 Ann 330 Bond
  254 Charlotte 282 Eliza Jane
  210 Elizabeth 136 Family
  252-254 Hannah 260 Joshua
  210 Lucinda 255 Ludo M 287
  Maria 272 280 Marietta 287
  288 Mary 329 Mary E 287 Ruth
  287 Sally 336 Sarah 254

LITTLE (continued)
Taylor 78 99 336 William 255
LOCKE, 56 98 Abigail 326 Betsey 314 Caroline 292 Chloe 318 Emeline 234 Family 179 312 313 James 37 Levi 12 Louisa 315 Maria 182 Peter 292 Polly 307 Sarah 300
LOCKWOOD, Mary E 178
LOGAN, William 8
LOOKE, James M 185
LOOMIS, Juliette A 104
LORD, Family 279 280 Jeremiah 44 45 80 84 Lois 84 Nancy 84 Priscilla 309 Rebecca 257 Stephen 21
LORIMER, Betsey 191 Family 243 Isabella 339 J 97 James B 244 Mary Jane 341 Mary P 244 Sarah 339 William 339
LOTHRIDGE, Elizabeth 169
LOVEJOY, Family 283 Jeremiah 69 Mary 282
LOVELACE, Hannah 134 James 134
LOVELAND, Quimby 214 Roana 214
LOVELL, Annis 270 Artemisia 270 Henry 270 John 270 Mary 315 Olive 270 Walter 270 Wm 315
LOWELL, Abigail 118 Dorcas 255 Luther 118 Mary 280 Rebecca 279
LUCAS, Margaret 320
LUCKEY, Samuel 85
LUDDEN, Daniel 92 Hannah 92
LUMSDEN, Magdalen 241
LUNT, Johnson 189 Sarah 189
LYFORD, Asenath 167 Family 182 183 Nancy 185 Nathaniel 201 Susan 201
LYMAN, Achsah 302 Dan 283 Hannah 283 308
M V RAILWAY, 356
MACDONALD, Alexander 95 Mr 96
MACK, Abigail 42 Abijah 39 40 43 220 Asa 41 D W 223 356 Daniel W 220 Delphine 224 Dorothy 202 Ebenezer 42 Elizabeth 42 223 Ethelinda 224

MACK (continued)
F 113 Family 226 227 Fanny 220 Franklin 41 110 111 225 Grace 42 John 42 Judith 166 Lurany 42 221 Lydia 42 231 Mary 42 Mary Ann 220 Nancy 228 Polly 225 228 232 Ruth 42 Sebre 110 228 Silas 41 42 224 Silas W 202 W B 166 Willard 43 William 42 43 Wm P 224 Zophar 42
MACPHERSON, James 108
MAGOG, Academy 105 Families 261
MAGOON, Betsey B 227 Calvin 280 Caroline 232 Elsie 268 Ezra 227 Family 240 241 Guilford 268 Jonathan 219 Lois 222 Martha J 223 Morrill 222 Sally 219 Sarah 223 224 Sophronia 268 Stewart 232 Sylvia 280
MAILS AND ROUTES, 16
MAJOR, Elizabeth 341
MANSERGH, Britania 269 George 269
MANSEUR, Daniel 207 Hannah 207 Huldah 208 John 208
MANSFIELD, Lydia 266 Miss 266
MANSUR, Betsey 202 226 Daniel 123 Family 171 John 55 Lois 123
MARLOW SETTLEMENT, 39
MARSH, Amasa 253 Dolly 340 Elder 97 Elmeda 206 Huldah 307 Jane A 286 Lucia 324 Lucius 286 Mary 259 Polly 252 259 Rosanna 138 Sarah 253 Thomas 324
MARSHALL, 34 Amy 315 Henry 133 Julia M 133 Julia Rose 133
MARSTON, Betsey 174 Marilla 287 Mr 174
MARTIN, Allen 206 Betsey 200 325 Comfort 268 Daniel 73 Electa 325 Family 143 144 204 205 338 339 H J 112 113 Hannah 206 Isabella 243 J W 12 14 James 199 L 243 Leonard 59 Lt 15 Lyman 243 Michael 325 Olive 200 Ruth 200 Sarah 137 222 243

MASON, ELeanor 176
MASONIC HALL BUILT 1860, 113
MASSAWIPPI OR W HATLEY, 49
MASSEY, Mehitable 168 177
MASTEE, J B 236
MASTEN, Asa 227 Charlotte 227
MATHER, Julia A 104
MATHEWS, Amanda 340 Horace 340
MATTISON, Levi 33
MAXDEL, Sarah 203
MAXFIELD, Caroline 210 Truman 210
MAY, Clarissa 121 Electa 206 Family 205 206 301 Maria 336 Mary 299 Philinda 335 Ruby 299 Willard 299
MCADAM, Mary 134 Michael 134
MCAULEY, M 102
MCCAFFEE, Mary 168 William 168
MCCAW, Betsey 134 Emily 133 Family 142 Hugh H 134 James 133 173 Jane 173 Sarah 173
MCCLARY, Family 142 143 179 180
MCCLEARY, Wm 37
MCCLURE, Margaret 188
MCCONNEL, John 6
MCCONNELL, Eliza 205 Family 272 273 John 64 Julia A 258 Roxana 247 T 247 Thomas Jr 49 64
MCCOY, Betsey 341 E P 341 Family 288 John 305 Lucretia 305 Sarah 293
MCCURDY, Catherine 182
MCDONALD, M 90 91 Malcolm 87 88
MCDUFF, James 174 Mary 174
MCDUFFEE, Elsie 134 Family 320 Julia A 133 Louisa 319 320 Mary 302 Moses 302 Nancy 319 Ruth 230
MCELROY, Agnes 142
MCEWEN, Alex 44
MCGAFFEE, Alvin 185 Florinda 197 John 160 Laura Ann 160 Mary A 185

MCGAFFEY, Family 342 Henry 169 Susan M 169
MCGIVERN, Bernard 278
MCGOOKIN, 56
MCHORN, Dorothy 314
MCINTYRE, John 200 Mary 200
MCKAY, Jane T 139
MCKEECH, Betsey 175 Euphrata 326 Lovell 15 175 Mary L 311 Matilda 298
MCLAREN, John 108 John J 355
MCLEAN, Ann 247 248
MCMACHIN, Margaret 314 William 314
MCMILLAN, Elizabeth 284
MCNICOL, Adelia 141 J 141
MCPHERSON, Alex 44
MEADER, Patience 306
MEARS, Emeline D 206 H 12 Mary B 134
MEIGS, Elizabeth C T 147 Family 146 147 John 108 147 355
MERRILL, 44 Betsey 199 200 Charles 57 Collins 199 David H 200 Family 193 194 Harriett 305 James 79 John 206 Jonathan Jr 198 Lillecta 200 Lucinda 198 Mary F 278 Nancy 223 Sarah 288 Sibyl 318 Thankful 206
MERRIMAN, Amasa 97 Amasa T 237 Charles 104 Clarissa 237 Family 269 270 Harvey 204 L P 106 Lorany 336 Mary L 303 Rozana 204
MERRY, Betsey 262 Daniel 276 Family 263 264 267 361 Florence L 275 John S 275 Julia A 292 Lucy 276 Olive 275 Polly 276 Ralph 50 105 265 Sally S 278 Susan 265
METHODISTS, 84
MIDDLEMAS, Eunice A 121 Mary 121 Peter 121
MILES, Mary A 314
MILITARY SERVICE, 11
MILLER, 43 Caroline 240 Daniel 41 Elijah 40 Elisha 39 41 213 Esther 225 Family 231-233 Ira 41 Mary 240 Phebe 42 Polly M

MILLER (continued)
227 Rufus 227 Sally 213 Willard 225 William 99 101
MILLIER, H 102
MILLIGAN, Almira 235
MILLS, Abigail 297 Anna 79 Dorcas 316 Mary Ann 129 W 129
MILNES, Robert Shore 3 4 37 38
MINER, Martha 167 Sarah 167
MIRICK, Martha 181
MITCHELL, 96 Almira 146 Dolphin 116 146 E 98 Margaret 268 Sarah 116 146 Sarah C 183 Sophia 268
MIX, Laura 226 Louisa 205 Samuel 226
MOE, Betsey 246 David 246 Lucy 246 Sewell 246
MOIR, Family 219 John 95 Olive J 228 William J 228 see also MOORE
MOLSON, Alexander 44
MONDOR, L Z 102 Z 103
MONRO, C 243 Family 244 John 106 Mary C 243
MONTAGUE, Mary 122 Moses 92 122 156 Susan 92 122 156
MOONEY, Joseph 202 Lydia H 268 Mary 202 Nancy 270
MOOR, Hannah 189 Hiram 189 see also MOORE
MOORE, A H 106 264 Agnes 117 Asenath 265 Betsey 285 Eliza 232 Ephraim 70 Family 291 292 Julia A 264 Louisa 166 Mary 168 181 232 235 Sarah A 196
MORDEN, Mark 310 Mary 310
MORE, see MOORE
MORELL, Adeline 250
MOREY, Benjamin 200 Betsey 223 Damaris 223 Emeline 200 Mary 253
MORGAN, Maria 222 Roxanna 323
MORKILL, Luvin 293 R D 293
MOROUGH, Robert 3
MORRILL, A W 35 Abigail 185 Abigail C 198 Almira 169 Archibald 156 Artemisia 235 Asenath 165 Azubah 156 B T 173 Benjamin B 126 Charles 34 Charlotte 142 D (Mrs) 156

MORRILL (continued)
David 157 David R 174 Deborah 157 Eugene 126 Evelina 170 Family 159-165 Fanny 184 Harriet 188 Harriet P 126 Henry 222 Jennie E 126 Jeremiah 156 233 Jerusha 197 Jonathan 28 Judith 156 Louisa 233 Lucinda 178 Malona 168 Malvina P 173 Maria 197 Mary 156 Nancy 222 Nathan 178 Ozro 34 35 142 356 Paul 184 Peletiah 235 Polly 184 Rhoda 156 Sarah J 174 Zelinda 184
MORRIS, Robert 112
MORRISON, C H 102 Jane 325 Mary 243
MORSE, Clarissa G 227 Emeline 133 Jesse 227 Leonard 276 Lizzie 256 Mary A 276 Sally 277
MOSELY, Ann 325 Cyrus 325 Miss 325
MOSES, Electa 278 James 37
MOSHER, 56 Betsey 186 312 Corner 55 Daniel 314 Elsie C 326 Family 314 Jemima 314 John 310 312 John M 186 Lois 297 Louisa 186 Margaret 311 Submit 310
MOULTON, Abial 98-100 182 Abigail 189 Albanus K 98 Avery 98 99 Betsey 285 David W 285 Family 165-167 Fanny 182 Grace 212 Harris 202 Hoel 282 James 282 L M 337 Lois 176 Louisa 187 291 Lydia 160 282 Lydia M 117 Mary 156 157 Naomi 168 Orrin N 183 Salome 204 Sarah 202 212 Sophronia 181 T P 100 291 Tabitha 282 Thomas P 98 100 William 98 212
MULLIN, Celia M 253 Michael 253
MUSTARD, Jennet 244
NASH, Catherine 126 Clarissa 92 121 Harriet 126 Martha 118 Oliver 109 121 Pamela 175
NASON, Hannah 171
NEAL, Morris 284 Sally 284
NELSON, Belinda 277 Isabel 189

NELSON (continued)
    Judith 253 Lorena 263 Manly 277 Marcia 265 Sibyl 121
NEW BOSTON, 56
NEWCOMB, Luther 108 Martin 215
NEWELL, S 327
NEWSPAPERS, 17
NEWTON, Anne 214 C 150 E D 105 Laura 150
NEWVILLE, 45
NICHOLLS, Willard 200
NICKLE, Col 15 Robert 14
NICOL, Sophia 219
NILES, Polly 192
NORCROSS, Harriet 197
NORRIS, 45 Dudley 201 Hannah 213 Mary 201 S 85
NORTH HATLEY & MAGOG, 50
NORTHCOPS, Mary 230
NORTON, 55 56 Betsey 327 Family 333-335 Helen 253 Issachar Jr 327 Jerusha 168 Matilda 315 Mr 44 Orissa 341 Porter 168 Rachel A 140
NOTES IN BRIEF, 351
NOTT, Amos 270 Sally 270
NOURSE, Polly 223
NOYCE, Abigail 291
NOYES, Adam 92 Family 137
NUTTER, Joel 172 Lodema 172
NYE, Almira 169 Solomon 169
O'CONNOR, Harriet 293 Marcella 106
O'DOMINIQUE, L N 102
O'DONNELL, J J J 102
OAKES, Phoebe 104
OGDEN, Isaac 3
OLIVER, Arvilla 275 E H 276 Edward 197 Electa 276 Esther 262 Family 266 267 George 247 275 Hester M 247 Lucy Ann 191 Mary 197 233 Polly 267 Sarah Ann 270 Susan 267 William 267 Wm 270
OLMSTEAD, Susan 331
ONTHANK, Lucretta 174 William 174
ORDWAY, Eliza 254
ORROCK, J M 274 John M 102 Josephine 274
OSAN, Mary Ann 226

OSBURN, Jane 324
OSGOOD, Betsey A 236 Family 293 J B 236 Jemima 195 Josiah 257 Mary Ann 257 Thaddeus 92 93 Thomas 181 Zelinda 293
OVITT, A W 35
PACKARD, 38 Anna 233 Chester B 233 Emeline 244 Family 234 235 Hollis 233 John 204 Laura W 191 Mary 233 238 Mary F 244 Matilda E 311 Mercy 266 Polly L 204 Richard 84 181 Richard C 311 Richards 97 Sally 84 T A 84
PAGE, A 304 Christopher 100 Lucinda 298 Phila 298 Samuel 298
PAINE, Lorana 333 Mary B 318 Phoebe 321 Rufus H 318
PALMER, Harriet 148 William B 148
PARADIS, Elizabeth 256 Family 328 Ruth 260 328 Thomas 260 328
PARKER, 55 59 96 A J 94 Adaline L 292 Alice A 339 Alpheus 306 Alvin 97 Asahel 292 Family 292 304-306 Fanny 224 Frederick 339 Harvey 331 Isaac 104 James 92 Joshua 297 Judith 297 Levi 295 Lucretia 288 Margaret 331 Sarah 295 Susan 306 W R 88
PARKHURST, Amy 323 Elias 325 Martha 172 Polly 325
PARKS, Harriet 118 Hiram 118 Lydia 118 Richard 100
PARMELEE, R 147 Sarah 147 Wm G 355
PARNELL, John 282 Polly 282
PARSONS, 45 Israel 128 169 Mary Jane 104 Nancy 128 Robert C 113 Ruth 169
PARTRIDGE, Amelia 252 Levi 252
PATCH, Lucy 272
PATRICK, Irene 193
PATTEE, Caroline 336
PATTERSON, Daniel 175 Jane 175
PATTON, A F B 131 Family 120

PATTON (continued)
Jane 131
PAUL, Erastus 180 Family 167 168 James 32 156 Lucius 172 Lydia L 172 Mary 156 Nancy A 180
PEAKE, Edwin 89
PEARCE, see PIERCE
PEARSOL, Adelia 221
PEARSON, Abigail 177
PEASE, Hannah 257
PEASLEE, Annis 223 259 Aurelia 240 Electa A 158 Family 208 209 Hiram 158 Huldah 171 James 110 James C 45 110 259 Nancy 119 Nason 240 Patience 307 Philip 307 Silas 44
PECK, Ebenezer 6 Mr 139
PEEBLE, Lizzie 191
PELL, J E 119 Laura 119
PELTIER, O 102
PENNOYER, Emeline 248 Henry 248 Jesse 52 77
PENWELL, Clara 330
PERCIVAL, Charles L 256 Emily 256 Family 283
PERKINS, Abbey 327 Albert C 281 Family 293 294 Hannah 218 295 Harriet 281 Henry B 218 John 296 Lent H 234 Maria 296 Sabrina C 186 Sally 234
PERRY, Emily 185 Family 193 Joshua 266 Marion 266 Mary 156 Sarah 121 267 William 185
PETTES, Abigail 146
PEVEY, Leonard 315 Sarah 315
PHELON, John 200
PHELPS, A E 149 Esther B 194 Heman 194 Mary A 117
PHILIPS, Elizabeth 290 S G 89 91
PHIPPS, Hollis 210 Martha 210
PICTE, M 102
PIERCE, Carlos 20 31 33 104 106 356 358 Caroline 293 Charles 34 Charles W 108 355 Family 128-131 H A 35 Henry F 126 Henry G 126 John N 326 Mary 326 Mary C 126 Nancy A 126 Olive 205 Rose Mary 126 T 35 Thomas 205 Wilder 28 104 110 132 Zilphia 314

PIGEON, M 102
PINKHAM, A 344 Betsey 209 Dorothy 325 Family 212 Joseph 165 Loella 157 Mary 156 158 Mary M 228 S S 228 Samuel 206 Sarah 165 205 Theodosia 206
PINNEY, Susan 317
PIPER, Betsey P 339 George 339 Nancy 298 301
PITMAN, Ann M 156 Anna M 158 159
PLUMLEY, Alden 273 Appleton 50 76 257 Family 258 Julia A 273 Lois 257
PLUMMER, Eunice 326 Samuel 326
POLLARD, Margaret 305
POMROY, Adeline 134 Aliva 207 B 107 108 156 355 Benj 355 359 Benjamin 343 356 358 360 Cordelia 125 Family 122-125 343 George 104 Hazen 27 118 171 Lois 171 Lucy 156 Mary 122 351 Mary Lee 343 Mr 32 Quartus 95 207 S J 328 Samuel 28 31 Selah 27 31 94 95 109 125 351 Wright 134
POND, Arvilla 157 Clarissa 169 Henry 157
POOL, Betsey 156 204 Eleanor 272 Family 292 293 Henry 272 J L 49 Ozro 250 Rufus 288 Sarah 156 192 288 Sarah M 272 Susanna 205 Theodore C 156
POPE, Amanda 189 Clarissa 207 Marshall 168 Mr 86 91 Philura 168 Richard 85 94
PORTER, 33 Abigail 334 Betsey 334 Cynthia 193 Family 218 James 214 Mr 193 Pamelia 214
POTTER, A B 271 Jerusha 271
POULIN, F X 103
POWELL, 96
PRATT, Freda 340 Nancy 308 Orrin 308
PRENTISS, Charles 104
PRESCOTT, Priscilla 166
PRESSEY, Sarah 183
PRICE, Mary 150
PRINCE, Albert 4

PROCTOR, Lydia 166 Mr 274 Sarah 274
PROUTY, Betsey 249 Elizabeth B 175
PUNSHON, W M 31 William Morley 108
PUTNAM, Olive 200
PUTNEY, Charlotte 253 Family 281 282 Henry 253 Sarah 284
PYER, Maria 317
QUIMBY, Coffin 14 Coffin M 160 Family 168 Henrietta 304 John M 166 Julia M 188 Malona 160 Nancy 188 Naomi 166 Orpha 157 Truman A 188
RAINE, John 86 90
RAMSAY, Anna 279
RAMSDELL, Amasa 268 Harriet 268
RANDALL, Esther 278 John 278 Martha 265 Samuel 265 Sarah 268
RANKIN, Andrew 94 James 46
RAWSON, Wellington 191
RAY, Stilman 35
RAYMOND, Emmons 358 359
REA, Ellen 243
REBELLION 1837-38, 12
REDFIELD, Harriet 147 Helen W 147 I F 132 Mary W 132 P 235 Sarah Abigail 235 Sidney P 147 T P 104 Timothy P 147
REDWAY, Dorothea 212 Ruth 294
REED, Eliza 253 John 34 Laura 137 Prussia 76 Sally 198 Samuel 34 73 76 111 Stephen 34 112 198 Thomas 253
REEVE, Sarah 263 Solomon 263
REID, Rev Mr 82
RELIGIOUS DENOMINATIONS, 81
REMICH, Betsey 328 Cassius 324 Edward 328 Family 267 268 Hannah 199 Mr 199 Polly 266 Ruthanna 324 Wealthy 207
REMICK, Amanda 255 Daniel 154 Elsie B 193 Mary 154 Page 55
RENAL, Mehitable 315
REXFORD, A 196 Abraham 247 Aluvia 278 Asenath 292 Betsey 234 Chester 292 Clarissa 247 Family 264-266 Isaac 67

REXFORD (continued) Joanna 190 Laura 198 Levi 278 Lucinda 262 Lucretia 271 Lucy 188 275 Lyman 275 Mercy 234 Olive 247 Rectina 262 Rice Jr 262 Roxana 196 Russell 247 Samuel 190 Susan 264 Whiting 234
REYNOLDS, Harriet 235
RHODES, Caroline 287 Miss 263
RICE, Catherine 264 S D 108 355
RICHARDSON, Betsey 192 C 184 C A 31 Family 139 Jonathan 222 Mary 222 Sylvia 211
RICHELIEU COUNTY, 2
RICKARD, 38 Family 191
RIDDELL, Sarah 319
RIDER, Betsey A 158 Carlos 197 Dorothy O 158 E B 113 Eizabeth 279 Emily 197 Ezra B 158 Family 239 G A 158
RIPLEY, Harriet E 228 Richard F 228
RIVERS, 23
RIX, Adeline 332 Eveline 165 Family 170 Hale 165 John 168 315 Martha 168 315 Mary 168 Mary A 208
ROBERTS, Family 174 John 203 Sally 203 Sarah 160
ROBERTSON, Andrew 104 Caroline 286 Catherine 150 G R 140 George 104 George R 132 George S 132 Gordon F 132 H A (Mrs) 31 Harriet A 132 Isabella F 132 James 150 James S 132 Josephine 132 140 Katherine E 132 L D 286 Margaret Selina 132 Mary Amanda 132 William Duncan 132
ROBIE, Mehitable 211
ROBINSON, George 215 282 Harriet 215 226 L R 35 LeRoy 18 Margaret 208 Mary Ann 291 Sally 282 William 291
ROCK ISLAND, 31
ROCKWOOD, Caroline 329
ROEDELL, Henry 241 Penelope 241
ROGERS, Almira 196 Ann 279 Betsey 207 Charles 188 279

ROGERS (continued)
  Elder 97 Family 186 187 201
  202 George 175 Hannah 159
  206 Hannah L 285 John 96
  Jonathan 205 Louisa 166 182
  Major 60 61 Maria E 175 Martha 172 Mary 188 Nancy 315
  Philip 166 Rebecca 205 Sarah
  206 Susan 183 Susanna 173
  William 98 Zeruiah 184
ROLLINS, Chestina 221 Luthera
  209 Sarah 211 Tristram 209
ROMAN CATHOLICS, 102
ROSE, Family 135 136 George
  170 George H 176 Julia Ann
  133 Mary 170 Nancy 176 Polly
  170 Sibyl 209 Timothy 108 109
  133
ROSS, M 354 W W 91
ROWE, Peter 226 Phebe 226
  Polly 176 Robert 176
ROWELL, Family 283 284 Lois
  136 Mary 256 Phebe 260
ROWSON, Rev Mr 91
ROYCE, Lucinda 246 Rebecca
  231 Sarah 155
RUGG, Amanda 299 Uriah J 299
RUGGLES, David 198 Susan 198
RUITER, Family 205 John 39
  Rebecca 201 Samuel 292 Sarah
  212 Susanna 292 Thomas 212
RUITOR, John 12
RUSSELL, Lucinda R 235
RYCKMAN, E B 31 88 107
SABIN, B 85 E 84 L 95
SADDLER, Elizabeth 275
SAGER, Susan 214
SALISBURY, William 28
SALMON, John 91
SAMPSON, Diana 282 Family 249
  Joseph 252 Judith 276 Mary
  252
SANBORN, Alina A 311 B 327
  David 302 Elizabeth 311
  Family 326 Jane M 185 Judge
  141 Mary 295 N 311 Ruth 302
  Sarah 165
SARGEANT, Abigail 268 Wm 268
SARGENT, Abiah 119 Charles 171
  Louisa 168 Ruth 171 Susan 171
  208

SARLES, Cyrus 312 Dianthe 318
  Family 209 Harry 318 Lucy M
  312 Luthera 324
SARTWELL, Judith 339
SAUNDERS, Esther 207 Family
  136
SAVAGE, John 154 Laura 170
  Lucy 154
SAWYER, 45 Family 174 G 100
  Maria 175 Narcissa 118 Polly
  141 Wm 108
SCALES, Wm 91
SCOTT, Diana 170 Jesse 170
SCRIBNER, E G 278
SCRUTEN, Hannah 307
SEARS, Deborah 157
SELLEY, J B 90 91
SEVA, Hannah 178
SEVRANCE, Elisha 118 Martha
  118
SHARP, Abbie A 143 Caroline A
  143 Edward 143 William 143
SHATTUCK, Eda T 172
SHAW, Elizabeth 149 Elmira 232
  Mary L 239 Miss 180 Silas 149
SHEDD, Josiah 138
SHEERAR, John 313 Lucy 313
SHELDON, Mary 256
SHEPPARD, Lucy Ann 182 Sarah
  195
SHERBROOKE, 359
SHERBURN, Lucy 167
SHERMAN, Abigail 179 Betsey A
  172 Elizabeth 197 John S 172
  Roger 197
SHERWIN, Abigail 191
SHIELDS, Eleanor 192 Lizzie 325
SHOFF, Valina A 300
SHONGO, Diana 285
SHOREY, Albert K 133 Betsey
  338 Charlotte 338 Family 337
  Fanny 338 Hollis 55 Laura P
  133 Lelia O 133 Lucy 338
  Samuel E 338 Samuel O 133
SHORT, Mr 139
SHUMWAY, Mary 315
SHURTLIFF, 38 Amos 36 Family
  195 287 288 329 330 Francis
  254 George 198 H (Mrs) 211
  Hannah 216 Harriet M 199
  Ichabod 199 Joel 253

SHURTLIFF (continued)
Louisa E 199 Lovisa 198
Mahala 199 Mary 253 Melissa
A 254 Nancy 211 Rebecca 275
Solon 275 T T 106 William
216
SIAS, Matilda 258 Nancy 180
Roxana 233 Sarah 295
SIMMONS, Polly 284 Rebecca 247
SIMONDS, Betsey 249 Emma 305
Family 252 George 315 Kate
244 Lavinia 249 Lowell 249
Melissa 315
SIMPSON, Family 243 244 Sally
184
SINCLAIR, Dianthe Jane 178
Sarah 245
SINGER, J A 102
SKETCHES OF SETTLEMENT
BY E GUSTIN ESQ, 41
SKINNER, Abigail 224 J F 274
Margaret 196
SLATER, 56
SLEEPER, Elizabeth 145 Family
343-345 Hannah 212 Harriet
203 Lewis L 57 145 Martha
272 Philinda 198 Wright 198
SLIGHT, B 91
SMALL, David 166 Edward A 337
Harriet G 210 Irene 199 Judith
223 Julia G 155 166 Laura E
337 Mary 199 Sarah 226
SMART, Mary 175
SMITH, 155 273 Abbie S 134 135
Abigail 216 Ahata 210 Amanda
92 Arvilla 307 Asher 85 Benjamin 317 Betsey 240 C M 354
Charlotte 124 Charlotte M 208
Cynthia 207 David 280 Delphine L 227 Dimmis 213 E 216
Elijah 207 Elizabeth 322 337
Esther 168 285 Ethelinda 227
Family 132 223 224 277
George 307 326 Hannah 240
326 Harrison 240 Ichabod 28
104 110 124 Israel 315 J 345
Joseph 174 Lebbeus 191 Levi
240 Lewis 321 Lucinda 191
Lucy 337 338 Lydia 240 Maria
209 Mary 317 Nancy 240 279
Olive 334 Oliver 337 338 Osmyn 241 Philip N 227

SMITH (continued)
Phoebe 321 Polly 176 280 R 99
Richard 92 Robinson 98 99
Roswell 96 334 Sally 241 315
335 Sarah 205 280 Solomon 168
Stephen 210 Susan 174
SNOW, Caroline 286 Charlotte
116 Jane 128 286 Miss 165 N
286 S W 31 Sarah 287 Shipley
W 128
SOMERS, Family 274 275
Florence L 264 Geo O 264
George O 105 274 Sarah A 274
SOMERVILLE, W C 345
SORNBERGER, D W 102
SOUTHMAYD, E S 56
SPALDING, Levi 34 150 Phineas
147 Reuben 104 Sarah 150
SPEAR, Sarah 256
SPENCER, Adeline 316 Harriet
167 Sophronia 127 William P
127
SPENDLOVE, Lois A 295 Robert
292 Rosina 292 William 295
SPRAGUE, 22 56 Betsey 317
Daniel 311 Dorothy 311
Frederick 317 Lydia 334 Mary
Ann 209 Orange 209
SQUIRE, Mary 116 Mr 91 Suviah
265 William 86 116
SREW, Joseph 268 Sally 268
STANDISH, Charlotte 160 Ellen
314 Gabriel 160
STANSTEAD, County 6 Families
116 Plain 26 Seminary 104
Township 18
STARKS, Maria 218
STATE OF SOCIETY, 8
STATER, Elizabeth 281
STEARNS, Aliva 124 Family 207
L A 183 Nathan 124 Pamelia
284 Ruth 183 Sarah 183 Susan
315
STEELE, Family 216-218 Mary
142 Mr 142 Sanford 36 95
Solomon 36 Theda 228 Zadock
Jr 228 Zadok 35 36
STERLING, Celina 275
STEVENS, Charles 307 Cordelia
A 227 Frances 285 Holland 282
Ira 202 Jane 314 Josephine H
104 158 Joshua 165 Lois 202

STEVENS (continued)
   Lyman 104 Mary 307 Samuel
   314 Sarah 165 282 Thaddeus
   165
STEVENSON, Thomas 113
STEWART, Charles 82 Chs 49
   Family 214 215 Horace 36
   John 89 Martha 138 R P 113
   Rev Dr 83 Rufus 108
STIMSON, Beulah 231 Clara 289
STODDARD, Abby 299 Abby A
   301 Alfonso 178 Phebe 205
STOKER, Abigail 182
STONE, Irene 281 Joseph 281
   Lianthe 232 Mary 118 Sally
   231 Simon 231 Sophia 120
   Webster B 118
STRAW, Betsey 310 Chase 310
   Family 339 Rosetta 309
STREETER, Squire 84
STRICKLAND, Prudence 321
STRONG, Elijah 108 Eliphalet
   294 Lemira 151 153 Mary 294
STUART, Georgia 158 John D 158
STUDDERT, E F G 155 Lydia 155
STURTEVANT, Polly 295
SUGAR MAKING, 25
SURVIVING PIONEERS & NAR-
   RATIVES, 61-74
SUTHERLAND, David 92
SUTTLE, Betsey 190 William
   190
SUTTON, Charlotte 330 Dean 206
   Family 335 336 John 205
   Joshua 319 Lorena 270 Luman
   270 P J 96 Phila 205 Robert
   325 Sarah 319 323 325 327
SWAIN, 45 Family 176 177
SWEENEY, James 14 John 275
   Sarah 275
SWEET, Harriet 275
SWETT, Elisha 185 Rachel 185
SYLVESTER, Sarah 263
SYMONDS, Elmira 157 158
TABOR, Betsey 299 Huldah 299
   Parker 299 Thomas 299
TAGGARD, Martha 321 Mr 321
TAPLIN, 38 Augustus 297 Betsey
   E 311 Family 190 191 324
   Horace 320 Huldah 297 Joanna
   266 John 92 204 Johnson 3 12
   26 27 92 122 Mr 31 32 52

TAPLIN (continued)
   Semira 320 Susan 204
TATTON, 24
TAYLOR, Abigail 184 Alice J 248
   Cynthia 180 Emma L 104 Es-
   ther 225 Family 173 180 181
   282 Horace 248 Jacob 73
   James 184 Jane 142 John 225
   Lucy 308 Maria 292 Mary 283
   N (Mrs) 69 Nathan 283 Reuben
   142 Reuel 308 Roxana 326
   Sally 320 Sarah 142 Sarah H
   298 Sophia 265 Squire W 265
   William 73
TEAL, Clarissa 118
TELDEN, James 326 Martha 326
TERRILL, Family 139-141
   George Frederick 131 H B 6 14
   Harriet 131 J L 106 Orrin 298
   T L 6 14 31 108 131 T Lee 354
   William Lee 131
THAYER, Abel 122 Hannah 122
   Lucy 117 Zabdiel 28
THIBODIER, T 102
THOMAS, Adelaide 143 Eliza 296
   Ellen 300 Family 341 George
   334 Harlowe H 300 Joseph 189
   Mary 41 176 189 270 299 301
   Orissa 334 William 176 Wm
   296
THOMPSON, Hannah 170 Lucy
   156 Margaret 229 Morilla 230
   W L 31 82 108
THORNELOE, George 83 John 89
THORNLOE, John 84
THORNTON, Family 328 329
   John 55 57 298 John Sr 327
   Lucy 298 327
THRASHER, Deborah 157 160
   Mary 159
THREAITS, Annis J 253
TIBBETS, Betsey 228 Caroline
   179 John 228
TICHWORTH, Phebe 342
TILDEN, Electa 261 Joel 261
   Mary 257
TILSON, Nancy 278 Richard C
   278
TILTON, Abigail 246 Asenath 118
   Benjamin 206 Comfort 191
   Emily 222 Esenath 159 Family
   165 Margaret 218 Miriam 222

TILTON (continued)
  Nathaniel 159 Persis 206
  Philinda 230
TODD, Julia 218
TOMKINS, John 87 88 91 119
  Maria 119
TOMLINSON, Julia A 134 R 134
TOPOGRAPHICAL VIEW, 7
TRIPP, Irene 198 Wm 37
TRUESDALE, Harriet 121 John 121
TRUMBULL, Catherine 241
  Robert H 241
TUCK, Adeline 141 John C 148
  Malcolm 106 Samuel 141
  Susan 148
TUCKER, Alice 304
TURNER, Charles 105 277
  Family 279 Nancy 277 Thomas 86 90
TUTTLE, Lucy 137 Mehitable 137
TYLER, Amos 100
UNDERWOOD, Narcissa 170
  Nathan 170
UNIVERALISTS, 101
UTTEN, Angeline 258 William 258
VANRIPER, George J 244 J M 244
VARNUM, Benjamin 200 Candace 200 Family 200 Hannah 188 Mary 194
VAUCAMP, Hannah 3 58
VENAN, Mary 172
VERBACK, Arvilla 199 Calvin 226 Family 222 223 Hannah 220 Lois 241 Lucretia 226 Lucy H 222 Luther 222 Philip 200 241 Roswell 220 Sarah 151 Thankful 200 William 112 113 Wm 110 151
VINCENT, Family 286 287 Robert 49
VINTON, Betsey 189 Lucindai 189
VIRGIN, Charles 84
VORNEY, Anna 258 Samuel 258
WADE, Sarah 193
WADLEIGH, 50 Alice 273
  Ephraim 77 99 Family 259-261
  Jesse 12 76 78 273 John 247

WADLEIGH (continued)
  Louisa 296 Lucy 251 296 Luke 284 Lydia 296 Malinda 247 282 Mary 210 255 Pamelia 247 248 Phebe 284 Roxana 255 Ruth 328 Sally 247 Taylor 247
WAIT, Betsey 199
WAKEFIELD, J 107 108 Nancy Temple 351
WALKER, Celestia 320 Clarinda 331 332 Emily 226 George 295 Hannah 285 James 285 John 320 Joseph 142 Judith 184 Levi 84 Mary 142 Mary M 295 Richard 184 Sibyl 135
WALLACE, 98 Abigail 118 Blake 204 Charles 247 Henrietta 249 Hepzibah 211 Irene 204 Lucy 247 Mehitable 185
WALLAHAN, Ruth 166 Samuel 166
WALLINGFORD, 98 David 119 Emeline 249 Family 182 Fanny 166 Gilbert 176 249 Ives 179 Malivna A 153 Marin 179 Mary Jane 119 Minerva 176 Samuel G 201
WALLIS, Caroline 180
WALTON, 34 J 91 J S 12 John 90
WARD, Amanda 132 Dorothy 267 Dr 58 Isabella 214 Joseph 101 Laura 267 Mary 92 Nathan 132
WARDNER, Margaret 225
WARFIELD, Ruby 104
WARREN, Isabella 243 Martha 316 Otis 33 34
WASHINGTON, G 107 108
WATERMAN, Jonathan 308 Sally 308
WATERS, Abigail 330
WATKINS, Angeline 330 Anne 330
WATSON, Hannah J 203 Helen 231 Susan 230
WATT, 9
WAY, 56 Charlotte 160 Delia 319 Esther 224 Ethelinda 227 Family 142 Harris 33 34 160 Sally 232
WAYVILLE, 56
WEARE, A M 104 Betsey 119 284 Family 171 172 Maria 157

WEARE (continued)
Sarah 186
WEBB, Family 174 Janet 244
John 244 Laura 104
WEBSTER, 34 73 Belinda 270
Betsey 289 David 148 Isabella 244 Martha 324 Mary 281 Mary A 148 330 Ruth 174 Samuel 174 Sylvia 176
WEEKS, Alva T 339 Ann C 339 Harriet M 316 Lydia 201 Newton 316 Phineas 201
WELCH, Hills 165 Kezia 236 Martha 324 Mary 233 Nancy 165 Sarah J 236
WELLMAN, Artemisia 236
WELLS, Abraham 73 Charlotte 151 Eliza 177 Elizabeth 308 Family 181 182 Horace 123 John R 151 Mary 150 196 282 Moses 97 Mr 84 Nancy M 123 Polly 256 257 Sophronia 166 Thomas 166
WESLEY, 9
WESLEYAN COLLEGE, 106 353
WEST, Mr 361
WESTON, Betsey 188 Charles 220 Charlotte 116 Family 285 286 James 109 John 49 Lydia 120 220 Marcia F 293 Mary 314 Nathan 314
WETHERELL, J T 279 Ruth 279
WHALER, Fanny 337
WHEELER, 89 Albert 303 323 Charity 315 Charles 303 Elias 321 Family 323 324 Huldah 303 Lucy 318 325 Lucy A 116 Mary Jane 323 Mehitable 303 Parley 323 Phebe 340 Sarah 279 321 323 Sylvia 306
WHIDDEN, Ann J 193 John 193
WHIPPLE, Martha 324
WHITCHER, Almira 176 C T 209 Dolly 92 118 Dr 43 74 E D 14 Erasmus D 202 Family 119 Isaac 109 118 Isaac N 176 Israel 92 Lavinia 202 Maria 104 Marietta 206 Mary Jane 182 Nancy 209
WHITCOMB, Amy 206 Cyrus 49 281 Elvira 281 Family 289 290 Lucy 281 Polly 296 Ruth 263

WHITCOMB (continued)
Thankful 275
WHITE, 55 96 Amantha 176 Caleb 40 Clarinda 223 David 35 213 Dexter 40 214 Eli S 55 Ellen 213 Emily 153 Erastus 223 268 Eunice 320 Family 221 222 336 337 Helen M 223 Hosea 41 Lavinia 297 Lemuel 297 Lucy 223 Lydia 268 Mary 223 Mary Ann 205 214 Rev Mr 94 Sally 252 Stephen A 176 Wm T 153 Zilpha 127
WHITECOMB, 45
WHITELAW, Mr 23
WHITING, Sophia 277
WHITMAN, Emma A 319
WHITNEY, Mary 297
WHITTACKER, Miss 276
WHITTAKER, Freedom 136 Lucretia 136 Sarah 156
WHYTE, Eliza 217 Joseph 217
WILCOX, Calvin Jr 224 Charlotte 224 Family 207 208 342 343
WILEY, 33
WILKIE, David 171 Mary 171
WILLARD, Emily A 247 George 283 Lucy 297 Sally 283 Samuel 297
WILLEY, Curtis 306 Esther 267 Jesse 36 239 Lyman 263 Mary 185 Olive 263 Orpha 306 Ruth 297 Sarah 239
WILLIAM, the Conqueror 122
WILLIAMS, Carlos 252 Deborah 212 307 Elizabeth 252 Family 218 Frances 137 330 G 107 Thomas 212
WILLIAMSON, Susanna 233
WILLIS, Caroline 340 Joseph 340 Sarah 176
WILMOTH, Celia 223
WILSON, Almira 218 Chester 192 Dalinda M 158 Horace 169 James 318 Lydia 326 Matilda 192 Obadiah 192 Olive 318 R 326 Ruby 192 Sarah 218 Sarepta 169
WINGATE, Mary 305
WINN, Agnes 242 Isaac 194 Jacob 151 Jenett 138 Mary 151 Mary G 194 Timothy 242

WINSLOW, William 44
WOLF HUNT, 79
WOOD, 33 Abigail 225 281 Agnes 233 Alonzo 286 Betsey 327 Charlotte 286 Elizabeth 156 Ellen 313 Ephraim 110 233 Family 116 117 George 289 Hiram O 324 Israel 3 14 27 92 122 167 Israel 3rd 118 James F 79 Joseph 314 Juliet 308 Lois 310 340 Lucina 280 Lucy 118 324 330 Lucy D 127 Lydia M 167 Matilda 218 Miriam 248 Patience 316 Phebe A 198 Polly 314 Reuben B 157 Rhoda M 157 Sarah 146 Squire 218 Stephen 313 W N 45 Willard 34
WOODBURY, Elizabeth 136 Luke 136 Mary 136 Sarah 136
WOODMAN, Calvin 294 Emeline 322 Family 295 Florinda 210 Hannah 294 Joshua S 210
WOODWARD, Abigail C 117 Albert 174 Betsey 174 Caroline 248 258 Edwin 254 290 Elvira 290 Emeline 257 Family 281 George J 292 Hiram 117 John 49 Lucinda 254 Lucy 290 Margaret 292 Mary J 273 Oscar 248 Roscoe 258
WOOLED, Abner 3
WOOLLEY, Jos 113

WOOLRYCHE, A J 83
WORTH, 45 Edward 80 Family 141 223 George 316 Joseph 80 Lydia 206 Mary 316 Miriam 207
WORTHEN, Augusta 273 Martha 312 Minerva 273 True 273
WORTHINGTON, David 157 Orenda 157
WRIGHT, Chester 92 Ellen 299 Esther 206 Family 228 341 Fanny 149 Grata 222 Ira 196 Lemuel 217 Lewis 302 Louisa 196 Malinda 228 Mary Ann 299 Nancy 226 Nehemiah 108 Philena 245 Sophia 302 Sylvia 196 Theda 217
WYMAN, Benj 34 35 Florinda 179 James 319 John 120 Lucy 292 Nancy 319 Oscar 179 Susan A 120
YARROW, Christina 244
YEMONS, Mary Ann 322
YOUNG, Ada 310 Adeline 124 Alexander 231 Andrew 3 12 28 32 80 81 Betsey 142 297 Cyrus 297 Emily 289 Family 134 135 340 James 124 Joab 101 John 355 Joseph 80 Joseph W 289 Lucinda 263 267 Lucy 174 Margaret 154 Mary 231 Mary J 289 Zabina 100